HSPT: Full Study Guide and Test Strategies for the High School Placement Test

Smart Edition Media
36 Gorham Street
Suite 1
Cambridge, MA 02138
800-496-5994

Email: info@smarteditionmedia.com

Library of Congress Cataloging-in-Publication Data
Smart Edition Media.
HSPT: Full Study Guide and Test Strategies for the High School Placement Test
ISBN: Print: 978-1-949147-30-8, 1st edition

1. HSPT Exam
2. Study Guides
3. High School Placement Test
4. High School Entrance Exam
5. Educational Assessment

Printed in the United States of America

HSPT: Full Study Guide and Test Strategies for the High School Placement Test/Smart Edition Media.

ISBN: Print: 978-1-949147-30-8
Ebook: 978-1-949147-36-0

Print and digital composition by Book Genesis, Inc.

HSPT Practice Online

Smart Edition Media's Online Learning Resources allow you the flexibility to study for your exam on your own schedule and are the perfect companion to help you reach your goals! You can access online content with an Internet connection from any computer, laptop, or mobile device.

Online Learning Resources

Designed to enable you to master the content in quick bursts of focused learning, these tools cover a complete range of subjects, including:

- English Language Arts
- Reading
- Math
- Science
- Writing

Our online resources are filled with test-taking tips and strategies, important facts, and practice problems that mirror questions on the exam.

Online Sample Tests & Flashcards

Access additional full-length practice tests online!

Use these tests as a diagnostic tool to determine areas of strength and weakness before embarking on your study program or to assess mastery of skills once you have completed your studies.

FLASHCARDS 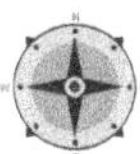 **GAMES** 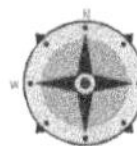 **QUIZZES** 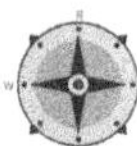 **TESTS**

Go to the URL: **https://smarteditionmedia.com/pages/HSPT-online-resources** and follow the password/login instructions.

TABLE OF CONTENTS

INTRODUCTION

AN OVERVIEW OF THE HSPT EXAM

The High School Placement Test (HSPT) is an exam used to help determine a student's admission qualifications for Catholic High Schools. The creators of this test, Scholastic Testing Service, Inc., have been producing this test since 1955 to assist Catholic schools determine candidates' qualifications for admission, scholarship selection, and curriculum placement.

The HSPT is administered at schools within the United States. The test is generally offered in the fall and winter to coincide with a school's application deadlines. Each school schedules their test dates independently with the Scholastic Testing Service, Inc. Students should contact the school directly to find out their testing date.

Unlike other standardized placement tests, the HSPT is designed to be taken only once. Whereas other standardized tests allow students to submit their best scores to their target schools, Scholastic Testing Service's policy is to submit a student's LOWEST score to schools. Your best strategy is to take the time to prepare diligently. The HSPT contains content that will be taught from elementary school through eighth grade; therefore, consider taking the HSPT at the latest date offered by your target school. This will allow you to be exposed to as many eighth grade concepts as possible simply by virtue of being in class longer before taking the test.

Also important to note: each correct answer on the HSPT is awarded 1 point. There are no deductions for incorrect answers. This means that you should answer all questions on the test, even if you are taking an educated guess. Use your time to answer the questions that you know with confidence, and in your remaining time, go back and make an educated guess on the questions that remain.

ABOUT THIS BOOK

This book provides you with an accurate and complete representation of the HSPT test and includes instructional content on the five core subjects of the exam: Verbal, Quantitative Skills, Reading, Mathematics, and Language Skills.

The instructional chapters are designed to provide the information and strategies you need to do well on the exam. The full-length practice tests are based on the HSPT and contain questions similar to those you can expect to encounter on the official test.

A detailed answer key follows each practice quiz and test. These answer keys provide explanations designed to help you completely understand the test material. Each explanation references the book chapter to allow you to go back to that section for additional review, if necessary.

How to Use This Book

Studies show that most people begin preparing for exams approximately 8 weeks before their test date. If you are scheduled to take your test in sooner than 8 weeks, do not despair! Smart Edition Media has designed this study guide to be flexible to allow you to concentrate on areas where you need the most support.

Whether you have 8 weeks to study – or much less than that – we urge you to take one of the online practice tests to determine areas of strength and weakness, if you have not done so already. These tests can be found in your online resources.

Once you have completed a practice test, use this information to help you create a study plan that suits your individual study habits and time frame. If you are short on time, look at your diagnostic test results to determine which subject matter could use the most attention and focus the majority of your efforts on those areas. While this study guide is organized to follow the order of the actual test, you are not required to complete the book from beginning to end, in that exact order.

How This Book Is Organized

Take a look at the Table of Contents. Notice that each **Section** in the study guide corresponds to a subtest of the exam. These sections are broken into **Chapters** that identify the major content categories of the exam.

Each chapter is further divided into individual **Lessons** that address the specific content and objectives required to pass the exam. Some lessons contain embedded example questions to assess your comprehension of the content "in the moment." All lessons contain a bulleted list called "**Let's Review**." Use this list to refresh your memory before taking a practice quiz, test, or the actual exam. A **Practice Quiz**, designed to check your progress as you move through the content, follows each chapter.

Whether you plan on working through the study guide from cover to cover, or selecting specific sections to review, each chapter of this book can be completed in one sitting. If you must end your study session before finishing a chapter, try to complete your current lesson in order to maximize comprehension and retention of the material.

Online Sample Tests

The purchase of this book grants you access to two additional full-length practice tests online. You can locate these exams on the Smart Edition Media website.

STUDY STRATEGIES AND TIPS

MAKE STUDY SESSIONS A PRIORITY.

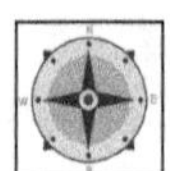

- Use a calendar to schedule your study sessions. Set aside a dedicated amount of time each day/week for studying. While it may seem difficult to manage, given your other responsibilities, remember that in order to reach your goals, it is crucial to dedicate the time now to prepare for this test. A satisfactory score on your exam is the key to unlocking a multitude of opportunities for your future success.
- Do you work? Have children? Other obligations? Be sure to take these into account when creating your schedule. Work around them to ensure that your scheduled study sessions can be free of distractions.

TIPS FOR FINDING TIME TO STUDY.

- Wake up 1-2 hours before your family for some quiet time
- Study 1-2 hours before bedtime and after everything has quieted down
- Utilize weekends for longer study periods
- Hire a babysitter to watch children

TAKE PRACTICE TESTS

- Smart Edition Media offers practice tests, both online and in print. Take as many as you can to help be prepared. This will eliminate any surprises you may encounter during the exam.

KNOW YOUR LEARNING STYLE

- Identify your strengths and weaknesses as a student. All students are different and everyone has a different learning style. Do not compare yourself to others.
- Howard Gardner, a developmental psychologist at Harvard University, has studied the ways in which people learn new information. He has identified seven distinct intelligences. According to his theory:

  "we are all able to know the world through language, logical-mathematical analysis, spatial representation, musical thinking, the use of the body to solve problems or to make things, an understanding of other individuals, and an understanding of ourselves. Where individuals differ is in the strength of these intelligences - the so-called profile of intelligences -and in the ways in which such intelligences are invoked and combined to carry out different tasks, solve diverse problems, and progress in various domains."

- Knowing your learning style can help you to tailor your studying efforts to suit your natural strengths.
- What ways help you learn best? Videos? Reading textbooks? Find the best way for you to study and learn/review the material.

WHAT IS YOUR LEARNING STYLE?

- **Visual-Spatial** – Do you like to draw, do jigsaw puzzles, read maps, daydream? Creating drawings, graphic organizers, or watching videos might be useful for you.
- **Bodily-kinesthetic** – Do you like movement, making things, physical activity? Do you communicate well through body language, or like to be taught through physical activity? Hands-on learning, acting out, role playing are tools you might try.
- **Musical** – Do you show sensitivity to rhythm and sound? If you love music, and are also sensitive to sounds in your environments, it might be beneficial to study with music in the background. You can turn lessons into lyricsor speak rhythmically to aid in content retention.
- **Interpersonal** – Do you have many friends, empathy for others, street smarts, and interact well with others? You might learn best in a group setting. Form a study group with other students who are preparing for the same exam. Technology makes it easy to connect, if you are unable to meet in person, teleconferencing or video chats are useful tools to aid interpersonal learners in connecting with others.
- **Intrapersonal** – Do you prefer to work alone rather than in a group? Are you in tune with your inner feelings, follow your intuition and possess a strong will, confidence and opinions? Independent study and introspection will be ideal for you. Reading books, using creative materials, keeping a diary of your progress will be helpful. Intrapersonal learners are the most independent of the learners.
- **Linguistic** – Do you use words effectively, have highly developed auditory skills and often think in words? Do you like reading, playing word games, making up poetry or stories? Learning tools such as computers, games, multimedia will be beneficial to your studies.
- **Logical-Mathematical** – Do you think conceptually, abstractly, and are able to see and explore patterns and relationships? Try exploring subject matter through logic games, experiments and puzzles.

CREATE THE OPTIMAL STUDY ENVIRONMENT

- Some people enjoy listening to soft background music when they study. (Instrumental music is a good choice.) Others need to have a silent space in order to concentrate. Which do you prefer? Either way, it is best to create an environment that is free of distractions for your study sessions.
- Have study guide – Will travel! Leave your house: Daily routines and chores can be distractions. Check out your local library, a coffee shop, or other quiet space to remove yourself from distractions and daunting household tasks will compete for your attention.
- Create a Technology Free Zone. Silence the ringer on your cell phone and place it out of reach to prevent surfing the Web, social media interactions, and email/texting exchanges. Turn off the television, radio, or other devices while you study.
- Are you comfy? Find a comfortable, but not *too* comfortable, place to study. Sit at a desk or table in a straight, upright chair. Avoid sitting on the couch, a bed, or in front of the TV. Wear clothing that is not binding and restricting.
- Keep your area organized. Have all the materials you need available and ready: Smart Edition study guide, computer, notebook, pen, calculator, and pencil/eraser. Use a desk lamp or overhead light that provides ample lighting to prevent eye-strain and fatigue.

HEALTHY BODY, HEALTHY MIND

- Consider these words of wisdom from Buddha, "To keep the body in good health is a duty – otherwise we shall not be able to keep our mind strong and clear."

KEYS TO CREATING A HEALTHY BODY AND MIND:

- Drink water – Stay hydrated! Limit drinks with excessive sugar or caffeine.
- Eat natural foods - Make smart food choices and avoid greasy, fatty, sugary foods.
- Think positively – You can do this! Do not doubt yourself, and trust in the process.
- Exercise daily – If you have a workout routine, stick to it! If you are more sedentary, now is a great time to begin! Try yoga or a low-impact sport. Simply walking at a brisk pace will help to get your heart rate going.
- Sleep well – Getting a good night's sleep is important, but too few of us actually make it a priority. Aim to get eight hours of uninterrupted sleep in order to maximize your mental focus, memory, learning, and physical wellbeing.

FINAL THOUGHTS

- Remember to relax and take breaks during study sessions.
- Review the testing material. Go over topics you already know for a refresher.
- Focus more time on less familiar subjects.

EXAM PREPARATION

In addition to studying for your upcoming exam, it is important to keep in mind that you need to prepare your mind and body as well. When preparing to take an exam as a whole, not just studying, taking practice exams, and reviewing math rules, it is critical to prepare your body in order to be mentally and physically ready. Often, your success rate will be much higher when you are *fully* ready.

Here are some tips to keep in mind when preparing for your exam:

SEVERAL WEEKS/DAYS BEFORE THE EXAM

- Get a full night of sleep, approximately 8 hours
- Turn off electronics before bed
- Exercise regularly
- Eat a healthy balanced diet, include fruits and vegetable
- Drink water

THE NIGHT BEFORE

- Eat a good dinner
- Pack materials/bag, healthy snacks, and water

- Gather materials needed for test: your ID and receipt of test. You do not want to be scrambling the morning of the exam. If you are unsure of what to bring with you, check with your testing center or test administrator.
- Map the location of test center, identify how you will be getting there (driving, public transportation, uber, etc.), when you need to leave, and parking options.
- Lay your clothes out. Wear comfortable clothes and shoes, do not wear items that are too hot/cold
- Allow minimum of ~8 hours of sleep
- Avoid coffee and alcohol
- Do not take any medications or drugs to help you sleep
- Set alarm

THE DAY OF THE EXAM 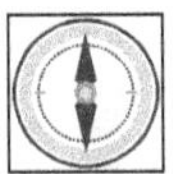

- Wake up early, allow ample time to do all the things you need to do and for travel
- Eat a healthy, well-rounded breakfast
- Drink water
- Leave early and arrive early, leave time for any traffic or any other unforeseeable circumstances
- Arrive early and check in for exam. This will give you enough time to relax, take off coat, and become comfortable with your surroundings.

<u>Take a deep breath, get ready, go! You got this!</u>

SECTION I. READING

CHAPTER 1 KEY IDEAS AND DETAILS

MAIN IDEAS, TOPIC SENTENCES, AND SUPPORTING DETAILS

To read effectively, you need to know how to identify the most important information in a text. You must also understand how ideas within a text relate to one other.

Main Ideas

The central or most important idea in a text is the **main idea**. As a reader, you need to avoid confusing the main idea with less important details that may be interesting but not central to the author's point.

The **topic** of a text is slightly different than the main idea. The topic is a word or phrase that describes roughly what a text is about. A main idea, in contrast, is a complete sentence that states the topic and explains what an author wants to say about it.

All types of texts can contain main ideas. Read the following informational paragraph and try to identify the main idea:

> The immune system is the body's defense mechanism. It fights off harmful bacteria, viruses, and substances that attack the body. To do this, it uses cells, tissues, and organs that work together to resist invasion.

The topic of this paragraph is the immune system. The main idea can be expressed in a sentence like this: "This paragraph defines and describes the immune system." Ideas about organisms and substances that invade the body are not the central focus. The topic and main idea must always be directly related to every sentence in the text, as the immune system is here.

Read the persuasive paragraph below and consider the topic and main idea:

> Football is not a healthy activity for kids. It causes head injuries that harm the ability to learn and achieve. It causes painful bodily injuries that can linger into adulthood. It teaches aggressive behavioral habits that make life harder for players after they have left the field.

The topic of this paragraph is youth football, and the main idea is that kids should not play the game. Note that if you are asked to state the main idea of a persuasive text, it is your job to be objective. This means you should describe the author's opinion, not make an argument of your own in response.

Both of the example paragraphs above state their main idea explicitly. Some texts have an implicit, or suggested, main idea. In this case, you need to figure out the main idea using the details as clues.

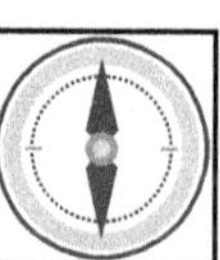

FOR EXAMPLE

The following fictional paragraph has an implicit main idea:

Daisy parked her car and sat gripping the wheel, not getting out. A few steps to the door. A couple of knocks. She could give him the news in two words. She'd already decided what she was going to do, so it didn't matter what he said, not really. Still, she couldn't make her feet carry her to the door.

The main idea here is that Daisy feels reluctant to speak to someone. This point is not stated outright, but it is clear from the details of Daisy's thoughts and actions.

Topic Sentences

Many paragraphs identify the topic and main idea in a single sentence. This is called a **topic sentence**, and it often appears at the beginning of a paragraph. However, a writer may choose to place a topic sentence anywhere in the text.

Some paragraphs contain an introductory sentence to grab the reader's attention before clearly stating the topic. A paragraph may begin by asking a rhetorical question, presenting a striking idea, or showing why the topic is important. When authors use this strategy, the topic sentence usually comes second:

> Have you ever wondered how your body fights off a nasty cold? **It uses a complex defense mechanism called the immune system.** The immune system fights off harmful bacteria, viruses, and substances that attack the body. To do this, it uses cells, tissues, and organs that work together to resist invasion.

Here, the first sentence grabs the attention, and the second, **boldfaced** topic sentence states the main idea. The remaining sentences provide further information, explaining what the immune system does and identifying its basic components.

COMPARE!

The informational paragraph above contains a question that grabs the attention at the beginning. The writer could convey the same information with a little less flair by omitting this device. The version you read in Section 1 does exactly this. (The topic sentence below is **boldfaced.**)

> **The immune system is the body's defense mechanism.** It fights off harmful bacteria, viruses, and substances that attack the body. To do this, it uses cells, tissues, and organs that work together to resist invasion.

Look back at the football paragraph from Section 1. Which sentence is the topic sentence?

Sometimes writers wait until the end of a paragraph to reveal the main idea in a topic sentence. When you're reading a paragraph that is organized this way, you may feel like you're reading a bit of a puzzle. It's not fully clear what the piece is about until you get to the end:

> It causes head injuries that harm the ability to learn and achieve. It causes painful bodily injuries that can linger through the passage of years. It teaches aggressive behavioral habits that make life harder for players after they have left the field. **Football is not a healthy activity for kids.**

Note that the topic—football—is not actually named until the final, **boldfaced** topic sentence. This is a strong hint that this final sentence is the topic sentence. Other paragraphs with this structure may contain several examples or related ideas and then tie them together with a summary statement near the end.

Supporting Details

The **supporting details** of a text develop the main idea, contribute further information, or provide examples.

All of the supporting details in a text must relate back to the main idea. In a text that sets out to define and describe the immune system, the supporting details could explain how the immune system works, define parts of the immune system, and so on.

> **Main Idea:** The immune system is the body's defense mechanism.
>
> **Supporting Detail:** It fights off harmful bacteria, viruses, and substances that attack the body.
>
> **Supporting Detail:** To do this, it uses cells, tissues, and organs that work together to resist invasion.

The above text could go on to describe white blood cells, which are a vital part of the body's defense system against disease. However, the supporting details in such a text should *not* drift off into descriptions of parts of the body that make no contribution to immune response.

Supporting details may be facts or opinions. A single text can combine both facts and opinions to develop a single main idea.

> **Main Idea:** Football is not a healthy activity for kids.
>
> **Supporting Detail:** It teaches aggressive behavioral habits that make life harder for players after they have left the field.
>
> **Supporting Detail:** In a study of teenage football players by Dr. Sophia Ortega at Harvard University, 28% reported involvement in fights or other violent incidents, compared with 19% of teenage boys who were not involved in sports.

The first supporting detail above states an opinion. The second is still related to the main idea, but it provides factual information to back up the opinion. Further development of this paragraph could contain other types of facts, including information about football injuries and anecdotes about real players who got hurt playing the game.

Let's Review!

- The main idea is the most important piece of information in a text.
- The main idea is often expressed in a topic sentence.
- Supporting details develop the main idea, contribute further information, or provide examples.

SUMMARIZING TEXT AND USING TEXT FEATURES

Effective readers need to know how to identify and restate the main idea of a text through summary. They must also follow complex instructions, figure out the sequence of events in a text that is not presented in order, and understand information presented in graphics.

Summary Basics

A **summary** is a text that restates the ideas from a different text in a new way. Every summary needs to include the main idea of the original. Some summaries may include information about the supporting details as well.

The content and level of detail in a summary vary depending on the purpose. For example, a journalist may summarize a recent scientific study in a newspaper profile of its authors. A graduate student might briefly summarize the same study in a paper questioning its conclusions. The journalist's version would likely use fairly simple language and restate only the main points. The student's version would likely use specialized scientific vocabulary and include certain supporting details, especially the ones most applicable to the argument the student intends to make later.

The language of a summary must be substantially different from the original. It should not retain the structure and word choice of the source text. Rather, it should provide a completely new way of stating the ideas.

Read the passage below and the short summary that follows:

> **Original:** There is no need for government regulations to maintain a minimum wage because free market forces naturally adjust wages on their own. Workers are in short supply in our thriving economy, and businesses must offer fair wages and working conditions to attract labor. Business owners pay employees well because common sense dictates that they cannot succeed any other way.
>
> **Effective Summary:** The author argues against minimum wage laws. He claims free market forces naturally keep wages high in a healthy economy with a limited labor supply.

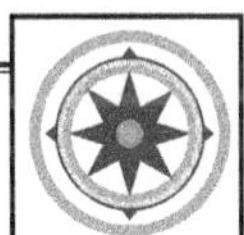

KEY POINT!

Many ineffective summaries attempt to imitate the structure of the original text and change only individual words. This makes the writing process difficult, and it can lead to unintentional plagiarism.

Ineffective Summary (Plagiarism): It is unnecessary for government regulations to create a minimum wage because capitalism adjusts wages without help. Good labor is rare in our excellent economy, and businesses need to offer fair wages and working conditions in order to attract workers.

The above text is an example of structural plagiarism. Summary writing does not just involve rewriting the original words one by one. An effective summary restates the main ideas of the text in a wholly original way.

The effective summary above restates the main ideas in a new but objective way. Objectivity is a key quality of an effective summary. A summary does not exaggerate, judge, or distort the author's original ideas.

> **Not a Summary:** The author makes a wild and unsupportable claim that minimum wage laws are unnecessary because market forces keep wages high without government intervention.

Although the above text might be appropriate in persuasive writing, it makes its own claims and judgments rather than simply restating the original author's ideas. It would not be an effective sentence in a summary.

In some cases, particularly dealing with creative works like fiction and poetry, summaries may mention ideas that are clearly implied but not stated outright in the original text. For example, a mobster in a thriller novel might turn to another character and say menacingly, "I wouldn't want anything to happen to your sweet little kids." A summary of this passage could objectively say the mobster had threatened the other character. But everything in the summary needs to be clearly supportable in the text. The summary could not go on to say how the other character feels about the threat unless the author describes it.

Attending to Sequence and Instructions

Events happen in a sequence. However, many written texts present events out of order to create an effect on the reader. Nonfiction writers such as journalists and history writers may use this strategy to create surprise or bring particular ideas to the forefront. Fiction writers may interrupt the flow of a plot to interweave bits of a character's history or to provide flashes of insight into future events. Readers need to know how to untangle this presentation of events and figure out what actually happened first, second, and third. Consider the following passage:

> The man in dark glasses was looking for something. He checked his pockets. He checked his backpack. He walked back to his car, unlocked the doors, and inspected the area around the seats. Shaking his head, he re-locked the doors and rubbed his forehead in frustration. When his hand bumped his sunglasses, he finally realized where he had put them.

This passage does not mention putting the sunglasses on until the end, but it is clear from context that the man put them on first, before beginning his search. You can keep track of sequence by paying attention to time words like *when* and *before,* noticing grammatical constructions *he had* that indicate when events happened, and making common sense observations like the fact that the man is wearing his dark glasses in the first sentence.

Sequence is also an important aspect of reading technical and functional documents such as recipes and other instructions. If such documents present many steps in a large text block without illustrations or visual breaks, you may need to break them down and categorize them yourself. Always read all the steps first and think about how to follow them before jumping in.

To see why, read the pancake recipe below:

> Combine flour, baking powder, sugar, and salt. Break the eggs into a separate bowl. Add milk and oil to the beaten eggs. Combine dry and liquid ingredients and stir. While you are doing the above, put a small amount of oil into a pan and heat it on medium heat. When it is hot, spoon batter onto the pan.

To follow directions like these effectively, a reader must break them down into categories, perhaps even rewriting them in a numbered list and noting when to start steps like heating the pan, which may be worth doing in a different order than it appears above.

Interpreting Graphics

Information is often presented in pictures, graphs, or diagrams. These **graphic elements** may provide information to back up an argument, illustrate factual information or instructions, or present key facts and statistics.

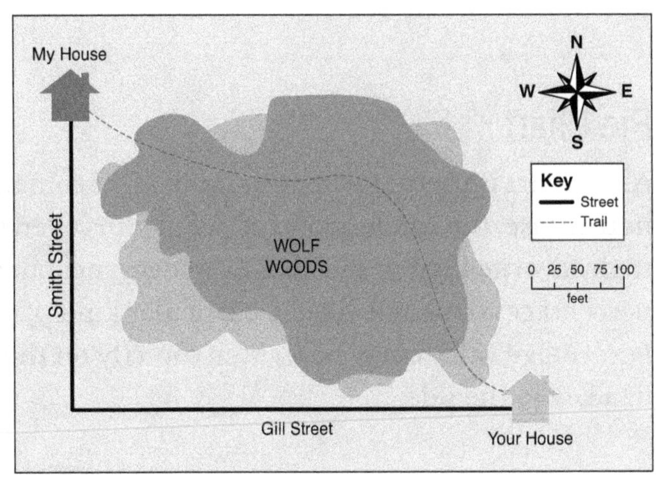

When you read charts and graphs, it is important to look carefully at all the information presented, including titles and labels, to be sure that you are interpreting the visuals correctly.

Diagram

A diagram presents a picture with labels that shows the parts of an object or functions of a mechanism. The diagram of a knee joint below shows the parts of the knee. Like many diagrams, it is placed in relation to a larger object—in this case, a leg—to clarify how the labeled parts fit into a larger context.

Flowchart

A flowchart shows a sequence of actions or decisions involved in a complex process. A flowchart usually begins with an oval-shaped box that asks a yes-no question or gives an instruction. Readers follow arrows indicating possible responses. This helps readers figure out how to solve a problem, or it illustrates how a complex system works.

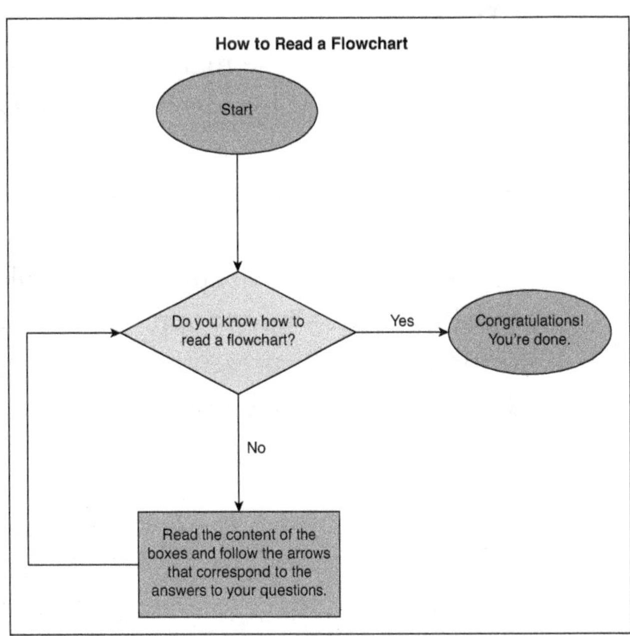

Bar Graph

A bar graph uses bars of different sizes to represent numbers. Larger bars show larger numbers to convey the magnitude of differences between two numeric values at a glance. In this case, each rectangle shows the number of candy bars of different types that a particular group of people ate.

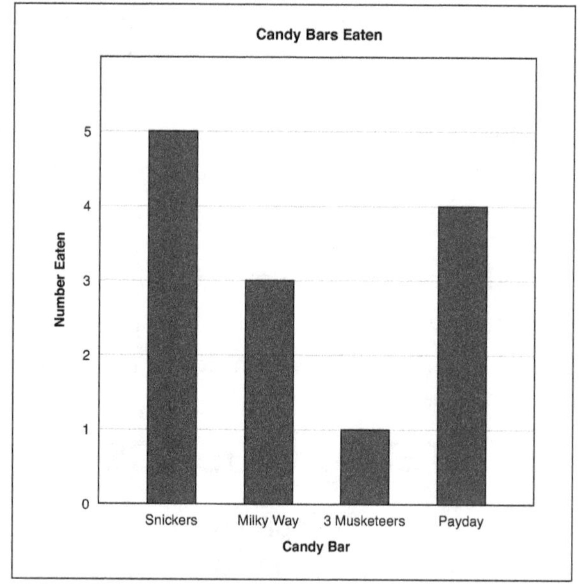

Pie Chart

A pie chart is useful for representing all of something—in this case, the whole group of people surveyed about their favorite kind of pie. Larger wedges mean larger percentages of people liked a particular kind of pie. Percentage values may be written directly on the chart or in a key to the side.

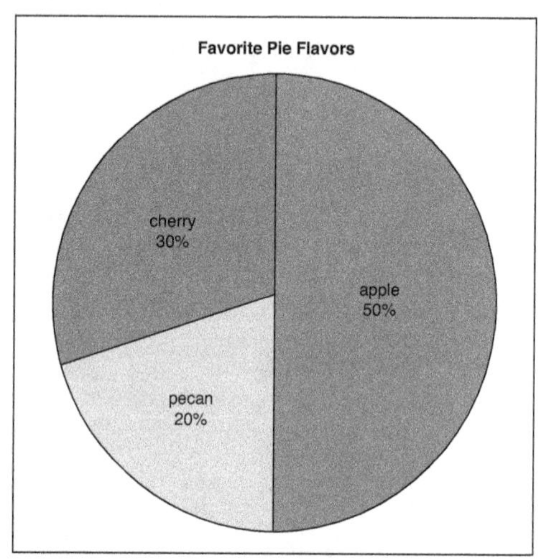

Let's Review!

- A summary restates the main ideas of a text in different words.
- A summary should objectively restate ideas in the present tense and give credit to the original author.
- Effective readers need to mentally reconstruct the basic sequence of events authors present out of order.
- Effective readers need to approach complex instructions by grouping steps into categories or considering how best to approach the steps.
- Information may be presented graphically in the form of diagrams, flowcharts, graphs, or charts.

Understanding Primary Sources, Making Inferences, and Drawing Conclusions

Effective readers must understand the difference between types of sources and choose credible sources of information to support research. Readers must also consider the content of their reading materials and draw their own conclusions.

Primary Sources

When we read and research information, we must differentiate between different types of sources. Sources are often classified depending on how close they are to the original creation or discovery of the information they present.

Primary sources include firsthand witness accounts of events, research described by the people who conducted it, and any other original information. Contemporary researchers can often access mixed media versions of primary sources such as video and audio recordings, photographs of original work, and so on. Note that original content is still considered primary even if it is reproduced online or in a book.

> **Examples:** Diaries, scientific journal articles, witness testimony, academic conference presentations, business memos, speeches, letters, interviews, and original literature and artwork.

Secondary sources respond to, analyze, summarize, or comment on primary sources. They add value to a discussion of the topic by giving readers new ways to think about the content. However, they may also introduce errors or layers of bias. Secondary sources may be very good sources of information, but readers must evaluate them carefully.

> **Examples:** Biographies, books and articles that summarize research for wider audiences, analyses of original literature and artwork, histories, political commentary.

Tertiary sources compile information in a general, highly summarized, and sometimes simplified way. Their purpose is not to add anything to the information, but rather to present the information in an accessible manner, often for audiences who are only beginning to familiarize themselves with a topic.

> **Examples:** Encyclopedias, guidebooks, literature study guides.

Source Materials in Action

Primary sources are often considered most trustworthy because they are closest to the original material and least likely to contain errors. However, readers must take a common sense approach to evaluating trustworthiness. For example, a single letter written by one biased witness of a historical event may not provide as much insight into what really happened as a secondary account by a historian who has considered the points of view of a dozen firsthand witnesses.

Tertiary sources are useful for readers attempting to gain a quick overview of understanding about a subject. They are also a good starting point for readers looking for keywords and subtopics to use for further research of a subject. However, they are not sufficiently detailed or credible to support an article, academic paper, or other document intended to add valuable analysis and commentary on a subject.

Evaluating Credibility

Not everything you read is equally trustworthy. Many sources contain mistakes, faulty reasoning, or deliberate misinformation designed to manipulate you. Effective readers seek out information from **credible**, or trustworthy, sources.

There is no single formula for determining credibility. Readers must make judgment calls based on individual texts and their purpose.

FOR EXAMPLE

Most sources should attempt to be objective. But if you're reading an article that makes an argument, you do not need to demand perfect objectivity from the source. The purpose of a persuasive article is to defend a point of view. As long as the author does this openly and defends the point of view with facts, logic, and other good argumentative techniques, you may trust the source.

Other sources may seem highly objective but not be credible. For example, some scientific studies meet all the criteria for credibility below except the one about trustworthy publishers. If a study is funded or conducted by a company that stands to profit from it, you should treat the results with skepticism no matter how good the information looks otherwise.

Sources and References

Credible texts are primary sources or secondary sources that refer to other trustworthy sources. If the author consults experts, they should be named, and their credentials should be explained. Authors should not attempt to hide where they got their information. Vague statements like "studies show" are not as trustworthy as statements that identify who completed a study.

Objectivity

Credible texts usually make an effort to be objective. They use clear, logical reasoning. They back arguments up with facts, expert opinions, or clear explanations. The assumptions behind the arguments do not contain obvious stereotypes.

Emotional arguments are acceptable in some argumentative writing, but they should not be manipulative. For example, photos of starving children may be acceptable for raising awareness of a famine, but they need to be respectful of both the victims and the audience—not just there for shock value.

Date of Publication

Information changes quickly in some fields, especially the sciences and technology. When researching a fast-changing topic, look for sources published in the last ten years.

Author Information

If an author and/or a respected organization take public credit for information, it is more likely to be reliable. Information published anonymously on the Internet may be suspicious because nobody is clearly responsible for mistakes. Authors with strong credentials such as university professors in a given field are more trustworthy than authors with no clear resume.

Publisher Information

Information published by the government, a university, a major national news organization, or another respected organization is often more credible. On the Internet, addresses ending in .edu or .gov may be more trustworthy than .com addresses. Publishers who stand to profit or otherwise benefit from the content of a text are always questionable.

BE CAREFUL!

Strong credentials only make a source more trustworthy if the credentials are related to the topic. A Columbia University Professor of Archeology is a credible source on ancient history. But if she writes a parenting article, it's not necessarily more credible than a parenting article by someone without a flashy university title.

Professionalism

Credible sources usually look professional and present information free of grammatical errors or major factual errors.

Making Inferences and Drawing Conclusions

In reading—and in life—people regularly make educated guesses based on limited information. When we use the information we have to figure out something nobody has told us directly, we are making an **inference**. People make inferences every day.

> **Example:** You hear a loud thump. Then a pained voice says, "Honey, can you bring the first aid kit?"

From the information above, it is reasonable to infer that the speaker is hurt. The thumping noise, the pain in the speaker's voice, and the request for a first aid kit all suggest this conclusion.

When you make inferences from reading, you use clues presented in the text to help you draw logical conclusions about what the author means. Before you can make an inference, you must read the text carefully and understand the explicit, or overt, meaning. Next, you must look for clues to any implied, or suggested, meanings behind the text. Finally, consider the clues in light of your prior knowledge and the author's purpose, and draw a conclusion about the meaning.

> As soon as Raizel entered the party, someone handed her a plate. She stared down at the hot dog unhappily.
>
> "What?" asked an unfamiliar woman nearby with an edge to her voice. "You don't eat dead animal?"

From the passage above, it would be reasonable to infer that the unfamiliar woman has a poor opinion of vegetarians. Several pieces of information suggest this: her combative tone, the edge in her voice, and the mocking question at the end.

When you draw inferences from a text, make sure your conclusion is truly indicated by the clues provided.

> Author Glenda Davis had high hopes for her children's book *Basketball Days*. But when the novel was released with a picture of a girl on the cover, boys refused to pick it up. The author reported this to her publisher, and the paperback edition was released with a new cover—this time featuring a dog and a basketball hoop. After that, many boys read the book. And Davis never heard anyone complain that the main character was a girl.

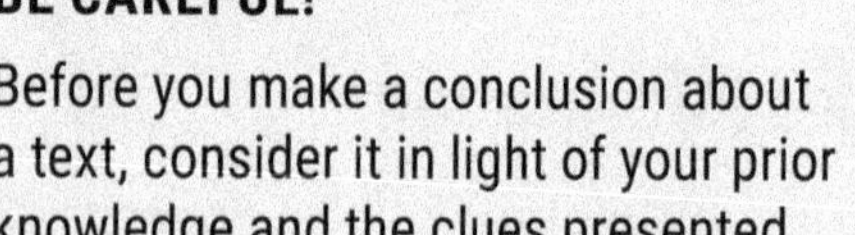

BE CAREFUL!

Before you make a conclusion about a text, consider it in light of your prior knowledge and the clues presented.

After reading the paragraph above, you might suspect that Raizel is a vegetarian. But the text does not fully support that conclusion. There are many reasons why Raizel might not want to eat a hot dog.

Perhaps she is keeping kosher, or she has social anxiety that makes it difficult to eat at parties, or she simply isn't hungry. The above inference about the unfamiliar woman's dislike for vegetarians is strongly supported. But you'd need further evidence before you could safely conclude that Raizel is actually a vegetarian.

The text above implies that boys are reluctant to read books with a girl on the cover. A hasty reader might stop reading early and conclude that boys are reluctant to read about girls—but this inference is not suggested by the full text.

Let's Review!

- Effective readers must consider the credibility of their sources.
- Primary sources are usually considered the most trustworthy.
- Readers must often make inferences about ideas that are implied but not explicitly stated in a text.

Chapter 1 Key Ideas and Details Practice Quiz 1

1. **Which type of graphic element would be most helpful for teaching the names of the parts of a bicycle?**

   A. Diagram
   B. Pie chart
   C. Bar graph
   D. Flowchart

Read the following sentence and answer questions 2-4.

Numerous robotic missions to Mars have revealed tantalizing evidence of a planet that may once have been capable of supporting life.

2. **Imagine this sentence is a *supporting detail* in a well-developed paragraph. Which of the following sentences would best function as a *topic sentence*?**

   A. Venus is an intensely hot planet surrounded by clouds full of drops of sulfuric acid.
   B. Of all the destinations within human reach, Mars is the planet most similar to Earth.
   C. Liquid water—a necessary ingredient of life—may once have flowed on the planet's surface.
   D. Space research is a costly, frivolous exercise that brings no clear benefit to people on Earth.

3. **Imagine this sentence is the *topic sentence* of a well-developed paragraph. Which of the following sentences would best function as a *supporting detail*?**

   A. Of all the destinations within human reach, Mars is the planet most similar to Earth.
   B. Venus is an intensely hot planet surrounded by clouds full of drops of sulfuric acid.
   C. Space research is a costly, frivolous exercise that brings no clear benefit to people on Earth.
   D. Liquid water—a necessary ingredient of life—may once have flowed on the planet's surface.

4. **How could this sentence function as a *supporting detail* in a persuasive text arguing that space research is worth the expense and effort because it teaches us more about Earth and ourselves?**

   A. By using statistics to back up an argument that needs support to be believed
   B. By showing how a space discovery could earn money for investors here on Earth
   C. By providing an example of a space discovery that enhances our understanding of life
   D. By developing the main idea that no space discovery can reveal information about Earth

The bar graph below provides information about book sales for a book called *The Comings,* which is the first book in a trilogy. Study the image and answer questions 5-6.

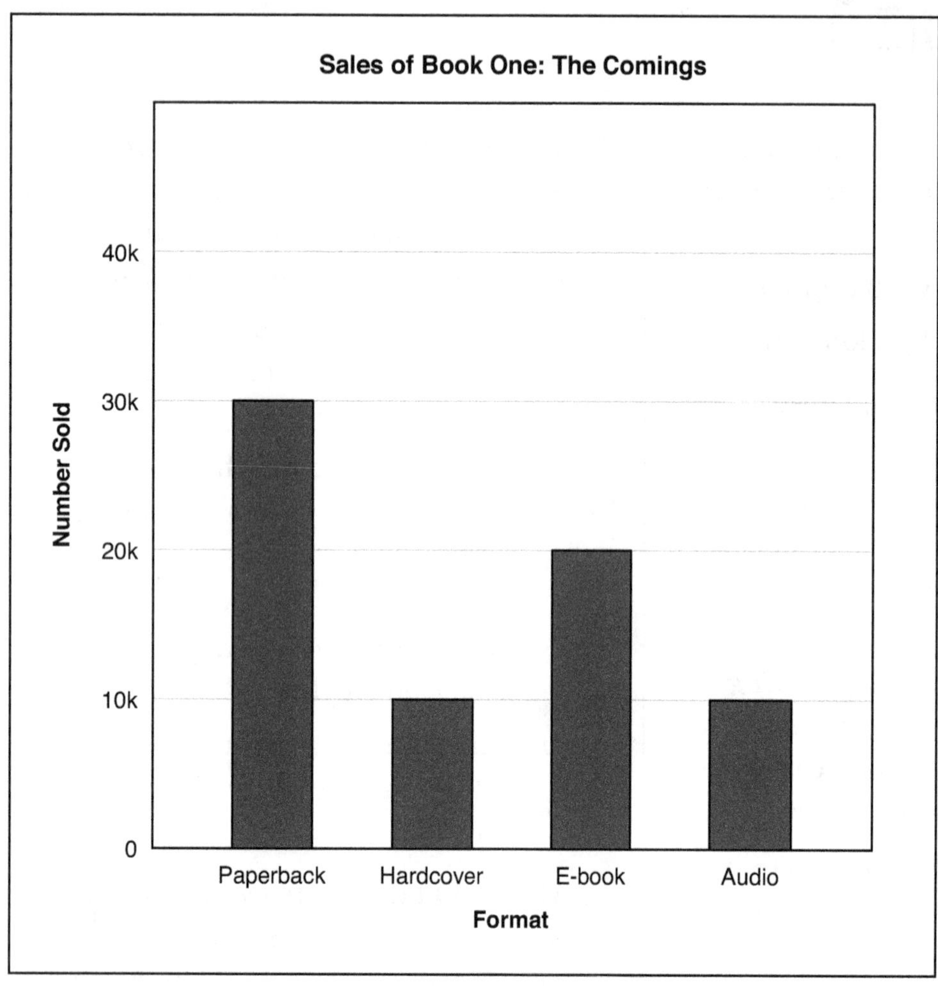

5. **Which type of book has sold the most copies?**

   A. E-book
   B. Hardcover
   C. Paperback
   D. Audio book

6. **The marketing director for *The Comings* wants to use a different strategy for publishing book two in the series. Which argument does the bar graph *best* support?**

   A. The first book in the trilogy has only sold 10,000 copies.
   B. The second book in the trilogy should not be released in hardcover.
   C. The second book in the trilogy should only be released as an e-book.
   D. The second and third books in the trilogy should be combined into one.

Study the infographic below and answer questions 7-9.

Credit: Center for Disease Control and Prevention. https://www.cdc.gov/nccdphp/dnpao/multimedia/infographics/getmoving.html

7. **Which of the following is not a sign that the infographic is credible?**
   A. The use of verifiable facts
   B. The list of source materials
   C. The professional appearance
   D. The inclusion of an author's name

8. **Zetta is unsure of the credibility of this source and has never heard of the Centers for Disease Control (CDC). Which fact could help her decide to trust it?**
   A. The CDC is located in Atlanta.
   B. The CDC has a .gov web address.
   C. The CDC creates many infographics.
   D. The CDC is also listed as a source consulted.

9. **What could a skeptical reader do to verify the facts on the infographic?**
   A. Interview one teenager to ask about his or her screen time.
   B. Follow the links for the sources and determine their credibility.
   C. Check a tertiary source like Wikipedia to verify the information.
   D. Find different values for screen time on someone's personal blog.

Chapter 1 Key Ideas and Details Practice Quiz 1 – Answer Key

1. **A.** A diagram illustrates complex visual ideas, so it could show which part of a bicycle is which and how they fit together. **See Lesson: Summarizing Text and Using Text Features.**

2. **B.** The sentence above conveys factual information about Mars in an excited tone that suggests a positive interest in the subject. This makes it most likely to fit into an informational paragraph sharing facts about Mars. **See Lesson: Main Ideas, Topic Sentences, and Supporting Details.**

3. **D.** If the above sentence were a topic sentence, its supporting details would likely share information to develop the idea that Mars may have supported life in the past. **See Lesson: Main Ideas, Topic Sentences, and Supporting Details.**

4. **C.** The sentence above could act as an example to show how space discoveries teach us about Earth and ourselves. **See Lesson: Main Ideas, Topic Sentences, and Supporting Details.**

5. **C.** Larger bars in a bar graph indicate higher numbers. This book has sold more paperback copies than any other. **See Lesson: Summarizing Text and Using Text Features.**

6. **B.** The bar graph shows fewer hardcover sales than any other kind. This could help support an argument that later books should only be released in electronic and paperback forms. **See Lesson: Summarizing Text and Using Text Features.**

7. **D.** It is usually a good sign if an author is clearly named in a source. Although this source is authored by an organization, the CDC, instead of a single author, there are many other signs it is credible. **See Lesson: Understanding Primary Sources Making Inferences and Drawing Conclusions.**

8. **B.** When presenting this type of information, a government organization with a .gov web address is typically considered a reputable source. **See Lesson: Understanding Primary Sources Making Inferences and Drawing Conclusions.**

9. **B.** One way to verify facts is to check the sources an author used. Verifying facts elsewhere may also be a good idea, but it is important to use reputable primary or secondary sources. **See Lesson: Understanding Primary Sources Making Inferences and Drawing Conclusions.**

CHAPTER 2 CRAFT AND STRUCTURE

FORMAL AND INFORMAL LANGUAGE

In English, there is formal language that is used most often in writing, and informal language that is most often used in speaking, but there are situations where one is more appropriate than the other. This lesson will cover differentiating contexts for (1) formal language and (2) informal language.

Formal Language

Formal language is often associated with writing for professional and academic purposes, but it is also used when giving a speech or a lecture. An essay written for a class will always use **formal language. Formal language** is used in situations where people are not extremely close and when one needs to show respect to another person. Certain qualities and contexts differentiate **formal language** from informal language.

Formal language does not use contractions.

- It doesn't have that - It does not have that.
- He's been offered a new job - He has been offered a new job.

Formal language also uses complete sentences.

- So much to tell you - I have so much to tell you.
- Left for the weekend - We left for the weekend.

Formal language includes more formal and polite vocabulary.

- The class starts at two - The class commences at two.
- I try to be the best person I can be - I endeavor to be the best person I can be.

Formal language is not personal and normally does not use the pronouns "I" and "We" as the subject of a sentence.

- I argue that the sky is blue - This essay argues that the sky is blue.
- We often associate green with grass - Green is often associated with grass.

Formal language also does not use slang.

- It's raining cats and dogs - It is raining heavily.
- Patients count on doctors to help them - Patients expect doctors to help them.

Informal Language

Informal language is associated with speaking, but is also used in text messages, emails, letters, and postcards. It is the language a person would use with their friends and family.

Informal language uses contractions.

- I can't go to the movie tomorrow.
- He doesn't have any manners.

Informal language can include sentence fragments.

- See you
- Talk to you later

Informal language uses less formal vocabulary such as slang.

- The dog drove me up the wall.
- I was so hungry I could eat a horse.
- I can always count on you.

Informal language is personal and uses pronouns such as "I" and "We" as the subject of a sentence.

- I am in high school.
- We enjoy going to the beach in the summer.

Let's Review!

- **Formal language** is used in professional and academic writing and talks. It does not have contractions, uses complete sentences, uses polite and formal vocabulary, not slang, and is not personal and generally does not use the pronouns "I" and "We" as the subject of a sentence.
- **Informal language** is used in daily life when communicating with friends and family through conversations, text messages, emails, letters, and postcards. It uses contractions, can be sentence fragments, uses less formal vocabulary and slang, and is personal and uses pronouns such as "I" and "We" as the subject of a sentence.

Tone, Mood, and Transition Words

Authors use language to show their emotions and to make readers feel something too. They also use transition words to help guide the reader from one idea to the next.

Tone and Mood

The **tone** of a text is the author's or speaker's attitude toward the subject. The tone may reflect any feeling or attitude a person can express: happiness, excitement, anger, boredom, or arrogance.

Readers can identify tone primarily by analyzing word choice. The reader should be able to point to specific words and details that help to establish the tone.

> **Example:** The train rolled past miles and miles of cornfields. The fields all looked the same. They swayed the same. They produced the same dull nausea in the pit of my stomach. I'd been sent out to see the world, and so I looked, obediently. What I saw was sameness.

Here, the author is expressing boredom and dissatisfaction. This is clear from the repetition of words like "same" and "sameness." There's also a sense of unpleasantness from phrases like "dull nausea" and passivity from words like "obediently."

Sometimes an author uses an ironic tone. Ironic texts often mean the opposite of what they actually say. To identify irony, you need to rely on your prior experience and common sense to help you identify texts with words and ideas that do not quite match.

> **Example:** With that, the senator dismissed the petty little problem of mass shootings and returned to the really important issue: his approval ratings.

Here the author flips around the words most people would usually use to discuss mass murder and popularity. By calling a horrific issue "petty" and a trivial issue "important," the author highlights what she sees as a politician's backwards priorities. Except for the phrase "mass shootings," the words here are light and airy—but the tone is ironic and angry.

BE CAREFUL!

When you're asked to identify the tone of a text, be sure to keep track of *whose* tone you're supposed to identify, and which part of the text the question is referencing. The author's tone can be different from that of the characters in fiction or the people quoted in nonfiction.

Example: The reporter walked quickly, panting to catch up to the senator's entourage. "Senator Biltong," she said. "Are you going to take action on mass shootings?"

"Sure, sure. Soon," the senator said vaguely. Then he turned to greet a newcomer. "Ah ha! Here's the man who can fix my approval ratings!" And with that, he returned to the really important issue: his popularity.

*

In the example above, the author's tone is ironic and angry. But the tone of the senator's dialogue is different. The line beginning with the words "Sure, sure" has a distracted tone. The line beginning with "Ah ha!" has a pleased tone.

A concept related to tone is **mood**, or the feelings an author produces in the reader. To determine the mood of a text, a reader can consider setting and theme as well as word choice and tone. For example, a story set in a haunted house may produce an unsettled or frightened feeling in a reader.

Tone and mood are often confused. This is because they are sometimes the same. For instance, in an op-ed article that describes children starving while food aid lies rotting, the author may use an outraged tone and simultaneously arouse an outraged mood in the reader.

However, tone and mood can be different. When they are, it's useful to have different words to distinguish between the author's attitude and the reader's emotional reaction.

> **Example:** I had to fly out of town at 4 a.m. for my trip to the Bahamas, and my wife didn't even get out of bed to make me a cup of coffee. I told her to, but she refused just because she'd been up five times with our newborn. I'm only going on vacation for one week, and she's been off work for a month! She should show me a little consideration.

Here, the tone is indignant. The mood will vary depending on the reader, but it is likely to be unsympathetic.

Transitions

Authors use connecting words and phrases, or **transitions**, to link ideas and help readers follow the flow of their thoughts. The number of possible ways to transition between ideas is almost limitless.

Below are a few common transition words, categorized by the way they link ideas.

Transitions	Examples
Time and sequence transitions orient the reader within a text. They can also help show when events happened in time.	*First, second, next, now, then, at this point, after, afterward, before this, previously, formerly, thereafter, finally, in conclusion*
Addition or emphasis transitions let readers know the author is building on an established line of thought. Many place extra stress on an important idea.	*Moreover, also, likewise, furthermore, above all, indeed, in fact*
Example transitions introduce ideas that illustrate a point.	*For example, for instance, to illustrate, to demonstrate*
Causation transitions indicate a cause-and-effect relationship.	*As a result, consequently, thus*
Contrast transitions indicate a difference between ideas.	*Nevertheless, despite, in contrast, however*

Transitions may look different depending on their function within the text. Within a paragraph, writers often choose short words or expressions to provide transitions and smooth the flow. Between paragraphs or larger sections of text, transitions are usually longer. They may use some of the key words or ideas above, but the author often goes into detail restating larger concepts and explaining their relationships more thoroughly.

Between Sentences: Students who cheat do not learn what they need to know. *As a result,* they get farther behind and face greater temptation to cheat in the future.

Between Paragraphs: *As a result of the cheating behaviors described above,* students find themselves in a vicious cycle.

Longer transitions like the latter example may be useful for keeping the reader clued in to the author's focus in an extended text. But long transitions should have clear content and function. Some long transitions, such as the very wordy "due to the fact that" take up space without adding more meaning and are considered poor style.

Let's Review!

- Tone is the author's or speaker's attitude toward the subject.
- Mood is the feeling a text creates in the reader.
- Transitions are connecting words and phrases that help readers follow the flow of a writer's thoughts.

The Author's Purpose and Point of View

In order to understand, analyze, and evaluate a text, readers must know how to identify the author's purpose and point of view. Readers also need to attend to an author's language and rhetorical strategies.

Author's Purpose

When writers put words on paper, they do it for a reason. This reason is the author's **purpose**. Most writing exists for one of three purposes: to inform, to persuade, or to entertain.

> **TEST TIP**
>
> You may have learned about a fourth purpose for writing: conveying an emotional experience. Many poems as well as some works of fiction, personal essays, and memoirs are written to give the reader a sense of how an event or moment might feel. This type of text is rarely included on placement tests, and if it is, it tends to be lumped in with literature meant to entertain.

If a text is designed to share knowledge, its purpose is to **inform**. Informational texts include technical documents, cookbooks, expository essays, journalistic newspaper articles, and many nonfiction books. Informational texts are based on facts and logic, and they usually attempt an objective tone. The style may otherwise vary; some informational texts are quite dry, whereas others have an engaging style.

If a text argues a point, its purpose is to **persuade**. A persuasive text attempts to convince a reader to believe a certain point of view or take a certain action. Persuasive texts include op-ed newspaper articles, book and movie reviews, project proposals, and argumentative essays. Key signs of persuasive texts include judgments, words like *should,* and other signs that the author is sharing opinions.

If a text is primarily for fun, its purpose is to **entertain**. Entertaining texts usually tell stories or present descriptions. Entertaining texts include novels, short stories, memoirs, and some poems. Virtually all stories are lumped into this category, even if they describe unpleasant experiences.

> **CONNECTIONS**
>
> You may have read elsewhere that readers can break writing down into the following basic categories. These categories are often linked to the author's purpose.
>
> **Narrative** writing tells a story and is usually meant to entertain.
> **Expository** writing explains an idea and is usually meant to inform.
> **Technical** writing explains a mechanism or process and is usually meant to inform.
> **Persuasive** writing argues a point and, as the label suggests, is meant to persuade.

A text can have more than one purpose. For example, many traditional children's stories come with morals or lessons. These are meant both to entertain children and persuade them to behave in ways society considers appropriate. Also, commercial nonfiction texts like popular science books are often written in an engaging or humorous style. The purpose of such a text is to inform while also entertaining the reader.

Point of View

Every author has a general outlook or set of opinions about the subject. These make up the author's **point of view**.

To determine point of view, a reader must recognize implicit clues in the text and use them to develop educated guesses about the author's worldview. In persuasive texts, the biggest clue is the author's explicit argument. From considering this argument, a reader can usually make some inferences about point of view. For instance, if an author argues that parents should offer kids opportunities to exercise throughout the day, it would be reasonable to infer that the author has an overall interest in children's health, and that he or she is troubled by the idea of kids pursuing sedentary behaviors like TV watching.

It is more challenging to determine point of view in a text meant to inform. Because the writer does not present an explicit argument, readers must examine assumptions and word choice to determine the writer's point of view.

> **Example:** Models suggest that at the current rate of global warming, hurricanes in 2100 will move 9 percent slower and drop 24 percent more rain. Longer storm durations and rainfall rates will likely translate to increased economic damage and human suffering.

It is reasonable to infer that the writer of this passage has a general trust for science and scientists. This writer assumes that global warming is happening, so it is clear he or she is not a global warming denier. Although the writer does not suggest a plan to prevent future storm damage, the emphasis on negative effects and the use of negative words like "damage" and "suffering" suggest that the author is worried about global warming.

Texts meant to entertain also contain clues about the author's point of view. That point of view is usually evident from the themes and deeper meanings. For instance, a memoirist who writes an upbeat story about a troubled but loving family is likely to believe strongly in the power of love. Note, however, that in this type of work, it is not possible to determine point of view merely from one character's words or actions. For instance, if a character says, "Your mother's love doesn't matter much if she can't take care of you," the reader should *not* automatically assume the writer agrees with that statement. Narrative writers often present a wide range of characters with varying outlooks on life. A reader can only determine the author's point of view by considering the work as a whole. The attitudes that are most emphasized and the ones that win out in the end are likely to reflect the author's point of view.

Rhetorical Strategies

Rhetorical strategies are the techniques an author uses to support an argument or develop a main idea. Effective readers need to study the language of a text and determine how the author is supporting his or her points.

One strategy is to appeal to the reader's reason. This is the foundation of effective writing, and it simply means that the writer relies on factual information and the logical conclusions that follow from it. Even persuasive writing uses this strategy by presenting facts and reasons to back up the author's opinions.

> **Ineffective:** Everyone knows *Sandra and the Lumps* is the best band of the new millennium.
>
> **Effective:** The three most recent albums by *Sandra and the Lumps* are the first, second, and third most popular records released since the turn of the millennium.

Another strategy is to establish trust. A writer can do this by choosing credible sources and by presenting ideas in a clear and professional way. In persuasive writing, writers may show they are trustworthy by openly acknowledging that some people hold contradicting opinions and by responding fairly to those positions. Writers should never attack or misrepresent their opponents' position.

> **Ineffective:** People who refuse to recycle are too lazy to protect their children's future.
>
> **Effective:** According to the annual Throw It Out Questionnaire, many people dislike the onerous task of sorting garbage, and some doubt that their effort brings any real gain.

A final strategy is to appeal to the reader's emotions. For instance, a journalist reporting on the opioid epidemic could include a personal story about an addict's attempts to overcome substance abuse. Emotional content can add a human dimension to a story that would be missing if the writer only included statistics and expert opinions. But emotions are easily manipulated, so writers who use this strategy need to be careful. Emotions should never be used to distort the truth or scare readers into agreeing with the writer.

> **Ineffective:** If you don't take action on gun control, you're basically killing children.
>
> **Effective:** Julie was puzzling over the Pythagorean Theorem when she heard the first gunshot.

Let's Review!

- Every text has a purpose.
- Most texts are meant to inform, persuade, or entertain.
- Texts contain clues that imply an author's outlook or set of opinions about the subject.
- Authors use rhetorical strategies to appeal to reason, establish trust, or invoke emotions.

Chapter 2 Craft and Structure Practice Quiz 1

1. **Which of the following sentences uses the MOST informal language?**
   A. The house creaked at night.
   B. I ate dinner with my friend.
   C. It's sort of a bad time.
   D. The water trickled slowly.

2. **In which of the following situations would it be best to use informal language?**
   A. In a seminar.
   B. Writing a postcard.
   C. Talking to your boss.
   D. Participating in a professional conference.

3. **Which of the following sentences uses the MOST formal language?**
   A. Thanks for letting me know.
   B. I want to thank you for telling me.
   C. Thank you for telling me about this issue.
   D. I appreciate you bringing this issue to my attention.

Read the passage below and answer questions 4-6.

The train was the most amazing thing ever even though it didn't go "choo choo." The toddler pounded on the railing of the bridge and supplied the sound herself. "Choo choo! Choo chooooooo!" she shouted as the train cars whizzed along below.

In the excitement, she dropped her favorite binky.

Later, when she noticed the binky missing, all the joy went out of the world. The wailing could be heard three houses down. The toddler's usual favorite activities were garbage—even waving to Hank the garbage man, which she refused to do, so that Hank went away looking mildly hurt. It was clear the little girl would never, ever, ever recover from her loss.

Afterward, she played at the park.

4. **Which adjectives best describe the tone of the passage?**
   A. Ironic, angry
   B. Earnest, angry
   C. Ironic, humorous
   D. Earnest, humorous

5. **Which sentence from the passage is clearly ironic?**
   A. "Choo choo! Choo chooooooo!" she shouted as the train cars whizzed along below.
   B. Later, when she noticed the binky missing, all the joy went out of the world.
   C. The wailing could be heard three houses down.
   D. Afterward, she played at the park.

6. The author of the passage first establishes the ironic tone by:

A. describing the child's trip to play at the park.

B. calling the train "the most amazing thing ever."

C. pretending that the child can make the sounds "choo choooooo!"

D. claiming inaccurately that the lost binky was the child's "favorite."

7. What is the most likely purpose of a popular science book describing recent advances in genetics?

A. To decide

B. To inform

C. To persuade

D. To entertain

8. Which phrase describes the set of techniques an author uses to support an argument or develop a main idea?

A. Points of view

B. Logical fallacies

C. Statistical analyses

D. Rhetorical strategies

9. What is the most likely purpose of an article that claims some genetic research is immoral?

A. To decide

B. To inform

C. To persuade

D. To entertain

Chapter 2 Craft and Structure Practice Quiz 1 – Answer Key

1. C. *It's sort of a bad time.* The sentence has contractions and uses informal and slang words. **See Lesson: Formal and Informal Language.**

2. B. *Writing a postcard.* It is an informal mode of communication between close friends and relatives. **See Lesson: Formal and Informal Language.**

3. D. *I appreciate you bringing this issue to my attention.* The sentence uses the most formal and polite vocabulary. **See Lesson: Formal and Informal Language.**

4. C. This passage ironically is a humorous description of a toddler's emotions, written by an adult who has enough experience to know that a toddler's huge emotions will pass. **See Lesson: Tone and Mood, Transition Words.**

5. B. Authors use irony when their words do not literally mean what they say. The joy does not really go out of the world when a toddler loses her binky—but it may seem that way to the child. **See Lesson: Tone and Mood, Transition Words.**

6. B. This passage establishes irony in the opening sentence by applying the superlative phrase "the most amazing thing ever" to an ordinary occurrence. **See Lesson: Tone and Mood, Transition Words.**

7. B. If a book is describing information, its purpose is to inform. **See Lesson: Understanding the Author's Purpose, Point of View, and Rhetorical Strategies.**

8. D. The techniques an author uses to support an argument or develop a main idea are called rhetorical strategies. **See Lesson: Understanding the Author's Purpose, Point of View, and Rhetorical Strategies.**

9. C. An article that takes a moral position is meant to persuade. **See Lesson: Understanding the Author's Purpose, Point of View, and Rhetorical Strategies.**

Chapter 3 Integration of Knowledge and Ideas

Facts, Opinions, and Evaluating an Argument

Nonfiction writing is based on facts and real events, but most nonfiction nevertheless expresses a point of view. Effective readers must evaluate the author's point of view and form their own conclusions about the points in the text.

Fact and Opinion

Many texts make an **argument**. In this context, the word *argument* has nothing to do with anger or fighting. It simply means the author is trying to convince readers of something.

Arguments are present in a wide variety of texts. Some relate to controversial issues, for instance by advocating support for a political candidate or change in laws. Others may defend a certain interpretation of facts or ideas. For example, a literature paper may argue that an author's story suggests a certain theme, or a science paper may argue for a certain interpretation of data. An argument may also present a plan of action such as a business strategy.

To evaluate an argument, readers must distinguish between **fact** and **opinion**. A fact is verifiably true. An opinion is someone's belief.

> **Fact:** Seattle gets an average of 37 inches of rain per year.
>
> **Opinion:** The dark, rainy, cloudy weather makes Seattle an unpleasant place to live in winter.

Meteorologists measure rainfall directly, so the above fact is verifiably true. The statement "it is unpleasant" clearly reflects a feeling, so the second sentence is an opinion.

The difference between fact and opinion is not always straightforward. For instance, a text may present a fact that contains an opinion within it:

> **Fact:** Nutritionist Fatima Antar questions the wisdom of extreme carbohydrate avoidance.

Assuming the writer can prove that this sentence genuinely reflects Fatima Antar's beliefs, it is a factual statement of her point of view. The reader may trust that Fatima Antar really holds this opinion, whether or not the reader is convinced by it.

If a text makes a judgment, it is not a fact:

Opinion: The patient's seizure drug regimen caused horrendous side effects.

This sentence uses language that different people would interpret in different ways. Because people have varying ideas about what they consider "horrendous," this sentence is an opinion as it is written, even though the actual side effects and the patient's opinion of them could both be verified.

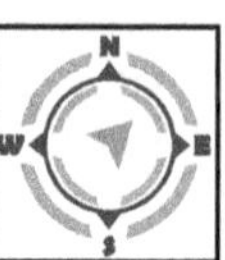
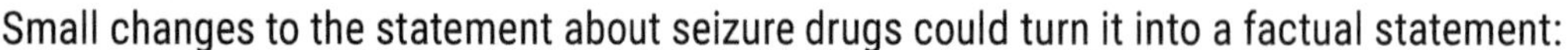

COMPARE!

Small changes to the statement about seizure drugs could turn it into a factual statement:

Fact: The patient's seizure drug regiment caused side effects such as migraines, confusion, and dangerously high blood pressure.

The above statement can be verified because the patient and other witnesses could confirm the exact nature of her symptoms. This makes it a fact.

Fact: The patient reported that her seizure drug regimen caused horrendous side effects.

This statement can also be verified because the patient can verify that she considers the side effects horrendous. By framing the statement in this way, the writer leaves nothing up to interpretation and is clearly in the realm of fact.

The majority of all arguments contain both facts and opinions, and strong arguments may contain both fact and opinion elements. It is rare for an argument to be composed entirely of facts, but it can happen if the writer is attempting to convince readers to accept factual information that is little-known or widely questioned. Most arguments present an author's opinion and use facts, reasoning, and expert testimony to convince readers.

Evaluating an Argument

Effective readers must evaluate an argument and decide whether or not it is valid. To do this, readers must consider every claim the author presents, including both the main argument and any supporting statements. If an argument is based on poor reasoning or insufficient evidence, it is not valid—even if you agree with the main idea.

KEY POINT!

Most of us want to agree with arguments that reflect our own beliefs. But it is inadvisable to accept an argument that is not properly rooted in good reasoning. Consider the following statements about global climate change:

Poor Argument: It just snowed fifteen inches! How can anyone say the world is getting warmer?

Poor Argument: It's seventy degrees in the middle of February! How can anyone deny global warming?

Both of these arguments are based on insufficient evidence. Each relies on *one* weather event in *one* location to support an argument that the entire world's climate is or is not changing. There is not nearly enough information here to support an argument on either side.

Beware of any argument that presents opinion information as fact.

False Claim of Fact: I know vaccines cause autism because my niece began displaying autism symptoms after receiving her measles vaccine.

The statement above states a controversial idea as fact without adequate evidence to back it up. Specifically, it makes a false claim of cause and effect about an incident that has no clear causal relationship.

Any claim that is not supported by sufficient evidence is an example of **faulty reasoning**.

Type of Faulty Reasoning	Definition	Example	Explanation
Circular Reasoning	Restating the argument in different words instead of providing evidence	Baseball is the best game in the world because it is more fun than any other game.	Here, everything after the word *because* says approximately the same thing as everything before it. It looks like the author is providing a reason, but no evidence has actually been offered.
Either/Or Fallacy	Presenting an issue as if it involves only two choices when in fact it is not so simple	Women should focus on motherhood, not careers.	This statement assumes that women cannot do both. It also assumes that no woman needs a career in order to provide for her children.
Overgeneralizations	Making a broad claim based on too little evidence	All elderly people have negative stereotypes of teenagers.	This statement lumps a whole category of people into a group and claims the whole group shares the same belief—always an unlikely prospect.

Most texts about evaluating arguments focus on faulty reasoning and false statements of fact. But arguments that attempt to misrepresent facts as opinions are equally suspicious. A careful reader should be skeptical of any text that denies clear physical evidence or questions the truth of events that have been widely verified.

Assumptions and Biases

A well-reasoned argument should be supported by facts, logic, and clearly explained opinions. But most arguments are also based on **assumptions,** or unstated and unproven ideas about what is true. Consider the following argument:

Argument: To improve equality of opportunity for all children, schools in underprivileged areas should receive as much taxpayer funding as schools in wealthy districts.

This argument is based on several assumptions. First is the assumption that all children should have equal opportunities. Another is that taxpayer-funded public schools are the best way to provide these opportunities. Whether or not you disagree with either of these points, it is worth noting that the second idea in particular is not the only way to proceed. Readers who examine the assumptions behind an argument can sometimes find points of disagreement even if an author's claims and logic are otherwise sound.

Examining an author's assumptions can also reveal a writer's biases. A **bias** is a preconceived idea that makes a person more likely to show unfair favor for certain thoughts, people, or groups. Because every person has a different experience of the world, every person has a different set of biases. For example, a person who has traveled widely may feel differently about world political events than someone who has always lived in one place.

Virtually all writing is biased to some degree. However, effective writing attempts to avoid bias as much as possible. Writing that is highly biased may be based on poor assumptions that render the entire argument invalid.

Highly biased writing often includes overgeneralizations. Words like *all, always, never,* and so on may indicate that the writer is overstating a point. While these words can exist in true statements, unbiased writing is more likely to qualify ideas using words like *usually, often,* and *rarely.*

Another quality of biased writing is excessively emotional word choice. When writers insult people who disagree with them or engage the emotions in a way that feels manipulative, they are being biased.

> **Biased:** Power-hungry politicians don't care that their standardized testing requirements are producing a generation of overanxious, incurious, impractical kids.
>
> **Less biased:** Politicians need to recognize that current standardized testing requirements are causing severe anxiety and other negative effects in children.

Biased writing may also reflect stereotypical thinking. A **stereotype** is a particularly harmful type of bias that applies specifically to groups of people. Stereotypical thinking is behind racism, sexism, homophobia, and so on. Even people who do not consider themselves prejudiced can use language that reflects common stereotypes. For example, the negative use of the word *crazy* reflects a stereotype against people with mental illnesses.

Historically, writers in English have used male nouns and pronouns to indicate all people. Revising such language for more inclusivity is considered more effective in contemporary writing.

> **Biased:** The history of the human race proves that man is a violent creature.
>
> **Less biased:** The history of the human race proves that people are violent.

Let's Review!

- A text meant to convince someone of something is making an argument.
- Arguments may employ both facts and opinions.
- Effective arguments must use valid reasoning.
- Arguments are based on assumptions that may be reasonable or highly biased.
- Almost all writing is biased to some degree, but strong writing makes an effort to eliminate bias.

EVALUATING AND INTEGRATING DATA

Effective readers do more than absorb and analyze the content of sentences, paragraphs, and chapters. They recognize the importance of features that stand out in and around the text, and they understand and integrate knowledge from visual features like maps and charts.

Text Features

Elements that stand out from a text are called **text features**. Text features perform many vital functions.

- **Introducing the Topic and Organizing Information**

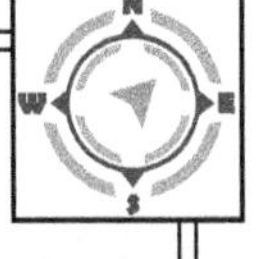

COMPARE!

The title on a fictional work does not always state the topic explicitly. While some titles do this, others are more concerned with hinting at a theme or setting up the tone.

- *Titles* – The title of a nonfiction text typically introduces the topic. Titles are guiding features of organization because they give clues about what is and is not covered. The title of this section, "Text Features," covers exactly that—not, for example, implicit ideas.
- *Headings and Subheadings* – Headings and subheadings provide subtopic information about supporting points and let readers scan to see how information is organized. The subheadings of this page organize text features according to the functions they perform.

- **Helping the Reader Find Information**

- *Table of Contents* – The table of contents of a long work lists chapter titles and other large-scale information so readers can predict the content. This helps readers to determine whether or not a text will be useful to them and to find sections relevant to their research.
- *Index* – In a book, the index is an alphabetical list of topics covered, complete with page numbers where the topics are discussed. Readers looking for information on one small subtopic can check the index to find out which pages to view.
- *Footnotes and Endnotes* – When footnotes and endnotes list sources, they allow the reader to find and evaluate the information an author is citing.

- **Emphasizing Concepts**

- *Formatting Features* – Authors may use formatting features such as *italics*, **boldfacing** or underlining to emphasize a word, phrase, or other important information in a text.
- *Bulleting and numbering* – Bullet points and numbered lists set off information and allow readers to scan for bits of information they do not know. It also helps to break down a list of steps.

- **Presenting Information and Illustrating Ideas**
    - *Graphic Elements* – Charts, graphs, diagrams, and other graphic elements present data succinctly, illustrate complex ideas, or otherwise convey information that would be difficult to glean from text alone.
- **Providing Peripheral Information**
    - *Sidebars* – Sidebars are text boxes that contain information related to the topic but not essential to the overall point.
    - *Footnotes and Endnotes* – Some footnotes and endnotes contain information that is not essential to the development of the main point but may nevertheless interest readers and researchers.[1]

> **FUN FACT!**
>
> Online, a sidebar is sometimes called a *doobly doo.*
>
> P.S. This is an example of a sidebar.

Maps and Charts

To read maps and charts, you need to understand what the labels, symbols, and pictures mean. You also need to know how to make decisions using the information they contain.

Maps

Maps are stylized pictures of places as seen from above. A map may have a box labeled "Key" or "Legend" that provides information about the meanings of colors, lines, or symbols. On the map below, the key shows that a solid line is a road and a dotted line is a trail.

There may also be a line labeled "scale" that helps you figure out how far you need to travel to get from one point on the map to another. In the example below, an inch is only 100 feet, so a trip from one end to the other is not far.

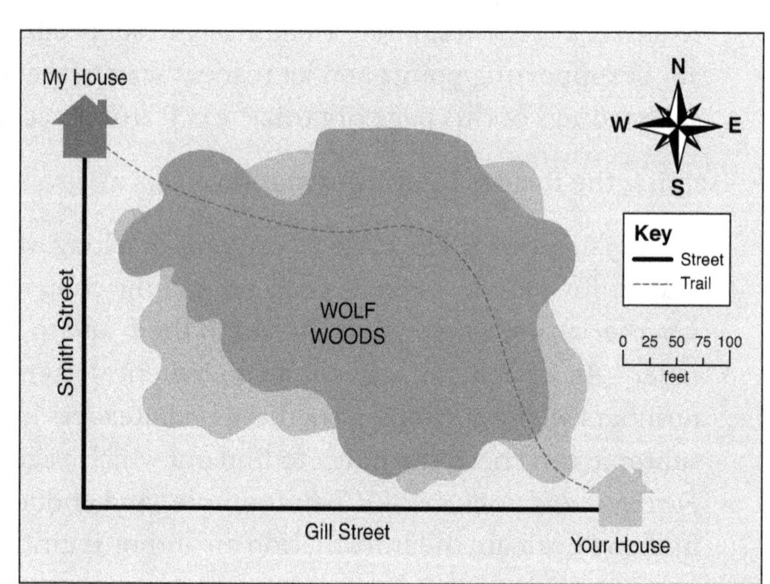

Some maps, including the example above, have compasses that show directions. If no compass is pictured, assume the top of the map is north.

1 Anthony Grafton's book *The Footnote: A Curious History* is an in-depth history of the origins and development of the footnote. (Also, this is an example of a footnote.)

Charts

Nutrition Facts Labels

Nutrition facts labels are charts many people see daily, but not everyone knows how to read them. The top third of the label lists calorie counts, serving sizes, and amount of servings in a package. If a package contains more than one serving, a person who eats the entire contents of the package may be consuming many times the number of calories listed per serving.

The label below lists the content of nutrients such as fats and carbohydrates, and so on. According to the label, a person who eats one serving of the product in the package will ingest 30 mg of cholesterol, or 10% of the total cholesterol he or she should consume in a day.

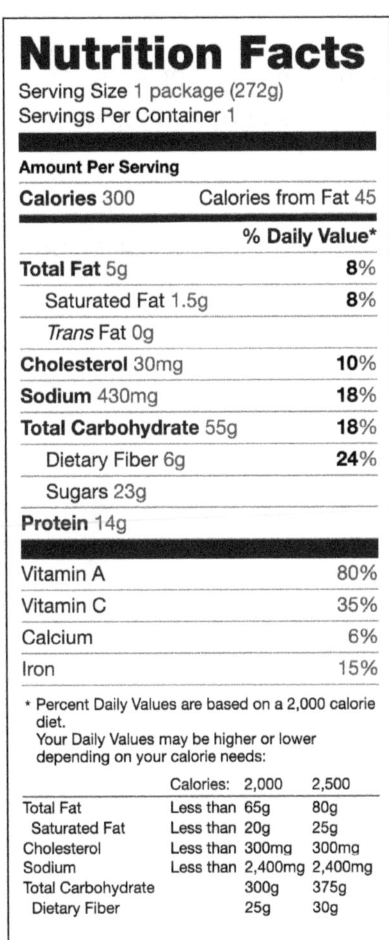

Nutrition Facts

Serving Size 1 package (272g)
Servings Per Container 1

Amount Per Serving

Calories 300	Calories from Fat 45
	% Daily Value*
Total Fat 5g	**8**%
Saturated Fat 1.5g	**8**%
Trans Fat 0g	
Cholesterol 30mg	**10**%
Sodium 430mg	**18**%
Total Carbohydrate 55g	**18**%
Dietary Fiber 6g	**24**%
Sugars 23g	
Protein 14g	
Vitamin A	80%
Vitamin C	35%
Calcium	6%
Iron	15%

* Percent Daily Values are based on a 2,000 calorie diet.
Your Daily Values may be higher or lower depending on your calorie needs:

	Calories:	2,000	2,500
Total Fat	Less than	65g	80g
Saturated Fat	Less than	20g	25g
Cholesterol	Less than	300mg	300mg
Sodium	Less than	2,400mg	2,400mg
Total Carbohydrate		300g	375g
Dietary Fiber		25g	30g

KEEP IN MIND . . .

The percentages on a Nutrition Facts label do not (and are not meant to) add up to 100. Instead, they show how much of a particular nutrient is contained in a serving of the product, as a proportion of a single person's Daily Value for that nutrient. The Daily Value is the total amount of a nutrient a person is supposed to eat in a day, based on a 2000-calorie diet.

In general, a percentage of 5% or less is considered low, whereas a percentage of 20% or more is considered high. A higher percentage can be good or bad, depending on whether or not a person should be trying to get more of a particular ingredient. People need to get plenty of vitamins, minerals, and fiber. In contrast, most people need to limit their intake of fat, cholesterol, and sodium.

Tables

Tables organize information into vertical columns and horizontal rows. Below is a table that shows how much water falls on areas of various sizes when it rains one inch. It shows, for instance, that a 40' x 70' roof receives 1,743 gallons of rain during a one-inch rainfall event.

Area	Area (square miles)	Area (square kilometers)	Amount of Water (gallons)	Amount of Water (liters)
My roof 40 x 70 feet	.0001	.000257	1,743 gallons	6,601 liters
1 acre (1 square mile = 640 acres)	.00156	.004	27,154 gallons	102,789 liters
1 square mile	1	2.6	17.38 million gallons	65.78 million liters
Atlanta, Georgia	132.4	342.9	2.293 billion gallons	8.68 billion liters
United States	3,537,438	9,161,922	61,474 billion gallons	232,700 billion liters

Let's Review!

- Readers must understand how and why text features make certain information stand out from the text.
- Readers must understand and interpret the content of maps and charts.

TYPES OF PASSAGES, TEXT STRUCTURES, GENRE AND THEME

To read effectively, you must understand what kind of text you are reading and how it is structured. You must also be able to look behind the text to find its deeper meanings.

Types of Passages

There are many ways of breaking texts down into categories. To do this, you need to consider the author's **purpose**, or what the text exists to do. Most texts exist to inform, persuade, or entertain. You also need to consider what the text does—whether it tells a story, describes facts, or develops a point of view.

Type of Passage	Examples
Narrative writing tells a story. The story can be fictional, or it can describe real events. The primary purpose of narrative writing is to entertain.	• An autobiography • A memoir • A short story • A novel
Expository writing provides an explanation or a description. Many academic essays and informational nonfiction books are expository writing. Stylistically, expository writing is highly varied. Although the explanations can be dry and methodical, many writers use an artful or entertaining style. Expository writing is nonfiction. Its primary purpose is to inform.	• A book about a historical event • An essay describing the social impacts of a new technology • A description of changing gender roles in marriages • A philosophical document exploring the nature of truth.
Technical writing explains a complex process or mechanism. Whereas expository writing is often academic, technical writing is used in practical settings such as businesses. The style of a technical document is almost always straightforward and impersonal. Technical writing is nonfiction, and its purpose is to inform.	• Recipes • Instructions • User manuals • Process descriptions
Persuasive writing makes an argument. It asks readers to believe something or do something. Texts that make judgments, such as movie reviews, are persuasive because they are attempting to convince readers to accept a point of view. Texts that suggest a plan are also persuasive because they are trying to convince readers to take an action. As the name "persuasive writing" indicates, the author's primary purpose is to persuade.	• Op-ed newspaper articles • Book reviews • Project proposals • Advertisements • Persuasive essays

BE CAREFUL!

Many texts have more than one purpose.

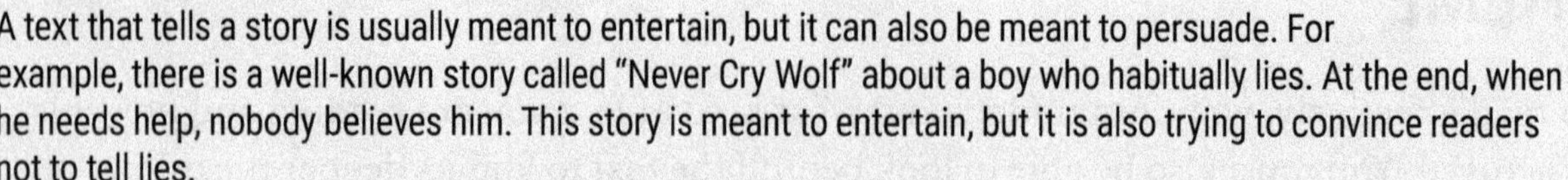

A text that tells a story is usually meant to entertain, but it can also be meant to persuade. For example, there is a well-known story called "Never Cry Wolf" about a boy who habitually lies. At the end, when he needs help, nobody believes him. This story is meant to entertain, but it is also trying to convince readers not to tell lies.

Similarly, many explanatory texts are meant to inform readers in an entertaining way. For example, a nonfiction author may describe a scientific topic using humor and wacky examples to make it fun for popular audiences to read.

Also, expository writing can look similar to persuasive writing, especially when it touches on topics that are controversial or emotional. For example, if an essay says social media is changing society, many readers assume it means social media is changing society *in a negative way.* If the writing makes this kind of value judgment or uses words like *should,* it is persuasive writing. But if the author is merely describing changes, the text is expository.

Text Structures

Authors rarely present ideas within a text in a random order. Instead, they organize their thoughts carefully. To read effectively, you must be able to recognize the **structure** of a text. That is, you need to identify the strategies authors use to organize their ideas. The five most common text structures are listed below.

Text Structure	Examples
In a **sequence** text, an author explains what happened first, second, third, and so on. In other words, a sequence text is arranged in **chronological order**, or time order. This type of text may describe events that have already happened or events that may happen in the future.	• A story about a birthday party. • A historical paper about World War II. • A list of instructions for baking a cake. • A series of proposed steps in a plan for business expansion.
A **compare/contrast** text explains the similarities and differences between two or more subjects. Authors may compare and contrast people, places, ideas, events, cultures, and so on.	• An essay describing the similarities and differences between women's experiences in medieval Europe and Asia. • A section in an op-ed newspaper article explaining the similarities and differences between two types of gun control.
A **cause/effect** text describes an event or action and its results. The causes and effects discussed can be actual or theoretical. That is, the author can describe the results of a historical event or predict the results of a possible future event.	• An explanation of ocean acidification and the coral bleaching that results. • A paper describing a proposed new law and its likely effects on the economy.
A **problem-solution** text presents a problem and outlines a solution. Sometimes it also predicts or analyzes the results of the solution. The solution can be something that already happened or a plan the author is proposing. Note that a problem can sometimes be expressed in terms of a wish or desire that the solution fulfills.	• An explanation of the problems smallpox caused and the strategies scientists used to eradicate it. • A business plan outlining a group of potential customers and the strategy a company should use to get their business.

Text Structure	Examples
A **description** text creates a mental picture for the reader by presenting concrete details in a coherent order. Description texts are usually arranged spatially. For instance, authors may describe the subject from top to bottom, or they may describe the inside first and then the outside, etc.	• An explanation of the appearance of a character in a story. • A paragraph in a field guide detailing the features of a bird. • A section on an instruction sheet describing how the final product should look.

CONNECTIONS

Different types of texts can use the same structures.

1. A story about a birthday party is a narrative, and its purpose is to entertain.
2. A historical paper about a war is an expository text meant to inform.
3. A list of instructions for baking a cake is a technical text meant to inform.
4. A series of proposed steps in a plan for business expansion is a persuasive text meant to persuade.

If all of these texts list ideas in chronological order, explaining what happened (or what may happen in the future) first, second, third, and so on, they are all using a sequence structure.

Genre and Theme

Literature can be organized into categories called **genres**. The two major genres of literature are fiction and nonfiction.

Fiction is made up. It can be broken down into many sub-genres, or sub-categories. The following are some of the common ones:

- Short story – Short work of fiction.
- Novel – Book-length work of fiction.
- Science fiction – A story set in the future
- Romance – A love story
- Mystery – A story that answers a concrete question, often about who committed a crime
- Mythology – A traditional story that reflects cultural traditions and beliefs but does not usually teach an explicit lesson
- Legends – Traditional stories that are presented as histories, even though they often contain fantastical or magical elements
- Fables – Traditional stories meant to teach an explicit lesson

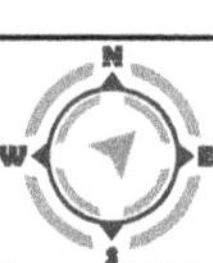

COMPARE!

The differences between myths and fables are sometimes hard to discern.

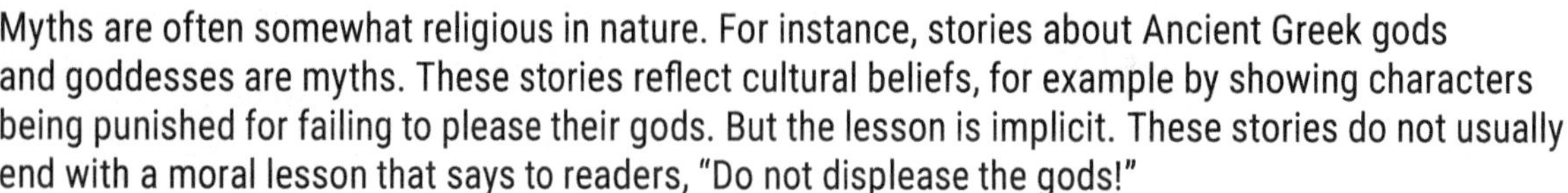

Myths are often somewhat religious in nature. For instance, stories about Ancient Greek gods and goddesses are myths. These stories reflect cultural beliefs, for example by showing characters being punished for failing to please their gods. But the lesson is implicit. These stories do not usually end with a moral lesson that says to readers, "Do not displease the gods!"

Fables are often for children, and they usually end with a sentence stating an explicit moral. For example, there's a story called "The Tortoise and the Hare," in which a tortoise and a hare agree to have a race. The hare, being a fast animal, gets cocky and takes a lot of breaks while the tortoise plods slowly toward the finish line without stopping. Because the tortoise keeps going, it eventually wins. The story usually ends with the moral, "Slow and steady win the race."

Nonfiction is true. Like fiction, it can be broken down into many sub-genres. The following are some of the common ones:

- Autobiography and memoir – The author's own life story
- Biography – Someone else's life story (not the author's)
- Histories – True stories about real events from the past
- Criticism and reviews – A response or judgment on another piece of writing or art
- Essay – A short piece describing the author's outlook or point of view.

CONNECTIONS

Everything under "Fiction" and several items under "Nonfiction" above are examples of narrative writing. We use labels like "narrative" and "persuasive" largely when we discuss writing tasks or the author's purpose. We could use these labels here too, but at the moment we're more concerned with the words that are most commonly used in discussions about literature's deeper meanings.

Literature reflects the human experience. Texts from different genres often share similar **themes**, or deeper meanings. Texts from different cultures do too. For example, a biography of a famous civil rights activist may highlight the same qualities of heroism and interconnectedness that appear in a work of mythology from Ancient India. Other common themes in literature may relate to war, love, survival, justice, suffering, growing up, and other experiences that are accessible to virtually all human beings.

Many students confuse the term *theme* with the term *moral*. A **moral** is an explicit message contained in the text, like "Don't lie" or "Crime doesn't pay." Morals are a common feature of fables and other traditional stories meant to teach lessons to children. Themes, in contrast, are implicit. Readers must consider the clues in the story and figure out themes for themselves. Because of this, themes are debatable. For testing purposes, questions focus on themes that are clearly and consistently indicated by clues within the text.

Let's Review!

- Written texts can be organized into the following categories: narrative, expository, technical, and persuasive.
- Texts of all categories may use the following organizational schemes or structures: sequence, compare/contrast, cause/effect, problem-solution, description.
- Literature can be organized into genres including fiction, nonfiction, and many sub-genres.
- Literature across genres and cultures often reflects the same deeper meanings, or themes.

KEEP IN MIND . . .

The text structures above do not always work in isolation. Authors often combine two or more structures within one text. For example, a business plan could be arranged in a problem-solution structure as the author describes what the business wants to achieve and how she proposes to achieve it. The "how" portion could also use a sequence structure as the author lists the steps to follow first, second, third, and so on.

Chapter 3 Integration of Knowledge and Ideas

Practice Quiz 1

1. **Which of the following is *not* a function of text features?**
   - A. Introducing the topic
   - B. Emphasizing a concept
   - C. Making the theme explicit
   - D. Providing peripheral information

2. **If a map does not have a compass, north is:**
   - A. up.
   - B. down.
   - C. right.
   - D. left.

3. **The purpose of an index is to tell readers:**
   - A. how to find sources that back up key ideas in the text.
   - B. who wrote the text and what his or her credentials are.
   - C. where to find information on a given subject within a book.
   - D. why the author believes the main idea of a text is important.

Read the following passage and answer questions 4-5.

Overworked public school teachers are required by law to spend extra time implementing

Individual Educational Plans for students with learning and attention challenges. This shortchanges children who are actually engaged in their education by depriving them of an equal amount of individualized attention.

4. **What assumption behind this passage reflects negative stereotypical thinking?**
   - A. Public school teachers are generally overworked and underpaid.
   - B. Students with learning disabilities are not engaged in their education.
   - C. Laws require teachers to provide accommodations to certain students.
   - D. Teachers have a finite amount of attention to divide between students.

5. **The above argument is invalid because the author:**
   - A. suggests that some students do not need as much attention because they learn the material more quickly.
   - B. uses derogatory and disrespectful word choice to describe people who think, learn, and process information differently.
   - C. describes public school teachers in a negative way that makes it seem as though they have no interest in helping students.
   - D. professes an interest in equality for all students while simultaneously suggesting some students are more worthy than others.

6. **Which statement, if true, is a fact?**
   A. The 1918 flu pandemic killed more people than World War I.
   B. The 1918 flu pandemic was more devastating than World War I.
   C. The 1918 flu pandemic was a terrifying display of nature's power.
   D. The 1918 flu pandemic caused greater social instability than the plague.

Read the following passage and answer questions 7-9.

There is inherent risk associated with the use of Rip Gym facilities. Although all Rip Gym customers sign a Risk Acknowledgment and Consent Form before gaining access to our grounds and equipment, litigation remains a possibility if customers suffer injuries due to negligence. Negligence complaints may include either staff mistakes or avoidable problems with equipment and facilities. It is therefore imperative that all Rip Gym employees follow the Safety Protocol in the event of a customer complaint.

Reports of Unsafe Equipment and Environs

Rip Gym employees must always respond promptly and seriously to any customer report of a hazard in our equipment or facilities, even if the employee judges the complaint frivolous. **Customers may not use rooms or equipment that have been reported unsafe until the following steps have been taken, in order, to confirm and/or resolve the problem.**

1. Place "Warning," "Out of Order," or "Off Limits" signs in the affected area or on the affected equipment, as appropriate. **Always follow this step first, before handling paperwork or attempting to resolve the reported problem.**
2. Fill out a Hazard Complaint Form. Include the name of the customer making the complaint and the exact wording of the problems being reported.
3. Visually check the area or equipment in question to verify the problem.
   a) If the report appears to be **accurate** and a resolution is necessary, proceed to step 4.
   b) If the report appears to be **inaccurate**, consult the manager on duty.
4. Determine whether you are qualified to correct the problem. Problems **all** employees are qualified to correct are listed on page 12 of the Employee Handbook.
   a) Employees who have **not** undergone training for equipment repair and maintenance must....

7. **This passage is best described as a(n):**
   A. narrative text.
   B. technical text.
   C. expository text.
   D. persuasive text.

8. **Which term best describes the structure of the opening paragraph?**
   A. Sequence
   B. Description
   C. Problem-solution
   D. Compare/Contrast

9. **Which term best describes the structure of the section under the subheading "Reports of Unsafe Equipment and Environs"?**
   A. Sequence
   B. Description
   C. Cause/effect
   D. Compare/contrast

Chapter 3 Integration of Knowledge and Ideas
Practice Quiz 1 – Answer Key

1. C. Although the title of a fictional work may hint at a theme, a theme is a message that is, by definition, not stated explicitly. **See Lesson: Evaluating and Integrating Data.**

2. A. By convention, north on a map is up. Mapmakers include a compass if they break this convention for some reason. **See Lesson: Evaluating and Integrating Data.**

3. C. An index lists subtopics of a book along with page numbers where those topics will be covered. **See Lesson: Evaluating and Integrating Data.**

4. B. The writer of this passage suggests implicitly that only students without learning and attention challenges are engaged in their education. This assumption reflects a negative stereotype that renders the entire argument faulty. **See Lesson: Facts, Opinions, and Evaluating an Argument.**

5. B. The author of the passage uses the phrase "students with learning and attention challenges" to refer to students who think and learn differently. This is not derogatory, but even so, the passage implies that people who experience these differences are less engaged in their education. **See Lesson: Facts, Opinions, and Evaluating an Argument.**

6. A. All of these statements contain beliefs or feelings that are subject to interpretation except the statement about the number of people killed in the 1918 flu pandemic compared to World War I. This is a verifiable piece of information, or a fact. **See Lesson: Facts, Opinions, and Evaluating an Argument.**

7. B. This is a technical text written to inform the reader about a complex process. **See Lesson: Types of Passages, Text Structures, Genre and Theme.**

8. C. The opening paragraph has a problem-solution structure. The problem it describes involves risks of injury and litigation, and the solution is that employees follow a process designed to minimize those risks. **See Lesson: Types of Passages, Text Structures, Genre and Theme.**

9. A. The step-by-step instructions under the subheading follow a sequential structure. Note key words and phrases such as "first" and "in order." **See Lesson: Types of Passages, Text Structures, Genre and Theme.**

Section II. Writing and Language

CHAPTER 4 CONVENTIONS OF STANDARD ENGLISH

SPELLING

Spelling correctly is important to accurately convey thoughts to an audience. This lesson will cover (1) vowels and consonants, (2) suffixes and plurals, (3) homophones and homographs.

Vowels and Consonants

Vowels and **consonants** are different speech sounds in English.

The letters A, E, I, O, U and sometimes Y are **vowels** and can create a variety of sounds. The most common are short sounds and long sounds. Long **vowel** sounds sound like the name of the letter such as the *a* in late. Short **vowel** sounds have a unique sound such as the *a* in cat. A rule for **vowels** is that when two vowels are walking, the first does the talking as in pain and meat.

Consonants include the other twenty-one letters in the alphabet. **Consonants** are weak letters and only make sounds when paired with **vowels**. That is why words always must have a **vowel**. This also means that **consonants** need to be doubled to make a stronger sound like sitting, grabbed, progress. Understanding general trends and patterns for **vowels** and **consonants** will help with spelling. The table below represents the difference between short and long **vowels** and gives examples for each.

	Symbol	Example Words
Short a	a	Cat, mat, hat, pat
Long a	ā	Late, pain, pay, they, weight, straight
Short e	e	Met, said, bread
Long e	ē	Breeze, cheap, dean, equal
Short i	i	Bit, myth, kiss, rip
Long i	ī	Cry, pie, high
Short o	o	Dog, hot, pop
Long o	ō	Snow, nose, elbow
Short u	u	Run, cut, club, gum
Long u	ū	Duty, rule, new, food
Short oo	oo	Book, foot, cookie
Long oo	ōō	Mood, bloom, shoot

Suffixes and Plurals

A **suffix** is a word part that is added to the ending of a root word. A **suffix** changes the meaning and spelling of words. There are some general patterns to follow with **suffixes**.

- Adding -er, -ist, or -or changes the root to mean *doer* or *performer*
    - Paint → Painter
    - Abolition → Abolitionist
    - Act → Actor
- Adding -ation or -ment changes the root to mean *an action* or *a process*
    - Ador(e) → Adoration
    - Develop → Development
- Adding -ism changes the root to mean *a theory or ideology*
    - Real → Realism
- Adding -ity, -ness, -ship, or -tude changes the root to mean *a condition, quality, or state*
    - Real → Reality
    - Sad → Sadness
    - Relation → Relationship
    - Soli(tary) → Solitude

Plurals are similar to suffixes as letters are added to the end of the word to signify more than one person, place, thing, or idea. There are also general patterns to follow when creating **plurals**.

- If a word ends in -s,-ss,-z,-zz,-ch, or -sh, add -es.
    - Bus → Buses
- If a word ends in a -y, drop the -y and add -ies.
    - Pony → Ponies
- If a word ends in an -f, change the f to a v and add -es.
    - Knife → Knives
- For all other words, add an -s.
    - Dog → Dogs

Homophones and Homographs

A **homophone** is a word that has the same sound as another word, but does not have the same meaning or spelling.

- To, too, and two
- There, their, and they're
- See and sea

A **homograph** is a word that has the same spelling as another word, but does not have the same sound or meaning.

- Lead (to go in front of) and lead (a metal)
- Bass (deep sound) and bass (a fish)

Let's Review!

- Vowels include the letters A, E, I, O, U and sometimes Y and have both short and long sounds.
- Consonants are the other twenty-one letters and have weak sounds. They are often doubled to make stronger sounds.
- Suffixes are word parts added to the root of a word and change the meaning and spelling.
- To make a word plural, add -es, -ies, -ves, or -s to the end of a word.
- Homophones are words that have the same sound, but not the same meaning or spelling.
- Homographs are words that have the same spelling, but not the same meaning or sound.

CAPITALIZATION

Correct capitalization helps readers understand when a new sentence begins and the importance of specific words. This lesson will cover the capitalization rules of (1) geographic locations and event names, (2) organizations and publication titles, (3) individual names and professional titles, and (4) months, days, and holidays.

Geographic Locations and Event Names

North, east, south, and west are not capitalized unless they relate to a **definite region**.

- Go north on I-5 for 200 miles.
- The West Coast has nice weather.

Words like northern, southern, eastern, and western are also not capitalized unless they describe **people or the cultural and political activities of people**.

- There is nothing interesting to see in eastern Colorado.
- Midwesterners are known for being extremely nice.
- The Western states almost always vote Democratic.

These words are not capitalized when placed before a name or region unless it is part of the **official name**.

- She lives in southern California.
- I loved visiting Northern Ireland.

Continents, countries, states, cities, and **towns** need to be capitalized.

- Australia has a lot of scary animals.
- Not many people live in Antarctica.
- Albany is the capital of New York.

Historical events should be capitalized to separate the specific from the general.

- The bubonic plague in the Middle Ages killed a large portion of the population in Europe.
- The Great Depression took place in the early 1930s.
- We are living in the twenty-first century.

Organizations and Publication Titles

The **names of national organizations** need to be capitalized. Short prepositions, articles, and conjunctions within the title are not capitalized unless they are the first word.

- The National American Woman Suffrage Association was essential in passing the Nineteenth Amendment.
- The House of Representatives is one part of Congress.

- Most kids' favorite holiday is Christmas.
- The new school year usually starts after Labor Day.
- It is nice to go to the beach over Memorial Day weekend.

The **seasons** are not capitalized.

- It gets too hot in the summer and too cold in the winter.
- The flowers and trees bloom so beautifully in the spring.

Let's Review!

- Only capitalize directional words like north, south, east, and, west when they describe a definite region, people, and their political and cultural activities, or when it is part of the official name.
- Historical periods and events are capitalized to represent their importance and specificity.
- Every word except short prepositions, conjunctions, and articles in the names of national organizations are capitalized.
- The titles of publications follow the same rules as organizations.
- The names of individual people need to be capitalized.
- Professional titles are capitalized if they precede a name or are used as a direct address.
- All months of the year, days of the week, and holidays are capitalized.
- Seasons are not capitalized.

- The National Football League consists of thirty-two teams.

The **titles of books, chapters, articles, poems, newspapers, and other publications** should be capitalized.

- Her favorite book is *A Wrinkle in Time.*
- I do the crossword in *The New York Times* every Sunday.
- *The Jabberwocky* by Lewis Carroll has many silly sounding words.

Individual Names and Professional Titles

People's names as well as their **familial relationship title** need to be capitalized.

- Barack Obama was our first African American president.
- Uncle Joe brought the steaks for our Memorial Day grill.
- Aunt Sarah lives in California, but my other aunt lives in Florida.

Professional titles need to be capitalized when they precede a name, or as a direct address. If it is after a name or is used generally, titles do not need to be capitalized.

- Governor Cuomo is trying to modernize the subway system in New York.
- Andrew Cuomo is the governor of New York.
- A governor runs the state. A president runs the country.
- Thank you for the recommendation, Mr. President.
- I need to see Doctor Smith.
- I need to see a doctor.

Capitalize the **title of high-ranking government officials** when an individual is referred to.

- The Secretary of State travels all over the world.
- The Vice President joined the meeting.

With **compound titles**, the prefixes or suffixes do not need to be capitalized.

- George W. Bush is the ex-President of the United States.

Months, Days, and Holidays

Capitalize **all months of the year** (January, February, March, April, May, June, July, August, September, October, November, December) and **days of the week** (Sunday, Monday, Tuesday, Wednesday, Thursday, Friday, Saturday).

- Her birthday is in November.
- People graduate from college in May or June.
- Saturdays and Sundays are supposed to be fun and relaxing.

Holidays are also capitalized.

PUNCTUATION

Punctuation is important in writing to accurately represent ideas. Without correct punctuation, the meaning of a sentence is difficult to understand. This lesson will cover (1) periods, question marks, and exclamation points, (2) commas, semicolons, and colons, and (3) apostrophes, hyphens, and quotation marks.

Terminal Punctuation Marks: Periods, Question Marks, and Exclamation Points

Terminal punctuation is used at the end of a sentence. Periods, question marks, and exclamation points are the three types of terminal punctuation.

Periods (.) mark the end of a declarative sentence, one that states a fact, or an imperative sentence, one that states a command or request). Periods can also be used in abbreviations.

- Doctors save lives.
- She has a B.A. in Psychology.

Question Marks (?) signify the end of a sentence that is a question. Where, when, who, whom, what, why, and how are common words that begin question sentences.

- Who is he?
- Where is the restaurant?
- Why is the sky blue?

Exclamation Points (!) indicate strong feelings, shouting, or emphasize a feeling.

- Watch out!
- That is incredible!
- I hate you!

Internal Punctuation: Commas, Semicolons, and Colons

Internal punctuation is used within a sentence to help keep words, phrases, and clauses in order. These punctuation marks can be used to indicate elements such as direct quotations and definitions in a sentence.

A **comma (,)** signifies a small break within a sentence and separates words, clauses, or ideas.

Commas are used before conjunctions that connect two independent clauses.

- I ate some cookies, and I drank some milk.

Commas are also used to set off an introductory phrase.

- After the test, she grabbed dinner with a friend.

Short phrases that emphasis thoughts or emotions are enclosed by **commas**.

- The school year, thankfully, ends in a week.

Commas set off the words yes and no.

- Yes, I am available this weekend.
- No, she has not finished her homework.

Commas set off a question tag.

- It is beautiful outside, isn't it?

Commas are used to indicate direct address.

- Are you ready, Jack?
- Mom, what is for dinner?

Commas separate items in a series.

- We ate eggs, potatoes, and toast for breakfast.
- I need to grab coffee, go to the store, and put gas in my car.

Semicolons (;) are used to connect two independent clauses without a coordinating conjunction like *and* or *but*. A **semicolon** creates a bond between two sentences that are related. Do not capitalize the first word after the **semicolon** unless it is a word that is normally capitalized.

- The ice cream man drove down my street; I bought a popsicle.
- My mom cooked dinner; the chicken was delicious.
- It is cloudy today; it will probably rain.

Colons (:) introduce a list.

- She teaches three subjects: English, history, and geography.

Within a sentence, **colons** can create emphasis of a word or phrase.

- She had one goal: pay the bills.

More Internal Punctuation: Apostrophes, Hyphens, and Quotation Marks

Apostrophes (') are used to indicate possession or to create a contraction.

- Bob has a car - Bob's car is blue.
- Steve's cat is beautiful.

For plurals that are also possessive, put the **apostrophe** after the s.

- Soldiers' uniforms are impressive.

Make contractions by combining two words.

- I do not have a dog - I don't have a dog
- I can't swim.

Its and it's do not follow the normal possessive rules. Its is possessive while it's means "it is."

- It's a beautiful day to be at the park.
- The dog has many toys, but its favorite is the rope.

Hyphens (-) are mainly used to create compound words.

- The documentary was a real eye-opener for me.
- We have to check-in to the hotel before midnight.
- The graduate is a twenty-two-year-old woman.

Quotation Marks (") are used when directly using another person's words in your own writing. Commas and periods, sometimes question marks and exclamation points, are placed within **quotation marks**. Colons and semicolons are placed outside of the **quotation marks**, unless they are part of the quoted material. If quoting an entire sentence, capitalize the first word. If it is a fragment, do not capitalize the first word.

- Ernest Hemingway once claimed, "There is nothing noble in being superior to your fellow man; true nobility is being superior to your former self."
- Steve said, "I will be there at noon."

An indirect quote which paraphrases what someone else said does not need **quotation marks**.

- Steve said he would be there at noon.

Quotation marks are also used for the titles of short works such as poems, articles, and chapters. They are not italicized.

- Robert Frost wrote "The Road Not Taken."

Let's Review!

- **Periods** (.) signify the end of a sentence or are used in abbreviations.
- **Question Marks** (?) are also used at the end of a sentence and distinguish the sentence as a question.
- **Exclamation Points** (!) indicate strong feelings, shouting, or emphasis and are usually at the end of the sentence.
- **Commas** (,) are small breaks within a sentence that separate clauses, ideas, or words. They are used to set off introductory phrases, the words yes and no, question tags, indicate direct address, and separate items in a series.
- **Semicolons** (;) connect two similar sentences without a coordinating conjunctions such as and or but.
- **Colons** (:) are used to introduce a list or emphasize a word or phrase.
- **Apostrophes** (') indicate possession or a contraction of two words.
- **Hyphens** (-) are used to create compound words.
- **Quotation Marks** (") are used when directly quoting someone else's words and to indicate the title of poems, chapters, and articles.

Chapter 4 Conventions of Standard English Practice Quiz 1

1. **Which word(s) in the following sentence should NOT be capitalized?**

   Can You Speak German?

   A. You and Speak
   B. Can and German
   C. Can, You, and Speak
   D. You, Speak, and German

2. **Fill in the blank with the correctly capitalized form.**

   Every week, they get together to watch ______.

   A. the bachelor
   B. The Bachelor
   C. The bachelor
   D. the Bachelor

3. **Choose the correct sentence.**

   A. They used to live in the pacific northwest.
   B. They used to live in the Pacific northwest.
   C. They used to live in the pacific Northwest.
   D. They used to live in the Pacific Northwest.

4. **What is the sentence with the correct use of punctuation?**

   A. Offcampus apartments are nicer.
   B. Off campus apartments are nicer.
   C. Off-campus apartments are nicer.
   D. Off-campus-apartments are nicer.

5. **Which of the following sentences is correct?**

   A. I asked Scott, How was your day?
   B. Scott said, it was awesome.
   C. He claimed, "My history presentation was great!"
   D. I said, That's wonderful!

6. **What is the mistake in the following sentence?**

   The highestranking officer can choose his own work, including his own hours.

   A. *Highestranking* needs a hyphen.
   B. There should be a comma after *officer*.
   C. There should be no comma after *work*.
   D. There should be a semicolon after *work*.

7. **Which of the following spellings is correct?**

   A. Busines
   B. Business
   C. Buseness
   D. Bussiness

8. **What is the correct plural of morning?**

   A. Morning
   B. Mornings
   C. Morninges
   D. Morningies

9. **On Earth, _____ are seven continents.**

   A. their
   B. there
   C. theer
   D. they're

Chapter 4 Conventions of Standard English
Practice Quiz 1 – Answer Key

1. **A.** *You and Speak.* Can is the first word in the sentence and needs to be capitalized. German is a nationality and needs to be capitalized. The other two words do not need to be capitalized. **See Lesson: Capitalization.**

2. **B.** *The Bachelor.* The names of TV shows are capitalized. *The* is capitalized here because it is the first word in the name. **See Lesson: Capitalization.**

3. **D.** *They used to live in the Pacific Northwest.* Specific geographic regions are capitalized. **See Lesson: Capitalization.**

4. **C.** *Off-campus apartments are nicer.* Hyphens are often used for compound words that are placed before the noun to help with understanding. **See Lesson: Punctuation.**

5. **C.** *He claimed, "My history presentation was great!"* Quotation marks enclose direct statements. **See Lesson: Punctuation.**

6. **A.** *Highestranking needs a hyphen.* Hyphens are used for compound words that describe a person or object. **See Lesson: Punctuation.**

7. **B.** *Business* is the only correct spelling. **See Lesson: Spelling.**

8. **B.** For most words ending in consonants, just add -s. **See Lesson: Spelling.**

9. **B.** *There* describes a place or position and is correctly spelled. **See Lesson: Spelling.**

CHAPTER 5 PARTS OF SPEECH

NOUNS

In this lesson, you will learn about nouns. A noun is a word that names a person, place, thing, or idea. This lesson will cover (1) the role of nouns in sentences and (2) different types of nouns.

Nouns and Their Role in Sentences

A **noun** names a person, place, thing, or idea.

Some examples of nouns are:

- Gandhi
- New Hampshire
- garden
- happiness

A noun's role in a sentence is as **subject** or **object**. A subject is the part of the sentence that does something, whereas the object is the thing that something is done to. In simple terms, the subject acts, and the object is acted upon.

Look for the nouns in these sentences.

1. The Louvre is stunning. (subject noun: The Louvre)
2. Marco ate dinner with Sara and Petra. (subject noun: Marco; object nouns: dinner, Sara, Petra)
3. Honesty is the best policy. (subject noun: honesty; object noun: policy)
4. After the election, we celebrated our new governor. (object nouns: governor, election)
5. I slept. (0 nouns)

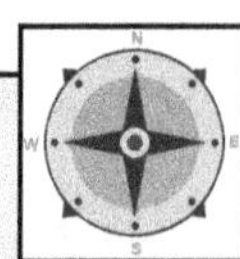

KEEP IN MIND . . .

The subjects *I* and *we* in the two sentences to the left are pronouns, not nouns.

Look for the nouns in these sentences.

1. Mrs. Garcia makes a great pumpkin pie. (subject noun: Mrs. Garcia; object noun: pie)
2. We really need to water the garden. (object noun: garden)
3. Love is sweet. (subject noun: love)
4. Sam loves New York in the springtime. (subject noun: Sam; object nouns: New York, springtime)
5. Lin and her mother and father ate soup, fish, potatoes, and fruit for dinner. (subject nouns: Lin, mother, father; object nouns: soup, fish, potatoes, fruit, dinner)

Why isn't the word *pumpkin* a noun in the first sentence? *Pumpkin* is often a noun, but here it is used as an adjective that describes what kind of *pie*.

Why isn't the word *water* a noun in the second sentence? Here, *water* is an **action verb**. To *water the garden* is something we do.

How is the word *love* a noun in the third sentence and not in the fourth sentence? *Love* is a noun (thing) in sentence 3 and a verb (action) in the sentence 4.

How many nouns can a sentence contain? As long as the sentence remains grammatically correct, it can contain an unlimited number of nouns.

BE CAREFUL!

Words can change to serve different roles in different sentences. A word that is usually a noun can sometimes be used as an adjective or a verb. Determine a word's function in a sentence to be sure of its part of speech.

Types of Nouns

Singular and Plural Nouns

Nouns can be **singular** or **plural**. A noun is singular when there is only one. A noun is plural when there are two or more.

- The book has 650 pages.

Book is a singular noun. *Pages* is a plural noun.

Often, to make a noun plural, we add *-s* at the end of the word: *cat/cats*. This is a **regular** plural noun. Sometimes we make a word plural in another way: *child/children*. This is an **irregular** plural noun. Some plurals follow rules, while others do not. The most common rules are listed here:

KEEP IN MIND . . .

Some nouns are countable, and others are not. For example, we eat *three blueberries*, but we **do not** drink *three milks*. Instead, we drink *three glasses of milk* or *some milk*.

Singular noun	Plural noun	Rule for making plural
star	stars	for most words, add *-s*
box	boxes	for words that end in *-j*, *-s*, *-x*, *-z*, *-ch* or *-sh*, add *-es*
baby	babies	for words that end in *-y*, change *-y* to *-i* and add *-es*
woman	women	irregular
foot	feet	irregular

Common and Proper Nouns

Common nouns are general words, and they are written in lowercase. **Proper nouns** are specific names, and they begin with an uppercase letter.

Examples:

Common noun	Proper noun
ocean	Baltic Sea
dentist	Dr. Marx
company	Honda
park	Yosemite National Park

Concrete and Abstract Nouns

Concrete nouns are people, places, or things that physically exist. We can use our senses to see or hear them. *Turtle, spreadsheet,* and *Australia* are concrete nouns.

Abstract nouns are ideas, qualities, or feelings that we cannot see and that might be harder to describe. *Beauty, childhood, energy, envy, generosity, happiness, patience, pride, trust, truth,* and *victory* are abstract nouns.

Some words can be either concrete or abstract nouns. For example, the concept of *art* is abstract, but *art* that we see and touch is concrete.

- We talked about *art.* (abstract)
- She showed me the *art* she had created in class. (concrete)

Let's Review!

- A noun is a person, place, thing, or idea.
- A noun's function in a sentence is as subject or object.
- Common nouns are general words, while proper nouns are specific names.
- Nouns can be concrete or abstract.

PRONOUNS

A pronoun is a word that takes the place of or refers to a specific noun. This lesson will cover (1) the role of pronouns in sentences and (2) the purpose of pronouns.

Pronouns and Their Role in Sentences

A **pronoun** takes the place of a noun or refers to a specific noun.

Subject, Object, and Possessive Pronouns

A pronoun's role in a sentence is as **subject, object,** or **possessive**.

Subject Pronouns	Object Pronouns	Possessive Pronouns
I	me	my, mine
you	you	your, yours
he	her	his
she	him	her, hers
it	it	its
we	us	ours
they	them	their, theirs

In simple sentences, subject pronouns come before the verb, object pronouns come after the verb, and possessive pronouns show ownership.

Look at the pronouns in these examples:

- She forgot her coat. (subject: she; possessive: her)
- I lent her mine. (subject: I; object: her; possessive: mine)
- She left it at school. (subject: she; object: it)
- I had to go and get it the next day. (subject: I; object: it)
- I will never lend her something of mine again! (subject: I; object: her; possessive: mine)

BE CAREFUL!

It is easy to make a mistake when you have multiple words in the role of subject or object.

Correct	Incorrect	Why?
John and I went out.	*John and me* went out.	*John and I* is a subject. *I* is a subject pronoun; *me* is not.
Johan took *Sam and me* to the show.	Johan took *Sam and I* to the show.	*Sam and me* is an object. *Me* is an object pronoun; *I* is not.

Relative Pronouns

Relative pronouns connect a clause to a noun or pronoun.

These are some relative pronouns:

who, whom, whoever, whose, that, which

- Steve Jobs, *who founded Apple,* changed the way people use technology.

The pronoun *who* introduces a clause that gives more information about Steve Jobs.

- This is the movie *that Emily told us to see.*

The pronoun *that* introduces a clause that gives more information about the movie.

Other Pronouns

Some other pronouns are:

this, that, what, anyone, everything, something

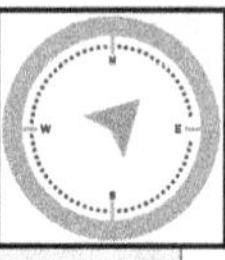
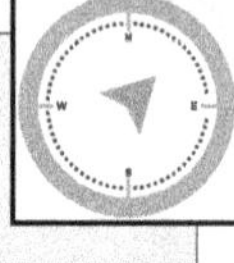

DID YOU KNOW?
Pronouns can sometimes refer to general or unspecified things.

Look for the pronouns in these sentences.

- What is that?
- There is something over there!
- Does anyone have a pen?

Pronouns and Their Purpose

The purpose of a pronoun is to replace a noun. Note the use of the pronoun *their* in the heading of this section. If we did not have pronouns, we would have to call this section *Pronouns and Pronouns' Purpose.*

What Is an Antecedent?

A pronoun in a sentence refers to a specific noun, and this noun called the **antecedent**.

- John Hancock signed the Declaration of Independence. He signed it in 1776.

The antecedent for *he* is John Hancock.
The antecedent for *it* is the Declaration of Independence.

BE CAREFUL!
Look out for unclear antecedents, such as in this sentence:

- Take the furniture out of the room and paint *it*.

What needs to be painted, the furniture or the room?

Find the pronouns in the following sentence. Then identify the antecedent for each pronoun.

Erin had an idea *that she* suggested to Antonio: "*I*'ll help *you* with *your* math homework if *you* help *me* with *my* writing assignment."

Pronoun	Antecedent
that	idea
she	Erin
I	Erin
you	Antonio
your	Antonio's
you	Antonio
me	Erin
my	Erin's

What Is Antecedent Agreement?

A pronoun must agree in **gender** and **number** with the antecedent it refers to. For example:

- Singular pronouns *I, you, he, she,* and *it* replace singular nouns.
- Plural pronouns *you, we,* and *they* replace plural nouns.
- Pronouns *he, she,* and *it* replace masculine, feminine, or neutral nouns.

Correct	Incorrect	Why?
Students should do their homework every night.	A student should do their homework every night.	The pronoun *their* is plural, so it must refer to a plural noun such as *students.*
When an employee is sick, he or she should call the office.	When an employee is sick, they should call the office.	The pronoun *they* is plural, so it must refer to a plural noun. *Employee* is not a plural noun.

Let's Review!

- A pronoun takes the place of or refers to a noun.
- The role of pronouns in sentences is as subject, object, or possessive.
- A pronoun must agree in number and gender with the noun it refers to.

Adjectives and Adverbs

An **adjective** is a word that describes a noun or a pronoun. An **adverb** is a word that describes a verb, an adjective, or another adverb.

Adjectives

An **adjective** describes, modifies, or tells us more about a **noun** or a **pronoun**. Colors, numbers, and descriptive words such as *healthy, good*, and *sharp* are adjectives.

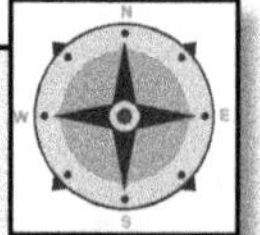

KEEP IN MIND . . .

Adjectives typically come **before the noun** in English. However, with **linking verbs** (non-action verbs such as *be, seem, look*), the adjective may come **after the verb** instead. Think of it like this: a linking verb **links** the adjective to the noun or pronoun.

Look for the adjectives in the following sentences:

	Adjective	Noun or pronoun it describes
I rode the blue bike.	blue	bike
It was a long trip.	long	trip
Bring two pencils for the exam.	two	pencils
The box is brown.	brown	box
She looked beautiful.	beautiful	she
That's great!	great	that

Multiple adjectives can be used in a sentence, as can multiple nouns. Look at these examples:

	Adjectives	Noun or pronoun it describes
The six girls were happy, healthy, and rested after their long beach vacation.	six, happy, healthy, rested; long, beach	girls; vacation
Leo has a good job, but he is applying for a better one.	good; better	job; one

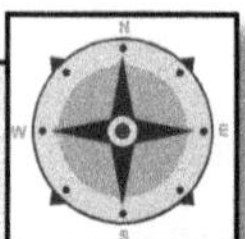

KEEP IN MIND . . .

Note comparative and superlative forms of adjectives, such as:

fast, faster, fastest

far, farther, farthest

good, better, best

bad, worse, worst

Articles: *A, An, The*

Articles are a unique part of speech, but they work like adjectives. An article tells more about a noun. *A* and *an* are **indefinite** articles. Use *a* before a singular **general** noun. Use *an* before a singular general noun that begins with a vowel.

The is a **definite** article. Use *the* before a singular or plural **specific** noun.

Look at how articles are used in the following sentences:

- I need *a* pencil to take *the* exam. (any pencil; specific exam)
- Is there *a* zoo in town? (any zoo)
- Let's go to *the* zoo today. (specific zoo)
- Can you get me *a* glass of milk? (any glass)
- Would you bring me *the* glass that's over there? (specific glass)

Adverbs

An **adverb** describes, modifies, or tells us more about a **verb**, an **adjective**, or another **adverb**. Many adverbs end in *-ly*. Often, adverbs tell when, where, or how something happened. Words such as *slowly, very,* and *yesterday* are adverbs.

Adverbs that Describe Verbs

Adverbs that describe verbs tell something more about the action.

Look for the adverbs in these sentences:

	Adverb	Verb it describes
They walked quickly.	quickly	walked
She disapproved somewhat of his actions, but she completely understood them.	somewhat; completely	disapproved; understood
The boys will go inside if it rains heavily.	inside; heavily	go; rains

Adverbs that Describe Adjectives

Adverbs that describe adjectives often add intensity to the adjective. Words like *quite, more,* and *always* are adverbs.

Look for the adverbs in these sentences:

	Adverb	Adjective it describes
The giraffe is very tall.	very	tall
Do you think that you are more intelligent than them?	more	intelligent
If it's really loud, we can make the volume slightly lower.	really; slightly	loud; lower

Adverbs that Describe Other Adverbs

Adverbs that describe adverbs often add intensity to the adverb.

Look for the adverbs in these sentences:

	Adverb	Adverb it describes
The mouse moved too quickly for us to catch it.	too	quickly
This store is almost never open.	almost	never
Those women are quite fashionably dressed.	quite	fashionably

Adjectives vs. Adverbs

Not sure whether a word is an adjective or an adverb? Look at these examples.

	Adjective	Adverb	Explanation
fast	You're a *fast* driver.	You drove *fast*.	The adjective *fast* describes *driver* (noun); the adverb *fast* describes *drove* (verb).
early	I don't like *early* mornings!	Try to arrive *early*.	The adjective *early* describes *mornings* (noun); the adverb *early* describes *arrive* (verb).
good/well	They did *good* work together.	They worked *well* together.	The adjective *good* describes *work* (noun); the adverb *well* describes *worked* (verb).
bad/badly	The dog is *bad*.	The dog behaves *badly*.	The adjective *bad* describes *dog* (noun); the adverb *badly* describes *behaves* (verb).

Let's Review!

- An **adjective** describes, modifies, or tells us more about a **noun** or a **pronoun**.
- An **adverb** describes, modifies, or tells us more about a **verb**, an **adjective**, or another **adverb**.

BE CAREFUL!

When an adverb ends in *-ly*, add *more* or *most* to make comparisons.

Correct: The car moved *more slowly*.

Incorrect: The car moved *slower*.

Conjunctions and Prepositions

A **conjunction** is a connector word; it connects words, phrases, or clauses in a sentence. A **preposition** is a relationship word; it shows the relationship between two nearby words.

Conjunctions

> **KEEP IN MIND . . .**
>
> A clause is a phrase that has a subject and a verb.
>
> Some clauses are **independent**. An independent clause can stand alone.
>
> Some clauses are **dependent**. A dependent clause relies on another clause in order to make sense.

A **conjunction** connects words, phrases, or clauses.

And, so, and *or* are conjunctions.

Types of Conjunctions

- **Coordinating** conjunctions connect two words, phrases, or independent clauses. The full list of coordinating conjunctions is: *and, or, but, so, for, nor, yet.*
- **Subordinating** conjunctions connect a main (independent) clause and a dependent clause. The conjunction may show a relationship or time order for the two clauses. Some subordinating conjunctions are: *after, as soon as, once, if, even though, unless.*
- **Correlative** conjunctions are pairs of conjunctions that work together to connect two words or phrases. Some correlative conjunctions are: *either/or, neither/nor, as/as.*

Example	Conjunction	What it is connecting
Verdi, Mozart, **and** *Wagner* are famous opera composers.	and	three nouns
Would you like *angel food cake, chocolate lava cake,* **or** *banana cream pie* for dessert?	or	three noun phrases
I took the bus to work, **but** *I walked home.*	but	two independent clauses
It was noisy at home, **so** *we went to the library.*	so	two independent clauses
They have to clean the house **before** *the realtor shows it.*	before	a main clause and a dependent clause
Use **either** *hers* **or** *mine.*	either/or	two pronouns
After *everyone leaves,* make sure you lock up.	after	a main clause and a dependent clause
I'd **rather** *fly* **than** *take the train.*	rather/than	two verb phrases
As soon as *they announced the winning number,* she looked at her ticket and shouted, "Whoopee!"	as soon as	a main clause and a dependent clause

> **DID YOU KNOW?**
>
> In the last example above, "*Whoopee!*" is an interjection. An **interjection** is a short phrase or clause that communicates emotion.
>
> Some other interjections are:
>
> - *Way to go!*
> - *Yuck.*
> - *Hooray!*
> - *Holy cow!*
> - *Oops!*

Prepositions

A **preposition** shows the relationship between two nearby words. Prepositions help to tell information such as direction, location, and time. *To*, *for*, and *with* are prepositions.

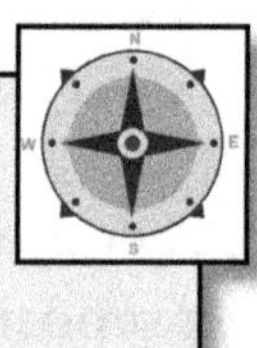

KEEP IN MIND . . .

Some prepositions are more than one word. *On top of* and *instead of* are prepositions.

Example	Preposition	What it tells us
The desk is in the classroom.	in	location
We'll meet you at 6:00.	at	time
We'll meet you at the museum.	at	place
The book is on top of the desk.	on top of	location

Prepositional Phrases

A preposition must be followed by an **object of the preposition**. This can be a noun or something that serves as a noun, such as a pronoun or a gerund.

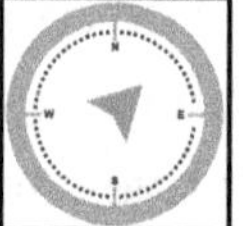

DID YOU KNOW?

A gerund is the *-ing* form a verb that serves as a noun. *Hiking* is a gerund in this sentence:

I wear these shoes for *hiking*.

A **prepositional phrase** is a preposition plus the object that follows it.

Look for the prepositional phrases in the following examples. Note that a sentence can have more than one prepositional phrase.

Example	Preposition	Object of the preposition
The tiny country won the war *against all odds*.	against	all odds
Look *at us*!	at	us
Why don't we go swimming *instead of sweating in this heat*?	instead of; in	sweating; this heat
Aunt Tea kept the trophy *on a shelf of the cabinet between the sofas in the living room*.	on; of; between; in	a shelf; the cabinet; the sofas; the living room

BE CAREFUL!

Sometimes a word looks like a preposition but is actually part of the verb. In this case, the verb is called a phrasal verb, and the preposition-like word is called a particle. Here is an example:

- *Turn on* the light. (*Turn on* has a meaning of its own; it is a phrasal verb. *On* is a particle here, rather than a preposition.)
- Turn *on that street.* (*On that street* shows location; it is a prepositional phrase. *On* is a preposition here.)

Let's Review!

- A **conjunction** connects words, phrases, or clauses. *And, so,* and *or* are conjunctions.
- A **preposition** shows the relationship between two nearby words. *To, for,* and *with* are prepositions.
- A **prepositional phrase** includes a preposition plus the object of the preposition.

VERBS AND VERB TENSES

A **verb** is a word that describes a **physical or mental action** or a **state of being**. This lesson will cover the role of verbs in sentences, verb forms and tenses, and helping verbs.

The Role of Verbs in Sentences

A verb describes an action or a state of being. A complete sentence must have at least one verb.

Verbs have different tenses, which show time.

Verb Forms

Each verb has three primary forms. The **base form** is used for simple present tense, and the **past form** is used for simple past tense. The **participle form** is used for more complicated time situations. Participle form verbs are accompanied by a helping verb.

Base Form	Past Form	Participle Form
end	ended	ended
jump	jumped	jumped
explain	explained	explained
eat	ate	eaten
take	took	taken
go	went	gone
come	came	come

Some verbs are **regular**. To make the **past** or **participle** form of a regular verb, we just add *-ed*. However, many verbs that we commonly use are **irregular**. We need to memorize the forms for these verbs.

In the chart above, *end, jump,* and *explain* are regular verbs. *Eat, take, go*, and *come* are irregular.

Using Verbs

A simple sentence has a **subject** and a **verb**. The subject tells us who or what, and the verb tells us the action or state.

Example	Subject	Verb	*Explanation/Time*
They ate breakfast together yesterday.	They	ate	*happened yesterday*
I walk to school.	I	walk	*happens regularly*
We went to California last year.	We	went	*happened last year*
She seems really tired.	She	seems	*how she seems right now*
The teacher is sad.	teacher	is	*her state right now*

You can see from the examples in this chart that **past tense verbs** are used for a time in the past, and **present tense verbs** are used for something that happens regularly or for a state or condition right now.

Often a sentence has more than one verb. If it has a connector word or more than one subject, it can have more than one verb.

- The two cousins live, work, and vacation together. (3 verbs)
- The girls planned by phone, and then they met at the movies. (2 verbs)

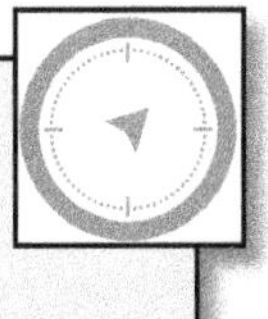

BE CAREFUL!

When you have more than one verb in a sentence, make sure both verb tenses are correct.

Helping Verbs and Progressive and Perfect Tenses

Helping Verbs

A **helping verb** is a supporting verb that accompanies a main verb.

Questions, negative sentences, and certain time situations require helping verbs.

forms of helping verb "to be"	forms of helping verb "to have"	forms of helping verb "to do"	some modals (used like helping verbs)
am, are, is, was, were, be, being, been	have, has, had, having	do, does, did, doing	will, would, can, could, must, might, should

Here are examples of helping verbs in questions and negatives.

- Where *is* he *going*?
- *Did* they *win*?
- I *do*n't *want* that.
- The boys *can*'t go.

Progressive and Perfect Tenses

Helping verbs accompany main verbs in certain time situations, such as when an action is or was ongoing, or when two actions overlap in time. To form these tenses, we use a **helping verb** with the **base form plus *-ing*** or with the **participle form** of the main verb.

The **progressive tense** is used for an action that is or was ongoing. It takes base form of the main verb plus *-ing*.

Example sentence	Tense	*Explanation/Time*
I am taking French this semester.	Present progressive	*happening now, over a continuous period of time*
I was working when you stopped by.	Past progressive	*happened over a continuous period of time in the past*

The **perfect tense** is used to cover two time periods. It takes the *participle* form of the main verb.

Example sentence	Tense	*Explanation/Time*
I have lived here for three years.	Present perfect	*started in the past and continues to present*
I had finished half of my homework when my computer stopped working.	Past perfect	*started and finished in the past, overlapping in time with another action*

Sometimes we use both the **progressive** and **perfect** tenses together.

Example sentence	Tense	*Explanation/Time*
I have been walking for hours!	Present perfect progressive	*started in the past, took place for a period of time, and continues to present*
She had been asking for a raise for months before she finally received one.	Past perfect progressive	*started in the past, took place for a period of time, and ended*

Let's Review!

- A verb describes an action or state of being.
- Each verb has three primary forms: base form, past form, and participle form.
- Verbs have different tenses, which are used to show time.
- Helping verbs are used in questions, negative sentences, and to form progressive and perfect tenses.

Chapter 5 Parts of Speech Practice Quiz 1

1. **Select the part of speech of the underlined word in the following sentence.**

   She did <u>quite</u> well on the exam.

   A. Noun
   B. Adverb
   C. Adjective
   D. Preposition

2. **Select the noun that the underlined adjectives describe.**

   Two weeks after his surgery, Henry felt <u>strong</u> and <u>healthy</u>.

   A. weeks
   B. his
   C. surgery
   D. Henry

3. **Which word is an adverb that describes the underlined verb?**

   The man <u>spoke</u> to us wisely.

   A. man
   B. to
   C. us
   D. wisely

4. **Identify the conjunction in the following sentence.**

   He is sick, yet he came to work.

   A. is
   B. yet
   C. came
   D. to

5. **Which is <u>not</u> a prepositional phrase?**

   Keep me informed about the status of the problem throughout the day.

   A. Keep me informed
   B. about the status
   C. of the problem
   D. throughout the day

6. **How many prepositions are in the following sentence?**

   The athletes traveled from Boston to Dallas for the competition.

   A. 0
   B. 1
   C. 2
   D. 3

7. **Which words in the following sentence are proper nouns?**

   Matthew had a meeting with his supervisor on Tuesday.

   A. Matthew, meeting
   B. Matthew, Tuesday
   C. meeting, supervisor
   D. supervisor, Tuesday

8. **How many plural nouns are in the following sentence?**

   Marie's father's appendix was taken out.

   A. 0
   B. 1
   C. 2
   D. 3

9. **Which of the following words is an abstract noun?**

   A. Car
   B. Tent
   C. Ruler
   D. Health

10. **Which word in the following sentence is a pronoun?**

    To whom should the applicant address the letter?

    A. To
    B. the
    C. whom
    D. should

11. Which pronoun correctly completes the following sentence?

Nigel introduced Van and ____ to the new administrator.

A. I
B. me
C. she
D. they

12. Select the noun to which the underlined pronoun refers.

Greta Garbo, <u>who</u> performed in both silent and talking pictures, is my favorite actress.

A. actress
B. pictures
C. performed
D. Greta Garbo

13. How many verbs are in the following sentence?

They toured the art museum and saw the conservatory.

A. 0
B. 1
C. 2
D. 3

14. Which word in the following sentence is a helping verb?

They did not ask for our help.

A. did
B. ask
C. for
D. our

15. Select the correct verb form to complete the following sentence.

William didn't think he would enjoy the musical, but he ____.

A. do
B. did
C. liked
D. would

Chapter 5 Parts of Speech Practice Quiz 1 – Answer Key

1. B. *Quite* is an adverb that describes the adverb *well.* **See Lesson: Adjectives and Adverbs.**

2. D. These adjectives describe *Henry.* **See Lesson: Adjectives and Adverbs.**

3. D. *Wisely* is an adverb that describes the verb *spoke.* **See Lesson: Adjectives and Adverbs.**

4. B. *Yet* is a conjunction. **See Lesson: Conjunctions and Prepositions.**

5. A. *Keep me informed* does not contain a preposition. *About, of,* and *throughout* are prepositions. **See Lesson: Conjunctions and Prepositions.**

6. D. *From, to,* and *for* are prepositions. **See Lesson: Conjunctions and Prepositions.**

7. B. *Matthew* and *Tuesday* are proper nouns. **See Lesson: Nouns.**

8. A. *Marie's* and *father's* are possessive; neither is plural. *Appendix* is a singular noun. **See Lesson: Nouns.**

9. D. *Health* is an abstract noun; it does not physically exist. **See Lesson: Nouns.**

10. C. *Whom* is a pronoun. **See Lesson: Pronouns.**

11. B. An object pronoun must be used here. **See Lesson: Pronouns.**

12. D. *Who* is a relative pronoun that refers to the subject *Greta Garbo.* **See Lesson: Pronouns.**

13. C. *Toured* and *saw* are verbs. **See Lesson: Verbs and Verb Tenses.**

14. A. *Did* is a helping verb; *ask* is the main verb. **See Lesson: Verbs and Verb Tenses.**

15. B. *Did* can be used here, for a shortened form of *did enjoy it.* **See Lesson: Verbs and Verb Tenses.**

CHAPTER 6 KNOWLEDGE OF LANGUAGE

TYPES OF SENTENCES

Sentences are a combination of words that communicate a complete thought. Sentences can be written in many ways to signal different relationships among ideas. This lesson will cover (1) simple sentences (2) compound sentences (3) complex sentences (4) parallel structure.

Simple Sentences

A **simple sentence** is a group of words that make up a **complete thought**. To be a complete thought, simple sentences must have one **independent clause.** An independent clause contains a single **subject** (who or what the sentence is about) and a **predicate** (a **verb** and something about the subject.)

Let's take a look at some simple sentences:

Simple Sentence	Subject	Predicate	Complete Thought?
The car was fast.	car	was fast (verb = was)	Yes
Sally waited for the bus.	Sally	waited for the bus (verb = waited)	Yes
The pizza smells delicious.	pizza	smells delicious (verb = smells)	Yes
Anton loves cycling.	Anton	loves cycling (verb = loves)	Yes

It is important to be able to recognize what a simple sentence is in order to avoid **run-ons** and **fragments**, two common grammatical errors.

A **run-on** is when two or more independent clauses are combined without proper punctuation:

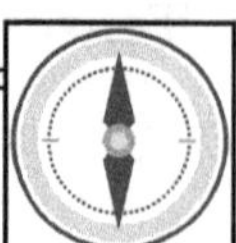

FOR EXAMPLE

Gregory is a very talented actor he was the lead in the school play.

If you take a look at this sentence, you can see that it is made up of 2 independent clauses or simple sentences:

1. *Gregory is a very talented actor*
2. *he was the lead in the school play*

You cannot have two independent clauses running into each other without proper punctuation.

You can fix this run-on in the following way:

Gregory is a very talented actor. He was the lead in the school play.

A **fragment** is a group of words that looks like a sentence. It starts with a capital letter and has end punctuation, but when you examine it closely you will see it is not a complete thought.

Let's put this information all together to determine whether a group of words is a simple sentence, a run-on, or a fragment:

Group of Words	Category
Mondays are the worst they are a drag.	Run-On: These are two independent clauses running into one another without proper punctuation. FIX: *Mondays are the worst. They are a drag.*
Because I wanted soda.	Fragment: This is a dependent clause and needs more information to make it a complete thought. FIX: *I went to the store because I wanted soda.*
Ereni is from Greece.	Simple Sentence: YES! This is a simple sentence with a subject (*Ereni*) and a predicate (*is from Greece*), so it is a complete thought.
While I was apple picking.	Fragment: This is a dependent clause and needs more information to make it a complete thought. FIX: *While I was apple picking, I spotted a bunny.*
New York City is magical it is my favorite place.	Run-On: These are two independent clauses running into one another without proper punctuation. FIX: *New York City is magical. It is my favorite place.*

Compound Sentences

A **compound sentence** is a sentence made up of two independent clauses connected with a **coordinating conjunction**.

Let's take a look at the following sentence:

Joe waited for the bus, but it never arrived.

If you take a close look at this compound sentence, you will see that it is made up of two independent clauses:

1. *Joe waited for the bus*
2. *it never arrived*

The word *but* is the coordinating conjunction that connects these two sentences. Notice that the coordinating conjunction has a comma right before it. This is the proper way to punctuate compound sentences.

Here are other examples of compound sentences:

FOR EXAMPLE

I want to try out for the baseball team, and I also want to try out for track.

Sally can play the clarinet in the band, ***or*** *she can play the violin in the orchestra.*

Mr. Henry is going to run the half marathon, ***so*** *he has a lot of training to do.*

All these sentences are compound sentences since they each have two independent clauses joined by a comma and a coordinating conjunction.

The following is a list of **coordinating conjunctions** that can be used in compound sentences. You can use the mnemonic device "FANBOYS" to help you remember them:

For

And

Nor

But

Or

Yet

So

Think back to Section 1: Simple Sentences. You learned about run-ons. Another way to fix run-ons is by turning the group of words into a compound sentence:

RUN-ON:	*Gregory is a very talented actor he was the lead in the school play.*
FIX:	*Gregory is a very talented actor,* **so** *he was the lead in the school play.*

Complex Sentences

A **complex** sentence is a sentence that is made up of an independent clause and one or more dependent clauses connected to it.

Think back to Section 1 when you learned about fragments. You learned about a **dependent clause**, the part of a sentence that cannot stand by itself. These clauses need other information to make them complete.

You can recognize a dependent clause because they always begin with a **subordinating conjunction**. These words are a key ingredient in complex sentences.

Here is a list of **subordinating conjunctions:**

after	although	as	because	before
despite	even if	even though	if	in order to
that	once	provided that	rather than	since
so that	than	that	though	unless
until	when	whenever	where	whereas
wherever	while	why		

Let's take a look at a few complex sentences:

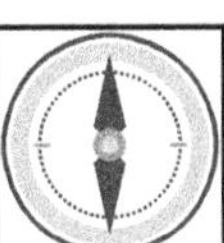

FOR EXAMPLE

Since the alarm clock didn't go off, I was late for class.

This is an example of a complex sentence because it contains:

A dependent clause: *Since the alarm clock didn't go off*
An independent clause: *I was late for class*
A subordinating conjunction: *since*

Sarah studied all night for the exam even though she did not receive an A.

This is an example of a complex sentence because it contains:

A dependent clause: *even though she did not receive an A*
An independent clause: *Sarah studied all night*
A subordinating conjunction: *even though*

***NOTE:** To make a complex sentence, you can either start with the dependent clause or the independent clause. When beginning with the dependent clause, you need a comma after it. When beginning with an independent clause, you do not need a comma after it.*

Parallel Structure

Parallel structure is the repetition of a grammatical form within a sentence to make the sentence sound more harmonious. Parallel structure comes into play when you are making a list of items. Stylistically, you want all the items in the list to line up with each other to make them sound better.

Let's take a look at when to use parallel structure:

1. Use parallel structure with verb forms:

   In a sentence listing different verbs, you want all the verbs to use the same form:

   Manuel likes hiking, biking, and mountain climbing.

   In this example, the words *hiking, biking* and *climbing* are all gerunds (having an -ing ending), so the sentence is balanced since the words are all using the gerund form of the verb.

   Manuel likes to hike, bike, and mountain climb.

In this example, the words *hike, bike* and *climb* are all infinitives (using the basic form of the verb), so the sentence is balanced.

You do not want to mix them up:

Manuel likes hiking, biking, and to mountain climb.

This sentence **does not** use parallel structure since *hiking* and *biking* use the gerund form of the verb and *to mountain climb* uses the infinitive form.

2. Use parallel structure with active and passive voice:

   In a sentence written in the **active voice**, the subject performs the action:

   Sally kicked the ball.

   Sally, the subject, is the one doing the action, kicking the ball.

   In a sentence written in the **passive voice**, the subject is acted on by the verb.

   The ball was kicked by Sally.

   When using parallel structure, you want to make sure your items in a list are either all in **active voice**:

   Raymond baked, frosted, and decorated the cake.

   Or all in **passive voice**:

   The cake was baked, frosted, and decorated by Raymond.

   You do not want to mix them up:

   The cake was baked, frosted, and Raymond decorated it.

   This sentence **does not** use parallel structure because it starts off with passive voice and then switches to active voice.

3. Use parallel structure with the length of terms within a list:

   When making a list, you should either have all short individual terms or all long phrases.

   Keep these consistent by either choosing short, individual terms:

   Cassandra is bold, courageous, and strong.

   Or longer phrases:

   Cassandra is brave in the face of danger, willing to take risks, and a force to be reckoned with.

   You do not want to mix them up:

   Cassandra is bold, courageous, and a force to be reckoned with.

This sentence **does not** use parallel structure because the first two terms are short, and the last one is a longer phrase.

Let's Review!

- A simple sentence consists of a clause, which has a single subject and a predicate.
- A compound sentence is made up of two independent clauses connected by a coordinating conjunction.
- A complex sentence is made up of a subordinating conjunction, an independent clause and one or more dependent clauses connected to it.
- Parallel structure is the repetition of a grammatical form within a sentence to make the sentence sound more harmonious.

TYPES OF CLAUSES

There are four types of clauses that are used to create sentences. Sentences with several clauses, and different types of clauses, are considered complex. This lesson will cover (1) independent clauses, (2) dependent clauses and subordinate clauses, and (3) coordinate clauses.

Independent Clause

An **independent clause** is a simple sentence. It has a subject, a verb, and expresses a complete thought.

- Steve went to the store.
- She will cook dinner tonight.
- The class was very boring.
- The author argues that listening to music helps productivity.

Two **independent clauses** can be connected by a semicolon. There are some common words that indicate the beginning of an **independent clause** such as: moreover, also, nevertheless, however, furthermore, consequently.

- I wanted to go to dinner; however, I had to work late tonight.
- She had a job interview; therefore, she dressed nicely.

Dependent and Subordinate Clauses

A **dependent clause** is not a complete sentence. It has a subject and a verb but does not express a complete thought. **Dependent clauses** are also called **subordinate clauses**, because they depend on the **independent or main clause** to complete the thought. A sentence that has both at least one **independent clause** and one **subordinate clause** are considered complex.

Subordinate clauses can be placed before or after the **independent clause**. When the **subordinate clause** begins the sentence, there should be a comma before the **main clause**. If the **subordinate clause** ends the sentence, there is no need for a comma.

Dependent clauses also have common indicator words. These are often called **subordinating conjunctions** because they connect a **dependent clause** to an **independent clause**. Some of these include: although, after, as, because, before, if, once, since, unless, until, when, whether, and while. Relative pronouns also signify the beginning of a **subordinate clause**. These include: that, which, who, whom, whichever, whoever, whomever, and whose.

- When I went to school...
- Since she joined the team...
- After we saw the play...
- *Because she studied hard*, she received an A on her exam.
- *Although the professor was late*, the class was very informative.
- I can't join you *unless I finish my homework*.

Coordinate Clause

A **coordinate clause** is a sentence or phrase that combines clauses of equal grammatical rank (verbs, nouns, adjectives, phrases, or independent clauses) by using a coordinating conjunction (and, but, for, nor, or so, yet). **Coordinating conjunctions** cannot connect a **dependent or subordinate clause** and an **independent clause.**

- She woke up, and he went to bed.
- We did not have cheese, so I went to the store to get some.
- Ice cream and candy taste great, but they are not good for you.
- Do you want to study, or do you want to go to Disneyland?

Let's Review!

- An **independent clause** is a simple sentence that has a noun, a verb, and a complete thought. Two **independent clauses** can be connected by a semicolon.
- A **dependent or subordinate clause** depends on the main clause to complete a thought. A **dependent or subordinate clause** can go before or after the **independent clause** and there are indicator words that signify the beginning of the **dependent or subordinate clause.**
- A **coordinate clause** connects two verbs, nouns, adjectives, phrases, or **independent clauses** using a **coordinating conjunction** (and, but, for, nor, or, so, yet).

SUBJECT AND VERB AGREEMENT

Every sentence must include a **subject** and a **verb**. The subject tells **who or what**, and the verb describes an **action or condition**. Subject and verb agree in number and person.

Roles of Subject and Verb

A complete sentence includes a **subject** and a **verb**. The verb is in the part of the sentence called the **predicate**. A predicate can be thought of as a verb phrase.

Simple Sentences

A sentence can be very simple, with just one or two words as the **subject** and one or two words as the **predicate**.

Sometimes, in a command, a subject is "understood," rather than written or spoken.

BE CAREFUL!
It's is a contraction of *it is*.
Its (without an apostrophe) is the possessive of the pronoun *it*.

Look at these examples of short sentences:

Sentence	Subject	Predicate, with main verb(s) underlined
I ate.	I	ate
They ran away.	They	ran away
It's OK.	It	is OK
Go and find the cat!	(You)	go and find the cat

Complex Sentences

Sometimes a subject or predicate is a long phrase or clause.

Some sentences have more than one subject or predicate, or even a predicate within a predicate.

Sentence	Subject(s)	Predicate(s), with main verb(s) underlined
My friend from work had a bad car accident.	My friend from work	had a bad car accident
John, his sister, and I plan to ride our bikes across the country this summer.	John, his sister, and I	plan to ride our bikes across the country this summer
I did so much for them, and they didn't even thank me.*	I; they	did so much for them; didn't even thank me
She wrote a letter that explained the problem.**	She	wrote a letter that explained the problem

*This sentence consists of two clauses, and each clause has its own subject and its own predicate.

**In this sentence, *that explained the problem* is part of the predicate, and it is also a relative clause with own subject and predicate.

Subject and Verb Agreement

Subjects and verbs must agree in **number** and **person**. This means that different subjects take different forms of a verb.

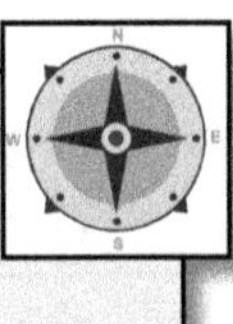

KEEP IN MIND . . .

The third person singular subject takes a different verb form than other subjects.

With **regular** verbs, simply add ***-s*** to the singular third person verb, as shown below:

	Singular		Plural	
	Subject	**Verb**	**Subject**	**Verb**
(first person)	I	play	we	play
(second person)	you	play	you	play
(third person)	he/she/it	plays	they	play

Some verbs are **irregular**, so simply adding *-s* doesn't work. For example:

Verb	Form for Third Person Singular Subject
have	has
do	does
fix	fixes

BE CAREFUL!

The verbs *be, have,* and *do* can be either main verbs or helping verbs.

Look for subject-verb agreement in the following sentences:

- *I* usually eat a banana for breakfast.
- *Marcy* does well in school.
- The *cat* licks its fur.

Subject-Verb Agreement for the Verb *Be*

Present		Past	
I am	we are	I was	we were
you are	you are	you were	you were
he/she/it is	they are	they were	they were

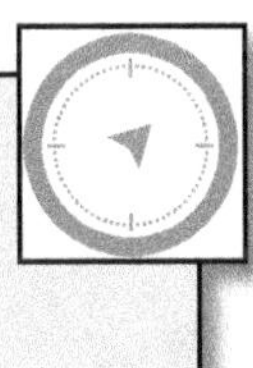

BE CAREFUL!

The verb ***be*** is very irregular. Its forms change with several subjects, in both present and past tense.

Things to Look Out For

Subject-verb agreement can be tricky. Be careful of these situations:

- **Sentences with more than one subject:** If two subjects are connected by *and,* the subject is **plural**. When two singular subjects are connected by *neither/nor,* the subject is **singular**.

Sandra and Luiz shop. (plural)
Neither Sandra nor Luiz has money. (singular)

- **Collective nouns:** Sometimes a noun stands for a group of people or things. If the subject is **one group**, it is considered **singular**.

Those students are still on chapter three. (plural)
That class is still on chapter three. (singular)

- ***There is* and *there are*:** With pronouns such as *there, what,* and *where,* the verb agrees with the noun or pronoun that follows it.

There's a rabbit! (singular)
Where are my shoes? (plural)

- **Indefinite pronouns:** Subjects such as *everybody, someone,* and *nobody* are **singular**. Subjects such as *all, none,* and *any* can be either **singular or plural**.

Everyone in the band plays well. (singular)
All of the students are there. (plural)
All is well. (singular)

Let's Review!

- Every sentence has a subject and a verb.
- The predicate is the part of the sentence that contains the verb.
- The subject and verb must agree in number and person.
- The third person singular subject takes a different verb form.

MODIFIERS

A modifier is a word, phrase, or clause that adds detail or changes (modifies) another word in the sentence. Descriptive words such as adjectives and adverbs are examples of modifiers.

The Role of Modifiers in a Sentence

Modifiers make a sentence more descriptive and interesting.

Look at these simple sentences. Notice how much more interesting they are with modifiers added.

Simple sentence	With Modifiers Added
I drove.	I drove my family along snowy roads to my grandmother's house.
They ate.	They ate a fruit salad of blueberries, strawberries, peaches, and apples.
The boy looked.	The boy in pajamas looked out the window at the birds eating from the feeder.
He climbed.	He climbed the ladder to fix the roof.

Look at the modifiers in bold type in the following sentences. Notice how these words add description to the basic idea in the sentence.

	Modifier	Word It Modifies	Type
The hungry man ate **quickly**.	1. the; 2. hungry; 3. quickly	1. man 2. man; 3. ate	1. article 2. adjective; 3. adverb
The small child, **who had scraped his knee**, cried **quietly**.	1. the; 2. small; 3. who had scraped his knee; 4. quietly	1. child; 2. child; 3. child; 4. cried	1. article; 2. adjective; 3. adjective clause; 4. adverb
The horse **standing near the fence** is **beautiful.**	1. the; 2. standing near the fence; 3. beautiful	1. horse; 2. horse; 3. horse	1. article; 2. participle phrase; 3. adjective
Hana and Mario stood **by the lake** and watched **a gorgeous** sunset.	1. by the lake; 2. a; 3. gorgeous	1. stood; 2. sunset; 3. sunset	1. prepositional phrase; 2. article; 3. adjective
They tried **to duck out of the way as the large spider dangled from the ceiling.**	1. to duck out of the way; 2. as the large spider dangled; 3. from the ceiling	1. tried; 2. duck; 3. dangled	1. infinitive phrase; 2. adverb clause; 3. prepositional phrase

DID YOU KNOW?

Adjectives and adverbs are not the only modifiers. With a participle phrase, **an -ing verb** can act as a modifier. For example, *eating from the feeder* modifies *the birds*. With an infinitive, ***to* plus the main form of a verb** can act as a modifier. For example, *to fix the roof* modifies *climbed.*

Misplaced and Dangling Modifiers

A **misplaced modifier** is a modifier that is placed incorrectly in a sentence, so that it modifies the wrong word.

A **dangling modifier** is a modifier that modifies a word that should be included in the sentence but is not.

Look at these examples.

- First, notice the modifier, in bold.
- Next, look for the word it modifies.

> **BE CAREFUL!**
> Sometimes there is a modifier within a modifier. For example, in the clause *as the large spider dangled, the* and *large* are words that modify *spider.*

Incorrect	Problem	How to Fix It	Correct
Sam wore his new shirt to school, **which was too big for him.**	Misplaced modifier. Notice the placement of the modifier ***which was too big for him.*** It is placed after the word *school,* which makes it seem like *school* is the word it describes. However, this was not the writer's intention. The writer intended for ***which was too big for him*** to describe the word *shirt.*	The modifier needs to be placed after the word *shirt,* rather than after the word *school.*	Sam wore his new shirt, **which was too big for him,** to school.
Running down the hallway, Maria's bag of groceries fell.	Dangling modifier. The modifier ***running down the hallway*** is placed before the phrase *Maria's bag of groceries,* which makes it seem this is what it describes. However, this was not the writer's intention; the *bag of groceries* cannot run! The correct reference would be the noun *Maria,* which was omitted from the sentence completely.	The modifier must reference *Maria,* rather than *Maria's bag of groceries.* This can be fixed by adding the noun *Maria* as a subject.	**Running down the hallway,** Maria dropped her bag of groceries.
With a leash on, my sister walked the dog.	Misplaced modifier. The modifier ***with a leash on*** is placed before *my sister,* which makes it seem like she is wearing a leash.	Move the modifier so that it is next to *the dog,* rather than *my sister.*	My sister walked the dog, **who had a leash on.**

Let's Review!

- A modifier is a word, phrase, or clause that adds detail by describing or modifying another word in the sentence.
- Adverbs, adjectives, articles, and prepositional phrases are some examples of modifiers.
- Misplaced and dangling modifiers have unclear references, leading to confusion about the meaning of a sentence.

> **BE CAREFUL!**
> A modifier should be placed next to the word it modifies. Misplaced and dangling modifiers lead to confusion about the meaning of a sentence.

Direct Objects and Indirect Objects

A direct or indirect object has a relationship with the action verb that precedes it. A direct object directly receives the action of the verb. An indirect object indirectly receives the action.

Direct and Indirect Objects in a Sentence

An **object** in grammar is something that is acted on. The **subject** does the action; the **object** receives it.

An object is usually a noun or a pronoun.

There are three types of objects:

- direct object
- indirect object
- object of the preposition

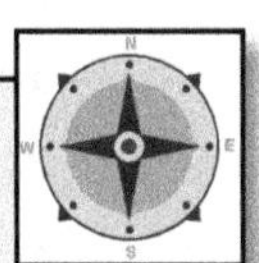

KEEP IN MIND . . .

When there is an **indirect object**, it will be placed between the verb and the direct object.

Many sentences have a direct object. Some sentences also have an indirect object.

Look at these examples:

- Kim threw *the ball. The ball* is the direct object. *Ask yourself:* What did she throw?
- Kim threw *Tommy* the ball. *Tommy* is the indirect object. *Ask yourself:* Who did she throw it to?

Look for the objects in the sentences below.

Sentence	Direct Object	Indirect Object	Be Careful!
Her mom poured her a glass of milk.	a glass of milk (*ask:* what did she pour?)	her (*ask:* who did she pour it for?)	The indirect object, when there is one, can be found between the verb and the direct object.
They work hard.			Not all sentences have objects. Here, *hard* is not an object. It is not the recipient of *work*. Instead, it is a modifier; it describes the work.
Kazu bought Katrina a present.	a present (*ask:* what did he buy?)	Katrina (*ask:* whom did he buy it for?)	
Kazu bought a present for Katrina.	a present (*ask*: what did he buy?)		Don't confuse indirect objects with prepositional phrases. *For* is a preposition, so *Katrina* is the object of the preposition; it is not an indirect object.

BE CAREFUL!

Some verbs can never take **direct objects**. These are:

- **Linking verbs** such as *is* and *seem*.
- **Intransitive verbs** such as *snore, go, sit*, and *die*.
- *Ask yourself:* Can you *snore* something? No. Therefore, this verb cannot take a direct object.

Let's Review!

- A direct object directly receives the action of the verb.
- An indirect object indirectly receives the action of the verb.
- An indirect object comes between the verb and the direct object.

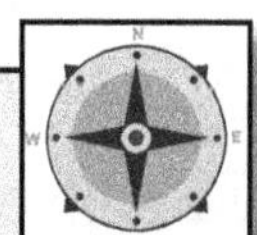

KEEP IN MIND . . .

If there is a preposition, the object is the **object of the preposition** rather than an **indirect object**.

Compare these two sentences:

- She made *me* dinner. (*Me* is an indirect object.)
- She made dinner *for me*. (*For me* is a prepositional phrase.)

Chapter 6 Knowledge of Language Practice Quiz 1

1. **Identify the direct object in the following sentence.**

   Paulo accidentally locked his keys in his car.

   A. Paulo
   B. accidentally
   C. his keys
   D. his car

2. **Select the word that is an object of the underlined verb.**

   The graduates held lit candles.

   A. The
   B. graduates
   C. lit
   D. candles

3. **Select the verb that acts on the underlined direct object in the following sentence.**

   We have no choice but to sit here and wait for these cows to cross the road!

   A. have
   B. sit
   C. wait
   D. cross

4. **Which modifier, if any, modifies the underlined word in the following sentence?**

   We always visit the bakery on the corner when we are in town.

   A. always
   B. on the corner
   C. when we are in town
   D. No modifier describes it.

5. **Identify the dangling or misplaced modifier, if there is one.**

   Having been repaired, we can drive the car again.

   A. Having been repaired
   B. we can drive
   C. the car again
   D. There is no dangling or misplaced modifier.

6. **Which ending does not create a sentence with a dangling modifier?**

   Trying to earn some extra money, ____.

   A. the new position paid more.
   B. he got a second job.
   C. the job was difficult.
   D. it was an extra shift.

7. **Select the "understood" subject with which the underlined verb must agree.**

   Watch out!

   A. You
   B. He
   C. I
   D. Out

8. **How many verbs must agree with the underlined subject in the following sentence?**

   Kareem Abdul-Jabbar, my favorite basketball player, dribbles, shoots, and scores to win the game!

   A. 0
   B. 1
   C. 2
   D. 3

9. Select the correct verb to complete the following sentence.

Our family ____ staying home for the holidays this year.

A. is
B. be
C. am
D. are

10. Fill in the blank with the correct subordinating conjunction.

You cannot go to the movies with your friends _____ you finish your homework.

A. If
B. Once
C. Since
D. Unless

11. Identify the dependent clause in the following sentence.

We decided to take our dog to the park although it was hot outside.

A. We decided to take our dog
B. to the park
C. although it was hot outside
D. to take our dog

12. Identify the independent clause in the following sentence.

After eating dinner, the couple went on a stroll through the park.

A. After eating dinner
B. The couple went on a stroll through the park
C. Through the park
D. Went on a stroll

13. Which of the following is an example of a simple sentence?

A. Tamara's sporting goods store.
B. Tamara has a sporting goods store in town.
C. Tamara has a sporting goods store it is in town.
D. Tamara's sporting goods store is in town, and she is the owner.

14. Which of the following uses a conjunction to combine the sentences below so the focus is on puppies requiring a lot of work?

Puppies are fun-loving animals. They do require a lot of work.

A. are fun-loving animals; they do require a lot of work.
B. Puppies are fun-loving animals, so they do require a lot of work.
C. Since puppies are fun-loving animals they do require a lot of work.
D. Although puppies are fun-loving animals, they do require a lot of work.

15. Which of the following options would complete the above sentence to make it a compound sentence?

The class of middle school students

_______________________________.

A. served food at.
B. served food at a soup kitchen.
C. served food at a soup kitchen, and they enjoyed the experience.
D. served food at a soup kitchen even though they weren't required to.

Chapter 6 Knowledge of Language Practice Quiz 1 – Answer Key

1. C. *His keys* is the direct object of the verb *locked.* **See Lesson: Direct Objects and Indirect Objects.**

2. D. *Candles* is the direct object of the verb *held.* **See Lesson: Direct Objects and Indirect Objects.**

3. D. *The road* is a direct object of the verb *cross.* **See Lesson: Direct Objects and Indirect Objects.**

4. B. *On the corner* modifies *bakery.* **See Lesson: Modifiers, misplaced modifiers, dangling modifiers.**

5. A. *Having been repaired* is placed where it references *we*, but it should reference *the car.* **See Lesson: Modifiers, misplaced modifiers, dangling modifiers**

6. B. Of these choices, *trying to earn some extra money* can only reference *he.* **See Lesson: Modifiers, misplaced modifiers, dangling modifiers.**

7. A. In a command like this one, the "understood" subject is *you.* **See Lesson: Subject and Verb Agreement.**

8. D. The verbs *dribbles, shoots,* and *scores* must agree with the subject *Kareem Abdul-Jabbar.* **See Lesson: Subject and Verb Agreement.**

9. A. The subject *family* is singular and takes the verb *is.* **See Lesson: Subject and Verb Agreement.**

10. D. Unless. The word "unless" signifies the beginning of a dependent clause and is the only conjunction that makes sense in the sentence. **See Lesson: Types of Clauses.**

11. C. Although it was hot outside. It is dependent because it does not express a complete thought and relies on the independent clause. The word "although" also signifies the beginning of a dependent clause. **See Lesson: Types of Clauses.**

12. B. The couple went on a stroll through the park. It is independent because it has a subject, verb, and expresses a complete thought. **See Lesson: Types of Clauses.**

13. B. This is a simple sentence since it contains one independent clause consisting of a simple subject and a predicate. **See Lesson: Types of Sentences.**

14. D. The subordinate conjunction "although" combines the sentences and puts the focus on puppies requiring a lot of work. **See Lesson: Types of Sentences.**

15. C. This option would make the sentence a compound sentence. **See Lesson: Types of Sentences.**

CHAPTER 7 VOCABULARY ACQUISITION

ROOT WORDS, PREFIXES, AND SUFFIXES

A root word is the most basic part of a word. You can create new words by: adding a prefix, a group of letters placed before the root word; or a suffix, a group of letters placed at the end of a root word. In this lesson you will learn about root words, prefixes, suffixes, and how to determine the meaning of a word by analyzing these word parts.

Root Words

Root words are found in everyday language. They are the most basic parts of words. Root words in the English language are mostly derived from Latin or Greek. You can add beginnings (prefixes) and endings (suffixes) to root words to change their meanings. To discover what a root word is, simply remove its prefix and/or suffix. What you are left with is the root word, or the core or basis of the word.

At times, root words can be stand-alone words.

Here are some examples of stand-alone root words:

Stand-Alone Root Word	Meaning
dress	*clothing*
form	*shape*
normal	*typical*
phobia	*fear of*
port	*carry*

Most root words, however, are **not** stand-alone words. They are not full words on their own, but they still form the basis of other words when you remove their prefixes and suffixes.

Here are some common root words in the English language:

Root Word	Meaning	Example
ami, amic	*love*	amicable
anni	*year*	anniversary
aud	*to hear*	auditory
bene	*good*	beneficial
biblio	*book*	bibliography
cap	*take, seize*	capture
cent	*one hundred*	century
chrom	*color*	chromatic

Root Word	Meaning	Example
chron	*time*	chronological
circum	*around*	circumvent
cred	*believe*	credible
corp	*body*	corpse
dict	*to say*	dictate
equi	*equal*	equality
fract; rupt	*to break*	fracture
ject	*throw*	eject
mal	*bad*	malignant
min	*small*	miniature
mort	*death*	mortal
multi	*many*	multiply
ped	*foot*	pedestrian
rupt	*break*	rupture
sect	*cut*	dissect
script	*write*	manuscript
sol	*sun*	solar
struct	*build*	construct
terr	*earth*	terrain
therm	*heat*	thermometer
vid, vis	*to see*	visual
voc	*voice; to call*	vocal

Prefixes

Prefixes are the letters added to the **beginning** of a root word to make a new word with a different meaning.

Prefixes on their own have meanings, too. If you add a prefix to a root word, it can change its meaning entirely.

Here are some of the most common prefixes, their meanings, and some examples:

Prefix	Meaning	Example
auto	*self*	autograph
con	*with*	conclude
hydro	*water*	hydrate
im, in, non, un	*not*	unimportant
inter	*between*	international
mis	*incorrect, badly*	mislead

Prefix	Meaning	Example
over	*too much*	over-stimulate
post	*after*	postpone
pre	*before*	preview
re	*again*	rewrite
sub	*under, below*	submarine
trans	*across*	transcribe

Let's look back at some of the root words from Section 1. By adding prefixes to these root words, you can create a completely new word with a new meaning:

Root Word	Prefix	New Word	Meaning
dress (*clothing*)	un (*remove*)	**un**dress	*remove clothing*
sect (*cut*)	inter (*between*)	**inter**sect	*cut across or through*
phobia (*fear*)	hydro (*water*)	**hydro**phobia	*fear of water*
script (*write*)	post (*after*)	**post**script	*additional remark at the end of a letter*

Suffixes

Suffixes are the letters added to the **end** of a root word to make a new word with a different meaning.

Suffixes on their own have meanings, too. If you add a suffix to a root word, it can change its meaning entirely.

Here are some of the most common suffixes, their meanings, and some examples:

Suffix	Meanings	Example
able, ible	*can be done*	agreeable
an, ean, ian	*belonging or relating to*	European
ed	*happened in the past*	jogged
en	*made of*	wooden
er	*comparative (more than)*	stricter
est	*comparative (most)*	largest
ful	*full of*	meaningful
ic	*having characteristics of*	psychotic
ion, tion, ation, ition	*act, process*	hospitalization
ist	*person who practices*	linguist
less	*without*	artless
logy	*study of*	biology

Let's look back at some of the root words from Section 1. By adding suffixes to these root words, you can create a completely new word with a new meaning:

Root Word	Suffix	New Word	Meaning
aud (*to hear*)	logy (*study of*)	audio**logy**	*the study of hearing*
form (*shape*)	less (*without*)	form**less**	*without a clear shape*
port (*carry*)	able (*can be done*)	port**able**	*able to be carried*
normal (*typical*)	ity (*state of*)	normal**ity**	*condition of being normal*

Determining Meaning

Knowing the meanings of common root words, prefixes, and suffixes can help you determine the meaning of unknown words. By looking at a word's individual parts, you can get a good sense of its definition.

If you look at the word *transportation*, you can study the different parts of the word to figure out what it means.

If you were to break up the word you would see the following:

PREFIX: *trans = across*	ROOT: *port = carry*	SUFFIX: *tion = act or process*

If you put all these word parts together, you can define transportation as: *the act or process of carrying something across.*

Let's define some other words by looking at their roots, prefixes and suffixes:

Word	Prefix	Root	Suffix	Working Definition
indestructible	in (*not*)	struct (*build*)	able (*can be done*)	Not able to be "un" built (torn down)
nonconformist	non (*not*) con (*with*)	form (*shape*)	ist (*person who practices*)	A person who can not be shaped (someone who doesn't go along with the norm)
subterranean	sub (*under, below*)	terr (*earth*)	ean (*belonging or relating to*)	Relating or belonging to something under the earth

Let's Review!

- A root word is the most basic part of a word.
- A prefix is the letters added to beginning of a root word to change the word and its meaning.
- A suffix is the letters added to the end of a root word to change the word and its meaning.
- You can figure out a word's meaning by looking closely at its different word parts (root, prefixes, and suffixes).

Context Clues and Multiple Meaning Words

Sometimes when you read a text, you come across an unfamiliar word. Instead of skipping the word and reading on, it is important to figure out what that word means so you can better understand the text. There are different strategies you can use to determine the meaning of unfamiliar words. This lesson will cover (1) how to determine unfamiliar words by reading context clues, (2) multiple meaning words, and (3) using multiple meaning words properly in context.

Using Context Clues to Determine Meaning

When reading a text, it is common to come across unfamiliar words. One way to determine the meaning of unfamiliar words is by studying other context clues to help you better understand what the word means.

Context means the other words in the sentences around the unfamiliar word.

You can look at these other words to find **clues** or **hints** to help you figure out what the word means.

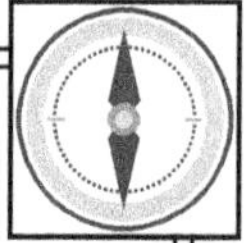

FOR EXAMPLE

Look at the following sentence:

Some of the kids in the cafeteria *ostracized* Janice because she dressed differently; they never allowed her to sit at their lunch table, and they whispered behind her back.

If you did not know what the word *ostracized* meant, you could look at the **other words** for **clues** to help you.

Here is what we know based on the clues in the sentence:

- Janice dressed differently
- Some kids did not allow her to sit at their table
- They whispered behind her back

We know that the kids **never allowed her to sit at their lunch** table and that they **whispered behind her back**. If you put all these clues together, you can conclude that the other students were **mistreating** Janice by **excluding** her.

Therefore, based on these context clues, *ostracized* means "excluded from the group."

Here's another example:

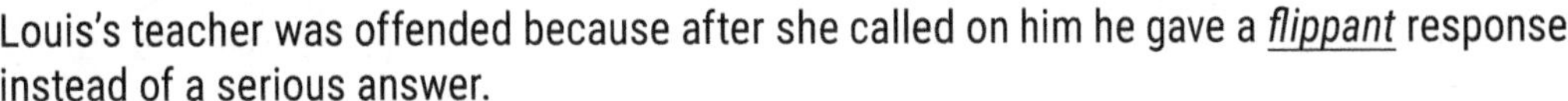

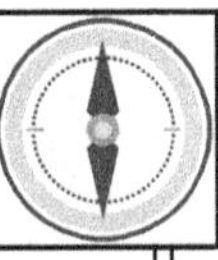

EXAMPLE 2

Look at this next sentence:

Louis's teacher was offended because after she called on him he gave a *flippant* response instead of a serious answer.

If you did not know what the word *flippant* meant, you could look at the **other words** for **clues** to help you.

Here is what we know based on the clues in the sentence:

- Louis's teacher was offended
- He gave a flippant response instead of a serious answer

We know that Louis said something that **offended** his teacher. Another keyword in this sentence is the word **instead**. This means that **instead of a serious answer** Louis gave the **opposite** of a serious answer.

Therefore, based on these context clues, *flippant* means "lacking respect or seriousness."

Multiple Meaning Words

Sometimes when we read words in a text, we encounter words that have **multiple meanings**.

Multiple meaning words are words that have **more than one definition** or meaning.

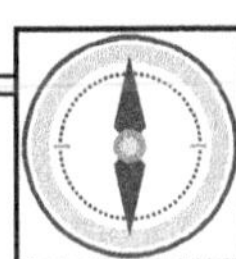

FOR EXAMPLE

The word **current** is a multiple meaning word. Here are the different definitions of *current:*

CURRENT:

1. adj: happening or existing in the present time

   Example: *It is important to keep up with current events so you know what's happening in the world.*
2. noun: the continuous movement of a body of water or air in a certain direction

   Example: *The river's current was strong as we paddled down the rapids.*
3. noun: a flow of electricity

   Example: *The electrical current was very weak in the house.*

Here are some other examples of words with multiple meanings:

Multiple Meaning Word	Definition #1	Definition #2	Definition #3
Buckle	noun: a metal or plastic device that connects one end of a belt to another	verb: to fasten or attach	verb: to bend or collapse from pressure or heat
Cabinet	noun: a piece of furniture used for storing things	noun: a group of people who give advice to a government leader	-
Channel	noun: a radio or television station	noun: a system used for sending something	noun: a long, narrow place where water flows
Doctor	noun: a person skilled in the science of medicine, dentistry, or one holding a PhD	verb: to change something in a way to trick or deceive	verb: to give medical treatment
Grave	noun: a hole in the ground for burying a dead body	adj: very serious	-
Hamper	noun: a large basket used for holding dirty clothes	verb: to slow the movement, action, or progress of	-
Plane	noun: a mode of transportation that has wings and an engine and can carry people and things in the air	noun: a flat or level surface that extends outward	noun: a level of though, development, or existence
Reservation	noun: an agreement to have something (such as a table, room, or seat) held for use at a later time	noun: a feeling of uncertainty or doubt	noun: an area of land kept separate for Native Americans to live an area of land set aside for animals to live for protection
Season	noun: one of the four periods in which a year is divided (winter, spring, summer, and fall)	noun: a particular period of time during the year	verb: to add spices to something to give it more flavor
Sentence	noun: a group words that expresses a statement, question, command, or wish	noun: the punishment given to someone by a court of law	verb: to officially state the punishment given by a court of law

From this chart you will notice that words with multiple meanings may have different **parts of speech**. A part of speech is a category of words that have the same grammatical properties. Some of the main parts of speech for words in the English language are: nouns, adjectives, verbs, and adverbs.

Part of Speech	Definition	Example
Noun	a person, place, thing, or idea	*Linda, New York City, toaster, happiness*
Adjective	a word that describes a noun or pronoun	*adventurous, young, red, intelligent*
Verb	an action or state of being	*run, is, sleep, become*
Adverb	a word that describes a verb, adjective, or other adverb	*quietly, extremely, carefully, well*

For example, in the chart above, *season* can be a **noun** or a **verb**.

Using Multiple Meaning Words Properly in Context

When you come across a **multiple meaning word** in a text, it is important to discern which meaning of the word is being used so you do not get confused.

You can once again turn to the **context clues** to clarify which meaning of the word is being used.

Let's take a look at the word *coach*. This word has several definitions:

COACH:

1. noun: a person who teaches and trains an athlete or performer
2. noun: a large bus with comfortable seating used for long trips
3. noun: the section on an airplane with the least expensive seats
4. verb: to teach or train someone in a specific area
5. verb: to give someone instructions on what to do or say in a certain situation

Since *coach* has so many definitions, you need to look at the **context clues** to figure out which definition of the word is being used:

The man was not happy that he had to sit in coach on the 24-hour flight to Australia.

In this sentence, the context clues **sit in** and **24-hour flight** help you see that *coach* means the least expensive seat on an airplane.

Let's look at another sentence using the word *coach*:

The lawyer needed to coach her witness so he would answer all the questions properly.

In this sentence, the context clues **so he would answer all the questions properly** help you see that the lawyer was giving the witness instructions on what to say.

Let's Review!

- When you come across an unfamiliar word in a text you can use context clues to help you define it.
- Context clues can also help you determine which definition of a multiple meaning word to use.

Synonyms, Antonyms, and Analogies

In order to utilize language to the best of your ability while reading, writing, or speaking, you must know how to interpret and use new vocabulary words, and also understand how these words relate to one another. Sometimes words have the same meaning. Sometimes words are complete opposites of each other. Understanding how the words you read, write, and speak with relate to each other will deepen your understanding of how language works. This lesson will cover (1) synonyms, (2) antonyms, and (3) analogies.

Synonyms

A **synonym** is a word that has the same meaning or close to the same meaning as another word. For example, if you look up the words *irritated* and *annoyed* in a dictionary, you will discover that they both mean "showing or feeling slight anger." Similarly, if you were to look up *blissful* and *joyful*, you will see that they both mean "extremely happy." The dictionary definition of a word is called its **denotation**. This is a word's literal or direct meaning.

When you understand that there are multiple words that have the same **denotation**, it will broaden your vocabulary.

It is also important to know that words with similar meanings have **nuances**, or subtle differences.

One way that words have nuances is in their **shades of meanings.** This means that although they have a similar definition, if you look closely, you will see that they have slight differences.

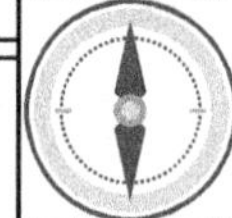

FOR EXAMPLE

If you quickly glance at the following words, you will see that they all have a similar meaning. However, if you look closely, you will see that their meanings have subtle differences. You can see their differences by looking at their various **levels** or **degrees**:

LEAST ⟶ MOST

nibble	bite	eat	devour
upset	angry	furious	irate
wet	soggy	soaked	drenched
good	great	amazing	phenomenal

Another way that words have nuance are in their **connotations.** A word's connotation is its **positive** or **negative** association. This can be the case even when two words have the same **denotations**, or dictionary definitions.

For example, the words *aroma* and *stench* both have a similar dictionary definition or **denotation**: "a smell." However, their **connotations** are quite different. *Aroma* has a **positive connotation** because it describes a *pleasant* smell. But *stench* has a **negative connotation** because it describes an unpleasant smell.

FOR EXAMPLE

Look at the following words. Although they have the same denotation, their connotations are very different:

Denotation	Positive Connotation	Negative Connotation
CLIQUE and *CLUB* both mean "a group of people."	*CLUB* has a positive connotation because it describes a group of people coming together to accomplish something.	*CLIQUE* has a negative connotation because it describes a group of people who exclude others.
INTERESTED and *NOSY* both mean "showing curiosity."	*INTERESTED* has a positive connotation because it means having a genuine curiosity about someone or something.	*NOSY* has a negative connotation because it describes who tries to pry information out of someone else to gossip or judge.
EMPLOY and *EXPLOIT* both mean "to use someone."	*EMPLOY* has a positive connotation because it means to use someone for a job.	*EXPLOIT* has a negative connotation because it means to use someone for one's own advantage.

Seeing that synonymous words have different **shades of meaning** and **connotations** will allow you to more precisely interpret and understand the nuances of language.

Antonyms

An **antonym** is a word that means the opposite or close to the opposite of another word. Think of an antonym as the direct opposite of a **synonym**. For example, *caring* and *apathetic* are antonyms because *caring* means "displaying concern and kindness for others" whereas *apathetic* means "showing no interest or concern."

Antonyms can fall under three categories:

Graded Antonyms:	Word pairs whose meanings are opposite and lie on a spectrum or continuum; there are many other words that fall between the two words. If you look at *hot* and *cold*, there are other words on this spectrum: *scalding,* ***hot****, warm, tepid, cool,* ***cold***
Relational Antonyms:	Word pairs whose opposites make sense only in the context of the relationship between the two meanings. These two words could not exist without the other: ***open - close***
Complementary Antonyms:	Word pairs that have no degree of meaning at all; there are only two possibilities, one or the other: ***dead - alive***

Here are some more examples of the three types of antonyms:

Graded Antonyms	Relational Antonyms	Complementary Antonyms
hard - soft	front - back	day - night
fast - slow	predator - prey	sink - float
bad - good	top - bottom	input - output
wet - dry	capture - release	interior - exterior
big - small	on - off	occupied - vacant

There are also common **prefixes** that help make antonyms. The most common prefixes for antonyms of words are: **UN**, **NON**, and **IN**. All these prefixes mean "not" or "without."

FOR EXAMPLE

UN:

likely – **un**likely
fortunate – **un**fortunate

IN:

tolerant – **in**tolerant
excusable – **in**excusable

NON:

conformist – **non**conformist
payment – **non**payment

Analogies

An **analogy** is a simple comparison between two things. Analogies help us understand the world around us by seeing how different things relate to one another.

In looking closely at words, analogies help us understand how they are connected.

In word analogies, they are usually set up using colons in the following way:

Pleasure: Smile :: Pain: ______________________________

This can be read as: Pleasure **IS TO** Smile **AS** Pain **IS TO** ______________________________

The answer: "grimace"

Sometimes you see analogies written out like this:

Pleasure is to Smile as Pain is to ______________________________

These are the common types of word analogies that illustrate how different words relate to one another:

Type of Analogy	Relationship	Example
Synonyms	Two words with the same meaning	Beginner : Novice:: Expert : Pro
Antonyms	Two words with the opposite meaning	Hot : Cold :: Up : Down
Part/Whole	One word is a part of another word	Stars : Galaxy :: Pages : Book
Cause/Effect	One word describes a condition or action, and the other describes an outcome	Tornado : Damage :: Joke : Laughter
Object/Function	One word describes something, and the other word describes what it's used for	Needle : Sew :: Saw : Cut

Category/Type	One word is a general category, and the other is something that falls in that category	Music : Folk :: Dance : Ballet
Performer/Related Action	One word is a person or object, and the other words is the action he/she/it commonly performs	Thief : Steal :: Surgeon : Operate
Degree of Intensity	These words have similar meanings, but one word is stronger or more intense than the other	Glad : Elated :: Angry : Furious

By recognizing the type of analogy two words have, you then can explore how they are connected.

Let's Review!

- Synonyms are words that have the same meaning. Synonyms also have nuances.
- Analogies are words that have an opposite meaning. There are three types of antonyms.
- Analogies show how words relate to each other. There are different types of analogy relationships to look for.
- Understanding how words relate to each other will help you better understand language, pull meaning from texts, and write and speak with a wider vocabulary.

Chapter 7 Vocabulary Acquisition Practice Quiz 1

1. **Select the word from the following sentence that has more than one meaning.**

   Cassandra's voice has a much different pitch than her brother's, so they sound great when they sing together.

   A. Voice
   B. Different
   C. Pitch
   D. Sing

2. **Select the correct definition of the underlined word that has multiple meanings in the sentence.**

   When the young boy saw his angry mother coming toward him, he made a <u>bolt</u> for the door.

   A. A large roll of cloth
   B. A quick movement in a particular direction
   C. A sliding bar that is used to lock a window or door
   D. A bright line of light appearing in the sky during a storm

3. **Select the meaning of the underlined word in the sentence based on the context clues.**

   When visiting the desert, the temperature tends to <u>fluctuate</u>, so you need to bring a variety of clothing.

   A. Rise
   B. Drop
   C. Change
   D. Stabilize

4. **The use of the suffix *ous* in the word parsimonious indicates what about a person?**

   A. He/she is full of stinginess
   B. He/she is against stinginess
   C. He/she is supportive of stinginess
   D. He/she is a person who studies stinginess

5. **Which of the following prefixes means <u>incorrect</u>?**

   A. un-
   B. non-
   C. mis-
   D. over-

6. **What is the best definition of the word <u>pugnacious</u>?**

   A. Rude
   B. Harmful
   C. Deceiving
   D. Combative

7. **The following words have the same denotation. Which word has a negative connotation?**

   A. Poised
   B. Assured
   C. Arrogant
   D. Confident

8. **Whisk : Mix :: Flashlight: ____________**

   A. Hike
   B. Light
   C. Camp
   D. Travel

9. **Which word in the list of synonyms shows the strongest degree of the word?**

   A. Amusing
   B. Comical
   C. Uproarious
   D. Entertaining

Chapter 7 Vocabulary Acquisition Practice Quiz 1 – Answer Key

1. C. The word "pitch" has more than one meaning. **See Lesson: Context Clues and Multiple Meaning Words.**

2. B. The meaning of <u>bolt</u> in the context of this sentence is "a quick movement in a particular direction. **See Lesson: Context Clues and Multiple Meaning Words.**

3. C. The meaning of <u>fluctuate</u> in the context of this sentence is "change." **See Lesson: Context Clues and Multiple Meaning Words.**

4. A. The suffix *ous* means "full of or possessing" so a parsimonious person is one who is full of stinginess. See **Lesson: Root Words, Prefixes, and Suffixes.**

5. C. The prefix that means "incorrect" is *mis.* **See Lesson: Root Words, Prefixes, and Suffixes.**

6. D. The root *pug* means "war," or "fight," so pugnacious means combative. **See Lesson: Root Words, Prefixes, and Suffixes.**

7. C. Arrogant has a negative connotation. **See Lesson: Synonyms, Antonyms, and Analogies.**

8. B. A whisk is a tool used to mix in the same way that a flashlight is a tool used to light. **See Lesson: Synonyms, Antonyms, and Analogies.**

9. C. Uproarious is the word that shows the strongest degree in the list of synonyms. **See Lesson: Synonyms, Antonyms, and Analogies.**

SECTION III. MATHEMATICS

CHAPTER 8 NUMBER AND QUANTITY

BASIC ADDITION AND SUBTRACTION

This lesson introduces the concept of numbers and their symbolic and graphical representations. It also describes how to add and subtract whole numbers.

Numbers

A **number** is a way to quantify a set of entities that share some characteristic. For example, a fruit basket might contain nine pieces of fruit. More specifically, it might contain three apples, two oranges, and four bananas. Note that a number is a quantity, but a **numeral** is the symbol that represents the number: 8 means the number eight, for instance.

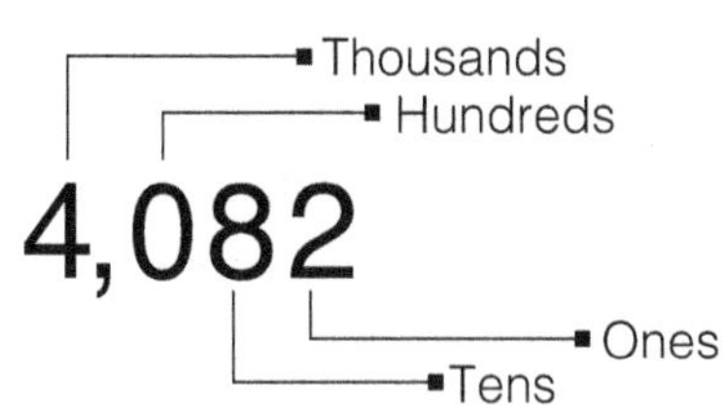

Although number representations vary, the most common is **base 10**. In base-10 format, each **digit** (or individual numeral) in a number is a quantity based on a multiple of 10. The base-10 system designates 0 through 9 as the numerals for zero through nine, respectively, and combines them to represent larger numbers. Thus, after counting from 1 to 9, the next number uses an additional digit: 10. That number means 1 group of 10 ones plus 0 additional ones. After 99, another digit is necessary, this time representing a hundred (10 sets of 10). This process of adding digits can go on indefinitely to express increasingly large numbers. For whole numbers, the rightmost digit is the ones place, the next digit to its left is the tens place, the next is the hundreds place, then the thousands place, and so on.

Classifying numbers can be convenient. The chart below lists a few common number sets.

Sets of Numbers	Members	Remarks
Natural numbers	1, 2, 3, 4, 5,...	The "counting" numbers
Whole numbers	0, 1, 2, 3, 4,...	The natural numbers plus 0
Integers	..., −3, −2, −1, 0, 1, 2, 3,...	The whole numbers plus all negative whole numbers
Real numbers	All numbers	The integers plus all fraction/decimal numbers in between
Rational numbers	All real numbers that can be expressed as p/q, where p and q are integers and q is nonzero	The natural numbers, whole numbers, and integers are all rational numbers
Irrational numbers	All real numbers that are not rational	The rational and irrational numbers together constitute the entire set of real numbers

Example

Jane has 4 pennies, 3 dimes, and 7 dollars. How many cents does she have?

A. 347 B. 437 C. 734 D. 743

The correct answer is **C**. The correct solution is 734. A penny is 1 cent. A dime (10 pennies) is 10 cents, and a dollar (100 pennies) is 100 cents. Place the digits in base-10 format: 7 hundreds, 3 tens, 4 ones, or 734.

The Number Line

The **number line** is a model that illustrates the relationships among numbers. The complete number line is infinite and includes every real number—both positive and negative. A ruler, for example, is a portion of a number line that assigns a **unit** (such as inches or centimeters) to each number. Typically, number lines depict smaller numbers to the left and larger numbers to the right. For example, a portion of the number line centered on 0 might look like the following:

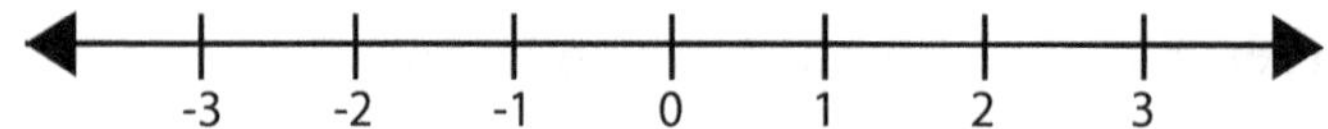

Because people learn about numbers in part through counting, they have a basic sense of how to order them. The number line builds on this sense by placing all the numbers (at least conceptually) from least to greatest. Whether a particular number is greater than or less than another is determined by comparing their relative positions. One number is greater than another if it is farther right on the number line. Likewise, a number is less than another if it is farther left on the number line. Symbolically, < means “is less than” and > means “is greater than.” For example, 5 > 1 and 9 < 25.

Example

Place the following numbers in order from greatest to least: 5, –12, 0.

A. 0, 5, –12
B. –12, 5, 0
C. 5, 0, –12
D. –12, 0, 5

The correct answer is **C**. The correct solution is 5, 0, –12. Use the number line to order the numbers. Note that the question says *from greatest to least*.

BE CAREFUL!
When ordering negative numbers, think of the number line. Although −10 > −2 may seem correct, it is incorrect. Because −10 is to the left of −2 on the number line, −10 < −2.

Addition

Addition is the process of combining two or more numbers. For example, one set has 4 members and another set has 5 members. To combine the sets and find out how many members are in the new set, add 4 and 5 to get the **sum**. Symbolically, the expression is 4 + 5, where + is the **plus sign**. Pictorially, it might look like the following:

$$\begin{matrix}\circ\circ\\\circ\circ\end{matrix} + \begin{matrix}\circ\circ\\\circ\circ\circ\end{matrix} = \begin{matrix}\circ\circ\circ\circ\\\circ\circ\circ\circ\circ\end{matrix}$$

To get the sum, combine the two sets of circles and then count them. The result is 9.

KEY POINT

The order of the numbers is irrelevant when adding.

Another way to look at addition involves the number line. When adding 4 + 5, for example, start at 4 on the number line and take 5 steps to the right. The stopping point will be 9, which is the sum.

Counting little pictures or using the number line works for small numbers, but it becomes unwieldy for large ones—even numbers such as 24 and 37 would be difficult to add quickly and accurately. A simple algorithm enables much faster addition of large numbers. It works with two or more numbers.

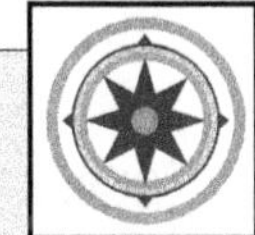

STEP BY STEP

Step 1. Stack the numbers, vertically aligning the digits for each place.

Step 2. Draw a plus sign (+) to the left of the bottom number and draw a horizontal line below the last number.

Step 3. Add the digits in the ones place.

Step 4. If the sum from Step 3 is less than 10, write it in the same column below the horizontal line. Otherwise, write the first (ones) digit below the line, then **carry** the second (tens) digit to the top of the next column.

Step 5. Going from right to left, repeat Steps 3–4 for the other places.

Step 6. If applicable, write the remaining carry digit as the leftmost digit in the sum.

Example

Evaluate the expression 154 + 98.

A. 250 B. 252 C. 352 D. 15,498

The correct answer is **B.** The correct solution is 252. Carefully follow the addition algorithm (see below). The process involves carrying a digit twice.

$$\begin{array}{r}154\\+\ 98\\\hline\end{array} \rightarrow \begin{array}{r}\scriptstyle 1\\154\\+\ 98\\\hline 2\end{array} \rightarrow \begin{array}{r}\scriptstyle 11\\154\\+\ 98\\\hline 52\end{array} \rightarrow \begin{array}{r}\scriptstyle 11\\154\\+\ 98\\\hline 252\end{array}$$

Subtraction

Subtraction is the inverse (opposite) of addition. Instead of representing the sum of numbers, it represents the difference between them. For example, given a set containing 15 members, subtracting 3 of those members yields a **difference** of 12. Using the **minus sign,** the expression for this operation is $15 - 3 = 12$. As with addition, two approaches are counting pictures and using the number line. The first case might involve drawing 15 circles and then crossing off 3 of them; the difference is the number of remaining circles (12). To use the number line, begin at 15 and move left 3 steps to reach 12.

Again, these approaches are unwieldy for large numbers, but the subtraction algorithm eases evaluation by hand. This algorithm is only practical for two numbers at a time.

STEP BY STEP

Step 1. Stack the numbers, vertically aligning the digits in each place. Put the number you are subtracting *from* on top.

Step 2. Draw a minus sign (–) to the left of the bottom number and draw a horizontal line below the stack of numbers.

Step 3. Start at the ones place. If the digit at the top is larger than the digit
below it, write the difference under the line. Otherwise, **borrow** from the top digit in the next-higher place by crossing it off, subtracting 1 from it, and writing the difference above it. Then add 10 to the digit in the ones place and perform the subtraction as normal.

Step 4. Going from right to left, repeat Step 3 for the rest of the places. If borrowing was necessary, make sure to use the new digit in each place, not the original one.

When adding or subtracting with negative numbers, the following rules are helpful. Note that x and y are used as placeholders for any real number.

$$x + (-y) = x - y$$

$$-x - y = -(x + y)$$

$$(-x) + (-y) = -(x + y)$$

$$x - y = -(y - x)$$

BE CAREFUL!

When dealing with numbers that have units (such as weights, currencies, or volumes), addition and subtraction are only possible when the numbers have the same unit. If necessary, convert one or more of them to equivalent numbers with the same unit.

Example

Kevin has 120 minutes to complete an exam. If he has already used 43, how many minutes does he have left?

A. 43 B. 77 C. 87 D. 163

The correct answer is **B.** The correct solution is 77. The first step is to convert this problem to a math expression. The goal is to find the difference between how many minutes Kevin has for the exam and how many he has left after 43 minutes have elapsed. The expression would be 120 – 43. Carefully follow the subtraction algorithm (see below). The process will involve borrowing a digit twice.

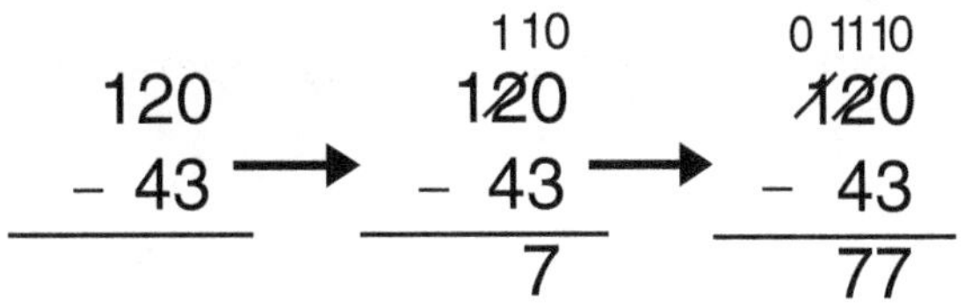

```
                1 10          0 11 10
  120           120            120
- 43    →     - 43     →     - 43
-----         -----          -----
                 7              77
```

Let's Review!

- Numbers are positive and negative quantities and often appear in base-10 format.
- The number line illustrates the ordering of numbers.
- Addition is the combination of numbers. It can be performed by counting objects or pictures, moving on the number line, or using the addition algorithm.
- Subtraction is finding the difference between numbers. Like addition, it can be performed by counting, moving on the number line, or using the subtraction algorithm.

Basic Multiplication and Division

This lesson describes the process of multiplying and dividing numbers and introduces the order of operations, which governs how to evaluate expressions containing multiple arithmetic operations.

Multiplication

Addition can be tedious if it involves multiple instances of the same numbers. For example, evaluating $29 + 29$ is easy, but evaluating $29 + 29 + 29 + 29 + 29$ is laborious. Note that this example contains five instances—or multiples—of 29. **Multiplication** replaces the repeated addition of the same number with a single, more concise operation. Using the **multiplication (or times) symbol** (×), the expression is

$29 + 29 + 29 + 29 + 29 = 5 \times 29$

The expression contains 5 multiples of 29. These numbers are the **factors** of multiplication. The result is called the **product.** In this case, addition shows that the product is 145. As with the other arithmetic operations, multiplication is easy for small numbers. Below is the multiplication table for whole numbers up to 12.

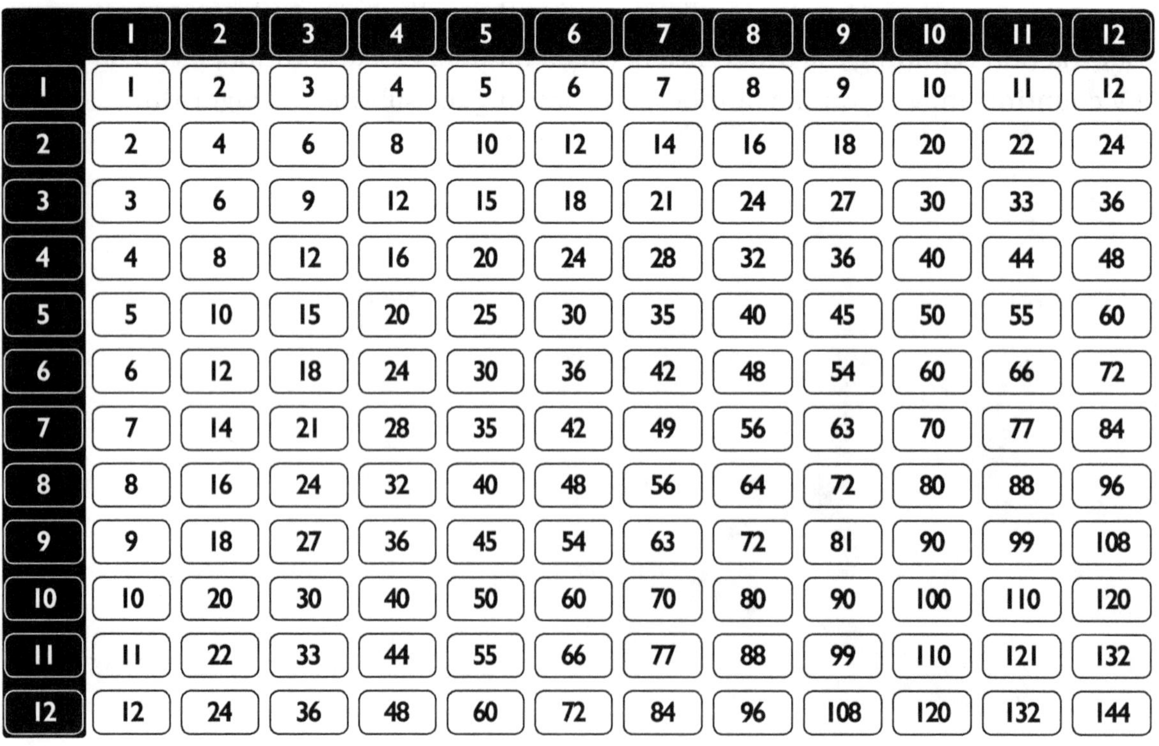

	1	2	3	4	5	6	7	8	9	10	11	12
1	1	2	3	4	5	6	7	8	9	10	11	12
2	2	4	6	8	10	12	14	16	18	20	22	24
3	3	6	9	12	15	18	21	24	27	30	33	36
4	4	8	12	16	20	24	28	32	36	40	44	48
5	5	10	15	20	25	30	35	40	45	50	55	60
6	6	12	18	24	30	36	42	48	54	60	66	72
7	7	14	21	28	35	42	49	56	63	70	77	84
8	8	16	24	32	40	48	56	64	72	80	88	96
9	9	18	27	36	45	54	63	72	81	90	99	108
10	10	20	30	40	50	60	70	80	90	100	110	120
11	11	22	33	44	55	66	77	88	99	110	121	132
12	12	24	36	48	60	72	84	96	108	120	132	144

When dealing with large numbers, the multiplication algorithm is more practical than memorization. The ability to quickly recall the products in the multiplication table is nevertheless crucial to using this algorithm.

STEP BY STEP

Step 1. Stack the two factors, vertically aligning the digits in each place.

Step 2. Draw a multiplication symbol (×) to the left of the bottom number and draw a horizontal line below the stack.

Step 3. Begin with the ones digit in the lower factor. Multiply it with the ones digit from the top factor.

Step 4. If the product from Step 3 is less than 10, write it in the same column below the horizontal line. Otherwise, write the first (ones) digit below the line and carry the second (tens) digit to the top of the next column.

Step 5. Perform Step 4 for each digit in the top factor, adding any carry digit to the result. If an extra carry digit appears at the end, write it as the leftmost digit in the product.

Step 6. Going right to left, repeat Steps 3–4 for the other places in the bottom factor, starting a new line in each case.

Step 7. Add the numbers below the line to get the product.

Example

A certain type of screw comes in packs of 35. If a contractor orders 52 packs, how many screws does he receive?

A. 2 B. 57 C. 245 D. 1,820

The correct answer is **D.** The first step is to convert this problem to a math expression. The goal is to find how many screws the contractor receives if he orders 52 packs of 35 each. The expression would be 52×35 (or 35×52). Carefully follow the multiplication algorithm (see below).

```
                1          1          1         1 1        1 1        1 1
   52          52         52         52          52         52         52
 x 35  -->   x 35  -->  x 35  -->  x 35  -->   x 35  -->  x 35  -->  x 35
 ----        ----       ----       ----        ----       ----       ----
                0        260        260         260        260        260
                                     6          56        156      + 156
                                                                   -----
                                                                   1,820
```

KEY POINT

As with addition, the order of numbers in a multiplication expression is irrelevant to the product. For example, $6 \times 9 = 9 \times 6$.

Division

Division is the inverse of multiplication, like subtraction is the inverse of addition. Whereas multiplication asks how many individuals are in 8 groups of 9 ($8 \times 9 = 72$), for example, division asks how many groups of 8 (or 9) are in 72. Division expressions use either the / or ÷ symbol. Therefore, $72 \div 9$ means: How many groups of 9 are in 72, or how many times does 9 go into 72? Thinking about the meaning of multiplication shows that $72 \div 9 = 8$ and $72 \div 8 = 9$. In the expression $72 \div 8 = 9$, 72 is the **dividend**, 8 is the **divisor**, and 9 is the **quotient**.

When the dividend is unevenly divisible by the divisor (e.g., $5 \div 2$), calculating the quotient with a **remainder** can be convenient. The quotient in this case is the maximum number of times the divisor goes into the dividend plus how much of the dividend is left over. To express the remainder, use an R. For example, the quotient of $5 \div 2$ is 2R1 because 2 goes into 5 twice with 1 left over.

Knowing the multiplication table allows quick evaluation of simple whole-number division. For larger numbers, the division algorithm enables evaluation by hand.

Unlike multiplication—but like subtraction—the order of the numbers in a division expression is important. Generally, changing the order changes the quotient.

STEP BY STEP

Step 1. Write the divisor and then the dividend on a single line.

Step 2. Draw a vertical line between them, connecting to a horizontal line over the dividend.

Step 3. If the divisor is smaller than the leftmost digit of the dividend, perform the remainder division and write the quotient (without the remainder) above that digit. If the divisor is larger than the leftmost digit, use the first two digits (or however many are necessary) until the number is greater than the divisor. Write the quotient over the rightmost digit in that number.

Step 4. Multiply the quotient digit by the divisor and write it under the dividend, vertically aligning the ones digit of the product with the quotient digit.

Step 5. Subtract the product from the digits above it.

Step 6. Bring down the next digit from the quotient.

Step 7. Perform Steps 3–6, using the most recent difference as the quotient.

Step 8. Write the remainder next to the quotient.

Example

Evaluate the expression 468 ÷ 26.

A. 18 B. 18R2 C. 494 D. 12,168

The correct answer is **A.** Carefully follow the division algorithm. In this case, the answer has no remainder.

$$26\overline{)468} \rightarrow \begin{array}{r} 1 \\ 26\overline{)468} \\ 26 \end{array} \rightarrow \begin{array}{r} 1 \\ 26\overline{)468} \\ \underline{-26} \\ 20 \end{array} \rightarrow \begin{array}{r} 1 \\ 26\overline{)468} \\ \underline{-26\downarrow} \\ 208 \end{array} \rightarrow \begin{array}{r} 18 \\ 26\overline{)468} \\ \underline{-26\downarrow} \\ 208 \\ \underline{-208} \\ 0 \end{array}$$

KEY POINT

Division by 0 is undefined. If it appears in an expression, something is wrong.

Signed Multiplication and Division

Multiplying and dividing signed numbers is simpler than adding and subtracting them because it only requires remembering two simple rules. First, if the two numbers have the same sign, their product or quotient is positive. Second, if they have different signs, their product or quotient is negative.

As a result, negative numbers can be multiplied or divided as if they are positive. Just keep track of the sign separately for the product or quotient. Note that negative numbers are sometimes written in parentheses to avoid the appearance of subtraction.

For Example:

$5 \times (-3) = -15$

$(-8) \times (-8) = 64$

$(-12) \div 3 = -4$

$(-100) \div (-25) = 4$

Example

Evaluate the expression (–7) × (–9).

A. –63 B. –16 C. 16 D. 63

The correct answer is **D.** Because both factors are negative, the product will be positive. Because the product of 7 and 9 is 63, the product of –7 and –9 is also 63.

Order of Operations

By default, math expressions work like most Western languages: they should be read and evaluated from left to right. However, some operations take precedence over others, which can change this default evaluation. Following this **order of operations** is critical. The mnemonic **PEMDAS** (**P**lease **E**xcuse **M**y **D**ear **A**unt **S**ally) helps in remembering how to evaluate an expression with multiple operations.

STEP BY STEP

P. Evaluate operations in parentheses (or braces/brackets). If the expression has parentheses within parentheses, begin with the innermost ones.

E. Evaluate exponential operations. (For expressions without exponents, ignore this step.)

MD. Perform all multiplication and division operations, going through the expression from left to right.

AS. Perform all addition and subtraction operations, going through the expression from left to right.

Because the order of numbers in multiplication and addition does not affect the result, the PEMDAS procedure only requires going from left to right when dividing or subtracting. At those points, going in the correct direction is critical to getting the right answer.

Calculators that can handle a series of numbers at once automatically evaluate an expression according to the order of operations. When available, calculators are a good way to check the results.

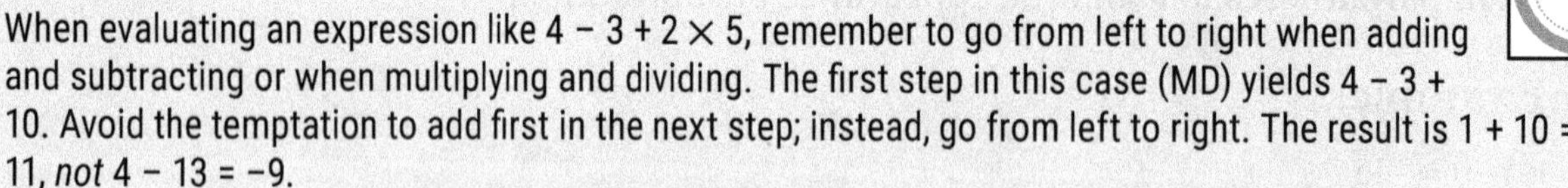

BE CAREFUL!

When evaluating an expression like $4 - 3 + 2 \times 5$, remember to go from left to right when adding and subtracting or when multiplying and dividing. The first step in this case (MD) yields $4 - 3 + 10$. Avoid the temptation to add first in the next step; instead, go from left to right. The result is $1 + 10 = 11$, *not* $4 - 13 = -9$.

Example

Evaluate the expression $8 \times (3 + 6) \div 3 - 2 + 5$.

A. 13 B. 17 C. 27 D. 77

The correct answer is **C**. Use the PEMDAS mnemonic. Start with parentheses. Then, do multiplication/division from left to right. Finally, do addition/subtraction from left to right.

$8 \times (3 + 6) \div 3 - 2 + 5$

$8 \times 9 \div 3 - 2 + 5$

$72 \div 3 - 2 + 5$

$24 - 2 + 5$

$22 + 5$

27

Let's Review!

- The multiplication table is important to memorize for both multiplying and dividing small whole numbers (up to about 12).
- Multiplication and division of large numbers by hand typically requires the multiplication and division algorithms.
- Multiplying and dividing signed numbers follows two simple rules: If the numbers have the same sign, the product or quotient is positive. If they have different signs, the product or quotient is negative.
- When evaluating expressions with several operations, carefully follow the order of operations; PEMDAS is a helpful mnemonic.

FACTORS AND MULTIPLES

This lesson shows the relationship between factors and multiples of a number. In addition, it introduces prime and composite numbers and demonstrates how to use prime factorization to determine all the factors of a number.

Factors of a Number

> **BE CAREFUL!**
>
> The term *factor* can mean any number being multiplied by another number, or it can mean a number by which another number is divisible. The two uses are related but slightly different. The context will generally clarify which meaning applies.

Multiplication converts two or more factors into a product. A given number, however, may be the product of more than one combination of factors; for example, 12 is the product of 3 and 4 and the product of 2 and 6. Limiting consideration to the set of whole numbers, a **factor of a number** (call it x) is a whole number whose product with any other whole number is equal to x. For instance, 2 is a factor of 12 because $12 \div 2$ is a whole number (6). Another way of expressing it is that 2 is a factor of 12 because 12 is **divisible** by 2.

A whole number always has at least two factors: 1 and itself. That is, for any whole number y, $1 \times y = y$. To test whether one number is a factor of a second number, divide the second by the first. If the quotient is whole, it is a factor. If the quotient is not whole (or it has a remainder), it is not a factor.

Example

Which number is not a factor of 54?

A. 1 B. 2 C. 4 D. 6

The correct answer is **C**. A number is a factor of another number if the latter is divisible by the former. The number 54 is divisible by 1 because $54 \times 1 = 54$, and it is divisible by 2 because $27 \times 2 = 54$. Also, $6 \times 9 = 54$. But $54 \div 4 = 13.5$ (or 13R2). Therefore, 4 is not a factor.

Multiples of a Number

Multiples of a number are related to factors of a number. A **multiple of a number** is that number's product with some integer. For example, if a hardware store sells a type of screw that only comes in packs of 20, customers must buy these screws in *multiples* of 20: that is, 20, 40, 60, 80, and so on. (Technically, 0 is also a multiple.) These numbers are equal to 20×1, 20×2, 20×3, 20×4, and so on. Similarly, measurements in feet represent multiples of 12 inches. A (whole-number) measurement in feet would be equivalent to 12 inches, 24 inches, 36 inches, and so on.

When counting by twos or threes, multiples are used. But because the multiples of a number are the product of that number with the integers, multiples can also be negative. For the number 2, the multiples are the set {..., −6, −4, −2, 0, 2, 4, 6,...}, where the ellipsis dots indicate that the set continues the pattern indefinitely in both directions. Also, the number can be any real number: the multiples of π (approximately 3.14) are {..., −3π, −2π, −1π, 0, 1π, 2π, 3π,...}. Note that the notation 2π, for example, means $2 \times \pi$.

The positive multiples (along with 0) of a whole number are all numbers for which that whole number is a factor. For instance, the positive multiples of 5 are 0, 5, 10, 15, 20, 25, 30, and so on. That full set contains all (whole) numbers for which 5 is a factor. Thus, one number is a multiple of a second number if the second number is a factor of the first.

Example

If a landowner subdivides a parcel of property into multiples of 7 acres, how many acres can a buyer purchase?

A. 1 B. 15 C. 29 D. 42

The correct answer is **D.** Because the landowner subdivides the property into multiples of 7 acres, a buyer must choose an acreage from the list 7 acres, 14 acres, 21 acres, and so on. That list includes 42 acres. Another way to solve the problem is to find which answer is divisible by 7 (that is, which number has 7 as a factor).

Prime and Composite Numbers

For some real-world applications, such as cryptography, factors and multiples play an important role. One important way to classify whole numbers is by whether they are prime or composite. A **prime** number is any whole (or natural) number greater than 1 that has only itself and 1 as factors. The smallest example is 2: because 2 only has 1 and 2 as factors, it is prime. **Composite** numbers have at least one factor other than 1 and themselves. The smallest composite number is 4: in addition to 1 and 4, it has 2 as a factor.

> **BE CAREFUL!**
> Avoid the temptation to call 1 a prime number. Although it only has itself and 1 as factors, those factors are the same number. Hence, 1 is fundamentally different from the prime numbers, which start at 2.

Determining whether a number is prime can be extremely difficult—hence its value in cryptography. One simple test that works for some numbers is to check whether the number is even or odd. An **even number** is divisible by 2; an **odd number** is not. To determine whether a number is even or odd, look at the last (rightmost) digit. If that digit is even (0, 2, 4, 6, or 8), the number is even. Otherwise, it is odd. Another simple test works for multiples of 3. Add all the digits in the number. If the sum is divisible by 3, the original number is also divisible by 3. This rule can be successively applied multiple times until the sum of digits is manageable. That number is then composite.

Example

Which number is prime?

A. 6 B. 16 C. 61 D. 116

The correct answer is **C.** When applicable, the easiest way to identify a number greater than 2 as composite rather than prime is to check whether it is even. All even numbers greater than 2 are composite. By elimination, 61 is prime.

Prime Factorization

Determining whether a number is prime, even for relatively small numbers (less than 100), can be difficult. One tool that can help both solve this problem and identify all factors of a number is **prime factorization.** One way to do prime factorization is to make a **factor tree.**

The procedure below demonstrates the process.

STEP BY STEP

Step 1. Write the number you want to factor.

Step 2. If the number is prime, stop. Otherwise, go to Step 3.

Step 3. Find any two factors of the number and write them on the line below the number.

Step 4. "Connect" the factors and the number using line segments. The result will look somewhat like an inverted tree, particularly as the process continues.

Step 5. Repeat Steps 2–4 for all composite factors in the tree.

The numbers in the factor tree are either "branches" (if they are connected downward to other numbers) or "leaves" (if they have no further downward connections). The leaves constitute all the prime factors of the original number: when multiplied together, their product is that number. Moreover, any product of two or more of the leaves is a factor of the original number. Thus, using prime factorization helps find any and all factors of a number, although the process can be tedious when performed by hand (particularly for large numbers). Below is a factor tree for the number 96. All the leaves are circled for emphasis.

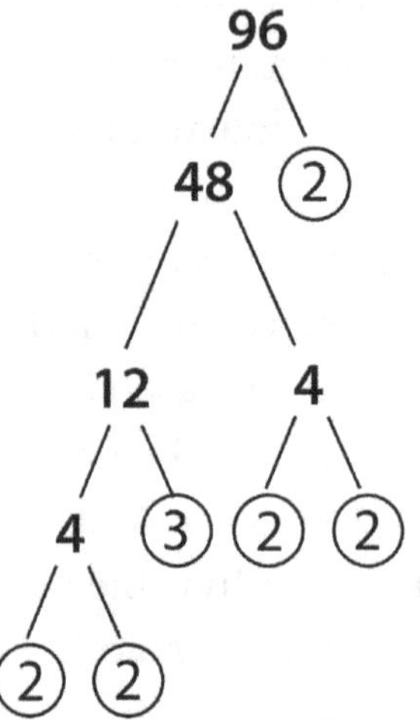

2x2x3x2x2x2=96

Example

Which list includes all the unique prime factors of 84?

A. 2, 3, 7   B. 3, 4, 7   C. 3, 5, 7   D. 1, 2, 3, 7

The correct answer is **A.** One approach is to find the prime factorization of 84. The factor tree shows that $84 = 2 \times 2 \times 3 \times 7$. Alternatively, note that answer D includes 1, which is not prime. Answer B includes 4, which is a composite number. Since answer C includes 5, which is not a factor of 84, the only possible answer is A.

Let's Review!

- A whole number is divisible by all of its factors, which are also whole numbers by definition.
- Multiples of a number are all possible products of that number and the integers.
- A prime number is a whole number greater than 1 that has no factors other than itself and 1.
- A composite number is a whole number greater than 1 that is not prime (that is, it has factors other than itself and 1).
- Even numbers are divisible by 2; odd numbers are not.
- Prime factorization yields all the prime factors of a number. The factor-tree method is one way to determine prime factorization.

STANDARDS OF MEASURE

This lesson discusses the conversion within and between the standard system and the metric system and between 12-hour clock time and military time.

Length Conversions

The basic units of measure of length in the standard measurement system are inches, feet, yards, and miles. There are 12 inches (in.) in 1 foot (ft.), 3 feet (ft.) in 1 yard (yd.), and 5,280 feet (ft.) in 1 mile (mi.).

The basic unit of measure of metric length is meters. There are 1,000 millimeters (mm), 100 centimeters (cm), and 10 decimeters (dm) in 1 meter (m). There are 10 meters (m) in 1 dekameter (dam), 100 meters (m) in 1 hectometer (hm), and 1,000 meters (m) in 1 kilometer (km).

BE CAREFUL!

There are some cases where multiple conversions must be performed to determine the correct units.

To convert from one unit to the other, multiply by the appropriate factor.

Examples

1. **Convert 27 inches to feet.**

   A. 2 feet B. 2.25 feet C. 3 feet D. 3.25 feet

   The correct answer is **B**. The correct solution is 2.25 feet. $27 \text{ in} \times \frac{1 \text{ ft}}{12 \text{ in}} = \frac{27}{12} = 2.25 \text{ ft}$.

2. **Convert 67 millimeters to centimeters.**

   A. 0.0067 centimeters
   B. 0.067 centimeters
   C. 0.67 centimeters
   D. 6.7 centimeters

   The correct answer is **D**. The correct solution is 6.7 centimeters. $67 \text{ mm} \times \frac{1 \text{ cm}}{10 \text{ mm}} = \frac{67}{10} = 6.7 \text{ cm}$.

Volume and Weight Conversions

There are volume conversion factors for standard and metric volumes.

The volume conversions for standard volume are shown in the table.

Measurement	Conversion
Pints (pt.) and fluid ounces (fl. oz.)	1 pint equals 16 fluid ounces
Quarts (qt.) and pints (pt.)	1 quart equals 2 pints
Quarts (qt.) and gallons (gal.)	1 gallon equals 4 quarts

The basic unit of volume for the metric system is liters. There are 1,000 milliliters (mL) in 1 liter (L) and 1,000 liters (L) in 1 kiloliter (kL).

There are weight conversion factors for standard and metric weights.

The basic unit of weight for the standard measurement system is pounds. There are

16 ounces (oz.) in 1 pound (lb.) and

2,000 pounds (lb.) in 1 ton (T).

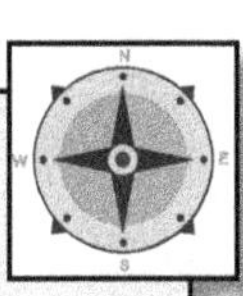

KEEP IN MIND

The conversions within the metric system are multiples of 10.

The basic unit of weight for the metric system is grams.

Measurement	Conversion
Milligrams (mg) and grams (g)	1,000 milligrams equals 1 gram
Centigrams (cg) and grams (g)	100 centigrams equals 1 gram
Kilograms (kg) and grams (g)	1 kilogram equals 1,000 grams
Metric tons (t) and kilograms (kg)	1 metric ton equals 1,000 kilograms

Examples

1. **Convert 8 gallons to pints.**

   A. 1 pint B. 4 pints C. 16 pints D. 64 pints

   The correct answer is **D.** The correct solution is 64 pints. $8 \text{ gal} \times \frac{4 \text{ qt}}{1 \text{ gal}} \times \frac{2 \text{ pt}}{1 \text{ qt}} = 64 \text{ pt}$.

2. **Convert 7.5 liters to milliliters.**

   A. 75 milliliters B. 750 milliliters C. 7,500 milliliters D. 75,000 milliliters

   The correct answer is **C.** The correct solution is 7,500 milliliters. $7.5 \text{ L} \times \frac{1{,}000 \text{ mL}}{1 \text{ L}} = 7{,}500 \text{ mL}$.

3. **Convert 12.5 pounds to ounces.**

   A. 142 ounces B. 150 ounces C. 192 ounces D. 200 ounces

   The correct answer is **D.** The correct solution is 200 ounces. $12.5 \text{ lb} \times \frac{16 \text{ oz}}{1 \text{ lb}} = 200 \text{ oz}$.

4. **Convert 84 grams to centigrams.**

   A. 0.84 centigrams B. 8.4 centigrams C. 840 centigrams D. 8,400 centigrams

   The correct answer is **D.** The correct solution is 8,400 centigrams. $84 \text{ g} \times \frac{100 \text{ cg}}{1 \text{ g}} = 8{,}400 \text{ cg}$.

Conversions between Standard and Metric Systems

The table shows the common conversions of length, volume, and weight between the standard and metric systems.

Measurement	Conversion
Centimeters (cm) and inches (in.)	2.54 centimeters equals 1 inch
Meters (m) and feet (ft.)	1 meter equals 3.28 feet
Kilometers (km) and miles (mi.)	1.61 kilometers equals 1 mile
Quarts (qt.) and liters (L)	1.06 quarts equals 1 liter
Liters (L) and gallons (gal.)	3.79 liters equals 1 gallon
Grams (g) and ounces (oz.)	28.3 grams equals 1 ounce
Kilograms (kg) and pounds (lb.)	1 kilogram equals 2.2 pounds

There are many additional conversion factors, but this lesson uses only the common ones. Most factors have been rounded to the nearest hundredth for accuracy.

STEP BY STEP

Step 1. Choose the appropriate conversion factor within each system, if necessary.

Step 2. Choose the appropriate conversion factor from the standard and metric conversion.

Step 3. Multiply and simplify to the nearest hundredth.

Examples

1. **Convert 12 inches to centimeters.**

A. 4.72 centimeters B. 14.54 centimeters C. 28.36 centimeters D. 30.48 centimeters

The correct answer is **D.** The correct solution is 30.48 centimeters. $12 \text{ in} \times \frac{2.54 \text{ cm}}{1 \text{ in}} = 30.48 \text{ cm}$.

2. **Convert 8 kilometers to feet.**

A. 13,118.01 feet B. 26,236.02 feet C. 34,003.20 feet D. 68,006.40 feet

The correct answer is **B.** The correct solution is 26,236.02 feet. $8 \text{ km} \times \frac{1 \text{ mi}}{1.61 \text{ km}} \times \frac{5{,}280 \text{ ft}}{1 \text{ mi}} = \frac{42{,}240}{1.61} = 26{,}236.02 \text{ ft}$.

3. **Convert 2 gallons to milliliters.**

A. 527 milliliters B. 758 milliliters C. 5,270 milliliters D. 7,580 milliliters

The correct answer is **D.** The correct solution is 7,580 milliliters.
$2 \text{ gal} \times \frac{3.79 \text{ L}}{1 \text{ gal}} \times \frac{1{,}000 \text{ mL}}{1 \text{ L}} = 7{,}580 \text{ mL}$.

4. Convert 16 kilograms to pounds.

A. 7.27 pounds B. 18.2 pounds C. 19.27 pounds D. 35.2 pounds

The correct answer is **D**. The correct solution is 35.2 pounds. $16 \text{ kg} \times \frac{2.2 \text{ lb}}{1 \text{ kg}} = 35.2 \text{ lb.}$

Time Conversions

Two ways to keep time are 12-hour clock time using a.m. and p.m. and military time based on a 24-hour clock. Keep these three key points in mind:

KEEP IN MIND

Midnight (12:00 a.m.) is 2400 or 0000 in military time.

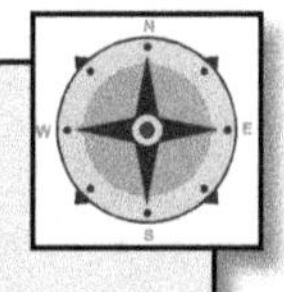

- The hours from 1:00 a.m. to 12:59 p.m. are the same in both methods. For example, 9:15 a.m. in 12-hour clock time is 0915 in military time.
- From 1:00 p.m. to 11:59 p.m., add 12 hours to obtain military time. For example, 4:07 p.m. in 12-hour clock time is 1607 in military time.
- From 12:01 a.m. to 12:59 a.m. in 12-hour clock time, military time is from 0001 to 0059.

Example

Identify 9:27 p.m. in military time.

A. 0927 B. 1927 C. 2127 D. 2427

The correct answer is **C**. The correct solution is 2127. Add 1200 to the time, 1200 + 927 = 2127.

Let's Review!

- To convert from one unit to another, choose the appropriate conversion factors.
- In many cases, it is necessary to use multiple conversion factors.

Chapter 8 Number and Quantity Practice Quiz 1

1. **Evaluate the expression 8 – 27.**

   A. –35
   B. –19
   C. 0
   D. 19

2. **Evaluate the expression 102 + 3 + 84 + 27.**

   A. 105
   B. 216
   C. 250
   D. 513

3. **How much change should a customer expect if she is buying a $53 item and hands the cashier two $50 bills?**

   A. $3
   B. $47
   C. $57
   D. $100

4. **When dealing with a series of multiplication and division operations, which is the correct approach to evaluating them?**

   A. Evaluate all division operations first.
   B. Evaluate the expression from left to right.
   C. Evaluate all multiplication operations first.
   D. None of the above.

5. **Evaluate the expression 28 × 43.**

   A. 71
   B. 196
   C. 1,204
   D. 1,960

6. **Evaluate the expression 3 + 1 – 5 + 2 – 6.**

   A. –9
   B. –5
   C. 0
   D. 17

7. **Which number is a factor of 128?**

   A. 3
   B. 6
   C. 12
   D. 16

8. **How many prime factors does 42 have?**

   A. 1
   B. 2
   C. 3
   D. 4

9. **If a factor tree for a prime factorization has four leaves—3, 2, 5, and 7—what is the number being factored?**

   A. 7
   B. 5
   C. 210
   D. Not enough information

10. **Convert 16,000 ounces to tons.**

    A. 0.5 ton
    B. 1 ton
    C. 1.5 tons
    D. 2 tons

11. **Convert 99 meters to kilometers.**

    A. 0.0099 kilometers
    B. 0.099 kilometers
    C. 0.9 centimeters
    D. 9.9 centimeters

12. **Identify 12:45 a.m. in military time.**

    A. 0045
    B. 0145
    C. 1245
    D. 1345

CHAPTER 8 NUMBER AND QUANTITY PRACTICE QUIZ 1 – ANSWER KEY

1. B. The correct solution is –19. Because the subtraction algorithm does not apply directly in this case (the first number is smaller than the second), first use the rule that $x - y = -(y - x)$. So, $8 - 27 = -(27 - 8)$. Applying the algorithm to 27 – 8 yields 19, then $-(27 - 8) = -19$. **See Lesson: Basic Addition and Subtraction.**

2. B. The correct solution is 216. Use the addition algorithm. Add the numbers two at a time or all at once. The latter approach will involve two carry digits. **See Lesson: Basic Addition and Subtraction.**

3. B. The correct solution is $47. The customer gives the cashier $100, which is the sum of $50 and $50. To find out how much change she receives, calculate the difference between $100 and $53, which is $47. **See Lesson: Basic Addition and Subtraction.**

4. B. Multiplication and division have equivalent priority in the order of operations. In this case, the expression must be evaluated from left to right. **See Lesson: Basic Multiplication and Division.**

5. C. Use the multiplication algorithm. It involves adding 84 and 1,120 to get the product of 1,204. **See Lesson: Basic Multiplication and Division.**

6. B. This expression only involves addition and subtraction, but its evaluation must go from left to right. **See Lesson: Basic Multiplication and Division.**

$3 + 1 - 5 + 2 - 6$

$4 - 5 + 2 - 6$

$(-1) + 2 - 6$

$1 - 6$

-5

7. D. To determine whether a number is a factor of another number, divide the second number by the first number. If the quotient is whole, the first number is a factor. In this case, 128 is only divisible by 16. **See Lesson: Factors and Multiples.**

8. C. The prime factorization—for example, using a factor tree—shows that 42 has the prime factors 2, 3, and 7 because $2 \times 3 \times 7 = 42$. **See Lesson: Factors and Multiples.**

9. C. The number being factored in a prime factorization is the product of all its prime factors. The leaves in a factor tree are these prime factors. Therefore, the number is their product. In this case, it is $3 \times 2 \times 5 \times 7 = 210$. **See Lesson: Factors and Multiples.**

10. A. The correct solution is 0.5 ton. $16{,}000\ oz \times \frac{1\ lb}{16\ oz} \times \frac{1T}{2{,}000\ lb} = \frac{16{,}000}{32{,}000} = 0.5\ T.$ **See Lesson: Standards of Measure.**

11. B. The correct solution is 0.099 kilometers. $99\ m \times \frac{1\ km}{1{,}000\ m} = \frac{99}{1{,}000} = 0.099\ km.$ **See Lesson: Standards of Measure.**

12. A. The correct solution is 0045. Subtract 1200 from the time, 1245 – 1200 = 0045. **See Lesson: Standards of Measure.**

CHAPTER 9 ALGEBRA

DECIMALS AND FRACTIONS

This lesson introduces the basics of decimals and fractions. It also demonstrates changing decimals to fractions, changing fractions to decimals, and converting between fractions, decimals, and percentages.

Introduction to Fractions

A fraction represents part of a whole number. The top number of a fraction is the **numerator,** and the bottom number of a fraction is the **denominator.** The numerator is smaller than the denominator for a **proper fraction.** The numerator is larger than the denominator for an **improper fraction.**

Proper Fractions	Improper Fractions
$\frac{2}{5}$	$\frac{5}{2}$
$\frac{7}{12}$	$\frac{12}{7}$
$\frac{19}{20}$	$\frac{20}{19}$

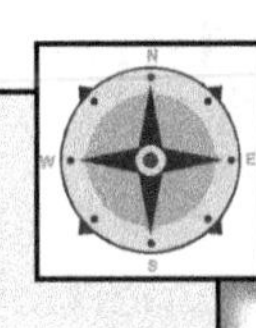

KEEP IN MIND

When comparing fractions, the denominators of the fractions must be the same.

An improper fraction can be changed to a **mixed number**. A mixed number is a whole number and a proper fraction. To write an improper fraction as a mixed number, divide the denominator into the numerator. The result is the whole number. The remainder is the numerator of the proper fraction, and the value of the denominator does not change. For example, $\frac{5}{2}$ is $2\frac{1}{2}$ because 2 goes into 5 twice with a remainder of 1. To write an improper fraction as a mixed number, multiply the whole number by the denominator and add the result to the numerator. The results become the new numerator. For example, $2\frac{1}{2}$ is $\frac{5}{2}$ because 2 times 2 plus 1 is 5 for the new numerator.

When comparing fractions, the denominators must be the same. Then, look at the numerator to determine which fraction is larger. If the fractions have different denominators, then a **least common denominator** must be found. This number is the smallest number that can be divided evenly into the denominators of all fractions being compared.

To determine the largest fraction from the group $\frac{1}{3}, \frac{3}{5}, \frac{2}{3}, \frac{2}{5}$, the first step is to find a common denominator. In this case, the least common denominator is 15 because 3 times 5 and 5 times 3 is 15. The second step is to convert the fractions to a denominator of 15.

The fractions with a denominator of 3 have the numerator and denominator multiplied by 5, and the fractions with a denominator of 5 have the numerator and denominator multiplied by 3, as shown below:

$$\frac{1}{3}\times\frac{5}{5}=\frac{5}{15},\ \frac{3}{5}\times\frac{3}{3}=\frac{9}{15},\ \frac{2}{3}\times\frac{5}{5}=\frac{10}{15},\ \frac{2}{5}\times\frac{3}{3}=\frac{6}{15}$$

Now, the numerators can be compared. The largest fraction is $\frac{2}{3}$ because it has a numerator of 10 after finding the common denominator.

Examples

1. **Which fraction is the least?**

   A. $\frac{3}{5}$ B. $\frac{3}{4}$ C. $\frac{1}{5}$ D. $\frac{1}{4}$

   The correct answer is **C**. The correct solution is $\frac{1}{5}$ because it has the smallest numerator compared to the other fractions with the same denominator. The fractions with a common denominator of 20 are $\frac{3}{5}=\frac{12}{20}, \frac{3}{4}=\frac{15}{20}, \frac{1}{5}=\frac{4}{20}, \frac{1}{4}=\frac{5}{20}$.

2. **Which fraction is the greatest?**

   A. $\frac{5}{6}$ B. $\frac{1}{2}$ C. $\frac{2}{3}$ D. $\frac{1}{6}$

   The correct answer is **A**. The correct solution is $\frac{5}{6}$ because it has the largest numerator compared to the other fractions with the same denominator. The fractions with a common denominator of 6 are $\frac{5}{6}=\frac{5}{6}, \frac{1}{2}=\frac{3}{6}, \frac{2}{3}=\frac{4}{6}, \frac{1}{6}=\frac{1}{6}$.

Introduction to Decimals

A **decimal** is a number that expresses part of a whole. Decimals show a portion of a number after a decimal point. Each number to the left and right of the decimal point has a specific place value. Identify the place values for 645.3207.

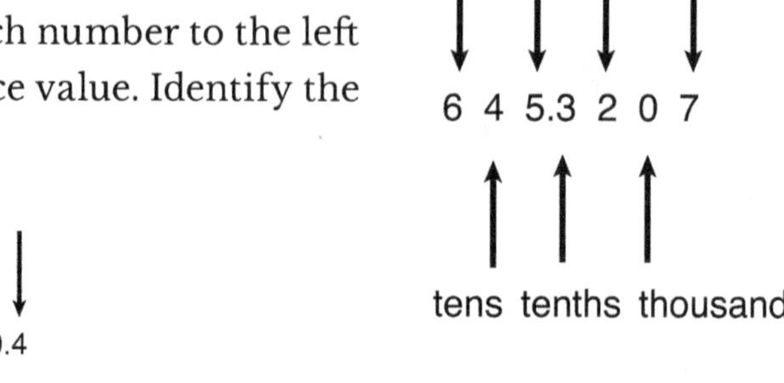

When comparing decimals, compare the numbers in the same place value. For example, determine the greatest decimal from the group 0.4, 0.41, 0.39, and 0.37. In these numbers, there is a value to the right of the decimal point. Comparing the tenths places, the numbers with 4 tenths (0.4 and 0.41) are greater than the numbers with three tenths (0.39 and 0.37).

0.4
0.41
0.39
0.37

KEEP IN MIND

When comparing decimals, compare the place value where the numbers are different.

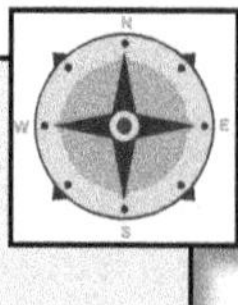

Then, compare the hundredths in the 4 tenths numbers. The value of 0.41 is greater because there is a 1 in the hundredths place versus a 0 in the hundredths place.

0.4

0.41

Here is another example: determine the least decimal of the group 5.23, 5.32, 5.13, and 5.31. In this group, the ones value is 5 for all numbers. Then, comparing the tenths values, 5.13 is the smallest number because it is the only value with 1 tenth.

Examples

1. **Which decimal is the greatest?**

   A. 0.07 B. 0.007 C. 0.7 D. 0.0007

   The correct answer is **C**. The solution is 0.7 because it has the largest place value in the tenths.

2. **Which decimal is the least?**

   A. 0.0413 B. 0.0713 C. 0.0513 D. 0.0613

   The correct answer is **A**. The correct solution is 0.0413 because it has the smallest place value in the hundredths place.

Changing Decimals and Fractions

Three steps change a decimal to a fraction.

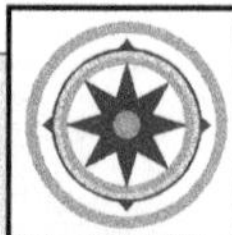

STEP BY STEP

Step 1. Write the decimal divided by 1 with the decimal as the numerator and 1 as the denominator.

Step 2. Multiply the numerator and denominator by 10 for every number after the decimal point. (For example, if there is 1 decimal place, multiply by 10. If there are 2 decimal places, multiply by 100).

Step 3. Reduce the fraction completely.

To change the decimal 0.37 to a fraction, start by writing the decimal as a fraction with a denominator of one, $\frac{0.37}{1}$. Because there are two decimal places, multiply the numerator and denominator by 100, $\frac{0.37 \times 100}{1 \times 100} = \frac{37}{100}$. The fraction does not reduce, so $\frac{37}{100}$ is 0.37 in fraction form.

Similarly, to change the decimal 2.4 to a fraction start by writing the decimal as a fraction with a denominator of one, $\frac{0.4}{1}$, and ignore the whole number. Because there is one decimal place, multiply the numerator and denominator by 10, $\frac{0.4 \times 10}{1 \times 10} = \frac{4}{10}$. The fraction does reduce: $2\frac{4}{10} = 2\frac{2}{5}$ is 2.4 in fraction form.

The decimal $0.\overline{3}$ as a fraction is $\frac{0.\overline{3}}{1}$. In the case of a repeating decimal, let $n = 0.\overline{3}$ *and* $10n = 3.\overline{3}$. Then, $10n - n = 3.\overline{3} - 0.\overline{3}$, resulting in $9n = 3$ and solution of $n = \frac{3}{9} = \frac{1}{3}$. The decimal $0.\overline{3}$ is $\frac{1}{3}$ as a fraction.

Examples

1. **Change 0.38 to a fraction. Simplify completely.**

   A. $\frac{3}{10}$ B. $\frac{9}{25}$ C. $\frac{19}{50}$ D. $\frac{2}{5}$

   The correct answer is **C**. The correct solution is $\frac{19}{50}$ because $\frac{0.38}{1} = \frac{38}{100} = \frac{19}{50}$.

2. **Change $1.\overline{1}$ to a fraction. Simplify completely.**

   A. $1\frac{1}{11}$ B. $1\frac{1}{9}$ C. $1\frac{1}{6}$ D. $1\frac{1}{3}$

   The correct answer is **B**. The correct solution is $1\frac{1}{9}$. Let $n = 1.\overline{1}$ and $10n = 11.\overline{1}$. Then, $10n - n = 11.\overline{1} - 1.\overline{1}$, resulting in $9n = 10$ and solution of $n = \frac{10}{9} = 1\frac{1}{9}$.

Two steps change a fraction to a decimal.

STEP BY STEP

Step 1. Divide the denominator by the numerator. Add zeros after the decimal point as needed.

Step 2. Complete the process when there is no remainder or the decimal is repeating.

To convert $\frac{1}{5}$ to a decimal, rewrite $\frac{1}{5}$ as a long division problem and add zeros after the decimal point, $1.0 \div 5$. Complete the long division and $\frac{1}{5}$ as a decimal is 0.2. The division is complete because there is no remainder.

To convert $\frac{8}{9}$ to a decimal, rewrite $\frac{8}{9}$ as a long division problem and add zeros after the decimal point, $8.00 \div 9$. Complete the long division, and $\frac{8}{9}$ as a decimal is $0.\overline{8}$. The process is complete because the decimal is complete.

To rewrite the mixed number $2\frac{3}{4}$ as a decimal, the fraction needs changed to a decimal. Rewrite $\frac{3}{4}$ as a long division problem and add zeros after the decimal point, $3.00 \div 4$. The whole number is needed for the answer and is not included in the long division. Complete the long division, and $2\frac{3}{4}$ as a decimal is 2.75.

Examples

1. **Change $\frac{9}{10}$ to a decimal. Simplify completely.**

   A. 0.75 B. 0.8 C. 0.85 D. 0.9

   The correct answer is **D**. The correct answer is 0.9 because $\frac{9}{10} = 9.0 \div 10 = 0.9$.

2. **Change $\frac{5}{6}$ to a decimal. Simplify completely.**

   A. 0.73 B. $0.7\overline{6}$ C. $0.8\overline{3}$ D. 0.86

   The correct answer is **C**. The correct answer is $0.8\overline{3}$ because $\frac{5}{6} = 5.000 \div 6 = 0.8\overline{3}$.

Convert among Fractions, Decimals, and Percentages

Fractions, decimals, and percentages can change forms, but they are equivalent values.

There are two ways to change a decimal to a percent. One way is to multiply the decimal by 100 and add a percent sign. 0.24 as a percent is 24%.

Another way is to move the decimal point two places to the right. The decimal 0.635 is 63.5% as a percent when moving the decimal point two places to the right.

Any decimal, including repeating decimals, can change to a percent. $0.\overline{3}$ as a percent is $0.\overline{3} \times 100 = 33.\overline{3}\%$.

Example

Write 0.345 as a percent.

A. 3.45% B. 34.5% C. 345% D. 3450%

The correct answer is **B.** The correct answer is 34.5% because 0.345 as a percent is 34.5%.

There are two ways to change a percent to a decimal. One way is to remove the percent sign and divide the decimal by 100. For example, 73% as a decimal is 0.73.

Another way is to move the decimal point two places to the left. For example, 27.8% is 0.278 as a decimal when moving the decimal point two places to the left.

Any percent, including repeating percents, can change to a decimal. For example, $44.\overline{4}\%$ as a decimal is $44.\overline{4} \div 100 = 0.\overline{4}$.

Example

Write 131% as a decimal.

A. 0.131 B. 1.31 C. 13.1 D. 131

The correct answer is **B.** The correct answer is 1.31 because 131% as a decimal is 131 ÷ 100 = 1.31.

Two steps change a fraction to a percent.

STEP BY STEP

Step 1. Divide the numerator and denominator.

Step 2. Multiply by 100 and add a percent sign.

To change the fraction $\frac{3}{5}$ to a decimal, perform long division to get 0.6. Then, multiply 0.6 by 100 and $\frac{3}{5}$ is the same as 60%.

To change the fraction $\frac{7}{8}$ to a decimal, perform long division to get 0.875. Then, multiply 0.875 by 100 and $\frac{7}{8}$ is the same as 87.5%.

Fractions that are repeating decimals can also be converted to a percent. To change the fraction $\frac{2}{3}$ to a decimal, perform long division to get $0.\overline{6}$. Then, multiply $0.\overline{6}$ by 100 and the percent is $66.\overline{6}\%$.

Example

Write $2\frac{1}{8}$ as a percent.

A. 21.2% B. 21.25% C. 212% D. 212.5%

The correct answer is **D.** The correct answer is 212.5% because $2\frac{1}{8}$ as a percent is 2.125 x 100 = 212.5%.

Two steps change a percent to a fraction.

STEP BY STEP

Step 1. Remove the percent sign and write the value as the numerator with a denominator of 100.

Step 2. Simplify the fraction.

Remove the percent sign from 45% and write as a fraction with a denominator of 100, $\frac{45}{100}$. The fraction reduces to $\frac{9}{20}$.

Remove the percent sign from 22.8% and write as a fraction with a denominator of 100, $\frac{22.8}{100}$. The fraction reduces to $\frac{228}{1000} = \frac{57}{250}$.

Repeating percentages can change to a fraction. Remove the percent sign from $16.\overline{6}\%$ and write as a fraction with a denominator of 100, $\frac{16.\overline{6}}{100}$. The fraction simplifies to $\frac{0.1\overline{6}}{1} = \frac{1}{6}$.

Example

Write 72% as a fraction.

A. $\frac{27}{50}$ B. $\frac{7}{10}$ C. $\frac{18}{25}$ D. $\frac{3}{4}$

The correct answer is **C**. The correct answer is $\frac{18}{25}$ because 72% as a fraction is $\frac{72}{100} = \frac{18}{25}$.

Let's Review!

- A fraction is a number with a numerator and a denominator. A fraction can be written as a proper fraction, an improper fraction, or a mixed number. Changing fractions to a common denominator enables you to determine the least or greatest fraction in a group of fractions.
- A decimal is a number that expresses part of a whole. By comparing the same place values, you can find the least or greatest decimal in a group of decimals.
- A number can be written as a fraction, a decimal, and a percent. These are equivalent values. Numbers can be converted between fractions, decimals, and percents by following a series of steps.

MULTIPLICATION AND DIVISION OF FRACTIONS

This lesson introduces how to multiply and divide fractions.

Multiplying a Fraction by a Fraction

The multiplication of fractions does not require changing any denominators like adding and subtracting fractions do. To multiply a fraction by a fraction, multiply the numerators together and multiply the denominators together. For example, $\frac{2}{3} \times \frac{4}{5}$ is $\frac{2 \times 4}{3 \times 5}$, which is $\frac{8}{15}$.

Sometimes, the final solution reduces. For example, $\frac{3}{5} \times \frac{1}{9} = \frac{3 \times 1}{5 \times 9} = \frac{3}{45}$. The fraction $\frac{3}{45}$ reduces to $\frac{1}{15}$.

Simplifying fractions can occur before completing the multiplication. In the previous problem, the numerator of 3 can be simplified with the denominator of 9: $\frac{13}{5} \times \frac{1}{39} = \frac{1}{15}$. This method of simplifying only occurs with the multiplication of fractions.

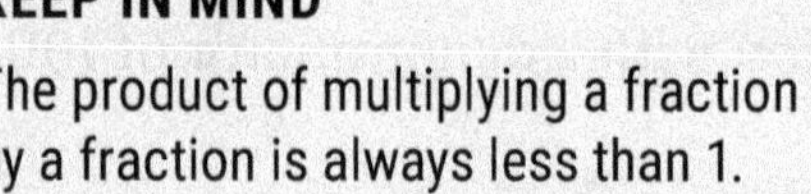
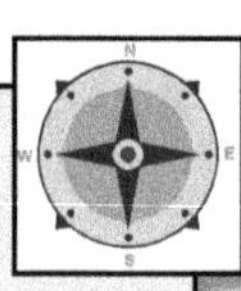

KEEP IN MIND

The product of multiplying a fraction by a fraction is always less than 1.

Examples

1. **Multiply $\frac{1}{2} \times \frac{3}{4}$.**

   A. $\frac{1}{4}$ B. $\frac{1}{2}$ C. $\frac{3}{8}$ D. $\frac{2}{3}$

   The correct answer is **C**. The correct solution is $\frac{3}{8}$ because $\frac{1}{2} \times \frac{3}{4} = \frac{3}{8}$.

2. **Multiply $\frac{2}{3} \times \frac{5}{6}$.**

   A. $\frac{1}{9}$ B. $\frac{5}{18}$ C. $\frac{5}{9}$ D. $\frac{7}{18}$

   The correct answer is **C**. The correct solution is $\frac{5}{9}$ because $\frac{2}{3} \times \frac{5}{6} = \frac{10}{18} = \frac{5}{9}$.

Multiply a Fraction by a Whole or Mixed Number

Multiplying a fraction by a whole or mixed number is similar to multiplying two fractions. When multiplying by a whole number, change the whole number to a fraction with a denominator of 1. Next, multiply the numerators together and the denominators together. Rewrite the final answer as a mixed number. For example: $\frac{9}{10} \times 3 = \frac{9}{10} \times \frac{3}{1} = \frac{27}{10} = 2\frac{7}{10}$.

When multiplying a fraction by a mixed number or multiplying two mixed numbers, the process is similar.

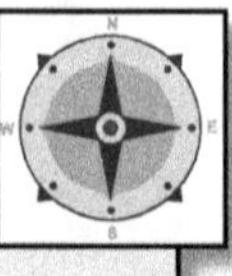

KEEP IN MIND

Always change a mixed number to an improper fraction when multiplying by a mixed number.

For example, multiply $\frac{10}{11} \times 3\frac{1}{2}$. Change the mixed number to an improper fraction, $\frac{10}{11} \times \frac{7}{2}$. Multiply the numerators together and multiply the denominators together, $\frac{70}{22}$. Write the improper fraction as a mixed number, $3\frac{4}{22}$. Reduce if necessary, $3\frac{2}{11}$.

This process can also be used when multiplying a whole number by a mixed number or multiplying two mixed numbers.

Examples

1. **Multiply $4 \times \frac{5}{6}$.**

   A. $\frac{5}{24}$ B. $2\frac{3}{4}$ C. $3\frac{1}{3}$ D. $4\frac{5}{6}$

   The correct answer is **C**. The correct solution is $3\frac{1}{3}$ because $\frac{4}{1} \times \frac{5}{6} = \frac{20}{6} = 3\frac{2}{6} = 3\frac{1}{3}$.

2. **Multiply $1\frac{1}{2} \times 1\frac{1}{6}$.**

   A. $1\frac{1}{12}$ B. $1\frac{1}{4}$ C. $1\frac{3}{8}$ D. $1\frac{3}{4}$

   The correct answer is **D**. The correct solution is $1\frac{3}{4}$ because $\frac{3}{2} \times \frac{7}{6} = \frac{21}{12} = 1\frac{9}{12} = 1\frac{3}{4}$.

Dividing a Fraction by a Fraction

Some basic steps apply when dividing a fraction by a fraction. The information from the previous two sections is applicable to dividing fractions.

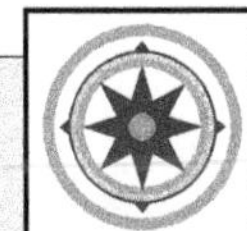

STEP BY STEP

Step 1. Leave the first fraction alone.

Step 2. Find the reciprocal of the second fraction.

Step 3. Multiply the first fraction by the reciprocal of the second fraction.

Step 4. Rewrite the fraction as a mixed number and reduce the fraction completely.

Divide, $\frac{3}{10} \div \frac{1}{2}$. Find the reciprocal of the second fraction, which is $\frac{2}{1}$.

Now, multiply the fractions, $\frac{3}{10} \times \frac{2}{1} = \frac{6}{10}$. Reduce $\frac{6}{10}$ to $\frac{3}{5}$.

Divide, $\frac{4}{5} \div \frac{3}{8}$. Find the reciprocal of the second fraction, which is $\frac{8}{3}$.

Now, multiply the fractions, $\frac{4}{5} \times \frac{8}{3} = \frac{32}{15}$. Rewrite the fraction as a mixed number, $\frac{32}{15} = 2\frac{2}{15}$.

Examples

1. **Divide $\frac{1}{2} \div \frac{5}{6}$.**

   A. $\frac{5}{12}$ B. $\frac{3}{5}$ C. $\frac{5}{6}$ D. $1\frac{2}{3}$

   The correct answer is **B**. The correct solution is $\frac{3}{5}$ because $\frac{1}{2} \times \frac{6}{5} = \frac{6}{10} = \frac{3}{5}$.

2. **Divide $\frac{2}{3} \div \frac{3}{5}$.**

A. $\frac{2}{15}$ B. $\frac{2}{5}$ C. $1\frac{1}{15}$ D. $1\frac{1}{9}$

The correct answer is **D**. The correct solution is $1\frac{1}{9}$ because $\frac{2}{3} \times \frac{5}{3} = \frac{10}{9} = 1\frac{1}{9}$.

Dividing a Fraction and a Whole or Mixed Number

Some basic steps apply when dividing a fraction by a whole number or a mixed number.

STEP BY STEP

Step 1. Write any whole number as a fraction with a denominator of 1. Write any mixed numbers as improper fractions.

Step 2. Leave the first fraction (improper fraction) alone.

Step 3. Find the reciprocal of the second fraction.

Step 4. Multiply the first fraction by the reciprocal of the second fraction.

Step 5. Rewrite the fraction as a mixed number and reduce the fraction completely.

Divide, $\frac{3}{10} \div 3$. Rewrite the expression as $\frac{3}{10} \div \frac{3}{1}$. Find the reciprocal of the second fraction, which is $\frac{1}{3}$. Multiply the fractions, $\frac{3}{10} \times \frac{1}{3} = \frac{3}{30} = \frac{1}{10}$. Reduce $\frac{3}{30}$ to $\frac{1}{10}$.

Divide, $2\frac{4}{5} \div 1\frac{3}{8}$. Rewrite the expression as $\frac{14}{5} \div \frac{11}{8}$. Find the reciprocal of the second fraction, which is $\frac{8}{11}$.

Multiply the fractions, $\frac{14}{5} \times \frac{8}{11} = \frac{112}{55} = 2\frac{2}{55}$. Reduce $\frac{112}{55}$ to $2\frac{2}{55}$.

Examples

1. **Divide $\frac{2}{3} \div 4$.**

A. $\frac{1}{12}$ B. $\frac{1}{10}$ C. $\frac{1}{8}$ D. $\frac{1}{6}$

The correct answer is **D**. The correct answer is $\frac{1}{6}$ because $\frac{2}{3} \times \frac{1}{4} = \frac{2}{12} = \frac{1}{6}$.

2. **Divide $1\frac{5}{12} \div 1\frac{1}{2}$.**

A. $\frac{17}{18}$ B. $1\frac{5}{24}$ C. $1\frac{5}{6}$ D. $2\frac{1}{8}$

The correct answer is **A**. The correct answer is $\frac{17}{18}$ because $\frac{17}{12} \div \frac{3}{2} = \frac{17}{12} \times \frac{2}{3} = \frac{34}{36} = \frac{17}{18}$.

Let's Review!

- The process to multiply fractions is to multiply the numerators together and multiply the denominators together. When there is a mixed number, change the mixed number to an improper fraction before multiplying.
- The process to divide fractions is to find the reciprocal of the second fraction and multiply the fractions. As with multiplying, change any mixed numbers to improper fractions before dividing.

EQUATIONS WITH ONE VARIABLE

This lesson introduces how to solve linear equations and linear inequalities.

One-Step Linear Equations

A **linear equation** is an equation where two expressions are set equal to each other. The equation is in the form $ax + b = c$, where a is a non-zero constant and b and c are constants. The exponent on a linear equation is always 1, and there is no more than one solution to a linear equation.

There are four properties to help solve a linear equation.

Property	Definition	Example with Numbers	Example with Variables
Addition Property of Equality	Add the same number to both sides of the equation.	$x–3 = 9$ $x–3 + 3 = 9 + 3$ $x = 12$	$x–a = b$ $x–a + a = b + a$ $x = a + b$
Subtraction Property of Equality	Subtract the same number from both sides of the equation.	$x + 3 = 9$ $x + 3–3 = 9–3$ $x = 6$	$x + a = b$ $x + a–a = b–a$ $x = b–a$
Multiplication Property of Equality	Multiply both sides of the equation by the same number.	$\frac{x}{3} = 9$ $\frac{x}{3} \times 3 = 9 \times 3$ $x = 27$	$\frac{x}{a} = b$ $\frac{x}{a} \times a = b \times a$ $x = ab$
Division Property of Equality	Divide both sides of the equation by the same number.	$3x = 9$ $\frac{3x}{3} = \frac{9}{3}$ $x = 3$	$ax = b$ $\frac{ax}{a} = \frac{b}{a}$ $x = \frac{b}{a}$

Example

Solve the equation for the unknown, $\frac{w}{2} = -6$.

A. −12   B. −8   C. −4   D. −3

The correct answer is **A**. The correct solution is −12 because both sides of the equation are multiplied by 2.

Two-Step Linear Equations

A two-step linear equation is in the form $ax + b = c$, where a is a non-zero constant and b and c are constants. There are two basic steps in solving this equation.

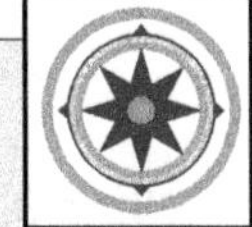

STEP BY STEP

Step 1. Use addition and subtraction properties of an equation to move the variable to one side of the equation and all number terms to the other side of the equation.

Step 2. Use multiplication and division properties of an equation to remove the value in front of the variable.

Examples

1. **Solve the equation for the unknown, $\frac{x}{-2} - 3 = 5$.**

A. −16　　B. −8　　C. 8　　D. 16

The correct answer is **A**. The correct solution is −16.

$\frac{x}{-2} = 8$	Add 3 to both sides of the equation.
$x = -16$	Multiply both sides of the equation by −2.

2. **Solve the equation for the unknown, $4x + 3 = 8$.**

A. −2　　B. $-\frac{5}{4}$　　C. $\frac{5}{4}$　　D. 2

The correct answer is **C**. The correct solution is $\frac{5}{4}$.

$4x = 5$	Subtract 3 from both sides of the equation.
$x = \frac{5}{4}$	Divide both sides of the equation by 4.

3. **Solve the equation for the unknown w, $P = 21 + 2w$.**

A. $2P - 21 = w$　　B. $\frac{P-21}{2} = w$　　C. $2P + 21 = w$　　D. $\frac{P+21}{2} = w$

The correct answer is **B**. The correct solution is $\frac{P-21}{2} = w$.

$P - 21 = 2w$	Subtract 21 from both sides of the equation.
$\frac{P-21}{2} = w$	Divide both sides of the equation by 2.

Multi-Step Linear Equations

In these basic examples of linear equations, the solution may be evident, but these properties demonstrate how to use an opposite operation to solve for a variable. Using these properties, there are three steps in solving a complex linear equation.

STEP BY STEP

Step 1. Simplify each side of the equation. This includes removing parentheses, removing fractions, and adding like terms.

Step 2. Use addition and subtraction properties of an equation to move the variable to one side of the equation and all number terms to the other side of the equation.

Step 3. Use multiplication and division properties of an equation to remove the value in front of the variable.

In Step 2, all of the variables may be placed on the left side or the right side of the equation. The examples in this lesson will place all of the variables on the left side of the equation.

When solving for a variable, apply the same steps as above. In this case, the equation is not being solved for a value, but for a specific variable.

Examples

1. **Solve the equation for the unknown, $2(4x+1)-5=3-(4x-3)$.**

   A. $\frac{1}{4}$ B. $\frac{3}{4}$ C. $\frac{4}{3}$ D. 4

   The correct answer is **B**. The correct solution is $\frac{3}{4}$.

$8x+2-5=3-4x+3$	Apply the distributive property.
$8x-3=-4x+6$	Combine like terms on both sides of the equation.
$12x-3=6$	Add $4x$ to both sides of the equation.
$12x=9$	Add 3 to both sides of the equation.
$x=\frac{3}{4}$	Divide both sides of the equation by 12.

2. **Solve the equation for the unknown, $\frac{2}{3}x+2=-\frac{1}{2}x+2(x+1)$.**

   A. 0 B. 1 C. 2 D. 3

   The correct answer is **A**. The correct solution is 0.

$\frac{2}{3}x+2=-\frac{1}{2}x+2x+2$	Apply the distributive property.
$4x+12=-3x+12x+12$	Multiply all terms by the least common denominator of 6 to eliminate the fractions.
$4x+12=9x+12$	Combine like terms on the right side of the equation.
$-5x=12$	Subtract $9x$ from both sides of the equation.
$-5x=0$	Subtract 12 from both sides of the equation.
$x=0$	Divide both sides of the equation by -5.

3. **Solve the equation for the unknown for x, $y-y_1 = m(x-x_1)$.**

A. $y-y_1 + mx_1$ B. $my - my_1 + mx_1$ C. $\frac{y-y_1+x_1}{m}$ D. $\frac{y-y_1+mx_1}{m}$

The correct answer is **D**. The correct solution is $\frac{y-y_1+mx_1}{m}$

$y-y_1 = mx-mx_1$	Apply the distributive property.
$y-y_1 + mx_1 = mx$	Add mx_1 to both sides of the equation.
$\frac{y-y_1+mx_1}{m} = x$	Divide both sides of the equation by m.

Solving Linear Inequalities

A **linear inequality** is similar to a linear equation, but it contains an inequality sign (<, >, ≤, ≥). Many of the steps for solving linear inequalities are the same as for solving linear equations. The major difference is that the solution is an infinite number of values. There are four properties to help solve a linear inequality.

Property	Definition	Example
Addition Property of Inequality	Add the same number to both sides of the inequality.	$x-3 < 9$ $x-3+3 < 9+3$ $x < 12$
Subtraction Property of Inequality	Subtract the same number from both sides of the inequality.	$x+3 > 9$ $x+3-3 > 9-3$ $x > 6$
Multiplication Property of Inequality (when multiplying by a positive number)	Multiply both sides of the inequality by the same number.	$\frac{x}{3} \geq 9$ $\frac{x}{3} \times 3 \geq 9 \times 3$ $x \geq 27$
Division Property of Inequality (when multiplying by a positive number)	Divide both sides of the inequality by the same number.	$3x \leq 9$ $\frac{3x}{3} \leq \frac{9}{3}$ $x \leq 3$
Multiplication Property of Inequality (when multiplying by a negative number)	Multiply both sides of the inequality by the same number.	$\frac{x}{-3} \geq 9$ $\frac{x}{-3} \times -3 \geq 9 \times -3$ $x \leq -27$
Division Property of Inequality (when multiplying by a negative number)	Divide both sides of the inequality by the same number.	$-3x \leq 9$ $\frac{-3x}{-3} \leq \frac{9}{-3}$ $x \geq -3$

Multiplying or dividing both sides of the inequality by a negative number reverses the sign of the inequality.

In these basic examples, the solution may be evident, but these properties demonstrate how to use an opposite operation to solve for a variable. Using these properties, there are three steps in solving a complex linear inequality.

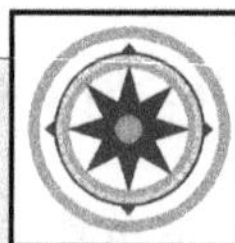

STEP BY STEP

Step 1. Simplify each side of the inequality. This includes removing parentheses, removing fractions, and adding like terms.

Step 2. Use addition and subtraction properties of an inequality to move the variable to one side of the equation and all number terms to the other side of the equation.

Step 3. Use multiplication and division properties of an inequality to remove the value in front of the variable. Reverse the inequality sign if multiplying or dividing by a negative number.

In Step 2, all of the variables may be placed on the left side or the right side of the inequality. The examples in this lesson will place all of the variables on the left side of the inequality.

Examples

1. **Solve the inequality for the unknown, $3(2+x) < 2(3x-1)$.**

   A. $x < -\frac{8}{3}$ B. $x > -\frac{8}{3}$ C. $x < \frac{8}{3}$ D. $x > \frac{8}{3}$

   The correct answer is **D**. The correct solution is $x > \frac{8}{3}$.

$6 + 3x < 6x - 2$	Apply the distributive property.
$6 - 3x < -2$	Subtract $6x$ from both sides of the inequality.
$-3x < -8$	Subtract 6 from both sides of the inequality.
$x > \frac{8}{3}$	Divide both sides of the inequality by -3.

2. **Solve the inequality for the unknown, $\frac{1}{2}(2x-3) \geq \frac{1}{4}(2x+1)-2$.**

   A. $x > -7$ B. $x > -3$ C. $x \geq -\frac{3}{2}$ D. $x \geq -\frac{1}{2}$

   The correct answer is **D**. The correct solution is $x \geq -\frac{1}{2}$.

$2(2x-3) \geq 2x + 1 - 8$	Multiply all terms by the least common denominator of 4 to eliminate the fractions.
$4x - 6 \geq 2x + 1 - 8$	Apply the distributive property.
$4x - 6 \geq 2x - 7$	Combine like terms on the right side of the inequality.
$2x - 6 \geq -7$	Subtract $2x$ from both sides of the inequality.
$2x \geq -1$	Add 6 to both sides of the inequality.
$x \geq -\frac{1}{2}$	Divide both sides of the inequality by 2.

Let's Review!

- A linear equation is an equation with one solution. Using opposite operations solves a linear equation.
- The process to solve a linear equation or inequality is to eliminate fractions and parentheses and combine like terms on the same side of the sign. Then, solve the equation or inequality by using inverse operations.

EQUATIONS WITH TWO VARIABLES

This lesson discusses solving a system of linear equations by substitution, elimination, and graphing, as well as solving a simple system of a linear and a quadratic equation.

Solving a System of Equations by Substitution

A **system of linear equations** is a set of two or more linear equations in the same variables. A solution to the system is an ordered pair that is a solution in all the equations in the system. The ordered pair (1, -2) is a solution for the system of equations $\begin{matrix} 2x + y = 0 \\ -x + 2y = -5 \end{matrix}$ because $\begin{matrix} 2(1) + (-2) = 0 \\ -1 + 2(-2) = -5 \end{matrix}$ makes both equations true.

One way to solve a system of linear equations is by substitution.

STEP BY STEP

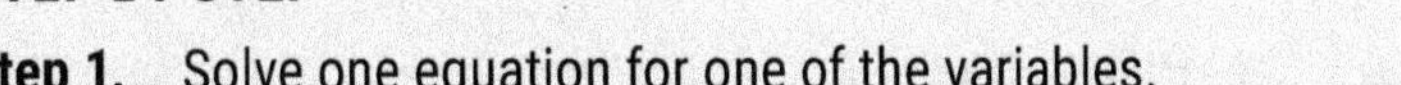

Step 1. Solve one equation for one of the variables.

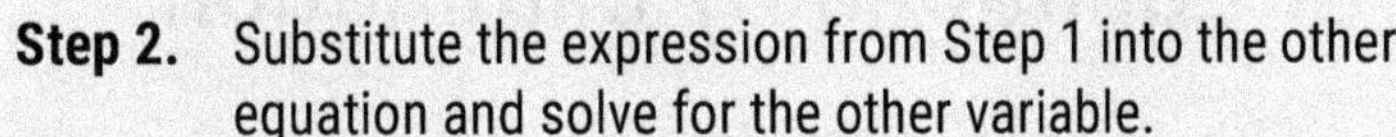

Step 2. Substitute the expression from Step 1 into the other equation and solve for the other variable.

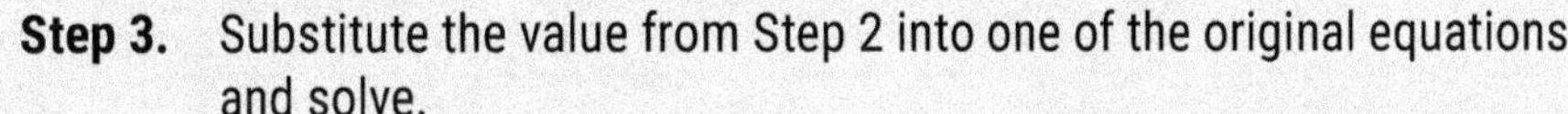

Step 3. Substitute the value from Step 2 into one of the original equations and solve.

All systems of equations can be solved by substitution for any one of the four variables in the problem. The most efficient way of solving is locating the $1x$ or $1y$ in the equations because this eliminates the possibility of having fractions in the equations.

Examples

1. **Solve the system of equations, $\begin{matrix} x = y + 6 \\ 4x + 5y = 60 \end{matrix}$.**

   A. (10, 12) B. (6, 12) C. (6, 4) D. (10, 4)

   The correct answer is **D**. The correct solution is (10, 4).

   The first equation is already solved for x.

$4(y + 6) + 5y = 60$	Substitute $y + 6$ in for x in the first equation.
$4y + 24 + 5y = 60$	Apply the distributive property.
$9y + 24 = 60$	Combine like terms on the left side of the equation.
$9y = 36$	Subtract 24 from both sides of the equation.
$y = 4$	Divide both sides of the equation by 9.
$x = 4 + 6$	Substitute 4 in the first equation for y.
$x = 10$	Simplify using order of operations.

2. Solve the system of equations, $\begin{matrix} 3x + 2y = 41 \\ -4x + y = -18 \end{matrix}$.

A. (5, 13) B. (6, 6) C. (7, 10) D. (10, 7)

The correct answer is **C**. The correct solution is (7, 10).

$y = 4x - 18$	Solve the second equation for y by adding $4x$ to both sides of the equation.
$3x + 2(4x - 18) = 41$	Substitute $4x - 18$ in for y in the first equation.
$3x + 8x - 36 = 41$	Apply the distributive property.
$11x - 36 = 41$	Combine like terms on the left side of the equation.
$11x = 77$	Add 36 to both sides of the equation.
$x = 7$	Divide both sides of the equation by 11.
$-4(7) + y = -18$	Substitute 7 in the second equation for x.
$-28 + y = -18$	Simplify using order of operations.
$y = 10$	Add 28 to both sides of the equation.

Solving a System of Equations by Elimination

Another way to solve a system of linear equations is by elimination.

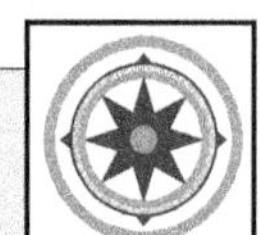

STEP BY STEP

Step 1. Multiply, if necessary, one or both equations by a constant so at least one pair of like terms has opposite coefficients.

Step 2. Add the equations to eliminate one of the variables.

Step 3. Solve the resulting equation.

Step 4. Substitute the value from Step 3 into one of the original equations and solve for the other variable.

All system of equations can be solved by the elimination method for any one of the four variables in the problem. One way of solving is locating the variables with opposite coefficients and adding the equations. Another approach is multiplying one equation to obtain opposite coefficients for the variables.

Examples

1. **Solve the system of equations,** $\begin{matrix}\mathbf{3x + 5y = 28} \\ \mathbf{-4x - 5y = -34}\end{matrix}$.

   A. (12, 6) B. (6, 12) C. (6, 2) D. (2, 6)

   The correct answer is **C.** The correct solution is (6, 2).

$-x = -6$	Add the equations.
$x = 6$	Divide both sides of the equation by -1.
$3(6) + 5y = 28$	Substitute 6 in the first equation for x.
$18 + 5y = 28$	Simplify using order of operations.
$5y = 10$	Subtract 18 from both sides of the equation.
$y = 2$	Divide both sides of the equation by 5.

2. **Solve the system of equations,** $\begin{matrix}\mathbf{-5x + 5y = 0} \\ \mathbf{2x - 3y = -3}\end{matrix}$.

   A. (2, 2) B. (3, 3) C. (6, 6) D. (9, 9)

   The correct answer is **B.** The correct solution is (3, 3).

$-10x + 10y = 0$	Multiply all terms in the first equation by 2.
$10x - 15y = -15$	Multiply all terms in the second equation by 5.
$-5y = -15$	Add the equations.
$y = 3$	Divide both sides of the equation by -5.
$2x - 3(3) = -3$	Substitute 3 in the second equation for y.
$2x - 9 = -3$	Simplify using order of operations.
$2x = 6$	Add 9 to both sides of the equation.
$x = 3$	Divide both sides of the equation by 2.

Solving a System of Equations by Graphing

Graphing is a third method of a solving system of equations. The point of intersection is the solution for the graph. This method is a great way to visualize each graph on a coordinate plane.

STEP BY STEP

Step 1. Graph each equation in the coordinate plane.

Step 2. Estimate the point of intersection.

Step 3. Check the point by substituting for x and y in each equation of the original system.

The best approach to graphing is to obtain each line in slope-intercept form. Then, graph the y-intercept and use the slope to find additional points on the line.

Example

Solve the system of equations by graphing, $\begin{matrix} y = 3x-2 \\ y = x-4 \end{matrix}$.

A.

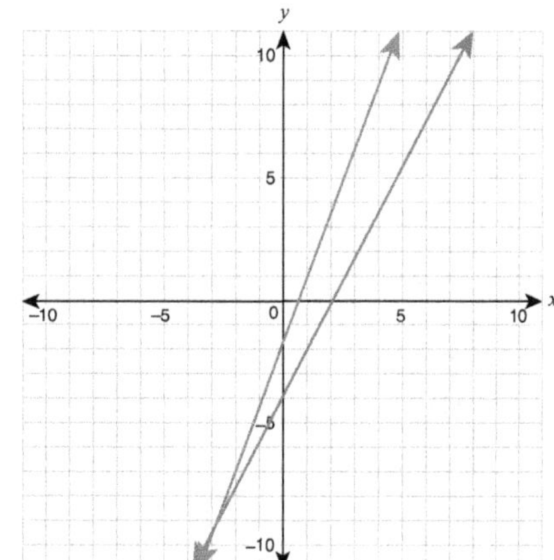

C.

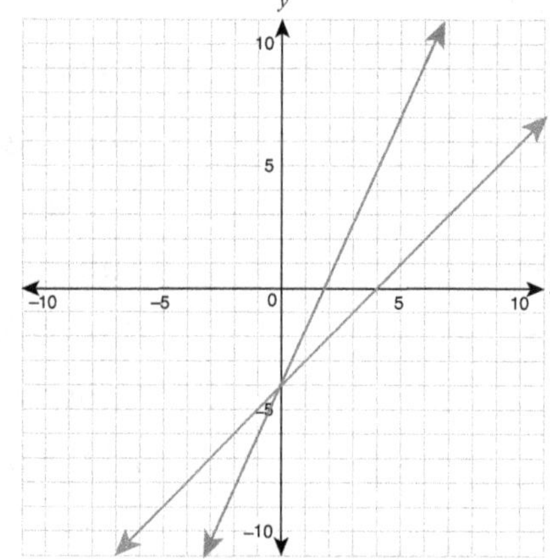

B.

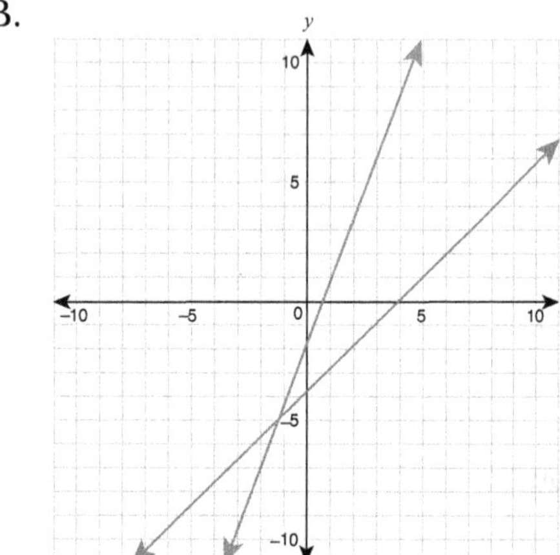

D.

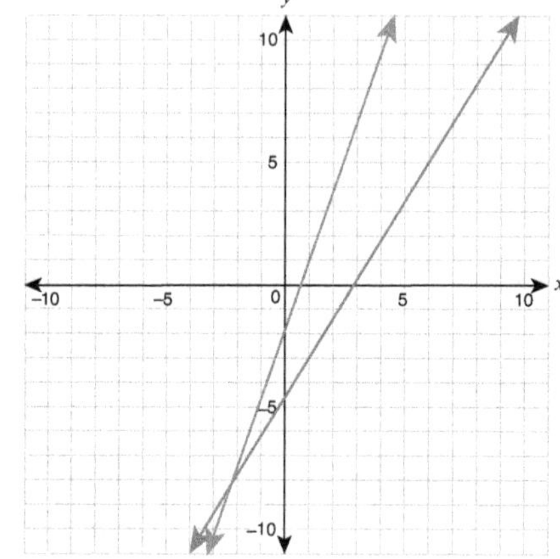

The correct answer is **B.** The correct graph has the two lines intersect at (-1, -5).

Solving a System of a Linear Equation and an Equation of a Circle

There are many other types of systems of equations. One example is the equation of a line $y = mx$ and the equation of a circle $x^2 + y^2 = r^2$ where r is the radius. With this system of equations, there can be two ordered pairs that intersect between the line and the circle. If there is one ordered pair, the line is tangent to the circle.

This system of equations is solved by substituting the expression mx in for y in the equation of a circle. Then, solve the equation for x. The values for x are substituted into the linear equation to find the value for y.

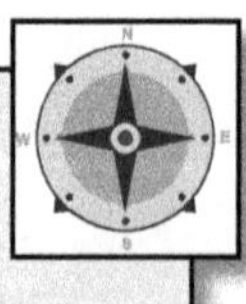

KEEP IN MIND

There will be two solutions in many cases with the system of a linear equation and an equation of a circle.

Example

Solve the system of equations, $\begin{matrix} y = -3x \\ x^2 + y^2 = 10 \end{matrix}$.

A. (1, 3) and (−1, −3)

B. (1, −3) and (−1, 3)

C. (−3, 10) and (3, −10)

D. (3, 10) and (−3, −10)

The correct answer is **B.** The correct solutions are (1, −3) and (−1, 3).

$x^2 + (-3x)^2 = 10$	Substitute $-3x$ in for y in the second equation.
$x^2 + 9x^2 = 10$	Apply the exponent.
$10x^2 = 10$	Combine like terms on the left side of the equation.
$x^2 = 1$	Divide both sides of the equation by 10.
$x = \pm 1$	Apply the square root to both sides of the equation.
$y = -3(1) = -3$	Substitute 1 in the first equation and multiply.
$y = -3(-1) = 3$	Substitute −1 in the first equation and multiply.

Let's Review!

- There are three ways to solve a system of equations: graphing, substitution, and elimination. Using any method will result in the same solution for the system of equations.
- Solving a system of a linear equation and an equation of a circle uses substitution and usually results in two solutions.

SOLVING REAL-WORLD MATHEMATICAL PROBLEMS

This lesson introduces solving real-world mathematical problems by using estimation and mental computation. This lesson also includes real-world applications involving integers, fractions, and decimals.

Estimating

Estimations are rough calculations of a solution to a problem. The most common use for estimation is completing calculations without a calculator or other tool. There are many estimation techniques, but this lesson focuses on integers, decimals, and fractions.

KEEP IN MIND

An estimation is an educated guess at the solution to a problem.

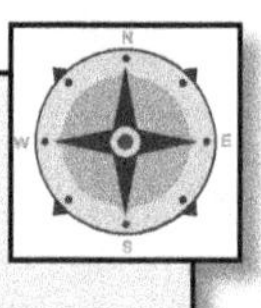

To round a whole number, round the value to the nearest ten or hundred. The number 142 rounds to 140 for the nearest ten and to 100 for the nearest hundred. The context of the problem determines the place value to which to round.

In most problems with fractions and decimals, the context of the problem requires rounding to the nearest whole number. Rounding these values makes calculation easier and provides an accurate estimation to the solution of the problem.

Other estimation strategies include the following:

- Using friendly or compatible numbers
- Using numbers that are easy to compute
- Adjusting numbers after rounding

Example

There are 168 hours in a week. Carson does the following:

- Sleeps 7.5 hours each day of the week
- Goes to school 6.75 hours five days a week
- Practices martial arts and basketball 1.5 hours each three times a week
- Reads and studies 1.75 hours every day
- Eats 1.5 hours every day

Estimate the remaining number of hours.

A. 30 B. 35 C. 40 D. 45

The correct answer is **C**. The correct solution is 40. He sleeps about 56 hours, goes to school for 35 hours, practices for 9 hours, reads and studies for about 14 hours, and eats for about 14 hours. This is 128 hours. Therefore, Carson has about 40 hours remaining.

Real-World Integer Problems

The following five steps can make solving word problems easier:

1. Read the problem for understanding.
2. Visualize the problem by drawing a picture or diagram.
3. Make a plan by writing an expression to represent the problem.
4. Solve the problem by applying mathematical techniques.
5. Check the answer to make sure it answers the question asked.

BE CAREFUL!

Make sure that you read the problem fully before visualizing and making a plan.

In basic problems, the solution may be evident, but make sure to demonstrate knowledge of writing the expression. In multi-step problems, first make a plan with the correct expression. Then, apply the correct calculation.

Examples

1. **The temperature on Monday was –9°F, and on Tuesday it was 8°F. What is the difference in temperature, in °F?**

   A. –17° B. –1° C. 1° D. 17°

   The correct answer is **D.** The correct solution is 17° because 8–(–9) = 17°F.

2. **A golfer's last 12 rounds were –2, +4, –3, –1, +5, +3, –4, –5, –2, –6, –1, and 0. What is the average of these rounds?**

   A. –12 B. –1 C. 1 D. 12

   The correct answer is **B.** The correct solution is –1. The total of the scores is –12. The average is –12 divided by 12, which is –1.

Real-World Fraction and Decimal Problems

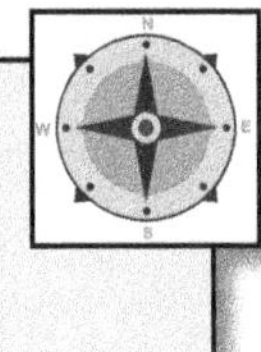

KEEP IN MIND

Estimating the solution first can help determine if a calculation is completed correctly.

The five steps in the previous section are applicable to solving real-world fraction and decimal problems. The expressions with one step require only one calculation: addition, subtraction, multiplication, or division. The problems with multiple steps require writing out the expressions and performing the correct calculations.

Examples

1. **The length of a room is $7\frac{2}{3}$ feet. When the length of the room is doubled, what is the new length in feet?**

A. $14\frac{2}{3}$ B. $15\frac{1}{3}$ C. $15\frac{2}{3}$ D. $16\frac{1}{3}$

The correct answer is **B.** The correct solution is $15\frac{1}{3}$. The length is multiplied by 2, $7\frac{2}{3} \times 2 = \frac{23}{3} \times \frac{2}{1} = \frac{46}{3} = 15\frac{1}{3}$ feet.

2. **A fruit salad is a mixture of $1\frac{3}{4}$ pounds of apples, $2\frac{1}{4}$ pounds of grapes, and $1\frac{1}{4}$ pounds of bananas. After the fruit is mixed, $1\frac{1}{2}$ pounds are set aside, and the rest is divided into three containers. What is the weight in pounds of one container?**

A. $1\frac{1}{5}$ B. $1\frac{1}{4}$ C. $1\frac{1}{3}$ D. $1\frac{1}{2}$

The correct answer is **B.** The correct solution is $1\frac{1}{4}$. The amount available for the containers is $1\frac{3}{4} + 2\frac{1}{4} + 1\frac{1}{4} - 1\frac{1}{2} = 5\frac{1}{4} - 1\frac{1}{2} = 5\frac{1}{4} - 1\frac{2}{4} = 4\frac{5}{4} - 1\frac{2}{4} = 3\frac{3}{4}$. This amount is divided into three containers, $3\frac{3}{4} \div 3 = \frac{15}{4} \times \frac{15}{12} = 1\frac{3}{12} = 1\frac{1}{4}$ pounds.

3. **In 2016, a town had 17.4 inches of snowfall. In 2017, it had 45.2 inches of snowfall. What is the difference in inches?**

A. 27.2 B. 27.8 C. 28.2 D. 28.8

The correct answer is **B.** The correct solution is 27.8 because 45.2–17.4 = 27.8 inches.

4. **Mike bought items that cost \$4.78, \$3.49, \$6.79, \$9.78, and \$14.05. He had a coupon worth \$5.00. If he paid with a \$50.00 bill, then how much change does he receive?**

A. \$16.11 B. \$18.11 C. \$21.11 D. \$23.11

The correct answer is **A.** The correct solution is \$16.11. The total bill is \$38.89, less the coupon is \$33.89. The amount of change is \$50.00–\$33.89 = \$16.11.

Let's Review!

- Using estimation is beneficial to determine an approximate solution to the problem when the numbers are complex.
- When solving a word problem with integers, fractions, or decimals, first read and visualize the problem. Then, make a plan, solve, and check the answer.

Chapter 9 Algebra Practice Quiz 1

1. **Which decimal is the greatest?**

   A. 1.7805　　C. 1.7085

   B. 1.5807　　D. 1.8057

2. **Change $0.\overline{63}$ to a fraction. Simplify completely.**

   A. $\frac{5}{9}$　　C. $\frac{2}{3}$

   B. $\frac{7}{11}$　　D. $\frac{5}{6}$

3. **Write $0.\overline{1}$ as a percent.**

   A. $0.\overline{1}\%$　　C. $11.\overline{1}\%$

   B. $1.\overline{1}\%$　　D. $111.\overline{1}\%$

4. **Solve the equation for the unknown, $4x + 3 = 8$.**

   A. -2　　C. $\frac{5}{4}$

   B. $-\frac{5}{4}$　　D. 2

5. **Solve the inequality for the unknown, $3x + 5-2(x + 3) > 4(1-x) + 5$.**

   A. $x > 2$　　C. $x > 10$

   B. $x > 9$　　D. $x > 17$

6. **Solve the equation for h, $SA = 2\pi rh + 2\pi r^2$.**

   A. $2\pi rSA-2\pi r^2 = h$

   B. $2\pi rSA + 2\pi r^2 = h$

   C. $\frac{SA-2\pi r^2}{2\pi r} = h$

   D. $\frac{SA + 2\pi r^2}{2\pi r} = h$

7. **Solve the system of equations, $\begin{matrix} y = -2x + 3 \\ y + x = 5 \end{matrix}$.**

   A. (-2, 7)　　C. (2, -7)

   B. (-2, -7)　　D. (2, 7)

8. **Solve the system of equations, $\begin{matrix} 2x-3y = -1 \\ x + 2y = 24 \end{matrix}$.**

   A. (7, 10)　　C. (6, 8)

   B. (10, 7)　　D. (8, 6)

9. **Divide $1\frac{5}{6} \div 1\frac{1}{3}$.**

   A. $1\frac{5}{18}$　　C. $2\frac{4}{9}$

   B. $1\frac{3}{8}$　　D. $3\frac{1}{6}$

10. **Multiply $1\frac{1}{4} \times 1\frac{1}{2}$.**

    A. $1\frac{1}{8}$　　C. $1\frac{2}{3}$

    B. $1\frac{1}{3}$　　D. $1\frac{7}{8}$

11. **Divide $\frac{1}{10} \div \frac{2}{3}$.**

    A. $\frac{1}{15}$　　C. $\frac{3}{20}$

    B. $\frac{1}{10}$　　D. $\frac{3}{5}$

12. **A store has 75 pounds of bananas. Eight customers buy 3.3 pounds, five customers buy 4.25 pounds, and one customer buys 6.8 pounds. How many pounds are left in stock?**

    A. 19.45　　C. 20.45

    B. 19.55　　D. 20.55

13. **A rectangular garden needs a border. The length is $15\frac{3}{5}$ feet, and the width is $3\frac{2}{3}$ feet. What is the perimeter in feet?**

    A. $18\frac{5}{8}$　　C. $37\frac{1}{4}$

    B. $19\frac{4}{15}$　　D. $38\frac{8}{15}$

14. Solve the system of equations by graphing, $\begin{matrix} 3x + y = -1 \\ 2x - y = -4 \end{matrix}$.

A.

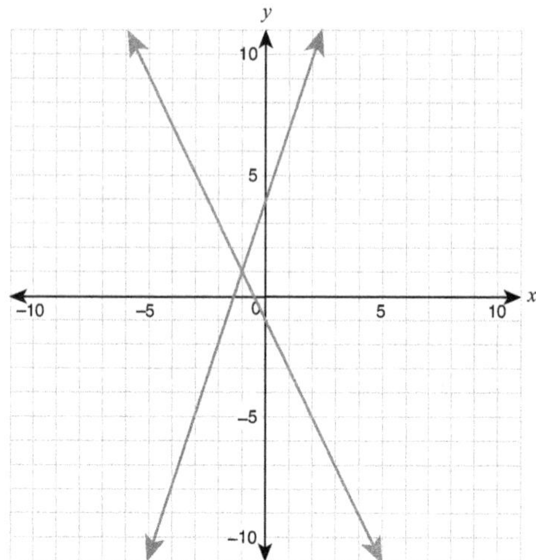

C.

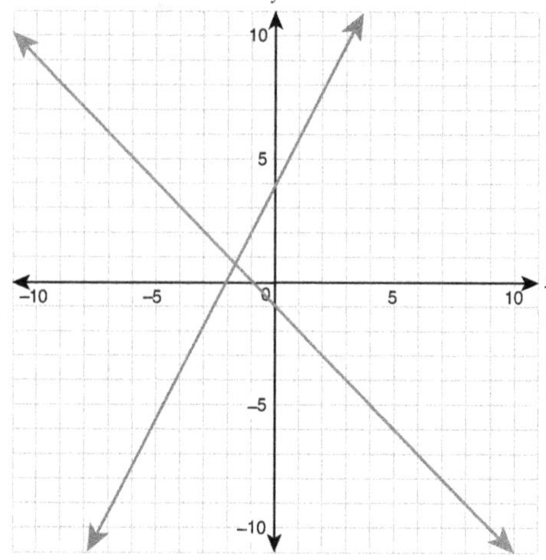

B.

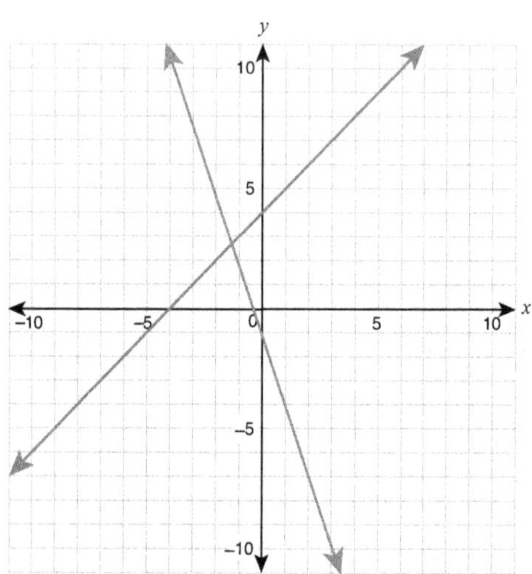

D.

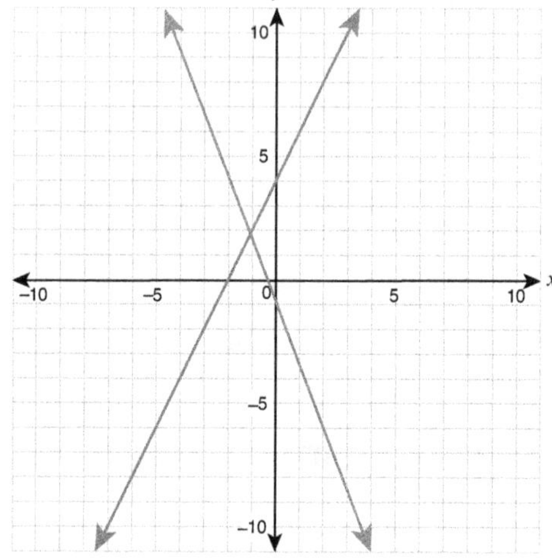

15. A historical society has 8 tours daily 5 days a week, with 32 people on each tour. Estimate the number of people who can be on the tour in 50 weeks.

A. 25,000

B. 50,000

C. 75,000

D. 100,000

Chapter 9 Algebra Practice Quiz 1 – Answer Key

1. **D.** The correct solution is 1.8057 because 1.8075 contains the largest value in the tenths place. **See Lesson: Decimals and Fractions.**

2. **B.** The correct solution is $\frac{7}{11}$. Let $n = 0.\overline{63}$ and $100n = 63.\overline{63}$ Then, $100n - n = 63.\overline{63} - 0.\overline{63}$resulting in $99n = 63$ and solution of $n = \frac{63}{99} = \frac{7}{11}$. **See Lesson: Decimals and Fractions.**

3. **C.** The correct answer is $11.\overline{1}\%$ because $0.\overline{1}$as a percent is $0.\overline{1} \times 100 = 11.\overline{1}\%$. **See Lesson: Decimals and Fractions.**

4. **C.** The correct solution is $\frac{5}{4}$.

$4x = 5$	Subtract 3 from both sides of the equation.
$x = \frac{5}{4}$	Divide both sides of the equation by 4.

See Lesson: Equations with One Variable.

5. **A.** The correct solution is $x > 2$.

$3x + 5 - 2x - 6 > 4 - 4x + 5$	Apply the distributive property.
$x - 1 > -4x + 9$	Combine like terms on both sides of the inequality.
$5x - 1 > 9$	Add $4x$ to both sides of the inequality.
$5x > 10$	Add 1 to both sides of the inequality.
$x > 2$	Divide both sides of the inequality by 5.

See Lesson: Equations with One Variable.

6. **C.** The correct solution is $\frac{SA - 2\pi r^2}{2\pi r} = h$.

$SA - 2\pi r^2 = 2\pi rh$	Subtract $2\pi r^2$ from both sides of the equation.
$\frac{SA - 2\pi r^2}{2\pi r} = h$	Divide both sides of the equation by $2\pi r$.

See Lesson: Equations with One Variable.

7. A. The correct solution is (-2, 7).

	The first equation is already solved for y.
$-2x + 3 + x = 5$	Substitute $-2x + 3$ in for y in the second equation.
$-x + 3 = 5$	Combine like terms on the left side of the equation.
$-x = 2$	Subtract 3 from both sides of the equation.
$x = -2$	Divide both sides of the equation by -1.
$y = -2(-2) + 3$	Substitute -2 in the first equation for x.
$y = 4 + 3 = 7$	Simplify using order of operations.

See Lesson: Equations with Two Variables.

8. B. The correct solution is (10, 7).

$-2x-4y = -48$	Multiply all terms in the second equation by -2.
$-7y = -49$	Add the equations.
$y = 7$	Divide both sides of the equation by -7.
$x + 2(7) = 24$	Substitute 7 in the second equation for y.
$x + 14 = 24$	Simplify using order of operations.
$x = 10$	Subtract 14 from both sides of the equation.

See Lesson: Equations with Two Variables.

9. B. The correct answer is $1\frac{3}{8}$ because $\frac{11}{6} \div \frac{4}{3} = \frac{11}{6} \times \frac{3}{4} = \frac{33}{24} = 1\frac{9}{24} = 1\frac{3}{8}$. **See Lesson: Multiplication and Division of Fractions.**

10. D. The correct solution is $1\frac{7}{8}$ because $\frac{5}{4} \times \frac{3}{2} = \frac{15}{8} = 1\frac{7}{8}$. **See Lesson: Multiplication and Division of Fractions.**

11. C. The correct solution is $\frac{3}{20}$ because $\frac{1}{10} \times \frac{3}{2} = \frac{3}{20}$. **See Lesson: Multiplication and Division of Fractions.**

12. D. The correct solution is 20.55 because the number of pounds purchased is $8(3.3) + 5(4.25) + 6.8 = 26.4 + 21.25 + 6.8 = 54.55$ pounds. The number of pounds remaining is $75-54.45 = 20.55$ pounds. **See Lesson: Solving Real World Mathematical Problems.**

13. D. The correct solution is $38\frac{8}{15}$ because $15\frac{3}{5} + 3\frac{2}{3} = 15\frac{9}{15} + 3\frac{10}{15} = 18\frac{19}{15}(2) = \frac{289}{15} \times \frac{2}{1} = \frac{578}{15} = 38\frac{8}{15}$ feet. **See Lesson: Solving Real World Mathematical Problems.**

14. D. The correct graph has the two lines intersect at (-1, 2). **See Lesson: Equations with Two Variables.**

15. C. The correct solution is 75,000 because by estimation $10(5)(30)(50) = 75{,}000$ people can be on the tour in 50 weeks. **See Lesson: Solving Real World Mathematical Problems.**

CHAPTER 10 FUNCTIONS

SOLVING QUADRATIC EQUATIONS

This lesson introduces solving quadratic equations by the square root method, completing the square, factoring, and using the quadratic formula.

Solving Quadratic Equations by the Square Root Method

A **quadratic equation** is an equation where the highest variable is squared. The equation is in the form $ax^2 + bx + c = 0$, where a is a non-zero constant and b and c are constants. There are at most two solutions to the equation because the highest variable is squared. There are many methods to solve a quadratic equation.

This section will explore solving a quadratic equation by the square root method. The equation must be in the form of $ax^2 = c$, or there is no x term.

STEP BY STEP

Step 1. Use multiplication and division properties of an equation to remove the value in front of the variable.

Step 2. Apply the square root to both sides of the equation.

Note: The positive and negative square root make the solution true. For the equation $x^2 = 9$, the solutions are –3 and 3 because $3^2 = 9$ and $(-3)^2 = 9$.

Example

Solve the equation by the square root method, $4x^2 = 64$.

A. 4 B. 8 C. ±4 D. ±8

The correct answer is **C**. The correct solution is ±4.

$x^2 = 16$	Divide both sides of the equation by 4.
$x = \pm 4$	Apply the square root to both sides of the equation.

Solving Quadratic Equations by Completing the Square

A quadratic equation in the form $x^2 + bx$ can be solved by a process known as completing the square. The best time to solve by completing the square is when the b term is even.

STEP BY STEP

Step 1. Divide all terms by the coefficient of x^2.

Step 2. Move the number term to the right side of the equation.

Step 3. Complete the square $\left(\frac{b}{2}\right)^2$ and add this value to both sides of the equation.

Step 4. Factor the left side of the equation.

Step 5. Apply the square root to both sides of the equation.

Step 6. Use addition and subtraction properties to move all number terms to the right side of the equation.

Examples

1. **Solve the equation by completing the square, $x^2 - 8x + 12 = 0$.**

   A. –2 and –6 B. 2 and –6 C. –2 and 6 D. 2 and 6

   The correct answer is **D**. The correct solutions are 2 and 6.

$x^2 - 8x = -12$	Subtract 12 from both sides of the equation.
$x^2 - 8x + 16 = -12 + 16$	Complete the square, $\left(-\frac{8}{2}\right)^2 = (-4)^2 = 16$.
	Add 16 to both sides of the equation.
$x^2 - 8x + 16 = 4$	Simplify the right side of the equation.
$(x-4)^2 = 4$	Factor the left side of the equation.
$x-4 = \pm 2$	Apply the square root to both sides of the equation.
$x = 4 \pm 2$	Add 4 to both sides of the equation.
$x = 4-2 = 2,\ x = 4 + 2 = 6$	Simplify the right side of the equation.

2. **Solve the equation by completing the square, $x^2 + 6x - 8 = 0$.**

   A. $-3 \pm \sqrt{17}$ B. $3 \pm \sqrt{17}$ C. $-3 \pm \sqrt{8}$ D. $3 \pm \sqrt{8}$

   The correct answer is **A**. The correct solutions are $-3 \pm \sqrt{17}$.

$x^2 + 6x = 8$	Add 8 to both sides of the equation.
$x^2 + 6x + 9 = 8 + 9$	Complete the square, $\left(\frac{6}{2}\right)^2 = 3^2 = 9$. Add 9 to both sides of the equation.
$x^2 + 6x + 9 = 17$	Simplify the right side of the equation.
$(x + 3)^2 = 17$	Factor the left side of the equation.
$x + 3 = \pm\sqrt{17}$	Apply the square root to both sides of the equation.
$x = -3 \pm \sqrt{17}$	Subtract 3 from both sides of the equation.

Solving Quadratic Equations by Factoring

Factoring can only be used when a quadratic equation is factorable; other methods are needed to solve quadratic equations that are not factorable.

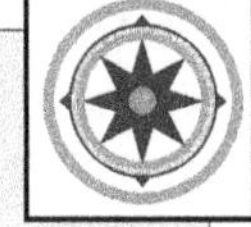

STEP BY STEP

Step 1. Simplify if needed by clearing any fractions and parentheses.

Step 2. Write the equation in standard form, $ax^2 + bx + c = 0$.

Step 3. Factor the quadratic equation.

Step 4. Set each factor equal to zero.

Step 5. Solve the linear equations using inverse operations.

The quadratic equation will have two solutions if the factors are different or one solution if the factors are the same.

Examples

1. **Solve the equation by factoring, $x^2 - 13x + 42 = 0$.**

   A. –6, –7 B. –6, 7 C. 6, –7 D. 6, 7

   The correct answer is **D**. The correct solutions are 6 and 7.

$(x-6)(x-7) = 0$	Factor the equation.
$(x-6) = 0$ or $(x-7) = 0$	Set each factor equal to 0.
$x-6 = 0$	Add 6 to both sides of the equation to solve for the first factor.
$x = 6$	
$x-7 = 0$	Add 7 to both sides of the equation to solve for the second factor.
$x = 7$	

2. **Solve the equation by factoring, $9x^2 + 30x + 25 = 0$.**

   A. $-\frac{5}{3}$ B. $-\frac{3}{5}$ C. $\frac{3}{5}$ D. $\frac{5}{3}$

   The correct answer is **A**. The correct solution is $-\frac{5}{3}$.

$(3x + 5)(3x + 5) = 0$	Factor the equation.
$(3x + 5) = 0$ or $(3x + 5) = 0$	Set each factor equal to 0.
$(3x + 5) = 0$	Set one factor equal to zero since both factors are the same.
$3x + 5 = 0$	Subtract 5 from both sides of the equation and divide both sides of the equation by 3 to solve.
$3x = -5$	
$x = -\frac{5}{3}$	

Solving Quadratic Equations by the Quadratic Formula

Many quadratic equations are not factorable. Another method of solving a quadratic equation is by using the quadratic formula. This method can be used to solve any quadratic equation in the form . Using the coefficients a, b, and c, the quadratic formula is $x = \frac{-b \pm \sqrt{b^2-4ac}}{2a}$. The values are substituted into the formula, and applying the order of operations finds the solution(s) to the equation.

The solution of the quadratic formula in these examples will be exact or estimated to three decimal places. There may be cases where the exact solutions to the quadratic formula are used.

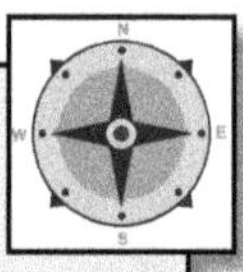

KEEP IN MIND

Watch the negative sign in the formula. Remember that a number squared is always positive.

Examples

1. **Solve the equation by the quadratic formula, $x^2-5x-6 = 0$.**

   A. –6 and –1 B. 6 and –1 C. –6 and 1 D. 6 and 1

   The correct answer is **B**. The correct solutions are 6 and –1.

   $x = \frac{-(-5) \pm \sqrt{(-5)^2-4(1)(-6)}}{2(1)}$ Substitute 1 for a, –5 for b, and –6 for c.

   $x = \frac{5 \pm \sqrt{25-(-24)}}{2}$ Apply the exponent and perform the multiplication.

   $x = \frac{5 \pm \sqrt{49}}{2}$ Perform the subtraction.

   $x = \frac{5 \pm 7}{2}$ Apply the square root.

   $x = \frac{5+7}{2}$, $x = \frac{5-7}{2}$ Separate the problem into two expressions.

   $x = \frac{12}{2} = 6$, $x = \frac{-2}{2} = -1$ Simplify the numerator and divide.

2. **Solve the equation by the quadratic formula, $2x^2 + 4x-5 = 0$.**

   A. –0.87 and –2.87 B. 0.87 and –2.87 C. –0.87 and 2.87 D. 0.87 and 2.87

   The correct answer is **B**. The correct solutions are –0.87 and –2.87.

   $x = \frac{-4 \pm \sqrt{4^2-4(2)(-5)}}{2(2)}$ Substitute 2 for a, 4 for b, and –5 for c.

   $x = \frac{-4 \pm \sqrt{16-(-40)}}{4}$ Apply the exponent and perform the multiplication.

   $x = \frac{-4 \pm \sqrt{56}}{4}$ Perform the subtraction.

   $x = \frac{-4 \pm 7.48}{4}$ Apply the square root.

   $x = \frac{-4+7.48}{4}$, $x = \frac{-4-7.48}{4}$ Separate the problem into two expressions.

   $x = \frac{3.48}{4} = 0.87$, $x = \frac{-11.48}{4} = -2.87$ Simplify the numerator and divide.

Let's Review!

There are four methods to solve a quadratic equation algebraically:

- The square root method is used when there is a squared variable term and a constant term.
- Completing the square is used when there is a squared variable term and an even variable term.
- Factoring is used when the equation can be factored.
- The quadratic formula can be used for any quadratic equation.

Polynomials

This lesson introduces adding, subtracting, and multiplying polynomials. It also explains polynomial identities that describe numerical expressions.

Adding and Subtracting Polynomials

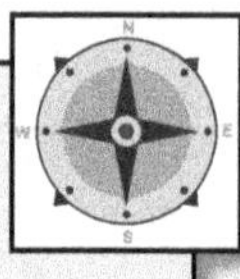

KEEP IN MIND

The solution is an expression, and a value is not calculated for the variable.

A **polynomial** is an expression that contains exponents, variables, constants, and operations. The exponents of the variables are only whole numbers, and there is no division by a variable. The operations are addition, subtraction, multiplication, and division. Constants are terms without a variable. A polynomial of one term is a **monomial**; a polynomial of two terms is a **binomial**; and a polynomial of three terms is a **trinomial.**

To add polynomials, combine like terms and write the solution from the term with the highest exponent to the term with the lowest exponent. To simplify, first rearrange and group like terms. Next, combine like terms.

$(3x^2 + 5x - 6) + (4x^3 - 3x + 4) = 4x^3 + 3x^2 + (5x - 3x) + (-6 + 4) = 4x^3 + 3x^2 + 2x - 2$

To subtract polynomials, rewrite the second polynomial using an additive inverse. Change the minus sign to a plus sign, and change the sign of every term inside the parentheses. Then, add the polynomials.

$(3x^2 + 5x - 6) - (4x^3 - 3x + 4) = (3x^2 + 5x - 6) + (-4x^3 + 3x - 4) = -4x^3 + 3x^2 + (5x + 3x) + (-6 - 4)$
$= -4x^3 + 3x^2 + 8x - 10$

Examples

1. **Perform the operation, $(2y^2 - 5y + 1) + (-3y^2 + 6y + 2)$.**

   A. $y^2 + y + 3$ B. $-y^2 - y + 3$ C. $y^2 - y + 3$ D. $-y^2 + y + 3$

   The correct answer is **D**. The correct solution is $-y^2 + y + 3$.

   $(2y^2 - 5y + 1) + (-3y^2 + 6y + 2) = (2y^2 - 3y^2) + (-5y + 6y) + (1 + 2) = -y^2 + y + 3$

2. **Perform the operation, $(3x^2y + 4xy - 5xy^2) - (x^2y - 3xy - 2xy^2)$.**

   A. $2x^2y - 7xy + 3xy^2$ C. $2x^2y + 7xy - 3xy^2$

   B. $2x^2y + 7xy + 3xy^2$ D. $2x^2y - 7xy - 3xy^2$

   The correct answer is **C**. The correct solution is $2x^2y + 7xy - 3xy^2$.

   $(3x^2y + 4xy - 5xy^2) - (x^2y - 3xy - 2xy^2) = (3x^2y + 4xy - 5xy^2) + (-x^2y + 3xy + 2xy^2)$
   $= (3x^2y - x^2y) + (4xy + 3xy) + (-5xy^2 + 2xy^2) = 2x^2y + 7xy - 3xy^2$

Multiplying Polynomials

BE CAREFUL!

Make sure that you apply the distributive property to all terms in the polynomials.

Multiplying polynomials comes in many forms. When multiplying a monomial by a monomial, multiply the coefficients and apply the multiplication rule for the power of an exponent.

$4xy(3x^2y) = 12x^3y^2$.

When multiplying a monomial by a polynomial, multiply each term of the polynomial by the monomial.

$4xy(3x^2y-2xy^2) = 4xy(3x^2y) + 4xy(-2xy^2) = 12x^3y^2-8x^2y^3$.

When multiplying a binomial by a binomial, apply the distributive property and combine like terms.

$(3x-4)(2x+5) = 3x(2x+5)-4(2x+5) = 6x^2+15x-8x-20 = 6x^2+7x-20$

When multiplying a binomial by a trinomial, apply the distributive property and combine like terms.

$(x+2)(3x^2-2x+3) = (x+2)(3x^2) + (x+2)(-2x) + (x+2)(3) = 3x^3+6x^2-2x^2-4x+3x+6 = 3x^3 +$

$4x^2-x+6$

Examples

1. **Multiply, $3xy^2(2x^2y)$.**

   A. $6x^2y^2$ B. $6x^3y^2$ C. $6x^3y^3$ D. $6x^2y^3$

   The correct answer is **C**. The correct solution is $6x^3y^3$. $3xy^2(2x^2y) = 6x^3y^3$.

2. **Multiply, $-2xy(3xy-4x^2y^2)$.**

   A. $-6x^2y^2+8x^3y^3$ B. $-6x^2y^2-8x^3y^3$ C. $-6xy+8x^3y^3$ D. $-6xy-8x^3y^3$

   The correct answer is **A**. The correct solution is $-6x^2y^2+8x^3y^3$.

   $-2xy(3xy-4x^2y^2) = -2xy(3xy)-2xy(-4x^2y^2) = -6x^2y^2+8x^3y^3$

Polynomial Identities

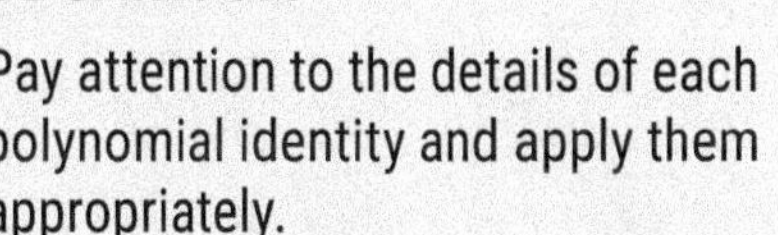

BE CAREFUL!

Pay attention to the details of each polynomial identity and apply them appropriately.

There are many polynomial identities that show relationships between expressions.

- Difference of two squares: $a^2-b^2 = (a-b)(a+b)$
- Square of a binomial: $(a+b)^2 = a^2+2ab+b^2$
- Square of a binomial: $(a-b)^2 = a^2-2ab+b^2$
- Sum of cubes: $a^3+b^3 = (a+b)(a^2-ab+b^2)$
- Difference of two cubes: $a^3-b^3 = (a-b)(a^2+ab+b^2)$

Examples

1. **Apply the polynomial identity to rewrite $x^2 + 6x + 9$.**

   A. $x^2 + 9$ B. $(x^2 + 3)^2$ C. $(x + 3)^2$ D. $(3x)^2$

   The correct answer is **C.** The correct solution is $(x + 3)^2$. The expression $x^2 + 6x + 9$ is rewritten as $(x + 3)^2$ because the value of a is x and the value of b is 3.

2. **Apply the polynomial identity to rewrite $8x^3 - 1$.**

   A. $(2x + 1)(4x^2 + 2x - 1)$
   C. $(2x + 1)(4x^2 - 2x + 1)$
   B. $(2x - 1)(4x^2 - 2x - 1)$
   D. $(2x - 1)(4x^2 + 2x + 1)$

   The correct answer is **D.** The correct solution is $(2x - 1)(4x^2 + 2x + 1)$. The expression $8x^3 - 1$ is rewritten as $(2x - 1)(4x^2 + 2x + 1)$ because the value of a is $2x$ and the value of b is 1.

Let's Review!

- Adding, subtracting, and multiplying are commonly applied to polynomials. The key step in applying these operations is combining like terms.
- Polynomial identities require rewriting polynomials into different forms.

RATIOS, PROPORTIONS, AND PERCENTAGES

This lesson reviews percentages and ratios and their application to real-world problems. It also examines proportions and rates of change.

Percentages

A **percent** or **percentage** represents a fraction of some quantity. It is an integer or decimal number followed by the symbol %. The word *percent* means "per hundred." For example, 50% means 50 per 100. This is equivalent to half, or 1 out of 2.

Converting between numbers and percents is easy. Given a number, multiply by 100 and add the % symbol to get the equivalent percent. For instance, 0.67 is equal to $0.67 \times 100 = 67\%$, meaning 67 out of 100. Given a percent, eliminate the % symbol and divide by 100. For instance, 23.5% is equal to $23.5 \div 100 = 0.235$.

Although percentages between 0% and 100% are the most obvious, a percent can be any real number, including a negative number. For example, $1.35 = 135\%$ and $-0.872 = -87.2\%$. An example is a gasoline tank that is one-quarter full: one-quarter is $\frac{1}{4}$ or 0.25, so the tank is 25% full. Another example is a medical diagnostic test that has a certain maximum normal result. If a patient's test exceeds that value, its representation can be a percent greater than 100%. For instance, a reading that is 1.22 times the maximum normal value is 122% of the maximum normal value. Likewise, when measuring increases in a company's profits as a percent from one year to the next, a negative percent can represent a decline. That is, if the company's profits fell by one-tenth, the change was –10%.

Example

If 15 out of every 250 contest entries are winners, what percentage of entries are winners?

A. 0.06%　　B. 6%　　C. 15%　　D. 17%

The correct answer is **B.** First, convert the fraction $\frac{15}{250}$ to a decimal: 0.06. To get the percent, multiply by 100% (that is, multiply by 100 and add the % symbol). Of all entries, 6% are winners.

Ratios

A **ratio** expresses the relationship between two numbers and is expressed using a colon or fraction notation. For instance, if 135 runners finish a marathon but 22 drop out, the ratio of finishers to non-finishers is 135:22 or $\frac{135}{22}$. These expressions are equal.

BE CAREFUL!

Avoid confusing standard ratios with odds (such as "3:1 odds"). Both may use a colon, but their meanings differ. In general, a ratio is the same as a fraction containing the same numbers.

Ratios also follow the rules of fractions. Performing arithmetic operations on ratios follows the same procedures as on fractions. Ratios should also generally appear in lowest terms. Therefore, the constituent numbers in a ratio represent the relative quantities of each side, not absolute quantities. For example, because the ratio 1:2 is equal to 2:4, 5:10, and 600:1,200, ratios are insufficient to determine the absolute number of entities in a problem.

Example

If the ratio of women to men in a certain industry is 5:4, how many people are in that industry?

A. 9
B. 20
C. 900
D. Not enough information

The correct answer is **D.** The ratio 5:4 is the industry's relative number of women to men. But the industry could have 10 women and 8 men, 100 women and 80 men, or any other breakdown whose ratio is 5:4. Therefore, the question provides too little information to answer. Had it provided the total number of people in the industry, it would have been possible to determine how many women and how many men are in the industry.

KEY POINT

Mathematically, ratios act just like fractions. For example, the ratio 8:13 is mathematically the same as the fraction $\frac{8}{13}$.

Proportions

A **proportion** is an equation of two ratios. An illustrative case is two equivalent fractions:

$$\frac{21}{28} = \frac{3}{4}$$

This example of a proportion should be familiar: going left to right, it is the conversion of one fraction to an equivalent fraction in lowest terms by dividing the numerator and denominator by the same number (7, in this case).

Equating fractions in this way is correct, but it provides little information. Proportions are more informative when one of the numbers is unknown. Using a question mark (?) to represent an unknown number, setting up a proportion can aid in solving problems involving different scales. For instance, if the ratio of maple saplings to oak saplings in an acre of young forest is 7:5 and that acre contains 65 oaks, the number of maples in that acre can be determined using a proportion: $\frac{7}{5} = \frac{?}{65}$

Note that to equate two ratios in this manner, the numerators must contain numbers that represent the same entity or type, and so must the denominators. In this example, the numerators represent maples and the denominators represent oaks.

$$\frac{7 \text{ maples}}{5 \text{ oaks}} = \frac{? \text{ maples}}{65 \text{ oaks}}$$

Recall from the properties of fractions that if you multiply the numerator and denominator by the same number, the result is an equivalent fraction. Therefore, to find the unknown in this proportion, first divide the denominator on the right by the denominator on the left. Then, multiply the quotient by the numerator on the left.

$65 \div 5 = 13$

$\frac{7 \times 13}{5 \times 13} = \frac{?}{65}$

The unknown (?) is $7 \times 13 = 91$. In the example, the acre of forest has 91 maple saplings.

DID YOU KNOW?

When taking the reciprocal of both sides of a proportion, the proportion still holds. When setting up a proportion, ensure that the numerators represent the same type and the denominators represent the same type.

Example

If a recipe calls for 3 parts flour to 2 parts sugar, how much sugar does a baker need if she uses 12 cups of flour?

A. 2 cups B. 3 cups C. 6 cups D. 8 cups

The correct answer is **D.** The baker needs 8 cups of sugar. First, note that "3 parts flour to 2 parts sugar" is the ratio 3:2. Set up the proportion using the given amount of flour (12 cups), putting the flour numbers in either the denominators or the numerators (either will yield the same answer): $\frac{3}{2} = \frac{12}{?}$

Since $12 \div 3 = 4$, multiply 2×4 to get 8 cups of sugar.

Rates of Change

Numbers that describe current quantities can be informative, but how they change over time can provide even greater insight into a problem. The rate of change for some quantity is the ratio of the quantity's difference over a specific time period to the length of that period. For example, if an automobile increases its speed from 50 mph to 100 mph in 10 seconds, the rate of change of its speed (its acceleration) is

$$\frac{100 \text{ mph}-50 \text{ mph}}{10 \text{ s}} = \frac{50 \text{ mph}}{10 \text{ s}} = 5 \text{ mph per second} = 5 \text{ mph/s}$$

The basic formula for the rate of change of some quantity is $\frac{x_f - x_i}{t_f - t_i}$, where t_f is the "final" (or ending) time and t_i is the "initial" (or starting) time. Also, x_f is the (final) quantity at (final) time t_f, and x_i is the (initial) quantity at (initial) time t_i. In the example above, the final time is 10 seconds and the initial time is 0 seconds—hence the omission of the initial time from the calculation.

According to the rules of fractions, multiplying the numerator and denominator by the same number yields an equivalent fraction, so you can reverse the order of the terms in the formula:

$$\frac{x_f - x_i}{t_f - t_i} = \frac{-1}{-1} \times \frac{x_f - x_i}{t_f - t_i} = \frac{x_i - x_f}{t_i - t_f}$$

The key to getting the correct rate of change is to ensure that the first number in the numerator and the first number in the denominator correspond to each other (that is, the quantity from the numerator corresponds to the time from the denominator). This must also be true for the second number.

TEST TIP

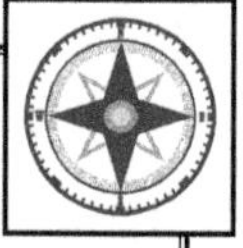

To convert a quantity's rate of change to a percent, divide it by the quantity at the *initial* time and multiply by 100%. To convert to a ratio, just skip the multiplication step.

Example

If the population of an endangered frog species fell from 2,250 individuals to 2,115 individuals in a year, what is that population's annual rate of increase?

A. –135% B. –6% C. 6% D. 135%

The correct answer is **B.** The population's rate of increase was –6%. The solution in this case involves two steps. First, calculate the population's annual rate of change using the formula. It will yield the change in the number of individuals.

$$\frac{2{,}115 - 2{,}250}{1 \text{ year} - 0 \text{ year}} = -135 \text{ per year}$$

Second, divide the result by the initial population. Finally, convert to a percent.

$$\frac{-135 \text{ per year}}{2{,}250} = -0.06 \text{ per year}$$

$$(-0.06 \text{ per year}) \times 100\% = -6\% \text{ per year}$$

Since the question asks for the *annual* rate of increase, the "per year" can be dropped. Also, note that the answer must be negative to represent the decreasing population.

Let's Review!

- A percent—meaning "per hundred"—represents a relative quantity as a fraction or decimal. It is the absolute number multiplied by 100 and followed by the % symbol.
- A ratio is a relationship between two numbers expressed using fraction or colon notation (for example, $\frac{3}{2}$ or 3:2). Ratios behave mathematically just like fractions.
- An equation of two ratios is called a proportion. Proportions are used to solve problems involving scale
- Rates of change are the speeds at which quantities increase or decrease. The formula $\frac{x_f - x_i}{t_f - t_i}$ provides the rate of change of quantity x over the period between some initial (i) time and final (f) time.

Powers, Exponents, Roots, and Radicals

This lesson introduces how to apply the properties of exponents and examines square roots and cube roots. It also discusses how to estimate quantities using integer powers of 10.

Properties of Exponents

An expression that is a repeated multiplication of the same factor is a **power**. The **exponent** is the number of times the **base** is multiplied. For example, 6^2 is the same as 6 times 6, or 36. There are many rules associated with exponents.

Property	Definition	Examples
Product Rule (Same Base)	$a^m \times a^n = a^{m+n}$	$4^1 \times 4^4 = 4^{1+4} = 4^5 = 1024$ $x^1 \times x^4 = x^{1+4} = x^5$
Product Rule (Different Base)	$a^m \times b^m = (a \times b)^m$	$2^2 \times 3^2 = (2 \times 3)^2 = 6^2 = 36$ $3^3 \times x^3 = (3 \times x)^3 = (3x)^3 = 27x^3$
Quotient Rule (Same Base)	$\frac{a^m}{a^n} = a^{m-n}$	$\frac{4^4}{4^2} = 4^{4-2} = 4^2 = 16$ $\frac{x^6}{x^3} = x^{6-3} = x^3$
Quotient Rule (Different Base)	$\frac{a^m}{b^m} = \left(\frac{a}{b}\right)^m$	$\frac{4^4}{3^4} = \left(\frac{4}{3}\right)^4$ $\frac{x^6}{y^6} = \left(\frac{x}{y}\right)^6$
Power of a Power Rule	$(a^m)^n = a^{mn}$	$(2^2)^3 = 2^{2\times3} = 2^6 = 64$ $(x^5)^8 = x^{5\times8} = x^{40}$
Zero Exponent Rule	$a^0 = 1$	$64^0 = 1$ $y^0 = 1$
Negative Exponent Rule	$a^{-m} = \frac{1}{a^m}$	$3^{-3} = \frac{1}{3^3} = \frac{1}{27}$ $\frac{1}{x^{-3}} = x^3$

For many exponent expressions, it is necessary to use multiplication rules to simplify the expression completely.

KEEP IN MIND

The expressions $(-2)^2 = (-2) \times (-2) = 4$ and $-2^2 = -(2 \times 2) = -4$ have different results because of the location of the negative signs and parentheses. For each problem, focus on each detail to simplify completely and correctly.

Examples

1. **Simplify $(3^2)^3$.**

   A. 18
   B. 216
   C. 243
   D. 729

   The correct answer is **D**. The correct solution is 729 because $(3^2)^3 = 3^{2\times3} = 3^6 = 729$.

2. **Simplify $(2x^2)^4$.**

A. $2x^8$ B. $4x^4$ C. $8x^6$ D. $16x^8$

The correct answer is **D.** The correct solution is $16x^8$ because $(2x^2)^4 = 2^4(x^2)^4 = 2^4x^{2\times4} = 16x^8$.

3. **Simplify $\left(\frac{x^{-2}}{y^2}\right)^3$.**

A. $\frac{1}{x^6y^6}$ B. $\frac{x^6}{y^6}$ C. $\frac{y^6}{x^6}$ D. x^6y^6

The correct answer is **A.** The correct solution is $\frac{1}{x^6y^6}$ because $\left(\frac{x^{-2}}{y^2}\right)^3 = \left(\frac{1}{x^2y^2}\right)^3 = \frac{1}{x^{2\times3}y^{2\times3}} = \frac{1}{x^6y^6}$.

Square Root and Cube Roots

The **square** of a number is the number raised to the power of 2. The **square root** of a number, when the number is squared, gives that number. $10^2 = 100$, so the square of 100 is 10, or $\sqrt{100} = 10$. **Perfect squares** are numbers with whole number square roots, such as 1, 4, 9, 16, and 25.

Squaring a number and taking a square root are opposite operations, meaning that the operations undo each other. This means that $\sqrt{x^2} = x$ and $(\sqrt{x})^2 = x$. When solving the equation $x^2 = p$, the solutions are $x = \pm\sqrt{p}$ because a negative value squared is a positive solution.

The **cube** of a number is the number raised to the power of 3. The **cube root** of a number, when the number is cubed, gives that number. $10^3 = 1000$, so the cube of 1,000 is 10, or $\sqrt[3]{1000} = 10$. **Perfect cubes** are numbers with whole number cube roots, such as 1, 8, 27, 64, and 125.

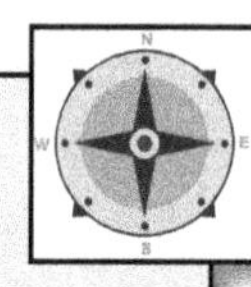

KEEP IN MIND

Most square roots and cube roots are not perfect roots.

Cubing a number and taking a cube root are opposite operations, meaning that the operations undo each other. This means that $\sqrt[3]{x^3} = x$ and $(\sqrt[3]{x})^3 = x$. When solving the equation $x^3 = p$, the solution is $x = \sqrt[3]{p}$.

If a number is not a perfect square root or cube root, the solution is an approximation. When this occurs, the solution is an irrational number. For example, $\sqrt{2}$ is the irrational solution to $x^2 = 2$.

Examples

1. **Solve $x^2 = 121$.**

A. –10, 10 B. –11, 11 C. –12, 12 D. –13, 13

The correct answer is **B.** The correct solution is –11, 11 because the square root of 121 is 11. The values of –11 and 11 make the equation true.

2. **Solve $x^3 = 125$.**

A. 1 B. 5 C. 10 D. 25

The correct answer is **B.** The correct solution is 5 because the cube root of 125 is 5.

Express Large or Small Quantities as Multiples of 10

KEEP IN MIND

A positive exponent in scientific notation represents a large number, while a negative exponent represents a small number.

Scientific notation is a large or small number written in two parts. The first part is a number between 1 and 10. In these problems, the first digit will be a single digit. The number is followed by a multiple to a power of 10. A positive integer exponent means the number is greater than 1, while a negative integer exponent means the number is smaller than 1.

The number 3×10^4 is the same as $3 \times 10{,}000 = 30{,}000$.

The number 3×10^{-4} is the same as $3 \times 0.0001 = 0.0003$.

For example, the population of the United States is about 3×10^8, and the population of the world is about 7×10^9. The population of the United States is 300,000,000, and the population of the world is 7,000,000,000. The world population is about 20 times larger than the population of the United States.

Examples

1. **The population of China is about 1×10^9, and the population of the United States is about 3×10^8. How many times larger is the population of China than the population of the United States?**

   A. 2　　B. 3　　C. 4　　D. 5

   The correct answer is **B.** The correct solution is 3 because the population of China is about 1,000,000,000 and the population of the United States is about 300,000,000. So the population is about 3 times larger.

2. **A red blood cell has a length of 8×10^{-6} meter, and a skin cell has a length of 3×10^{-5} meter. How many times larger is the skin cell?**

   A. 1　　B. 2　　C. 3　　D. 4

   The correct answer is **D.** The correct solution is 4 because 3×10^{-5} is 0.00003 and 8×10^{-6} is 0.000008. So, the skin cell is about 4 times larger.

Let's Review!

- The properties and rules of exponents are applicable to generate equivalent expressions.
- Only a few whole numbers out of the set of whole numbers are perfect squares. Perfect cubes can be positive or negative.
- Numbers expressed in scientific notation are useful to compare large or small numbers.

Chapter 10 Functions Practice Quiz 1

1. **Multiply, $(x–1)(x^2 + 2x + 3)$.**

   A. $x^3 + x^2 + x–3$
   C. $x^3 + x^2–x–3$
   B. $x^3–x^2–x–3$
   D. $x^3–x^2 + x–3$

2. **Apply the polynomial identity to rewrite $9x^2–30x + 25$.**

   A. $(3x + 5)(3x–5)$
   C. $(3x–5)(3x–1)$
   B. $(3x–5)^2$
   D. $(3x–5)(3x + 1)$

3. **Perform the operation, $(3y^2 + 4y)–(5y^3–2y^2 + 3)$.**

   A. $-5y^3 + y^2 + 4y–3$
   B. $-5y^3 + 5y^2 + 4y + 3$
   C. $-5y^3 + y^2 + 4y + 3$
   D. $-5y^3 + 5y^2 + 4y–3$

4. **Solve $x^3 = 343$.**

   A. 6
   C. 8
   B. 7
   D. 9

5. **One online seller has about 6×10^8 online orders, and another online seller has about 5×10^7 online orders. How many times more orders does the first company have?**

   A. 12
   C. 20
   B. 15
   D. 32

6. **Simplify $\frac{x^2y^{-2}}{x^{-3}y^3}$.**

   A. $\frac{x^5}{y^5}$
   C. $\frac{1}{x^5y^5}$
   B. $\frac{y^5}{x^5}$
   D. x^5y^5

7. **What is 15% of 64?**

   A. 5:48
   C. 48:5
   B. 15:64
   D. 64:15

8. **Which number satisfies the proportion $\frac{378}{?} = \frac{18}{7}$?**

   A. 18
   C. 972
   B. 147
   D. 2,646

9. **If a tree grows an average of 4.2 inches in a day, what is the rate of change in its height per month? Assume a month is 30 days.**

   A. 0.14 inches per month
   B. 4.2 inches per month
   C. 34.2 inches per month
   D. 126 inches per month

10. **Solve the equation by the quadratic formula, $11x^2–14x + 4 = 0$.**

    A. -0.84 and -0.43
    B. 0.84 and -0.43
    C. -0.84 and 0.43
    D. 0.84 and 0.43

11. **Solve the equation by any method, $3x^2–5 = 22$.**

    A. 0
    C. ±2
    B. ±1
    D. ±3

12. **Solve the equation by the square root method, $5x^2 + 10 = 10$.**

    A. 0
    C. 2
    B. 1
    D. 3

Chapter 10 Functions Practice Quiz 1 – Answer Key

1. **A.** The correct solution is $\boldsymbol{x^3 + x^2 + x–3}$.

$$(x–1)(x^2 + 2x + 3) = (x–1)(x^2) + (x–1)(2x) + (x–1)(3)$$
$$= x^3 – x^2 + 2x^2 – 2x + 3x – 3 = x^3 + x^2 + x – 3$$

See Lesson: Polynomials.

2. **B.** The correct solution is $(3x–5)^2$. The expression $9x^2–30x + 25$ is rewritten as $(3x–5)^2$ because the value of a is $3x$ and the value of b is 5. **See Lesson: Polynomials.**

3. **D.** The correct solution is $–5\boldsymbol{y^3} + 5\boldsymbol{y^2} + 4\boldsymbol{y}–3$.

$$(3y^2 + 4y)–(5y^3–2y^2 + 3) = (3y^2 + 4y) + (–5y^3 + 2y^2–3)$$
$$= –5y^3 + (3y^2 + 2y^2) + 4y–3 = –5y^3 + 5y^2 + 4y–3$$

See Lesson: Polynomials.

4. **B.** The correct solution is 7 because the cube root of 343 is 7. **See Lesson: Powers, Exponents, Roots, and Radicals.**

5. **A.** The correct solution is 12 because the first company has about 600,000,000 orders and the second company has about 50,000,000 orders. So, the first company is about 12 times larger. **See Lesson: Powers, Exponents, Roots, and Radicals.**

6. **A.** The correct solution is $\frac{x^5}{y^5}$ because $\frac{x^2y^{-2}}{x^{-3}y^3} = x^{2-(-3)}y^{-2-3} = x^5y^{-5} = \frac{x^5}{y^5}$. **See Lesson: Powers, Exponents, Roots, and Radicals.**

7. **C.** Either set up a proportion or just note that this question is asking for a fraction of a specific number: 15% (or $\frac{3}{20}$) of 64. Multiply $\frac{3}{20}$ by 64 to get $\frac{48}{5}$, or 48:5. **See Lesson: Ratios, Proportions, and Percentages.**

8. **B.** The number 147 satisfies the proportion. First, divide 378 by 18 to get 21. Then, multiply 21 by 7 to get 147. Check your answer by dividing 147 by 7: the quotient is also 21, so 147 satisfies the proportion. **See Lesson: Ratios, Proportions, and Percentages.**

9. **D.** The rate of change is 126 inches per month. One approach is to set up a proportion.

$$\frac{1\ day}{4.2\ inches} = \frac{30\ days}{?}$$

Since 1 month is equivalent to 30 days, multiply the rate of change per day by 30 to get the rate of change per month. 4.2 inches multiplied by 30 is 126 inches. Thus, the growth rate is 126 inches per month. **See Lesson: Ratios, Proportions, and Percentages.**

10. **D.** The correct solutions are 0.84 and 0.43.

$x = \frac{-(-14) \pm \sqrt{(-14)^2-4(11)(4)}}{2(11)}$	Substitute 11 for a, –14 for b, and 4 for c.
$x = \frac{14 \pm \sqrt{196-176}}{22}$	Apply the exponent and perform the multiplication.
$x = \frac{14 \pm \sqrt{20}}{22}$	Perform the subtraction.
$x = \frac{14 \pm 4.47}{22}$	Apply the square root.
$x = \frac{14 + 4.47}{22}, x = \frac{14-4.47}{22}$	Separate the problem into two expressions.
$x = \frac{18.47}{22} = 0.84, x = \frac{9.53}{22} = 0.43$	Simplify the numerator and divide.

See Lesson: Solving Quadratic Equations.

11. D. The correct solutions are ±3. Solve this equation by the square root method.

$3x^2 = 27$	Add 5 to both sides of the equation.
$x^2 = \pm 9$	Divide both sides of the equation by 3.
$x = \pm 3$	Apply the square root to both sides of the equation.

See Lesson: Solving Quadratic Equations.

12. A. The correct solution is 0.

$5x^2 = 0$	Subtract 10 from both sides of the equation.
$x^2 = 0$	Divide both sides of the equation by 5.
$x = 0$	Apply the square root to both sides of the equation.

See Lesson: Solving Quadratic Equations.

CHAPTER 11 GEOMETRY

CONGRUENCE

This lesson discusses basic terms for geometry. Many polygons have the property of lines of symmetry, or rotational symmetry. Rotations, reflections, and translations are ways to create congruent polygons.

Geometry Terms

The terms *point*, *line*, and *plane* help define other terms in geometry. A point is an exact location in space with no size and has a label with a capital letter. A line has location and direction, is always straight, and has infinitely many points that extend in both directions. A plane has infinitely many intersecting lines that extend forever in all directions.

The diagram shows point W, point X, point Y, and point Z. The line is labeled as $\overleftrightarrow{WX}$, and the plane is Plane A or Plane WYZ (or any three points in the plane).

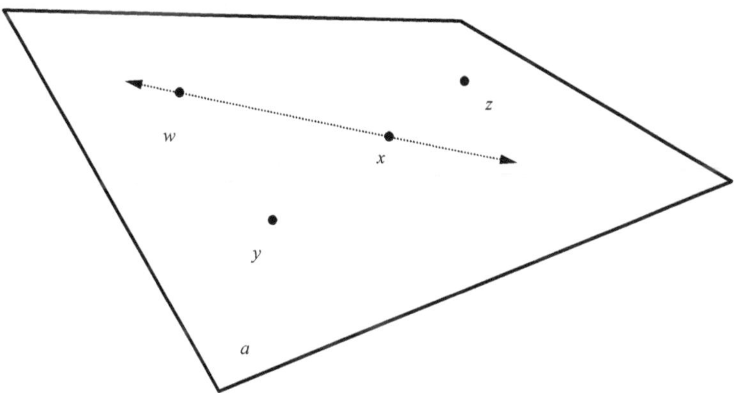

With these definitions, many other geometry terms can be defined. *Collinear* is a term for points that lie on the same line, and *coplanar* is a term for points and/or lines within the same plane. A line segment is a part of a line with two endpoints. For example, $\overline{WX}$ has endpoints W and X. A ray has an endpoint and extends forever in one direction. For example, $\longrightarrow AB$ has an endpoint of A, and $\longrightarrow BA$ has an endpoint of B. The intersection of lines, planes, segment, or rays is a point or a set of points.

Some key statements that are evident in geometry are

- There is exactly one straight line through any two points.
- There is exactly one plane that contains any three non-collinear points.
- A line with points in the plane lies in the plane.
- Two lines intersect at a point.
- Two planes intersect at a line.

Two rays that share an endpoint form an angle. The vertex is the common endpoint of the two rays that form an angle. When naming an angle, the vertex is the center point. The angle below is named $\angle ABC$ or $\angle CBA$.

An acute angle has a measure between 0° and 90°, and a 90° angle is a right angle. An obtuse angle has a measure between 90° and 180°, and a 180° angle is a straight angle.

There are two special sets of lines. Parallel lines are at least two lines that never intersect within the same plane. Perpendicular lines intersect at one point and form four angles.

Example

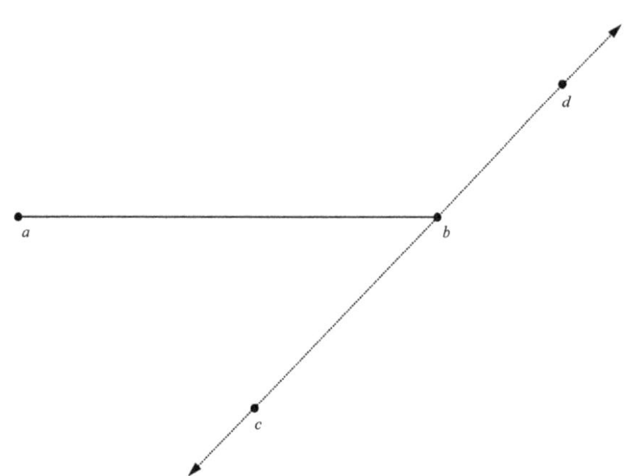

BE CAREFUL!

Lines are always named with two points, a plane can be named with three points, and an angle is named with the vertex as the center point.

Describe the diagram.

A. Points A, B, C, and D are collinear.

B. Points A, C, and D are collinear.

C. $\overline{CD}$ intersects $\overleftrightarrow{AB}$ at point B.

D. $\overline{AB}$ intersects $\overleftrightarrow{CD}$ at point B.

The correct answer is **D.** The correct solution is $\overline{AB}$ intersects $\overleftrightarrow{CD}$ at point B. The segment intersects the line at point B.

Line and Rotational Symmetry

Symmetry is a reflection or rotation of a shape that allows that shape to be carried onto itself. Line symmetry, or reflection symmetry, is when two halves of a shape are reflected onto each other across a line. A shape may have none, one, or several lines of symmetry. A kite has one line of symmetry, and a scalene triangle has no lines of symmetry.

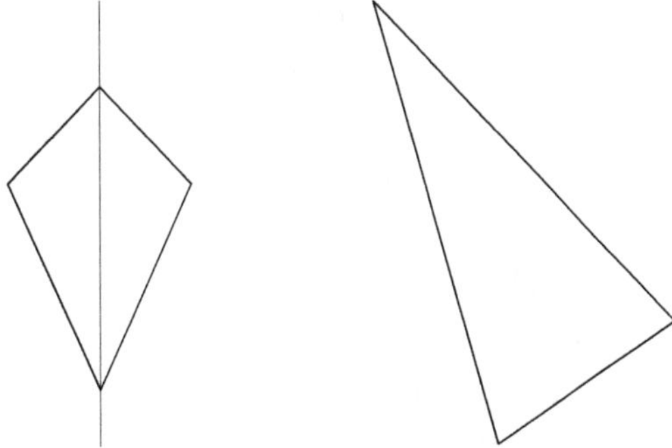

Rotational symmetry is when a figure can be mapped onto itself by a rotation about a point through any angle between 0° and 360°. The order of rotational symmetry is the number of times the object can be rotated. If there is no rotational symmetry, the order is 1 because the object can only be rotated 360° to map the figure onto itself. A square has 90° rotational symmetry and is order 4 because it can be rotated 90°, 180°, 270°, and 360°. A trapezoid has no rotational symmetry and is order 1 because it can only be rotated 360° to map onto itself.

KEEP IN MIND

A polygon can have both, neither, or either reflection and rotational symmetry.

Example

What is the rotational symmetry for a regular octagon?

A. 30° B. 45° C. 60° D. 75°

The correct answer is **B.** The correct solution is 45°. For a regular polygon, divide 360° by the eight sides of the octagon to obtain 45°.

Rotations, Reflections, and Translations

There are three types of transformations: rotations, reflections, and translations. A rotation is a turn of a figure about a point in a given direction. A reflection is a flip over a line of symmetry, and a translation is a slide horizontally, vertically, or both. Each of these transformations produces a congruent image.

A rotation changes ordered pairs (x, y) in the coordinate plane. A 90° rotation counterclockwise about the point becomes $(-y, x)$, a 180° rotation counterclockwise about the point becomes $(-x, -y)$, and a 270° rotation the point becomes $(y, -x)$. Using the point (6, −8),

- 90° rotation counterclockwise about the origin (8, 6)
- 180° rotation counterclockwise about the origin (−6, 8)
- 270° rotation counterclockwise about the origin (−8, −6)

A reflection also changes ordered pairs (x, y) in the coordinate plane. A reflection across the x-axis changes the sign of the y-coordinate, and a reflection across the y-axis changes the sign of the x-coordinate. A reflection over the line $y = x$ changes the points to (y, x), and a reflection over the line $y = -x$ changes the points to $(-y, -x)$. Using the point (6, −8),

- A reflection across the x-axis (6, 8)
- A reflection across the y-axis (−6, −8)
- A reflection over the line $y = x$ (−8, 6)
- A reflection over the line $y = -x$ (8, −6)

KEEP IN MIND

A rotation is a turn, a reflection is a flip, and a translation is a slide.

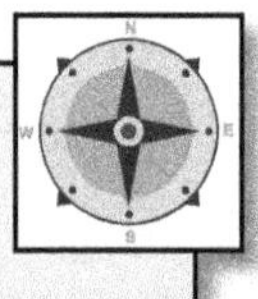

A translation changes ordered pairs (x, y) left or right and/or up or down. Adding a positive value to an x-coordinate is a translation to the right, and adding a negative value to an x-coordinate is a translation to the left. Adding a positive value to a y-coordinate is a translation up, and adding a negative value to a y-coordinate is a translation down. Using the point (6, −8),

- A translation of $(x + 3)$ is a translation right 3 units (9, −8)
- A translation of $(x - 3)$ is a translation left 3 units (3, −8)
- A translation of $(y + 3)$ is a translation up 3 units (6, −5)
- A translation of $(y - 3)$ is a translation down 3 units (6, −11)

Example

ΔABC has points A (3, −2), B (2, −1), and C (−1, 4), which after a transformation become A' (2, 3), B' (1, 2), and C' (−4, −1). What is the transformation between the points?

A. Reflection across the x-axis

B. Reflection across the y-axis

C. Rotation of 90° counterclockwise

D. Rotation of 270° counterclockwise

The correct answer is **C**. The correct solution is a rotation of 90° counterclockwise because the points (x, y) become $(y, -x)$.

Let's Review!

- The terms *point*, *line*, and *plane* help define many terms in geometry.
- Symmetry allows a figure to carry its shape onto itself. This can be reflectional or rotational symmetry.
- Three transformations are rotation (turn), reflection (flip), and translation (slide).

SIMILARITY, RIGHT TRIANGLES, AND TRIGONOMETRY

This lesson defines and applies terminology associated with coordinate planes. It also demonstrates how to find the area of two-dimensional shapes and the surface area and volume of three-dimensional cubes and right prisms.

Coordinate Plane

The **coordinate plane** is a two-dimensional number line with the horizontal axis called the ***x*-axis** and the vertical axis called the ***y*-axis**. Each **ordered pair** or **coordinate** is listed as (x, y). The center point is the origin and has an ordered pair of (0, 0). A coordinate plane has four quadrants.

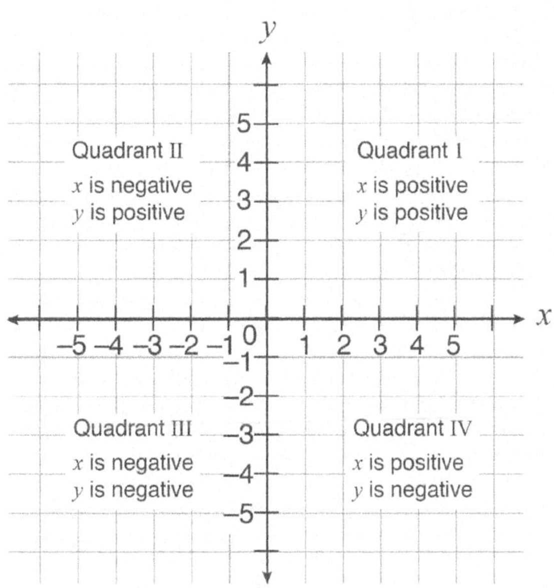

KEEP IN MIND

The *x*-coordinates are positive to the right of the *y*-axis. The *y*-coordinates are positive above the *x*-axis.

To graph a point in the coordinate plane, start with the x-coordinate. This point states the number of steps to the left (negative) or to the right (positive) from the origin. Then, the y-coordinate states the number of steps up (positive) or down (negative) from the x-coordinate.

Given a set of ordered pairs, points can be drawn in the coordinate plane to create polygons. The length of a segment can be found if the segment has the same first coordinate or the same second coordinate.

Examples

1. **Draw a triangle with the coordinates (–2, –1), (–3, 5), (–4, 2).**

A.

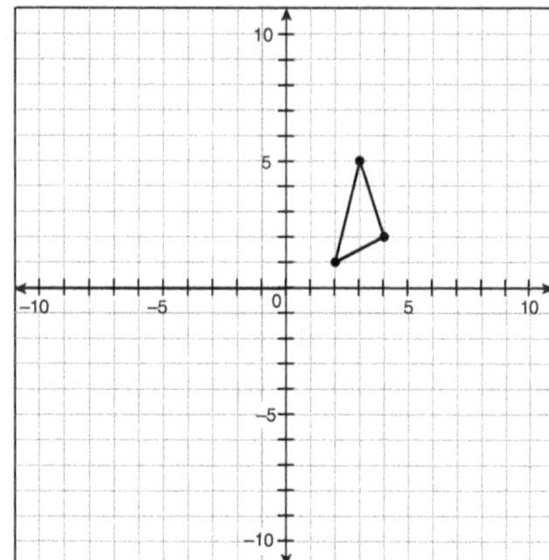

C.

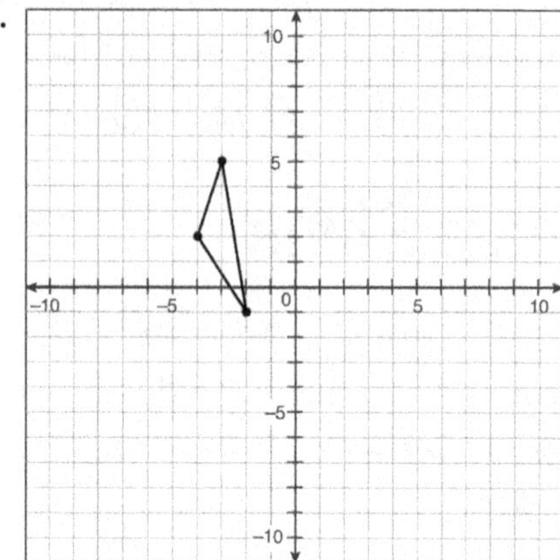

B.

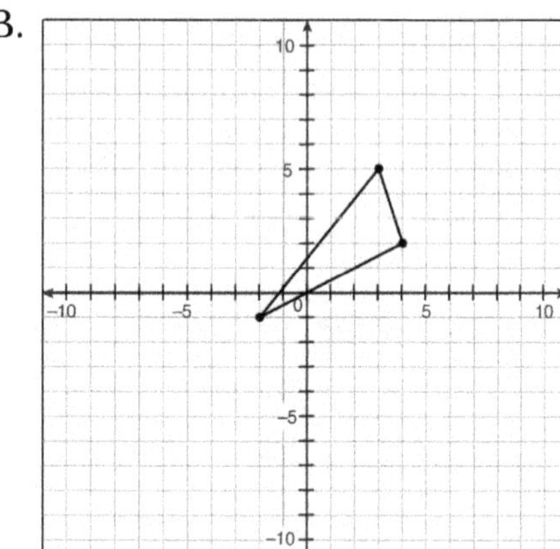

D.

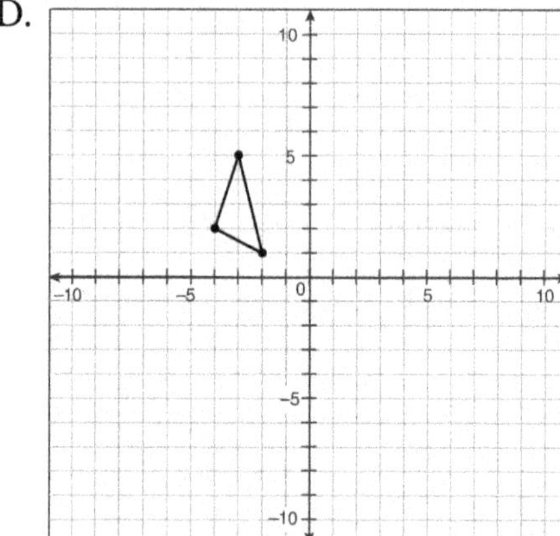

The correct answer is **C**. The first point is in the third quadrant because x is negative and y is negative, and the last two points are in the second quadrant because x is negative and y is positive.

2. **Given the coordinates for a rectangle (4, 8), (4, –2), (–1, –2), (–1, 8), find the length of each side of the rectangle.**

A. 3 units and 6 units
B. 3 units and 10 units
C. 5 units and 6 units
D. 5 units and 10 units

The correct answer is **D**. The correct solution is 5 units and 10 units. The difference between the x-coordinates is $4-(-1) = 5$ units, and the difference between the y-coordinates is $8-(-2) = 10$ units.

3. **The dimensions for a soccer field are 45 meters by 90 meters. One corner of a soccer field on the coordinate plane is (–45, –30). What could a second coordinate be?**

A. (–45, 30)
B. (–45, 45)
C. (–45, 60)
D. (–45, 75)

The correct answer is **C**. The correct solution is (–45, 60) because 90 can be added to the y-coordinate, $-30 + 90 = 60$.

Area of Two-Dimensional Objects

BE CAREFUL!

Make sure that you apply the correct formula for area of each two-dimensional object.

The **area** is the number of unit squares that fit inside a two-dimensional object. A unit square is one unit long by one unit wide, which includes 1 foot by 1 foot and 1 meter by 1 meter. The unit of measurement for area is units squared (or feet squared, meters squared, and so on). The following are formulas for calculating the area of various shapes.

- Rectangle: The product of the length and the width, $A = lw$.
- Parallelogram: The product of the base and the height, $A = bh$.
- Square: The side length squared, $A = s^2$.
- Triangle: The product of one-half the base and the height, $A = \frac{1}{2}bh$.
- Trapezoid: The product of one-half the height and the sum of the bases, $A = \frac{1}{2}h(b_1 + b_2)$.
- Regular polygon: The product of one-half the **apothem** (a line from the center of the regular polygon that is perpendicular to a side) and the sum of the perimeter, $A = \frac{1}{2}ap$.

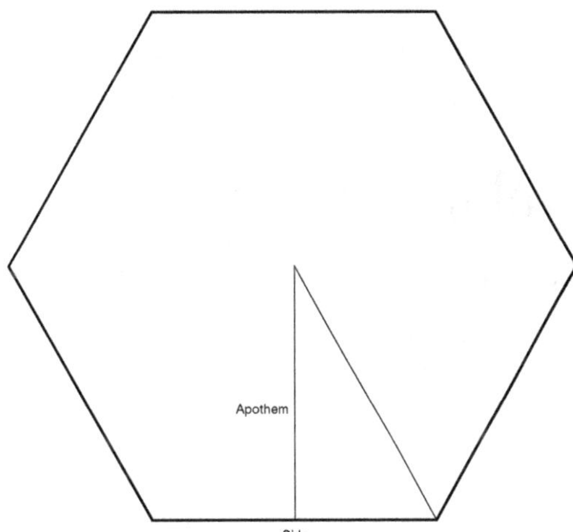

Examples

1. **A trapezoid has a height of 3 centimeters and bases of 8 centimeters and 10 centimeters. Find the area in square centimeters.**

   A. 18 B. 27 C. 52 D. 55

   The correct answer is **B**. The correct solution is 27. Substitute the values into the formula and simplify using the order of operations, $A = \frac{1}{2}h(b_1 + b_2) = \frac{1}{2}(3)(8 + 10) = \frac{1}{2}(3)(18) = 27$ square centimeters.

2. **A regular decagon has a side length of 12 inches and an apothem of 6 inches. Find the area in square inches.**

   A. 120 B. 360 C. 720 D. 960

   The correct answer is **B.** The correct solution is 360. Simplify using the order of operations, $A = \frac{1}{2}ap = \frac{1}{2}(6)(12(10)) = 360$ square inches.

3. **Two rectangular rooms need to be carpeted. The dimensions of the first room are 18 feet by 19 feet, and the dimensions of the second room are 12 feet by 10 feet. What is the total area to be carpeted in square feet?**

   A. 118 B. 236 C. 342 D. 462

   The correct answer is **D.** The correct solution is 462. Substitute the values into the formula and simplify using the order of operations, $A = lw + lw = 18(19) + 12(10) = 342 + 120 = 462$ square feet.

4. **A picture frame is in the shape of a right triangle with legs 12 centimeters and 13 centimeters and hypotenuse of 17 centimeters. What is the area in square centimeters?**

   A. 78 B. 108 C. 117 D. 156

   The correct answer is **A.** The correct solution is 78. Substitute the values into the formula and simplify using the order of operations, $A = \frac{1}{2}bh = \frac{1}{2}(12)(13) = 78$ square centimeters.

Surface Area and Volume of Cubes and Right Prisms

A three-dimensional object has length, width, and height. **Cubes** are made up of six congruent square faces. A **right prism** is made of three sets of congruent faces, with at least two sets of congruent rectangles.

BE CAREFUL!

Surface area is a two-dimensional calculation, and volume is a three-dimensional calculation.

The **surface area** of any three-dimensional object is the sum of the area of all faces. The formula for the surface area of a cube is $SA = 6s^2$ because there are six congruent faces. For a right rectangular prism, the surface area formula is $SA = 2lw + 2lh + 2hw$ because there are three sets of congruent rectangles. For a triangular prism, the surface area formula is twice the area of the base plus the area of the other three rectangles that make up the prism.

The **volume** of any three-dimensional object is the amount of space inside the object. The volume formula for a cube is $V = s^3$. The volume formula for a rectangular prism is the area of the base times the height, or $V = Bh$.

Examples

1. **A cube has a side length of 5 centimeters. What is the surface area in square centimeters?**

   A. 20 B. 25 C. 125 D. 150

   The correct answer is **D**. The correct solution is 150. Substitute the values into the formula and simplify using the order of operations, $SA = 6s^2 = 6(5^2) = 6(25) = 150$ square centimeters.

2. **A cube has a side length of 5 centimeters. What is the volume in cubic centimeters?**

   A. 20 B. 25 C. 125 D. 180

   The correct answer is **C**. The correct solution is 125. Substitute the values into the formula and simplify using the order of operations, $V = s^3 = 5^3 = 125$ cubic centimeters.

3. **A right rectangular prism has dimensions of 4 inches by 5 inches by 6 inches. What is the surface area in square inches?**

   A. 60 B. 74 C. 120 D. 148

   The correct answer is **D**. The correct solution is 148. Substitute the values into the formula and simplify using the order of operations, $SA = 2lw + 2lh + 2hw = 2(4)(5) + 2(4)(6) + 2(6)(5) = 40 + 48 + 60 = 148$ square inches.

4. **A right rectangular prism has dimensions of 4 inches by 5 inches by 6 inches. What is the volume in cubic inches?**

   A. 60 B. 62 C. 120 D. 124

   The correct answer is **C**. The correct solution is 120. Substitute the values into the formula and simplify using the order of operations, $V = lwh = 4(5)(6) = 120$ cubic inches.

Let's Review!

- The coordinate plane is a two-dimensional number line that is used to display ordered pairs. Two-dimensional shapes can be drawn on the plane, and the length of the objects can be determined based on the given coordinates.
- The area of a two-dimensional object is the amount of space inside the shape. There are area formulas to use to calculate the area of various shapes.
- For a three-dimensional object, the surface area is the sum of the area of the faces and the volume is the amount of space inside the object. Cubes and right rectangular prisms are common three-dimensional solids.

CIRCLES

This lesson introduces concepts of circles, including finding the circumference and the area of the circle.

Circle Terminology

A **circle** is a figure composed of points that are equidistant from a given point. The **center** is the point from which all points are equidistant. A **chord** is a segment whose endpoints are on the circle, and the **diameter** is a chord that goes through the center of the circle. The **radius** is a segment with one endpoint at the center of the circle and one endpoint on the circle. **Arcs** have two endpoints on the circle and all points on a circle between those endpoints.

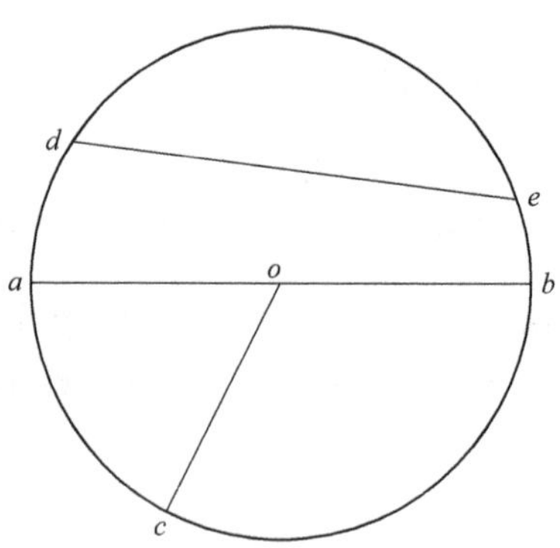

In the circle at the right, O is the center, $\overline{OC}$ is the radius, $\overline{AB}$ is the diameter, $\overline{DE}$ is a chord, and $\widehat{AD}$ is an arc.

Example

Identify a diameter of the circle.

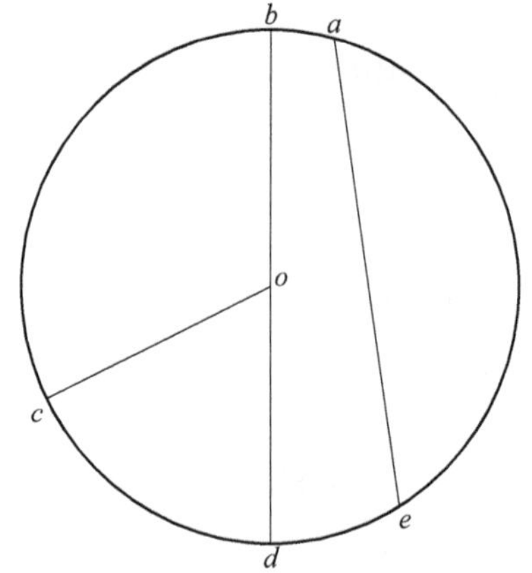

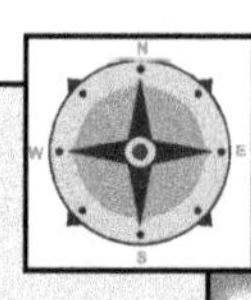

KEEP IN MIND

The radius is one-half the length of the diameter of the circle.

A. $\overline{BD}$ B. $\overline{OC}$ C. $\overline{DO}$ D. $\overline{AE}$

The correct answer is **A**. The correct solution is $\overline{BD}$ because points B and D are on the circle and the segment goes through the center O.

Circumference and Area of a Circle

The **circumference** of a circle is the perimeter, or the distance, around the circle. There are two ways to find the circumference. The formulas are the product of the diameter and pi or the product of twice the radius and pi. In symbol form, the formulas are $C = \pi d$ or $C = 2\pi r$.

BE CAREFUL!
Make sure that you apply the correct formula for circumference and area of a circle.

The **area** of a circle is the amount of space inside a circle. The formula is the product of pi and the radius squared. In symbol form, the formula is $A = \pi r^2$. The area is always expressed in square units.

Given the circumference or the area of a circle, the radius and the diameter can be determined. The given measurement is substituted into the appropriate formula. Then, the equation is solved for the radius or the diameter.

Examples

1. **Find the circumference in centimeters of a circle with a diameter of 8 centimeters. Use 3.14 for π.**

   A. 12.56 B. 25.12 C. 50.24 D. 100.48

   The correct answer is **B.** The correct solution is 25.12 because $C = \pi d \approx 3.14(8) \approx 25.12$ centimeters.

2. **Find the area in square inches of a circle with a radius of 15 inches. Use 3.14 for π.**

   A. 94.2 B. 176.63 C. 706.5 D. 828.96

   The correct answer is **C.** The correct solution is 706.5 because $A = \pi r^2 \approx 3.14(15)^2 \approx$ $3.14(225) \approx 706.5$ square inches.

3. **A circle has a circumference of 70 centimeters. Find the diameter to the nearest tenth of a centimeter. Use 3.14 for π.**

   A. 11.1 B. 22.3 C. 33.5 D. 44.7

   The correct answer is **B.** The correct solution is 22.3 because $C = \pi d; 70 = 3.14d; d \approx 22.3$ centimeters.

4. **A circle has an area of 95 square centimeters. Find the radius to the nearest tenth of a centimeter. Use 3.14 for π.**

   A. 2.7 B. 5.5 C. 8.2 D. 10.9

   The correct answer is **B.** The correct solution is 5.5 because $A = \pi r^2; 95 = 3.14r^2; 30.25 = r^2;\ r \approx 5.5$ centimeters.

Finding Circumference or Area Given the Other Value

Given the circumference of a circle, the area of the circle can be found. First, substitute the circumference into the formula and find the radius. Substitute the radius into the area formula and simplify.

Reverse the process to find the circumference given the area. First, substitute the area into the area formula and find the radius. Substitute the radius into the circumference formula and simplify.

BE CAREFUL!

Pay attention to the details with each formula and apply them in the correct order.

Examples

1. **The circumference of a circle is 45 inches. Find the area of the circle in square inches. Round to the nearest tenth. Use 3.14 for π.**

   A. 51.8 B. 65.1 C. 162.8 D. 204.5

   The correct answer is **C**. The correct solution is 162.8.

   $C = 2\pi r; 45 = 2(3.14)r; 45 = 6.28r; r \approx 7.2$ inches. $A = \pi r^2 \approx 3.14(7.2)^2 \approx 3.14(51.84) \approx 162.8$ square inches.

2. **The area of a circle is 60 square centimeters. Find the circumference of the circle in centimeters. Round to the nearest tenth. Use 3.14 for π.**

   A. 4.4 B. 13.8 C. 19.1 D. 27.6

   The correct answer is **D**. The correct solution is 27.6.

   $A = \pi r^2; 60 = 3.14r^2; 19.11 = r^2; r \approx 4.4$ centimeters. $C = 2\pi r; C = 2(3.14)4.4 \approx 27.6$ centimeters.

Let's Review!

- Key terms related to circles are *radius, diameter, chord,* and *arc*. Note that the diameter is twice the radius.
- The circumference or the perimeter of a circle is the product of pi and the diameter or twice the radius and pi.
- The area of the circle is the product of pi and the radius squared.

MEASUREMENT AND DIMENSION

This lesson applies the formulas of volume for cylinders, pyramids, cones, and spheres to solve problems.

Volume of a Cylinder

A **cylinder** is a three-dimensional figure with two identical circular bases and a rectangular lateral face.

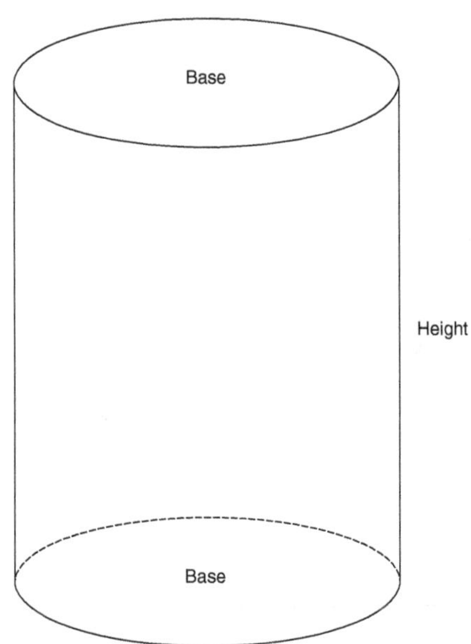

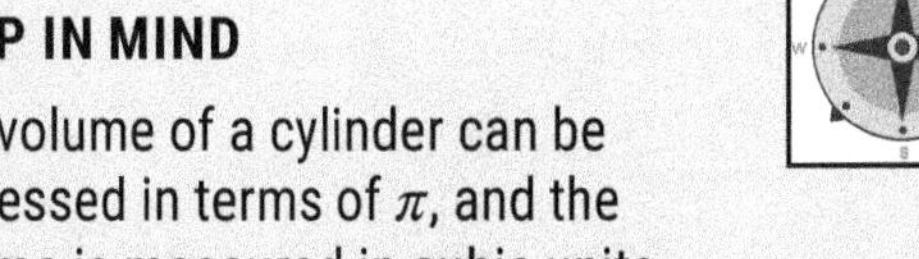

KEEP IN MIND

The volume of a cylinder can be expressed in terms of π, and the volume is measured in cubic units.

The volume of a cylinder equals the product of the area of the base and the height of the cylinder. This is the same formula used to calculate the volume of a right prism. In this case, the area of a base is a circle, so the formula is $V = Bh = \pi r^2 h$. The height is the perpendicular distance between the two circular bases.

Example

Find the volume of a cylinder in cubic centimeters with a radius of 13 centimeters and a height of 12 centimeters.

A. 156π B. 312π C. $1{,}872\pi$ D. $2{,}028\pi$

The correct answer is **D**. The correct solution is $2{,}028\pi$. Substitute the values into the formula and simplify using the order of operations, $V = \pi r^2 h = \pi 13^2(12) = \pi(169)(12) = 2{,}028\pi$ cubic centimeters.

Volume of a Pyramid and a Cone

A **pyramid** is a three-dimensional solid with one base and all edges from the base meeting at the top, or apex. Pyramids can have any two-dimensional shape as the base. A **cone** is similar to a pyramid, but it has a circle instead of a polygon for the base.

BE CAREFUL!

Make sure that you apply the correct formula for area of the base for a pyramid.

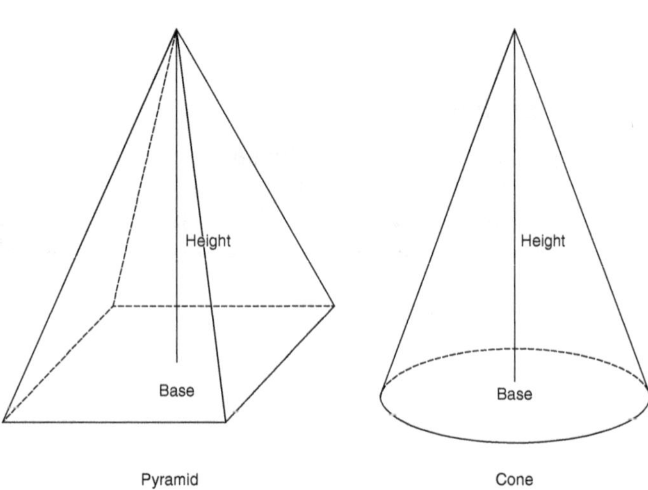

The formula for the volume of a pyramid is similar to a prism, $V = \frac{1}{3}Bh$ where B is the area of the base. The base is a circle for a cone, and the formula for the volume is $V = \frac{1}{3}Bh = \frac{1}{3}\pi r^2 h$.

Examples

1. **A regular hexagonal pyramid has base with side lengths of 5 centimeters and an apothem of 3 centimeters. If the height is 6 centimeters, find the volume in cubic centimeters.**

   A. 90 B. 180 C. 270 D. 360

   The correct answer is **A.** The correct solution is 90. Substitute the values into the formula and simplify using the order of operations, $V = \frac{1}{3}Bh = \frac{1}{3}\left(\frac{1}{2}ap\right)h = \frac{1}{3}\left(\frac{1}{2}(3)(30)\right)6 = 90$ cubic centimeters.

2. **A cone has a radius of 10 centimeters and a height of 9 centimeters. Find the volume in cubic centimeters.**

   A. 270π B. 300π C. 810π D. 900π

   The correct answer is **B.** The correct solution is 300π. Substitute the values into the formula and simplify using the order of operations, $V = \frac{1}{3}\pi r^2 h = \frac{1}{3}\pi 10^2(9) = \frac{1}{3}\pi(100)(9) = 300\pi$ cubic centimeters.

Volume of a Sphere

A **sphere** is a round, three-dimensional solid, with every point on its surface equidistant to the center. The formula for the volume of a sphere is represented by just the radius of the sphere. The volume of a sphere is $V = \frac{4}{3}\pi r^3$. The volume of a hemi (half) of a sphere is $V = \left(\frac{1}{2}\right)\frac{4}{3}\pi r^3 = \frac{2}{3}\pi r^3$.

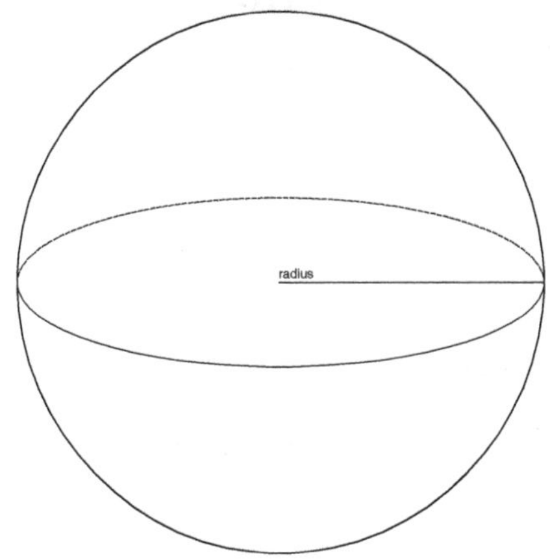

BE CAREFUL!

The radius is cubed, not squared, for the volume of a sphere.

Example

A sphere has a radius of 3 centimeters. Find the volume of a sphere in cubic centimeters.

A. 18π B. 27π C. 36π D. 45π

The correct answer is **C**. The correct solution is 36π. Substitute the values into the formula and simplify using the order of operations, $V = \frac{4}{3}\pi r^3 = \frac{4}{3}\pi 3^3 = \frac{4}{3}\pi(27) = 36\pi$ cubic centimeters.

Let's Review!

- The volume is the capacity of a three-dimensional object and is expressed in cubic units.
- The volume formula for a cylinder is the product of the area of the base (which is a circle) and the height of the cylinder.
- The volume formula for a pyramid or cone is one-third of the product of the area of the base (a circle in the case of the cone) and the height of the pyramid or cone.
- The volume formula for a sphere is $V = \frac{4}{3}\pi r^3$.

Chapter 11 Geometry Practice Quiz 1

1. **The bottom of a plastic pool has an area of 64 square feet. What is the radius to the nearest tenth of a foot? Use 3.14 for π.**

   A. 2.3
   B. 4.5
   C. 6.9
   D. 10.2

2. **The area of a circular hand mirror is 200 square centimeters. Find the circumference of the mirror to the nearest tenth of a centimeter. Use 3.14 for π.**

   A. 25.1
   B. 50.2
   C. 75.3
   D. 100.4

3. **The circumference of a pie is 300 centimeters. Find the area of one-fourth of the pie to the nearest tenth of a square centimeter. Use 3.14 for π.**

   A. 1,793.6
   B. 2,284.8
   C. 7,174.4
   D. 14,348.8

4. **A regular hexagon has a rotational order of 6. What is the smallest number of degrees for the figure to be rotated onto itself?**

   A. 30°
   B. 60°
   C. 90°
   D. 120°

5. **A right triangle has a base of 6 inches and a hypotenuse of 10 inches. Find the height in inches of the triangle if the area is 24 square inches.**

   A. 4
   B. 6
   C. 8
   D. 10

6. **ΔGHI has points $G(2, 7)$, $H(-3, -8)$, and $I(-6, 0)$. After a transformation, the points are $G'(7, 2)$, $H'(-8, -3)$, and $I'(0, -6)$. What is the transformation between the points?**

   A. Reflection across the x-axis
   B. Reflection across the y-axis
   C. Reflection across the line of $y = x$
   D. Reflection across the line of $y = -x$

7. **Name the right angle in the diagram.**

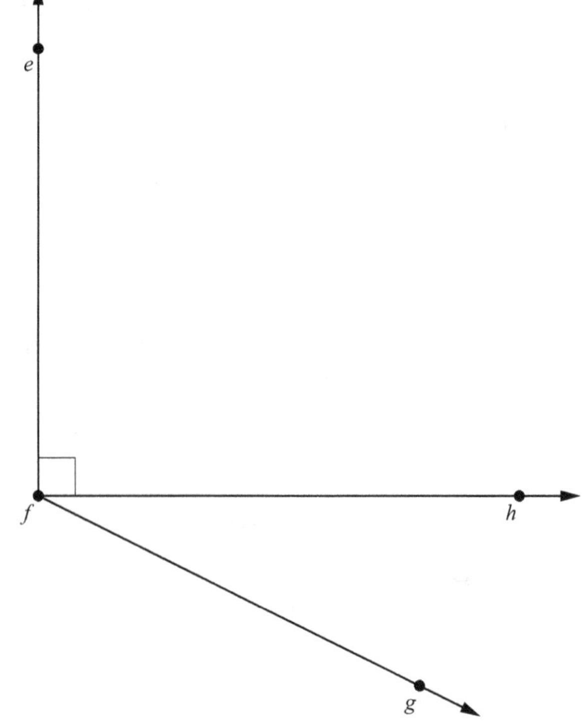

   A. $\angle EHF$
   B. $\angle EFG$
   C. $\angle EFH$
   D. $\angle EGF$

8. Draw a rectangle with the coordinates (5,7), (5,1), (1,1), (1,7).

A.

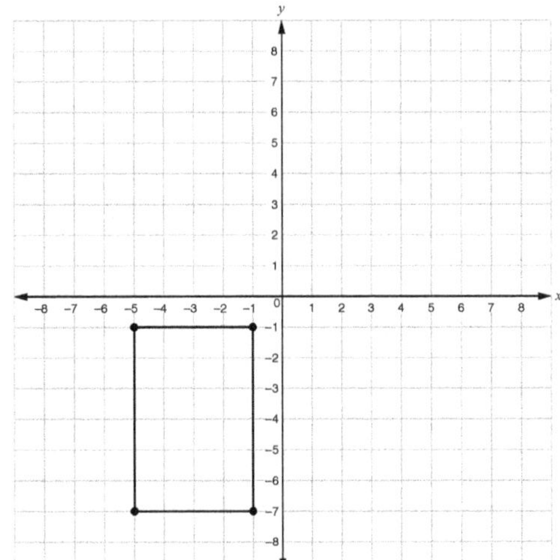

C.

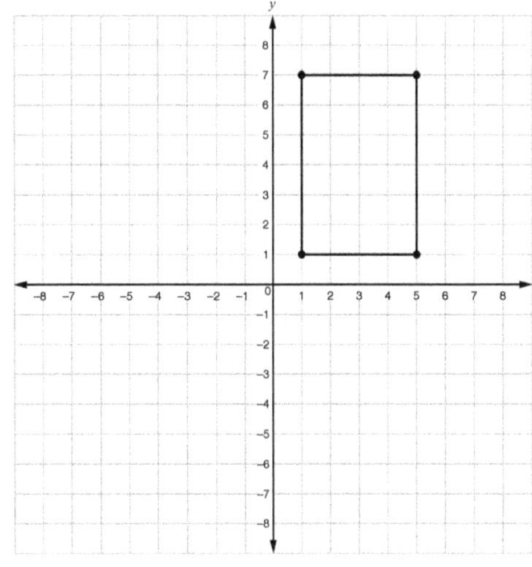

B.

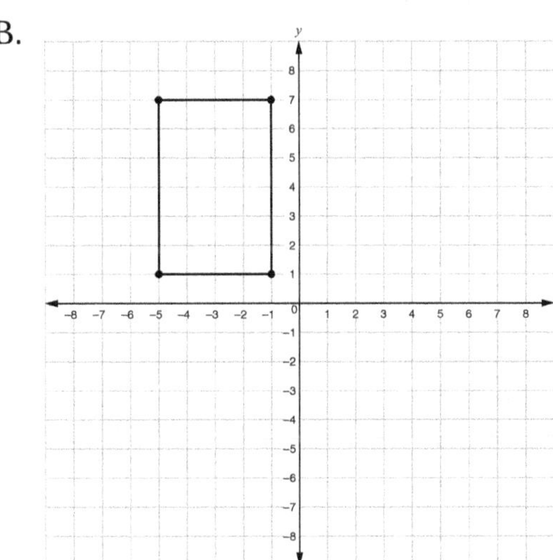

D.

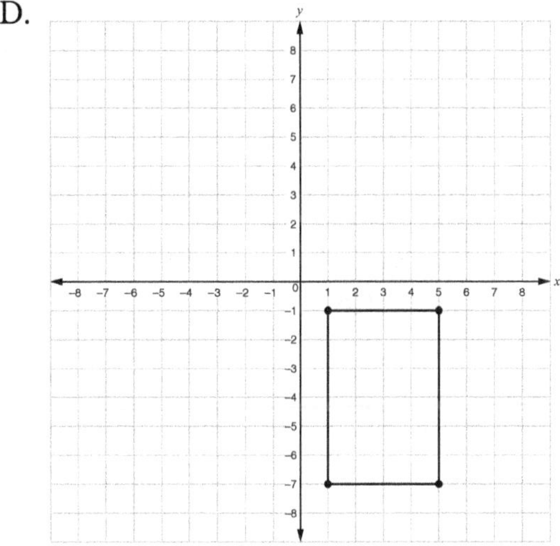

9. The volume of a cone is 28π cubic inches, and its diameter is 2 inches. What is the height of the cone?

A. 2 inches

B. 4 inches

C. 6 inches

D. 8 inches

10. A hemi-sphere has a radius of 6 centimeters. Find the volume in cubic centimeters.

A. 72π

B. 144π

C. 288π

D. 576π

11. A rectangular pyramid has a height of 7 meters and a volume of 112 cubic meters. Find the area of the base in square meters.

A. 16

B. 28

C. 42

D. 48

12. A right rectangular prism has dimensions of 3 inches by 6 inches by 9 inches. What is the surface area in square inches?

A. 162

B. 198

C. 232

D. 286

Chapter 11 Geometry Practice Quiz 1 – Answer Key

1. B. The correct solution is 4.5 because $A = \pi r^2; 64 = 3.14r^2; 20.38 = r^2$; $r \approx$ 4.5 feet. **See Lesson: Circles.**

2. B. The correct solution is 50.2. $A = \pi r^2; 200 = 3.14r^2; 63.69 = r^2; r \approx$ 8.0 centimeters. $C = 2\pi r; C = 2(3.14)8.0 \approx$ 50.2 centimeters. **See Lesson: Circles.**

3. A. The correct solution is 1,793.6. $C = 2\pi r; 300 = 2(3.14)r; 300 = 6.28r; r \approx$ 47.8 centimeters. $A = \frac{1}{4}\pi r^2 \approx \frac{1}{4}(3.14)(47.8)^2 \approx \frac{1}{4}3.14(2{,}284.84) \approx$ 1793.6 square centimeters. **See Lesson: Circles.**

4. B. The correct solution is 60°. For a regular hexagon, divide 360° by the six sides to obtain 60°. **See Lesson: Congruence.**

5. C. The correct solution is 8. Substitute the values into the formula, $24 = \frac{1}{2}(6)h$ and simplify the right side of the equation, $24 = 3h$. Divide both sides of the equation by 3, $h = 8$ inches. **See Lesson: Similarity, Right Triangles, and Trigonometry.**

6. C. The correct solution is a reflection across the line of $y = x$ because the points (x, y) become (y, x). **See Lesson: Congruence.**

7. C. The correct solution is $\angle EFH$ because the vertex of the right angle is F and the other two points are E and H. **See Lesson: Congruence.**

8. C. All points are in the first quadrant. **See Lesson: Similarity, Right Triangles, and Trigonometry.**

9. C. The correct solution is 6 inches. Substitute the values into the formula, $2\pi = \frac{1}{3}\pi(1)^2 h$ and simplify using the right side of the equation by applying the exponent and multiplying, $2\pi = \frac{1}{3}\pi(1)h$, $2\pi = \frac{1}{3}\pi h$. Multiply both sides of the equation by 3 to get a solution of 6 inches. **See Lesson: Measurement and Dimension.**

10. B. The correct solution is 144π. Substitute the values into the formula and simplify using the order of operations, $V = \frac{4}{3}\pi r^3 = \frac{4}{3}\pi(6^3) = \frac{4}{3}\pi(216) = 144\pi$ cubic centimeters. **See Lesson: Measurement and Dimension.**

11. D. The correct solution is 48. Substitute the values into the formula, $112 = \frac{1}{3}B(7)$ and simplify the right side of the equation, $112 = \frac{7}{3}B$. Multiply both sides of the equation by the reciprocal, $B = 48$ square meters. **See Lesson: Measurement and Dimension.**

12. B. The correct solution is 198. Substitute the values into the formula and simplify using the order of operations, $SA = 2lw + 2lh + 2hw = 2(3)(6) + 2(6)(9) + 2(9)(3) = 36 + 108 + 54 = 198$ square inches. **See Lesson: Similarity, Right Triangles, and Trigonometry.**

Chapter 12 Statistics and Probability

Interpreting Graphics

This lesson discusses how to create a bar, line, and circle graph and how to interpret data from these graphs. It also explores how to calculate and interpret the measures of central tendency.

Creating a Line, Bar, and Circle Graph

A line graph is a graph with points connected by segments that examines changes over time. The horizontal axis contains the independent variable (the input value), which is usually time. The vertical axis contains the dependent variable (the output value), which is an item that measures a quantity. A line graph will have a title and an appropriate scale to display the data. The graph can include more than one line.

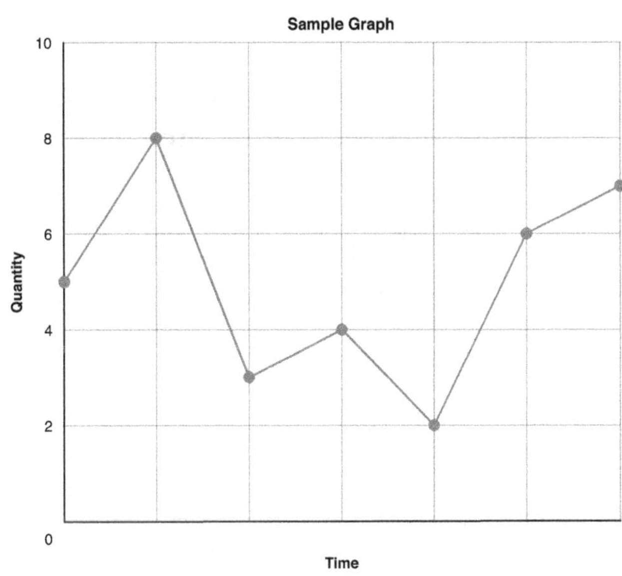

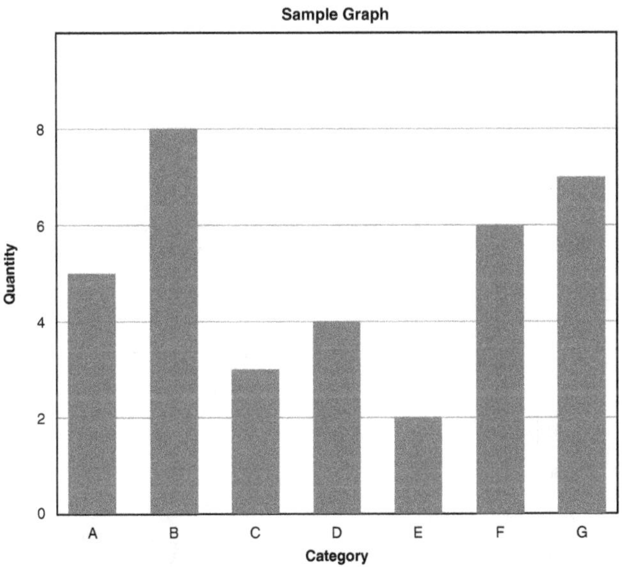

A bar graph uses rectangular horizontal or vertical bars to display information. A bar graph has categories on the horizontal axis and the quantity on the vertical axis. Bar graphs need a title and an appropriate scale for the frequency. The graph can include more than one bar.

BE CAREFUL

Make sure to use the appropriate scale for each type of graph.

A circle graph is a circular chart that is divided into parts, and each part shows the relative size of the value. To create a circle graph, find the total number and divide each part by the total to find the percentage. Then, to find the part of the circle, multiply each percent by 360°. Draw each part of the circle and create a title.

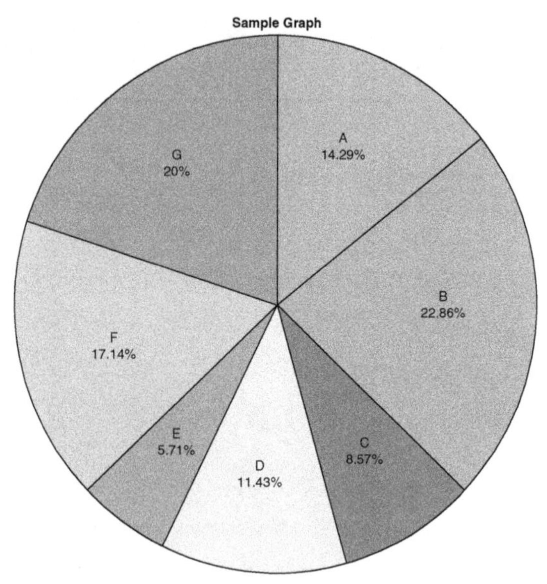

Examples

1. **The table shows the amount of rainfall in inches. Select the line graph that represents this data.**

Day	1	2	3	4	5	6	7	8	9	10	11	12
Rainfall Amount	0.5	0.2	0.4	1.1	1.6	0.9	0.7	1.3	1.5	0.8	0.5	0.1

A.

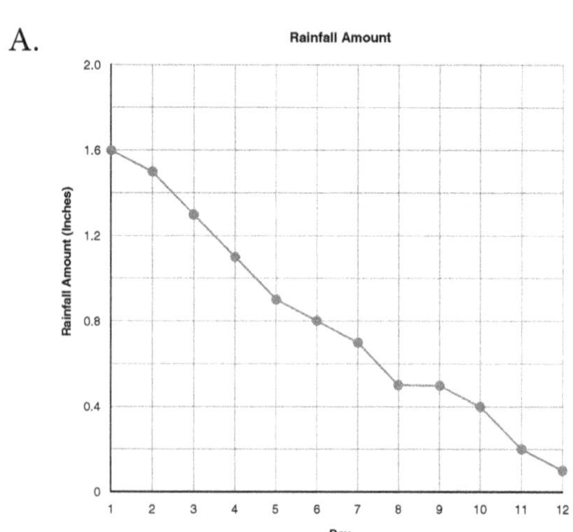

C.

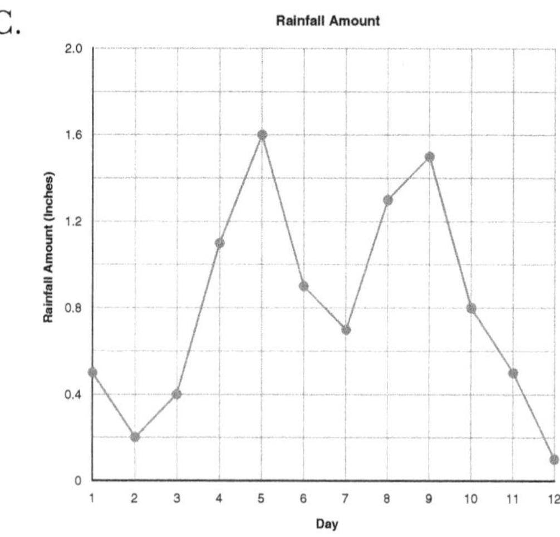

B.

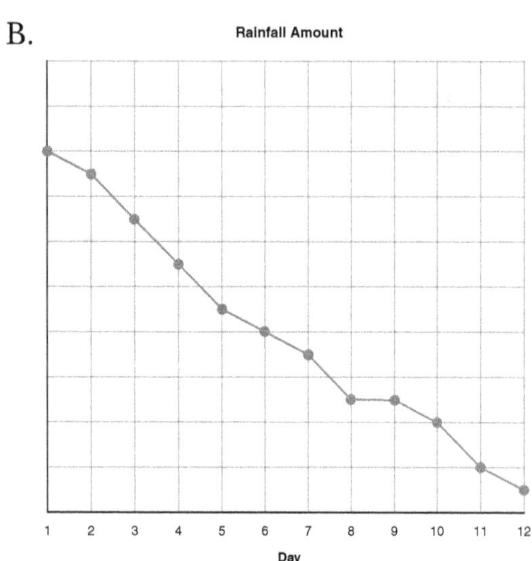

D.

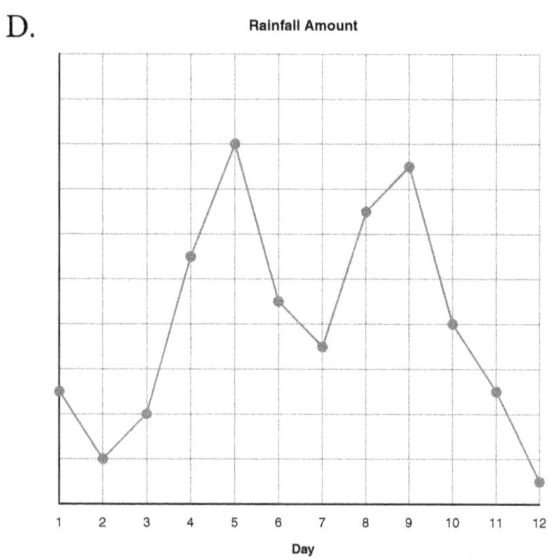

The correct answer is **C**. The graph is displayed correctly for the days with the appropriate labels.

2. **Students were surveyed about their favorite pet, and the table shows the results. Select the bar graph that represents this data.**

Pet	Quantity
Dog	14
Cat	16
Fish	4
Bird	8
Gerbil	7
Pig	3

A.

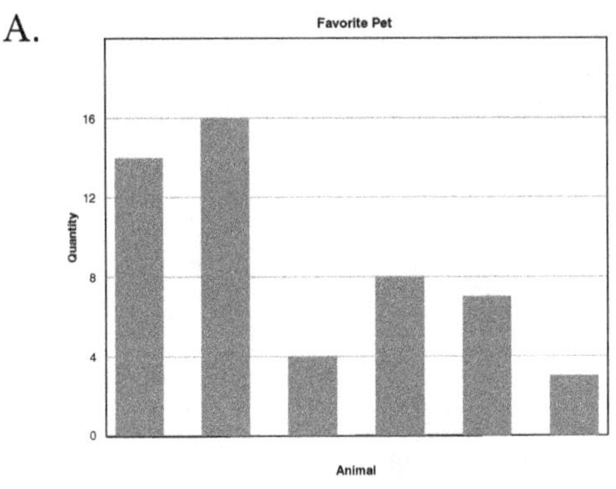

C.

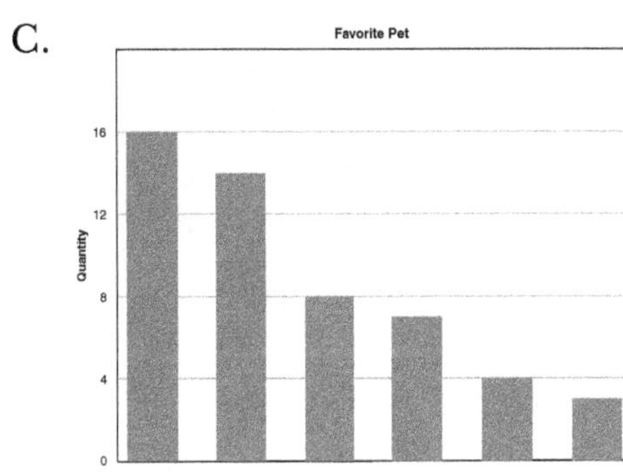

B.

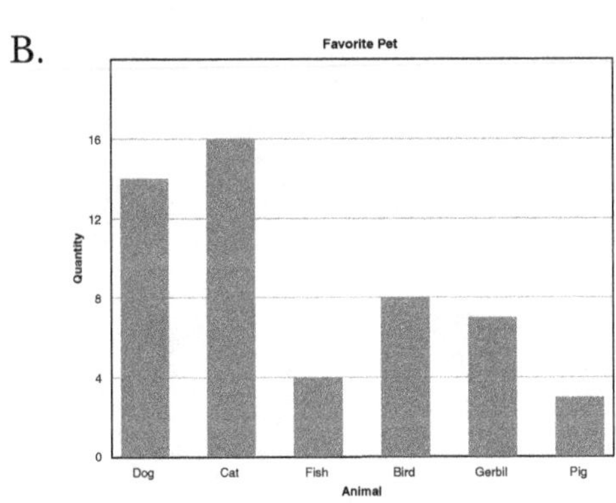

D.

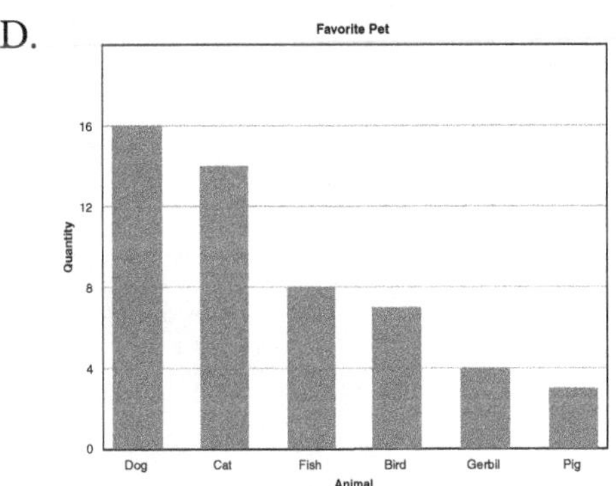

The correct answer is **B**. The bar graph represents each pet correctly and is labeled correctly.

3. The table shows the amount a family spends each month. Select the circle graph that represents the data.

Item	Food/Household Items	Bills	Mortgage	Savings	Miscellaneous
Amount	$700	$600	$400	$200	$100

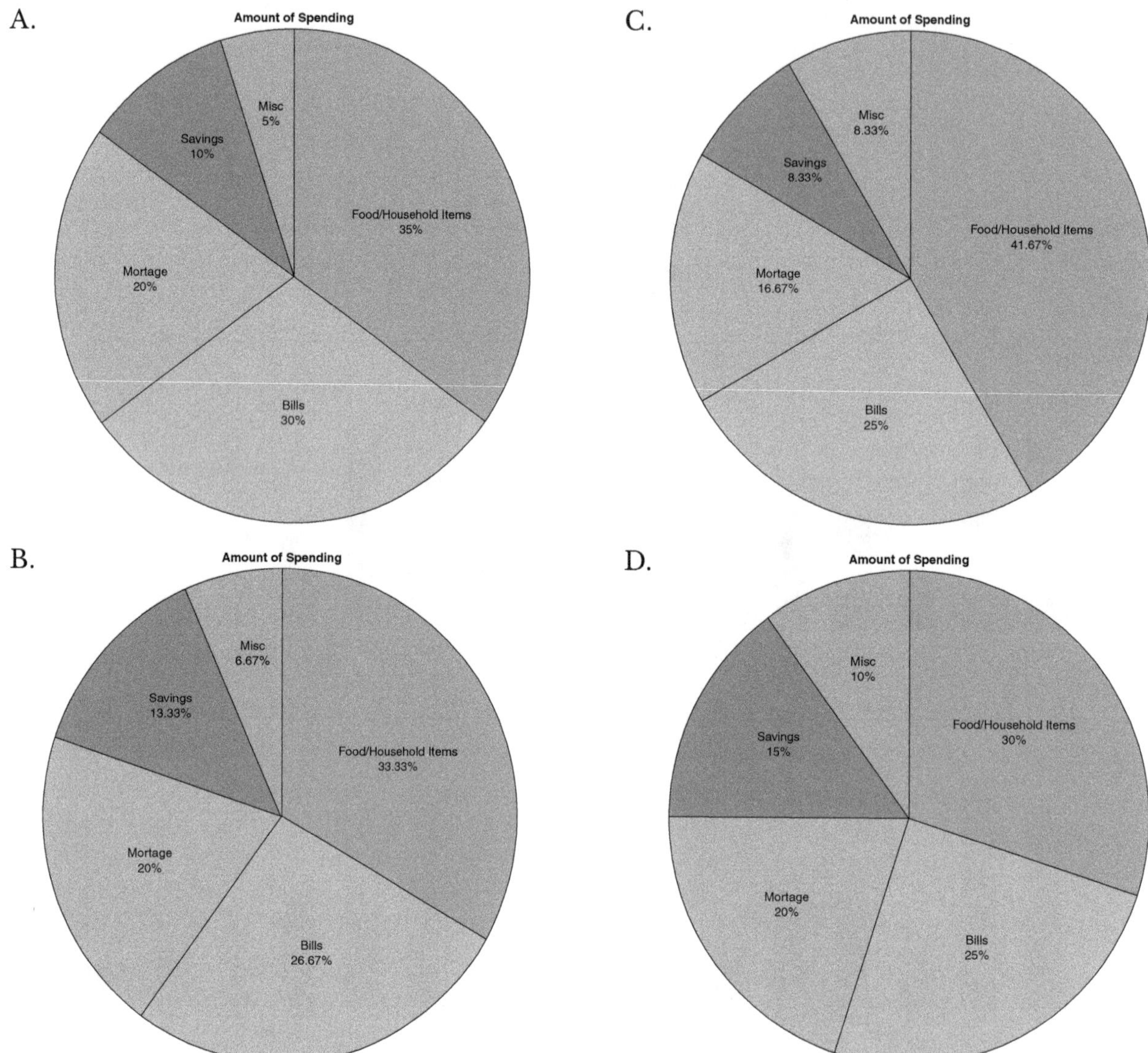

The correct answer is **A.** The total amount spent each month is $2,000. The section of the circle for food and household items is $\frac{700}{2,000} = 0.35 = 35\%$. The section of the circle for bills is $\frac{600}{2,000} = 0.30 = 30\%$. The section of the circle for mortgage is $\frac{400}{2,000} = 0.20 = 20\%$. The section of the circle for savings is $\frac{200}{2,000} = 0.10 = 10\%$. The section of the circle for miscellaneous is $\frac{100}{2,000} = 0.05 = 5\%$.

Interpreting and Evaluating Line, Bar, and Circle Graphs

Graph and charts are used to create visual examples of information, and it is important to be able to interpret them. The examples from Section 1 can show a variety of conclusions.

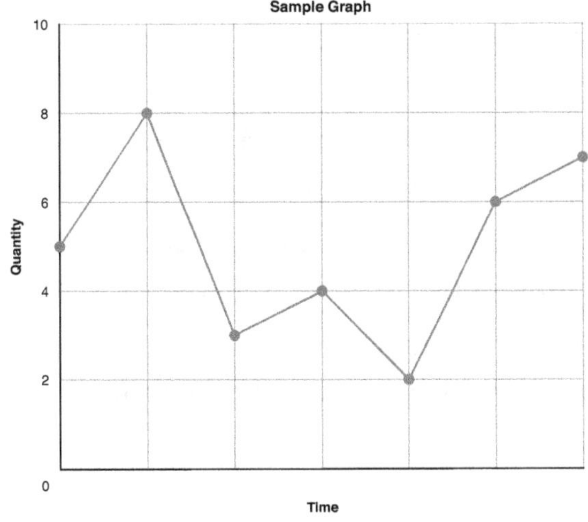

- The minimum value is 2, and the maximum value is 8.
- The largest decrease is between the second and third points.
- The largest increase is between the fifth and sixth points.

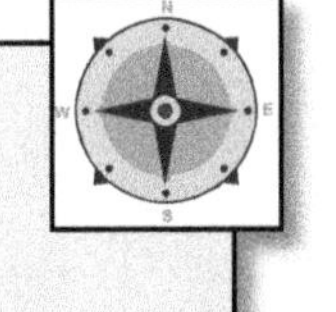

KEEP IN MIND

Read and determine the parts of the graph before answering questions related to the graph.

- Category B is the highest with 8.
- Category E is the lowest with 2.
- There are no categories that are the same.

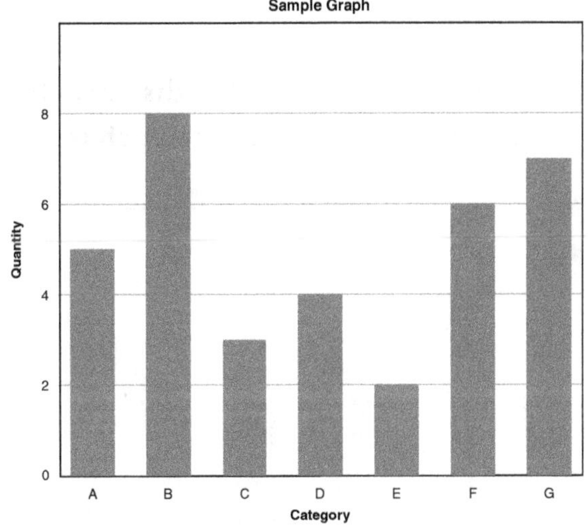

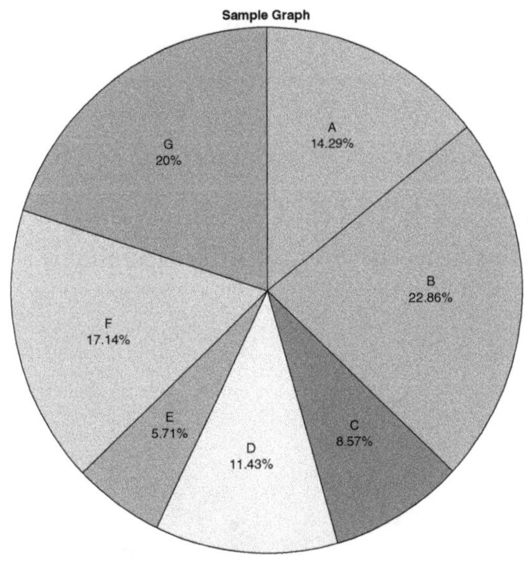

- Category B is the largest with 22.86%.
- Category E is the smallest with 5.71%.
- All of the categories are less than one-fourth of the graph.

Examples

1. **The line chart shows the number of minutes a commuter drove to work during a month. Which statement is true for the line chart?**

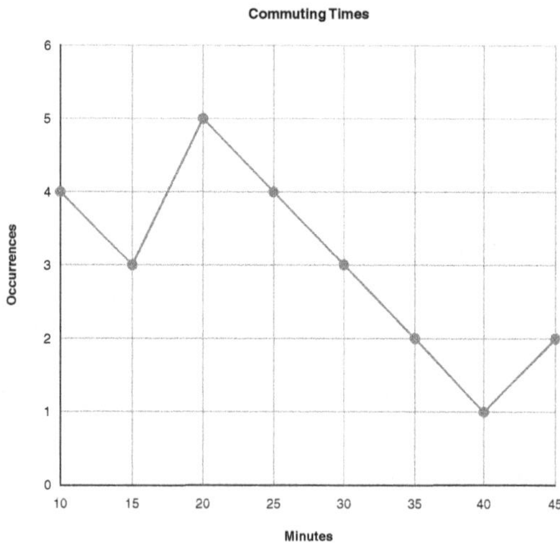

A. The commuter drove 25 minutes to work the most times

B. The commuter drove 25 minutes to work the fewest times.

C. The commuter took 10 minutes and 25 minutes twice during the month.

D. The commuter took 35 minutes and 45 minutes twice during the month.

The correct answer is **D.** The commuter took 35 minutes and 45 minutes twice during the month.

2. **The bar chart shows the distance different families traveled for summer vacation. Which statement is true for the bar chart?**

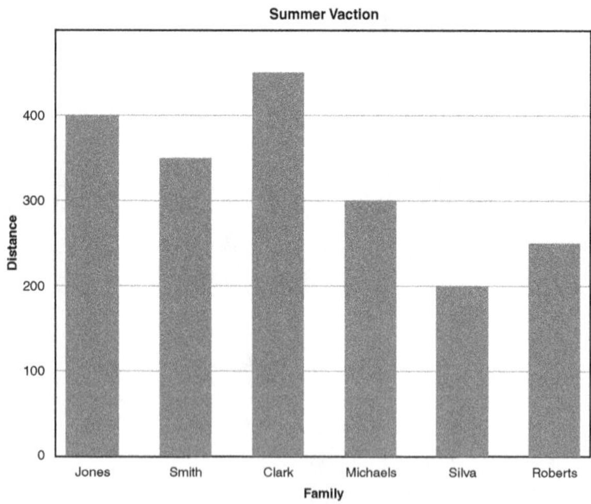

A. All families drove more than 200 miles.

B. The Clark family traveled 250 miles more than the Silva family.

C. The Roberts family traveled more miles than the Michaels family.

D. The Jones family is the only family that traveled 400 miles or more.

The correct answer is **B.** The correct solution is the Clark family traveled 250 miles more than the Silva family. The Clark family traveled 450 miles, and the Silva family traveled 200 miles, making the difference 250 miles.

3. Students were interviewed about their favorite subject in school. The circle graph shows the results. Which statement is true for the circle graph?

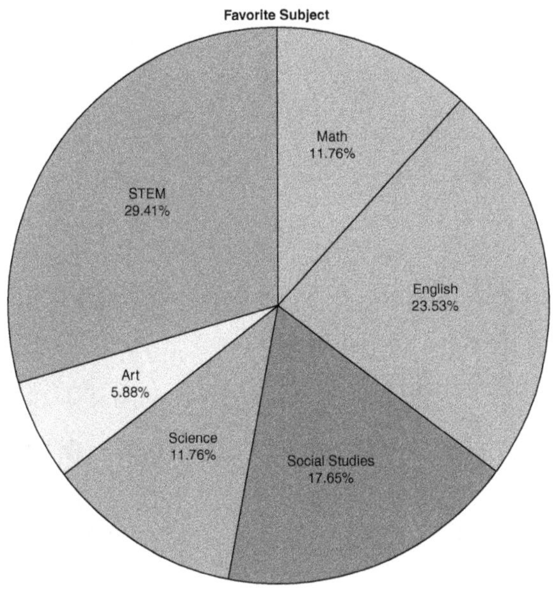

A. Math is the smallest percent for favorite subject.

B. The same number of students favor science and social studies.

C. English and STEM together are more than half of the respondents.

D. English and social students together are more than half of the respondents.

The correct answer is **C**. The correct solution is English and STEM together are more than half of the respondents because these values are more than 50% combined.

Mean, Median, Mode, and Range

The mean, median, mode, and range are common values related to data sets. These values can be calculated using the data set 2, 4, 7, 6, 8, 5, 6, and 3.

The mean is the sum of all numbers in a data set divided by the number of elements in the set. The sum of items in the data set is 41. Divide the value of 41 by the 8 items in the set. The mean is 5.125.

The median is the middle number of a data set when written in order. If there are an odd number of items, the median is the middle number. If there are an even number of items, the median is the mean of the middle two numbers. The numbers in order are 2, 3, 4, 5, 6, 6, 7, 8. The middle two numbers are 5 and 6. The mean of the two middle numbers is 5.5, which is the median.

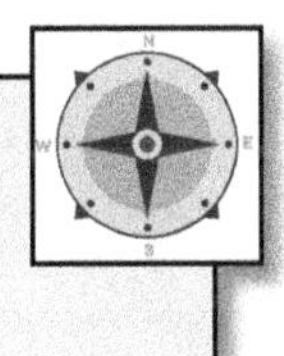

KEEP IN MIND

The mean, median, mode, and range can have the same values, depending on the data set.

The mode is the number or numbers that occur most often. There can be no modes, one mode, or many modes. In the data set, the number 6 appears twice, making 6 the mode.

The range is the difference between the highest and lowest values in a data set. The highest value is 8 and the lowest value is 2, for a range of 6.

Examples

1. **Find the mean and the median for the data set 10, 20, 40, 20, 30, 50, 40, 60, 30, 10, 40, 20, 50, 70, and 80.**

   A. The mean is 40, and the median is 38.

   B. The mean is 38, and the median is 40.

   C. The mean is 36, and the median is 50.

   D. The mean is 50, and the median is 36.

   The correct answer is **B**. The correct solution is the mean is 38 and the median is 40. The sum of all items is 570 divided by 15, which is 38. The data set in order is 10, 10, 20, 20, 20, 30, 30, 40, 40, 40, 50, 50, 60, 70, 80. The median number is 40.

2. **Find the mode and the range for the data set 10, 20, 40, 20, 30, 50, 40, 60, 30, 10, 40, 20, 50, 70, and 80.**

   A. The mode is 20, and the range is 70.

   B. The mode is 40, and the range is 70.

   C. The modes are 20 and 40, and the range is 70.

   D. The modes are 20, 40, and 70, and the range is 70.

   The correct answer is **C**. The correct solution is the modes are 20 and 40 and the range is 70. The modes are 20 and 40 because each of these numbers appears three times. The range is the difference between 80 and 10, which is 70.

Let's Review!

- A bar graph, line graph, and circle graph are different ways to summarize and represent data.
- The mean, median, mode, and range are values that can be used to interpret the meaning of a set of numbers.

STATISTICAL MEASURES

This lesson explores the different sampling techniques using random and non-random sampling. The lesson also distinguishes among different study techniques. In addition, it provides simulations that compare results with expected outcomes.

Probability and Non-Probability Sampling

A population includes all items within a set of data, while a sample consists of one or more observations from a population.

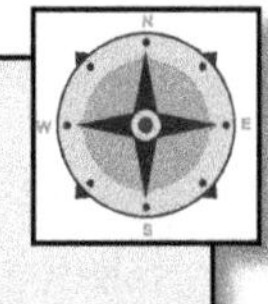

KEEP IN MIND

Probability sampling is random, and non-probability sampling is not random.

The collection of data samples from a population is an important part of research and helps researcher draw conclusions related to populations. Probability sampling creates a sample from a population by using random sampling techniques. Every person within a population has an equal chance of being selected for a sample. Non-probability sampling creates a sample from a population without using random sampling techniques.

There are four types of probability sampling. Simple random sampling is assigning a number to each member of a population and randomly selecting numbers. Stratified sampling uses simple random sampling after the population is split into equal groups. Systematic sampling chooses every n^{th} member from a list or a group. Cluster random sampling uses natural groups in a population: the population is divided into groups, and random samples are collected from groups.

Each type of probability sampling has an advantage and a disadvantage when finding an appropriate sample.

Probability Sampling	Advantage	Disadvantage
Simple random sampling	Most cases have a sample representative of a population	Not efficient for large samples
Stratified random sampling	Creates layers of random samples from different groups representative of a population	Not efficient for large samples
Systematic sampling	Creates a sample representative of population without a random number selection	Not as random as simple random sampling
Cluster random sampling	Relatively easy and convenient to implement	Might not work if clusters are different from one another

There are four types of non-probability sampling. Convenience sampling produces samples that are easy to access. Volunteer sampling asks for volunteers or recommendations for a sample. Purposive sampling bases samples on specific characteristics by selecting samples from a group that meets the qualifications of the study. Quota sampling is choosing samples of groups of the subpopulation.

Examples

1. **A factory is studying the quality of beverage samples. There are 50 bottles randomly chosen from one shipment every 60 minutes. What type of sampling is used?**

   A. Systematic sampling
   B. Simple random sampling
   C. Cluster random sampling
   D. Stratified random sampling

   The correct answer is **C.** The correct solution is cluster random sampling because bottles of beverage are selected within specific boundaries.

2. **A group conducting a survey asks a person for his or her opinion. Then, the group asks the person being surveyed for the names of 10 friends to obtain additional options. What type of sampling is used?**

   A. Quota sampling
   B. Volunteer sampling
   C. Purposive sampling
   D. Convenience sampling

   The correct answer is **B.** The correct solution is volunteer sampling because the group is looking for recommendations.

Census, Surveys, Experiments, Observational Studies

Various sampling techniques are used to collect data from a population. These are in the form of a census, a survey, observational studies, or experiments.

KEEP IN MIND

A census includes everyone within a population, and a survey includes every subject of a sample. An observational study involves watching groups randomly, and an experiment involves assigning groups.

A census collects data by asking everyone in a population the same question. Asking everyone at school or everyone at work are examples of a census. A survey collects data on every subject within a sample. The subjects can be determined by convenience sampling or by simple random sampling. Examples of surveys are asking sophomores at school or first shift workers at work.

In an observational study, data collection occurs by watching or observing an event. Watching children who play outside and observing if they drink water or sports drinks is an example. An experiment is way of finding information by assigning people to groups and collecting data on observations. Assigning one group of children to drink water and another group to drink sports drinks after playing and making comparisons is an example of an experiment.

Examples

1. **A school wants to create a census to identify students' favorite subject in school. Which group should the school ask?**

   A. All staff
   B. All students
   C. All sophomores
   D. All male students

   The correct answer is **B**. The correct solution is all students because this gathers information on the entire population.

2. **A researcher records the arrival time of employees at a job based on their actual start time. What type of study is this?**

   A. Census
   B. Survey
   C. Experiment
   D. Observational study

   The correct answer is **D**. The correct solution is observational study because the researcher is observing the time the employees arrive at work.

3. **The local county wants to test the water quality of a stream by collecting samples. What should the county collect?**

   A. The water quality at one spot
   B. The water quality under trees
   C. The water quality under bridges
   D. The water quality at different spots

   The correct answer is **D**. The correct solution is the water quality at different spots because this survey allows for the collection of different samples.

Simulations

A simulation enables researchers to study real-world events by modeling events. Advantages of simulations are that they are quick, easy, and inexpensive; the disadvantage is that the results are approximations. The steps to complete a simulation are as follows:

KEEP IN MIND

A simulation is only useful if the results closely mirror real-world outcomes.

- Describe the outcomes.
- Assign a random value to the outcomes.
- Choose a source to generate the outcomes.
- Generate values for the outcomes until a consistent pattern emerges.
- Analyze the results.

Examples

1. **A family has two children and wants to simulate the gender of the children. Which object would be beneficial to use for the simulation?**

   A. Coin
   B. Four-section spinner
   C. Six-sided number cube
   D. Random number generator

   The correct answer is **B**. The correct solution is a four-section spinner because there are four possible outcomes of the event (boy/boy, boy/girl, girl/boy, and girl/girl).

2. **There are six options from which to choose a meal at a festival. A model using a six-sided number cube is used to represent the simulation.**

Hamburger	Chicken	Hot Dog	Bratwurst	Pork Chop	Fish	Total
1	2	3	4	5	6	
83	82	85	89	86	75	500

   Choose the statement that correctly answers whether the simulation of using a six-sided number cube is consistent with the actual number of dinners sold and then explains why or why not.

   A. The simulation is consistent because it has six equally likely outcomes.
   B. The simulation is consistent because it has two equally likely outcomes.
   C. The simulation is not consistent because of the limited number of outcomes.
   D. The simulation is not consistent because of the unlimited number of outcomes.

   The correct answer is **A**. The correct solution is the simulation is consistent because it has six equally likely outcomes. The six-sided number cube provides consistent outcomes because there is an equal opportunity to select any dinner.

Let's Review!

- Probability (random) sampling and non-probability (not random) sampling are ways to collect data.
- Censuses, surveys, experiments, and observational studies are ways to collect data from a population.
- A simulation is way to model random events and compare the results to real-world outcomes.

STATISTICS & PROBABILITY: THE RULES OF PROBABILITY

This lesson explores a sample space and its outcomes and provides an introduction to probability, including how to calculate expected values and analyze decisions based on probability.

Sample Space

A **sample space** is the set of all possible outcomes. Using a deck of cards labeled 1–10, the sample space is 1, 2, 3, 4, 5, 6, 7, 8, 9, and 10. An **event** is a subset of the sample space. For example, if a card is drawn and the outcome of the event is an even number, possible results are 2, 4, 6, 8, 10.

The **union** of two events is everything in both events, and the notation is $A \bigcup B$. The union of events is associated with the word *or*. For example, a card is drawn that is either a multiple of 3 or a multiple of 4. The set containing the multiples of 3 is 3, 6, and 9. The set containing the multiples of 4 is 4 and 8. The union of the set is 3, 4, 6, 8, and 9.

KEEP IN MIND

The intersection of an event can have no values. The intersection of drawing a card that is even and odd is a set with no values because a card cannot be both even and odd. The complement of an event is the "not," or the opposite of, the event.

The **intersection** of two events is all of the events in both sets, and the notation is $A \bigcap B$. The intersection of events is associated with the word *and*. For example, a card is drawn that is even and a multiple of 4. The set containing even numbers is 2, 4, 6, 8, and 10. The set containing the multiples of 4 is 4 and 8. The intersection is 4 and 8 because these numbers are in both sets.

The **complement** of an event is an outcome that is not part of the set. The complement of an event is associated with the word *not*. A card is drawn and is not a multiple of 5. The set not containing multiples of 5 is 1, 2, 3, 4, 6, 7, 8, and 9. The complement of not a multiple of 5 is 1, 2, 3, 4, 6, 7, 8, and 9.

Examples

Use the following table of the results when rolling two six-sided number cubes.

1, 1	1, 2	1, 3	1, 4	1, 5	1, 6
2, 1	2, 2	2, 3	2, 4	2, 5	2, 6
3, 1	3, 2	3, 3	3, 4	3, 5	3, 6
4, 1	4, 2	4, 3	4, 4	4, 5	4, 6
5, 1	5, 2	5, 3	5, 4	5, 5	5, 6
6, 1	6, 2	6, 3	6, 4	6, 5	6, 6

1. **How many possible outcomes are there for the union of rolling a sum of 3 or a sum of 5?**

   A. 2 B. 4 C. 6 D. 8

   The correct answer is **C.** The correct solution is 6 possible outcomes. There are two options for the first event (2, 1) and (1, 2). There are 4 options for the second event (4, 1), (3, 2), (2, 3), and (1, 4). The union of two events is six possible outcomes.

2. **How many possible outcomes are there for the intersection of rolling a double and a multiple of 3?**

   A. 0 B. 2 C. 4 D. 6

   The correct answer is **B.** The correct solution is 2 possible outcomes. There are six options for the first event (1, 1), (2, 2), (3, 3), (4, 4), (5, 5), and (6, 6). There are 12 options for the second event of the multiple of three. The intersection is (3, 3) and (6, 6) because these numbers meet both requirements.

3. **How many possible outcomes are there for the complement of rolling a 3 and a 5?**

   A. 16 B. 18 C. 27 D. 36

   The correct answer is **A.** The correct solution is 16 possible outcomes. There are 16 options of not rolling a 3 or a 5.

Probability

The **probability** of an event is the number of favorable outcomes divided by the total number of possible outcomes.

BE CAREFUL!

Make sure that you apply the correct formula for the probability of an event.

$$Probability = \frac{\textit{number of favorable outcomes}}{\textit{number of possible outcomes}}$$

Probability is a value between 0 (event does not happen) and 1 (event will happen). For example, the probability of getting heads when a coin is flipped is $\frac{1}{2}$ because heads is 1 option out of 2 possibilities. The probability of rolling an odd number on a six-sided number cube is $\frac{3}{6} = \frac{1}{2}$ because there are three odd numbers, 1, 3, and 5, out of 6 possible numbers.

The probability of an "or" event happening is the sum of the events happening. For example, the probability of rolling an odd number or a 4 on a six-sided number cube is $\frac{4}{6}$. The probability of rolling an odd number is $\frac{3}{6}$, and the probability of rolling a 4 is $\frac{1}{6}$. Therefore, the probability is $\frac{3}{6} + \frac{1}{6} = \frac{4}{6} = \frac{2}{3}$.

The probability of an "and" event happening is the product of the probability of two or more events. The probability of rolling 6 three times in a row is $\frac{1}{216}$. The probability of a single event is $\frac{1}{6}$, and this fraction is multiplied three times to find the probability, $\frac{1}{6} \times \frac{1}{6} \times \frac{1}{6}$. There are cases of "with replacement" when the item is returned to the pile and "without replacement" when the item is not returned to the pile.

The probability of a "not" event happening is 1 minus the probability of the event occurring. For example, the probability of not rolling 6 three times in a row is $1 - \frac{1}{216} = \frac{215}{216}$.

Examples

1. **A deck of cards contains 40 cards divided into 4 colors: red, blue, green, and yellow. Each group has cards numbered 0–9. What is the probability of selecting an 8?**

   A. $\frac{1}{10}$ B. $\frac{1}{8}$ C. $\frac{1}{4}$ D. $\frac{1}{2}$

   The correct answer is **A**. The correct solution is $\frac{1}{10}$. There are 4 cards out of 40 that contain the number 8, making the probability $\frac{4}{40} = \frac{1}{10}$.

2. **A deck of cards contains 40 cards divided into 4 colors: red, blue, green, and yellow. Each group has cards numbered 0–9. What is the probability of selecting an even or a red card?**

   A. $\frac{1}{4}$ B. $\frac{3}{8}$ C. $\frac{5}{8}$ D. $\frac{3}{4}$

   The correct answer is **C**. The correct solution is $\frac{5}{8}$. There are 20 even cards and 10 red cards. The overlap of 5 red even cards is subtracted from the probability, $\frac{20}{40} + \frac{10}{40} - \frac{5}{40} = \frac{25}{40} = \frac{5}{8}$.

3. **A deck of cards contains 40 cards divided into 4 colors: red, blue, green, and yellow. Each group has cards numbered 0–9. What is the probability of selecting a blue card first, replacing the card, and selecting a 9?**

   A. $\frac{1}{100}$ B. $\frac{1}{80}$ C. $\frac{1}{40}$ D. $\frac{1}{20}$

   The correct answer is **C**. The correct solution is $\frac{1}{40}$. There are 10 blue cards and 4 cards that contain the number 9. The probability of the event is $\frac{10}{40} \times \frac{4}{40} = \frac{40}{1600} = \frac{1}{40}$.

4. **A deck of cards contains 40 cards divided into 4 colors: red, blue, green, and yellow. Each group has cards numbered 0–9. What is the probability of NOT selecting a green card?**

   A. $\frac{1}{4}$ B. $\frac{3}{8}$ C. $\frac{1}{2}$ D. $\frac{3}{4}$

   The correct answer is **D**. The correct solution is $\frac{3}{4}$. There are 10 cards that are green, making the probability of NOT selecting a green card $1 - \frac{10}{40} = \frac{30}{40} = \frac{3}{4}$.

Calculating Expected Values and Analyzing Decisions Based on Probability

The **expected value** of an event is the sum of the products of the probability of an event times the payoff of an event. A good example is calculating the expected value for buying a lottery ticket. There is a one in a hundred million chance that a person would win $50 million. Each ticket costs $2. The expected value is

$$\frac{1}{100{,}000{,}000}(50{,}000{,}000-2) + \frac{99{,}999{,}999}{100{,}000{,}000}(-2) = \frac{49{,}999{,}998}{100{,}000{,}000} - \frac{199{,}999{,}998}{100{,}000{,}000} = -\frac{150{,}000{,}000}{100{,}000{,}000} = -\$1.50$$

On average, one should expect to lose $1.50 each time the game is played. Analyzing the information, the meaning of the data shows that playing the lottery would result in losing money every time.

BE CAREFUL!

The expected value will not be the same as the actual value unless the probability of winning is 100%.

Examples

1. **What is the expected value of an investment if the probability is $\frac{1}{5}$ of losing \$1,000, $\frac{1}{4}$ of no gain, $\frac{2}{5}$ of making \$1,000, and $\frac{3}{20}$ of making \$2,000?**

   A. \$0 B. \$200 C. \$500 D. \$700

   The correct answer is **C**. The correct solution is \$500. The expected value is $\frac{1}{5}(-1{,}000) + \frac{1}{4}(0) + \frac{2}{5}(1{,}000) + \frac{3}{20}(2{,}000) = -200 + 0 + 400 + 300 = \$500$.

2. **The table below shows the value of the prizes and the probability of winning a prize in a contest.**

Prize	\$10	\$100	\$5,000	\$50,000
Probability	1 in 50	1 in 1,000	1 in 50,000	1 in 250,000

   Calculate the expected value.

   A. \$0.10 B. \$0.20 C. \$0.50 D. \$0.60

   The correct answer is **D**. The correct solution is \$0.60. The probability for each event is

Prize	\$10	\$100	\$5,000	\$50,000	Not Winning
Probability	1 in 50 = 0.02	1 in 1,000 = 0.001	1 in 50,000 = 0.00002	1 in 250,000 = 0.000004	0.978976

   The expected value is $0.02(10) + 0.001(100) + 0.00002(5{,}000) + 0.000004(50{,}000) + 0.978976(0) =$

   $0.2 + 0.1 + 0.1 + 0.2 + 0 = \$0.60$.

3. **Which option results in the largest loss on a product?**

   A. 40% of gaining \$100,000 and 60% of losing \$100,000

   B. 60% of gaining \$250,000 and 40% of losing \$500,000

   C. 30% of gaining \$400,000 and 70% of losing \$250,000

   D. 60% of gaining \$250,000 and 40% of losing \$450,000

   The correct answer is **C**. The correct solution is 30% of gaining \$400,000 and 70% of losing \$250,000. The expected value is $0.30(400{,}000) + 0.7(-250{,}000) = 120{,}000 + (-175{,}000) = -55{,}000$.

Let's Review!

- The sample space is the number of outcomes of an event. The union, the intersection, and the complement are related to the sample space.
- The probability of an event is the number of possible events divided by the total number of outcomes. There can be "and," "or," and "not" probabilities.
- The expected value of an event is based on the payout and probability of an event occurring.

INTERPRETING CATEGORICAL AND QUANTITATIVE DATA

This lesson discusses how to represent and interpret data for a dot plot, a histogram, and a box plot. It compares multiple sets of data by using the measures of center and spread and examines the impact of outliers.

Representing Data on a Number Line

There are two types of data: quantitative and categorical. Quantitative variables are numerical, such as number of people in a household, bank account balance, and number of cars sold. Categorical variables are not numerical, and there is no inherent way to order them. Example are classes in college, types of pets, and party affiliations. The information for these data sets can be arranged on a number line using dot plots, histograms, and box plots.

A dot plot is a display of data using dots. The dots represent the number of times an item appears. Below is a sample of a dot plot.

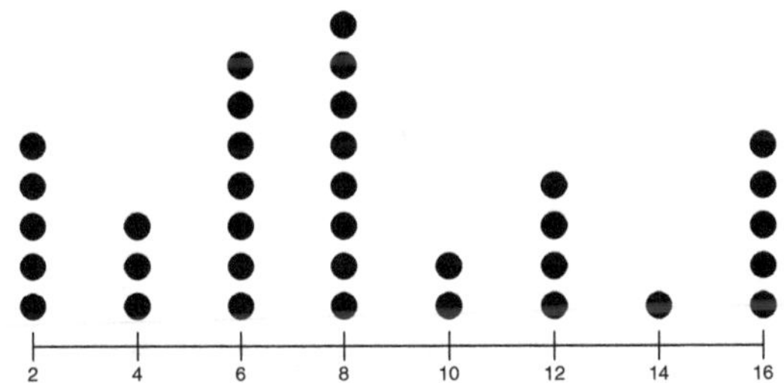

The mean and median can be determined by looking at a dot plot. The mean is the sum of all items divided by the number of dots. The median is the middle dot or the average of the middle two dots.

A histogram is a graphical display that has bars of various heights. It is similar to a bar chart, but the numbers are grouped into ranges. The bins, or ranges of values, of a histogram have equal lengths, such as 10 or 50 units. Continuous data such as weight, height, and amount of time are examples of data shown in a histogram. In the histogram to the right, the bin length is 8 units.

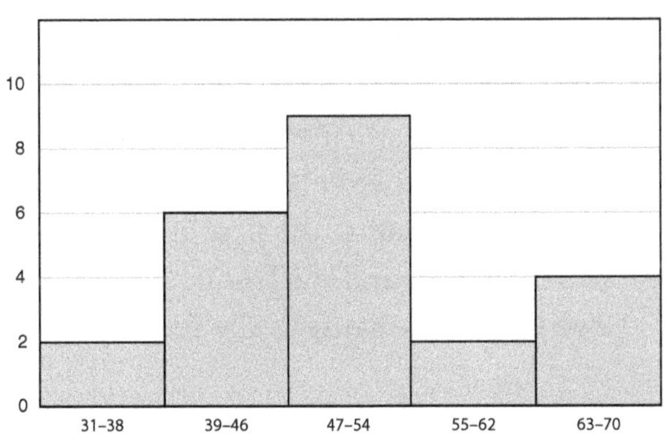

It is not possible to calculate the mean and median by looking at a histogram because there is a bin size rather than a single value on the horizontal axis. Histograms are beneficial when working with a large set of data.

BE CAREFUL!

Make sure to carefully interpret the data for any graphical display.

A box plot (or box-and-whisker plot) is a graphical display of the minimum, first quartile, median, third quartile, and maximum of a set of data. Recall the minimum is the smallest value and the maximum is the largest value in a set of data. The median is the middle number when the data set is written in order. The first quartile is the middle number between the minimum and the median. The third quartile is the middle number between the median and the maximum.

In the data display below, the minimum is 45, the first quartile is 50, the median is 57, the third quartile is 63, and the maximum is 75. With most box-and-whisker plots, the data is not symmetrical.

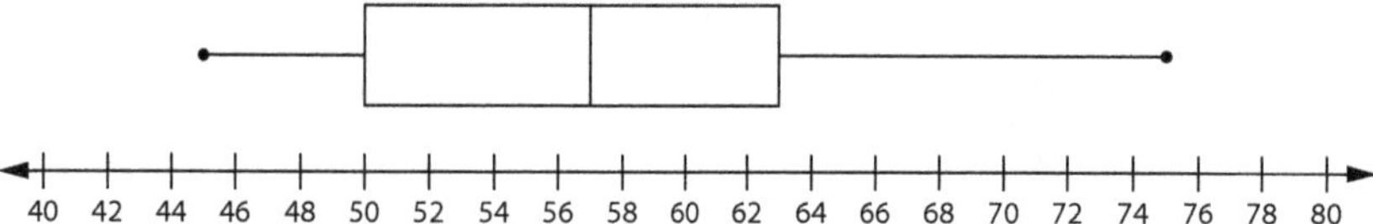

Example

The histogram below shows a basketball team's winning margin during the season. Which statement is true for the histogram?

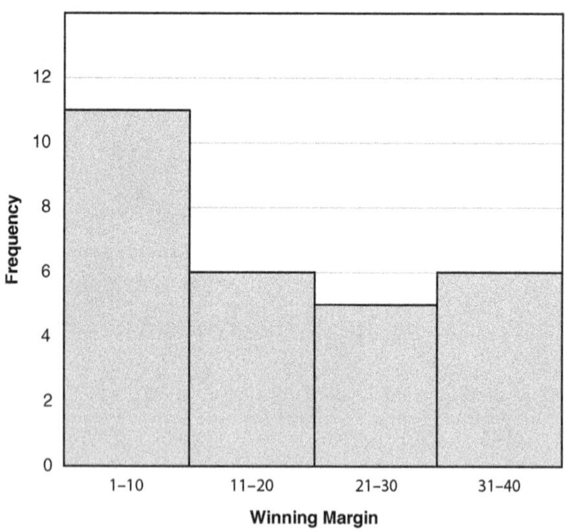

A. The team played a total of 30 games.

B. The frequency for 20–30 points is the same as for 30–40 points.

C. The sum of the frequency for the last two bins is the same as the first bin.

D. The frequency for 0–10 is twice the frequency for any other winning margin.

The correct answer is **C**. The correct solution is the sum of the frequency for the last two bins is the same as the first bin. The frequency of the first bin is 11, the frequency of the third bin is 5, and the frequency of the fourth bin is 6. The sum of the frequency of the last two bins is the same as the first bin.

Comparing Center and Spread of Multiple Data Sets

The measures of center are the mean (average) and median (middle number when written in order). These values describe the expected value of a data set. Very large or very small numbers affect the mean, but they do not affect the median.

The measures of spread are standard deviation (how far the numbers of a data set are from the mean) and interquartile range (the difference between the third and first quartile values).

To find the standard deviation:

- Find the mean.
- Find the difference between the mean and each member of the date set and square that result.
- Find the mean of the squared differences from the previous step.
- Apply the square root.

The larger the value for the standard deviation, the greater the spread of values from the mean. The larger the value for the interquartile range, the greater the spread of the middle 50% of values from the median.

Symmetric data has values that are close together, and the mean, median, and mode occur near the same value. The mean and standard deviation are used to explain multiple data sets and are evident in dot plots.

For example, consider this data set.

10, 10, 11, 11, 11, 12, 12, 12, 12, 12, 13, 13, 13, 14, 14

The mean is found by finding the sum of the numbers in the data set and dividing it by the number of items in the set, as follows:

$$10 + 10 + 11 + 11 + 11 + 12 + 12 + 12 + 12 + 12 + 13 + 13 + 13 + 14 + 14 = 180 \div 15 = 12.$$

The standard deviation calculation is shown in the table below.

Data	Data – Mean	(Data – Mean)^2
10	−2	4
10	−2	4
11	−1	1
11	−1	1
11	−1	1
12	0	0
12	0	0
12	0	0
12	0	0

Data	Data – Mean	(Data – Mean)^2
12	0	0
13	1	1
13	1	1
13	1	1
14	2	4
14	2	4

The sum of the last column is 22. The standard deviation is $\sqrt{\frac{22}{15}} \approx 1.211$.

Next, consider this data set.

8, 8, 9, 10, 11, 12, 12, 12, 12, 12, 13, 14, 15, 16, 16

The mean is $8 + 8 + 9 + 10 + 11 + 12 + 12 + 12 + 12 + 12 + 13 + 14 + 15 + 16 + 16 = 180 \div 15 = 12$.

The standard deviation calculation is shown in the table below.

Data	Data – Mean	(Data – Mean)^2
8	−4	16
8	−4	16
9	−3	9
10	−2	4
11	−1	1
12	0	0
12	0	0
12	0	0
12	0	0
12	0	0
13	1	1
14	2	4
15	3	9
16	4	16
16	4	16

The sum of the last column is 92. The standard deviation is $\sqrt{\frac{92}{15}} \approx 2.476$.

Therefore, the second set of data has values that are farther from the mean than the first data set.

When data is skewed, a group of its values are close and the remaining values are evenly spread. The median and interquartile range are used to explain multiple data sets and are evident in dot plots and box plots.

KEEP IN MIND

Compare the same measure of center or variation to draw accurate conclusions when comparing data sets.

The data set 10, 10, 11, 11, 11, 11, 11, 11, 12, 12, 12, 13, 13, 14, 15 has a median of 11 and an interquartile range of 2. The data set 10, 11, 12, 12, 13, 13, 14, 14, 14, 14, 14, 14, 14, 15, 15 has a median of 14 and an interquartile range of 2. The median is greater in the second data set, but the spread of data is the same for both sets of data.

Example

The box plots below show the heights of students in inches for two classes. Choose the statement that is true for the median and the interquartile range.

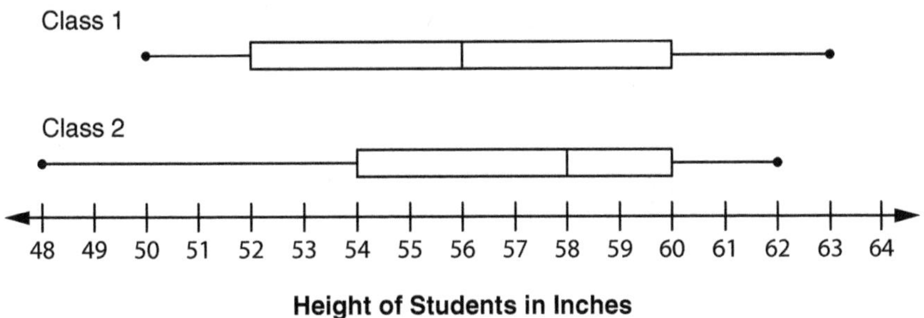

A. The median and interquartile range are greater for class 1.

B. The median and interquartile range are greater for class 2.

C. The median is greater for class 1, and the interquartile range is greater for class 2.

D. The median is greater for class 2, and the interquartile range is greater for class 1.

The correct answer is **D**. The correct solution is the median is greater for class 2, and the interquartile range is greater for class 1. The median is 58 inches for class 2 and 56 inches for class 1. The interquartile range is 8 inches for class 1 and 6 inches for class 2.

Determining the Effect of Extreme Data Points

An outlier is a value that is much smaller or much larger than rest of the values in a data set. This value has an impact on the mean and standard deviation values and occasionally has an impact on the median and interquartile range values.

The data set of 10, 10, 11, 11, 11, 12, 12, 12, 12, 12, 13, 13, 13, 14, 14 has a mean of 12 and a standard deviation of 1.211. If an outlier of 50 is added, the data set has a mean of has a mean of 14.38 and a standard deviation of 9.273. The outlier has increased the mean by more than 2, and the spread of the data has increased significantly.

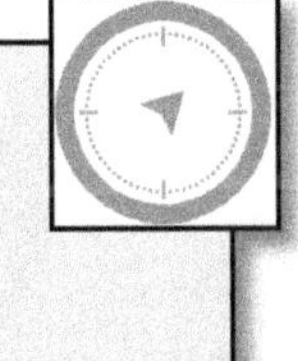

BE CAREFUL!

There may be a high outlier and a low outlier that may not have an impact on data.

The data set 10, 10, 11, 11, 11, 11, 11, 11, 12, 12, 12, 13, 13, 14, 15 has a median of 11 and an interquartile range of 2. If an outlier of 50 is added, the median slightly increases to 11.5 and the interquartile range remains 2.

Example

A little league basketball team scores 35, 38, 40, 36, 41, 42, 39, 35, 29, 32, 37, 33 in its first 12 games. In its next game, the team scores 12 points. Which statement describes the mean and standard deviation?

A. The mean increases, and the standard deviation increases.

B. The mean decreases, and the standard deviation increases.

C. The mean increases, and the standard deviation decreases.

D. The mean decreases, and the standard deviation decreases.

The correct answer is **B**. The correct solution is the mean decreases, and the standard deviation increases. The outlier value is lower than all other values, which results in a decrease for the mean. The standard deviation increases because the outlier of 12 is a value far away from the mean.

Let's Review!

- Dot plots, histograms, and box plots summarize and represent data on a number line.
- The mean and standard deviation are used to compare symmetric data sets.
- The median and interquartile range are used to compare skewed data sets.
- Outliers can impact measures of center and spread, particularly mean and standard deviation.

Chapter 12 Statistics and Probability Practice Quiz 1

1. **Two companies have made a chart of paid time off. Which statement describes the mean and standard deviation?**

Paid Time off for Employees at Company A

Paid Time off for Employees at Company B

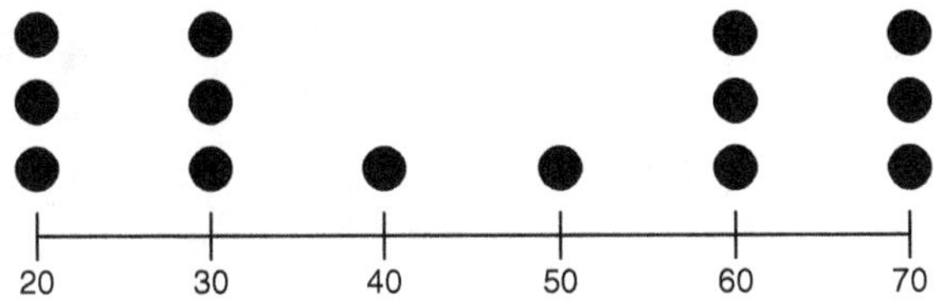

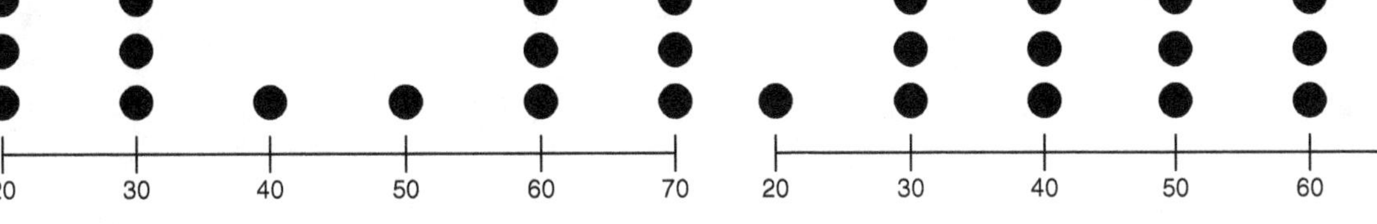

A. The means are the same, but the standard deviation is smaller for Company B.

B. The means are the same, but the standard deviation is smaller for Company A.

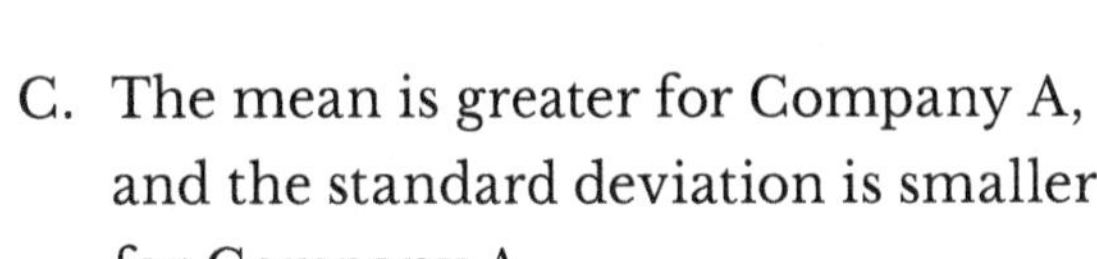

C. The mean is greater for Company A, and the standard deviation is smaller for Company A.

D. The mean is greater for Company B, and the standard deviation is smaller for Company B.

2. **A basketball player scores 18, 17, 20, 23, 15, 24, 22, 28, 5. What is the effect of removing the outlier on the mean and standard deviation?**

A. The mean and the standard deviation increase.

B. The mean and the standard deviation decrease.

C. The standard deviation increases, but the mean decreases.

D. The standard deviation decreases, but the mean increases.

3. **Find the median from the dot plot.**

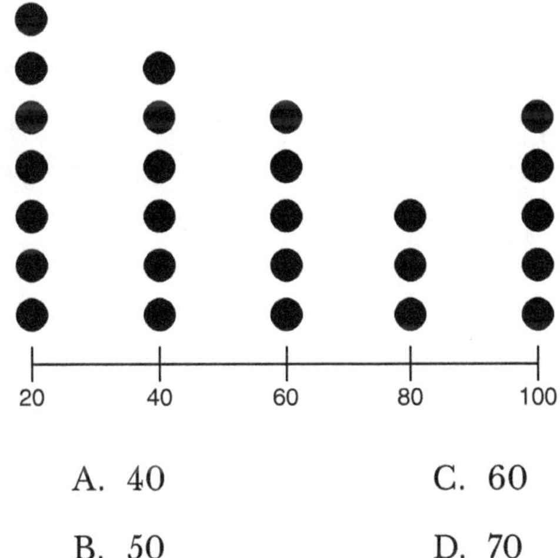

A. 40

B. 50

C. 60

D. 70

4. The table shows the number of students in grades kindergarten through sixth grade. Select the correct bar graph for this data.

Grade	Kindergarten	1st	2nd	3rd	4th	5th	6th
Number of Students	135	150	140	155	145	165	170

A.

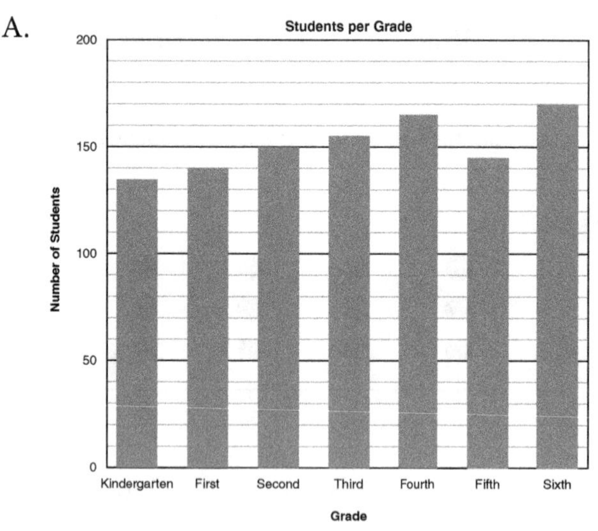

C.

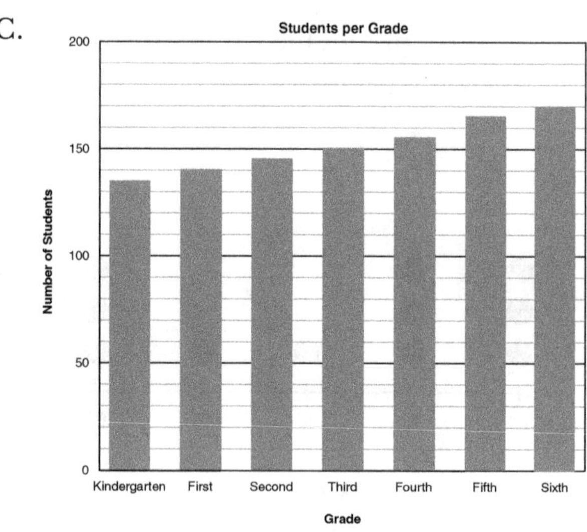

B.

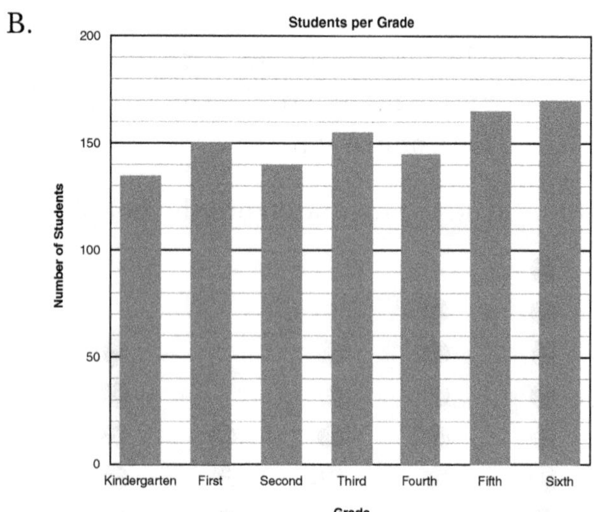

D.

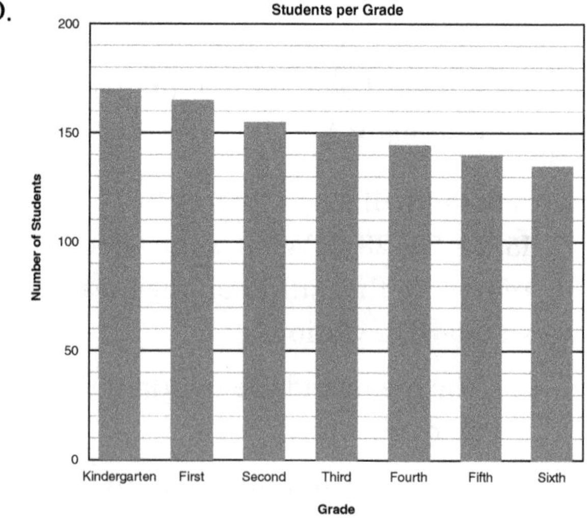

5. **The bar chart shows the number of items collected for a charity drive. Which statement is true for the bar chart?**

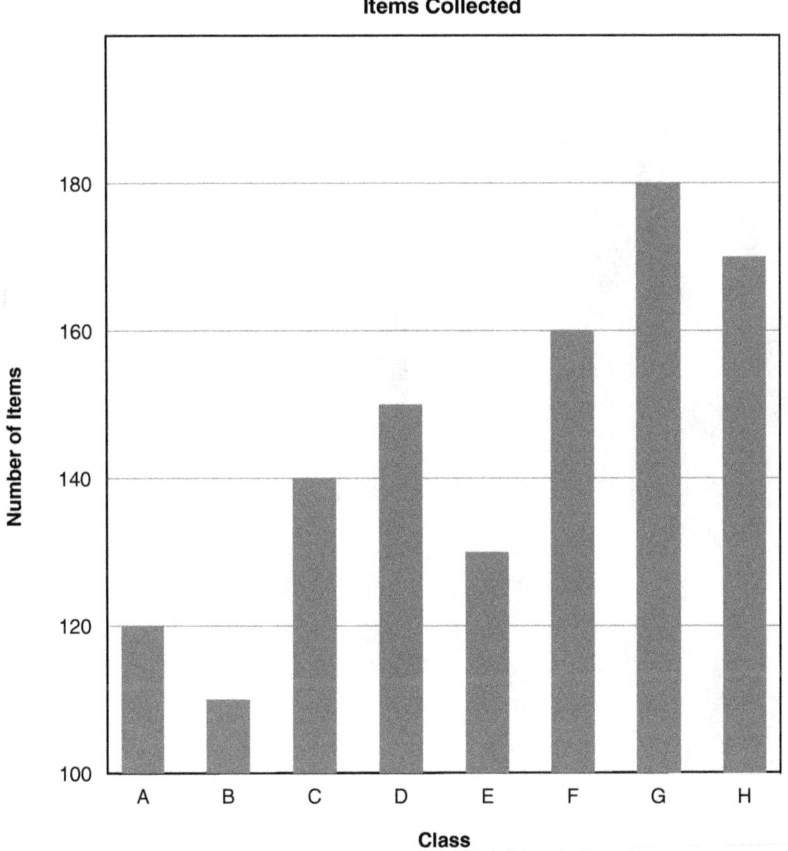

A. Classes F, G, and H each collected more than 150 items.

B. Classes D, F, and G each collected more than 150 items.

C. Classes C, D, and E each collected more than 140 items.

D. Classes A, B, and C each collected more than 140 items.

6. **The circle graph shows the number of votes for each candidate. How many votes were cast for candidate D if there were 25,000 voters?**

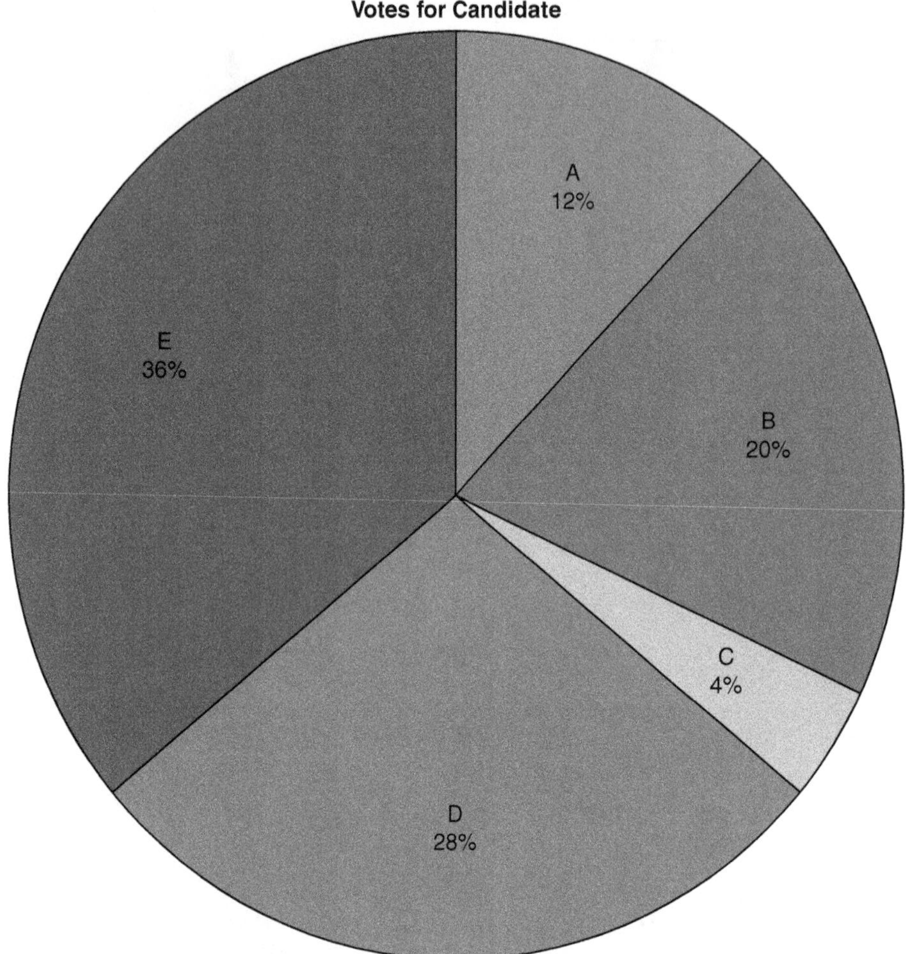

A. 3,000 votes
B. 5,000 votes
C. 7,000 votes
D. 9,000 votes

7. **A factory is investigating defects in screwdrivers that have been placed in containers to be shipped to stores. Random containers are selected for the team leader to review. What type of sampling is used?**

A. Systematic sampling
B. Simple random sampling
C. Cluster random sampling
D. Stratified random sampling

8. **A study looked at a random sample of people and watched their use of social media on mobile devices. The researcher looked at which group of users were happier. What type of study is this?**

A. Census
B. Survey
C. Experiment
D. Observational study

9. There are four available pen colors to choose. A simulation is used to represent the number of times each pen is used.

Red	Blue	Black	Green	Total
1,248	1,260	1,247	1,245	5,000

Choose the statement that correctly explains why or why not seeing these results questions the probability of one out of four for each color.

A. Yes, because of the limited number of outcomes

B. Yes, because not enough simulations were completed

C. No, because the probability of each color is not exactly one out of four

D. No, because the probability of each color is very close to one out of four

10. A bag contains 10 red marbles, 8 black marbles, and 7 white marbles. What is the probability of selecting a black marble first and a red marble second with no replacement?

A. $\frac{8}{25}$

C. $\frac{2}{15}$

B. $\frac{16}{125}$

D. $\frac{7}{75}$

11. Which option results in the greatest gain on an investment?

A. 100% of gaining $1,000

B. 60% of gaining $2,500 and 40% of gaining $0

C. 75% of gaining $1,000 and 25% of gaining $1,500

D. 70% of gaining $1,500 and 30% of gaining $1,000

12. There are 60 students attending classes in town. There are 40 students in dance class and 30 students in art class. Find the number of students in either dance or art class.

A. 30

C. 50

B. 40

D. 60

Chapter 12 Statistics and Probability Practice Quiz 1 – Answer Key

1. A. The correct solution is the means are the same, but the standard deviation is smaller for Company B. The standard deviation is smaller for Company B because more values are closer to the mean. **See Lesson: Interpreting Categorical and Quantitative Data.**

2. D. The correct solution is the standard deviation decreases, but the mean increases. The standard deviation from 6.226 and 3.951 when the low outlier is removed. The mean increases from 19.11 to 20.88 because the outlier, 5, is the lowest value. **See Lesson: Interpreting Categorical and Quantitative Data.**

3. B. The correct solution is 50. The middle two values are 40 and 60, and the average of these values is 50. **See Lesson: Interpreting Categorical and Quantitative Data.**

4. B. The correct solution is B because the number of students for each grade is correct. **See Lesson: Interpreting Graphics.**

5. A. The correct solution is classes F, G, and H collected more than 150 items. Class F collected 160 items, class G collected 180 items, and class H collected 170 items. **See Lesson: Interpreting Graphics.**

6. C. The correct solution is 7,000 votes because 28% of 25,000 is 7,000 voters. **See Lesson: Interpreting Graphics.**

7. D. The correct solution is stratified random sampling because the screwdrivers are placed into containers and the containers are randomly selected. **See Lesson: Statistical Measures.**

8. D. The correct solution is observational study because people were not randomly assigned to group and their behaviors were observed. **See Lesson: Statistical Measures.**

9. D. The correct solution is no, because the probability of each color is very close to one out of four. The more simulations, the closer the results will be to the actual probability of one out of four for each color. **See Lesson: Statistical Measures.**

10. C. The correct solution is $\frac{2}{15}$. There are 8 marbles out of 25 for the first event and 10 marbles out of 24 for the second event. The probability of the event is $\frac{8}{25} \times \frac{10}{24} = \frac{80}{600} = \frac{2}{15}$. **See Lesson: Statistics & Probability: The Rules of Probability.**

11. B. The correct solution is 60% of gaining \$2,500 and 40% of gaining \$0. The expected value is $0.60(2{,}500) + 0.40(0) = \$1{,}500$. **See Lesson: Statistics & Probability: The Rules of Probability.**

12. C. The correct solution 50 because there are 70 students in both classes less the total students is 10 students. Then, subtract 10 students from the total, which is 50 students. **See Lesson: Statistics & Probability: The Rules of Probability.**

SECTION IV. FULL-LENGTH PRACTICE EXAMS

HSPT Practice Exam 1

Section I. Verbal Skills

1. Mary attends Northern Heights High School. Sally attends the same school as Mary. Sally attends Northern Heights High School. If the first to statements are true, the third is

   A. true.
   B. false.
   C. uncertain.

2. Construct : Building

   A. Drive : Car
   B. Ride : Bike
   C. Cook : Dinner
   D. Watch : Television

3. Select the one word that is most nearly the same in meaning as the word in capital letters.

   ABASE

   A. Diminish
   B. Elevate
   C. Praise
   D. Value

4. Select the one word that does not have the same meaning as the word in capital letters.

   AGGREGATE

   A. Amass
   B. Distribute
   C. Gather
   D. Heaped

5. The science fair selects one student in each class for an award. Kayla received an award for her science project. Her classmate Ted also received an award. If the first to statements are true, the third is

   A. true.
   B. false.
   C. uncertain.

6. Select the one word that is most nearly the same in meaning as the word in capital letters.

   BRAZEN

   A. Bold
   B. Humble
   C. Meek
   D. Timid

7. Select the one word that does not have the same meaning as the word in capital letters.

   BUFFET

   A. Assist
   B. Hit
   C. Pound
   D. Strike

8. Couch : Room

   A. Chair : Table
   B. Stove : Kitchen
   C. Staircase : Upstairs
   D. Ladder : Attic

9. Select the one word that is most nearly the same in meaning as the word in capital letters.

   CAPTIVATE

   A. Allure
   B. Dissuade
   C. Disturb
   D. Offend

10. Select the answer option that does not have the same meaning as the word in bold letters.

    DICTATE

    A. Command
    B. Decree
    C. Mandate
    D. Request

11. Taylor and Jacob leave the house at the same time. It takes each of them twenty minutes to arrive to their destination. Taylor and Jacob went to the same destination. If the first to statements are true, the third is

A. true. C. uncertain.

B. false.

12. Select the one word that is most nearly the same in meaning as the word in capital letters.

EXTRAVAGANT

A. Indulgent C. Usual

B. Modest D. Wise

13. Select the answer option that does not have the same meaning as the word in bold letters.

INDICTMENT

A. Absolve C. Prosecute

B. Charge D. Question

14. Shark : Ocean

A. Lion : Jungle

B. Dog : Yard

C. Bird : Sky

D. Dolphin : Aquarium

15. Select the one word that is most nearly the same in meaning as the word in capital letters.

GREGARIOUS

A. Affable C. Reclusive

B. Frigid D. Reserved

16. Select the answer option that does not have the same meaning as the word in bold letters.

LAUD

A. Approve C. Glorify

B. Denounce D. Revere

17. Today is Saturday. Halloween is one week away from today. Halloween will be on a Saturday. If the first to statements are true, the third is

A. true. C. uncertain.

B. false.

18. Select the one word that is most nearly the same in meaning as the word in capital letters.

INCLINATION

A. Averse C. Indifferent

B. Distaste D. Prone

19. Select the one word that does not have the same meaning as the word in capital letters.

MALLEABLE

A. Adaptable C. Mold

B. Firm D. Transform

20. School : Learn

A. Post Office : Write

B. Home : Work

C. Hospital : Doctor

D. Store : Shop

21. Select the one word that is most nearly the same in meaning as the word in capital letters.

MALICIOUS

A. Detrimental C. Pleasant

B. Moral D. Useful

22. Select the one word that does not have the same meaning as the word in capital letters.

PARIAH

A. Friend
B. Outcast
C. Stray
D. Wretch

23. Tracy opens a box of envelopes. Tracy takes out every envelope to mail her letters. The box has no more envelopes inside. If the first to statements are true, the third is

A. true.
B. false.
C. uncertain.

24. Select the one word that is most nearly the same in meaning as the word in capital letters.

PUGNACIOUS

A. Calm
B. Combative
C. Dulcify
D. Tranquil

25. Select the one word that does not have the same meaning as the word in capital letters.

PORTLY

A. Burly
B. Hefty
C. Lean
D. Rotund

26. Select the one word that is most nearly the same in meaning as the word in capital letters.

UNIFORM

A. Abrupt
B. Constant
C. Different
D. Varied

27. Stripes : Tiger

A. Leaves : Tree
B. Seat : Car
C. Stomach : Body
D. Grapes : Juice

28. Select the one word that does not have the same meaning as the word in capital letters.

RETALIATE

A. Counter
B. Fight
C. Repay
D. Sympathize

29. Henry attends the afternoon portion of a golf tournament. The golf tournament began in the morning and ended in the early evening. Henry attended the entire golf tournament. If the first to statements are true, the third is

A. true.
B. false.
C. uncertain.

30. Select the one word that is not related to the others.

A. activate
B. liven
C. mobilize
D. weaken

31. Select the one word that is not related to the others.

A. passive
B. critical
C. gentle
D. mild

32. Select the one word that is most nearly the same in meaning as the word in capital letters.

COMATOSE

A. bustling
B. conscious
C. flourishing
D. lethargic

33. **Select the one word that is not related to the others.**

A. calming
B. distressing
C. endurable
D. reasonable

34. **Mouse : Rodent :: Fern : __________**

A. Plant
B. Crop
C. Vine
D. Weed

35. **Select the one word that is most nearly the same in meaning as the word in capital letters.**

TERSE

A. diffuse
B. gentle
C. polite
D. short

36. **Garfield always finishes his dinner. Garfield eats lasagna for dinner one night. Garfield doesn't finish the lasagna. If the first to statements are true, the third is**

A. true.
B. false.
C. uncertain.

37. **Select the one word that is not related to the others.**

A. adept
B. inept
C. unable
D. unskilled

38. **Select the one word that is not related to the others.**

A. agitate
B. irritate
C. pacify
D. trouble

39. **Select the one word that is most nearly the same in meaning as the word in capital letters.**

SAGACIOUS

A. foolish
B. irrational
C. obtuse
D. wise

40. **Select the one word that is not related to the others.**

A. cheap
B. mild
C. steep
D. temperate

41. **Amiable : Friendly :: Sadistic : __________**

A. Monster
B. Sin
C. Cruel
D. Villain

42. **Oak trees can grow to be over one hundred feet tall. There is a tree in Sam's yard that stands over one hundred feet tall. The tree in Sam's yard is an oak tree. If the first to statements are true, the third is**

A. true.
B. false.
C. uncertain.

43. **Select the one word that is not related to the others.**

A. cheerful
B. depressed
C. heavy
D. pallid

44. **Select the one word that is most nearly the same in meaning as the word in capital letters.**

INCLEMENT

A. bitter
B. clear
C. fair
D. mild

45. **Select the one word that is not related to the others.**

A. drab
B. nebulous
C. opaque
D. transparent

46. **Select the one word that is not related to the others.**

A. creditable
B. kind
C. respectable
D. shameful

47. Lady bugs have spots on their wings. Susan finds a lady bug with ten spots on its wings. Lady bugs always have ten spots on their wings. If the first to statements are true, the third is

A. true.
B. false.
C. uncertain.

48. Pacify : Baby :: Kindle : __________

A. Belongings
B. Supplies
C. Fire
D. Home

49. Select the one word that is not related to the others.

A. difficult
B. effortless
C. laborious
D. profound

50. Select the one word that is not related to the others.

A. consolidate
B. divide
C. loosen
D. disperse

51. Select the one word that is most nearly the same in meaning as the word in capital letters.

RANCID

A. pure
B. rotten
C. sharp
D. sweet

52. Select the one word that is not related to the others.

A. calculated
B. designed
C. hapless
D. lucky

53. There are twenty-four hours in the day. Sally slept for half of the day. Sally was awake for half of the day. If the first to statements are true, the third is

A. true.
B. false.
C. uncertain.

54. Select the one word that is most nearly the same in meaning as the word in capital letters.

PERSPICUOUS

A. clear
B. inconspicuous
C. obscure
D. partial

55. Predict : Psychic :: Analyze : __________

A. Conclude
B. Results
C. Report
D. Judge

56. Select the one word that is not related to the others.

A. dehydrate
B. dry
C. infiltrate
D. translucent

57. Select the one word that is not related to the others.

A. auspicious
B. encouraging
C. foreboding
D. stealthy

58. Insult : Slander :: Respect : __________

A. Compliment
B. Flatter
C. Appease
D. Honor

59. Select the one word that is not related to the others.

A. demolish
B. grow
C. repair
D. win

60. Select the one word that is not related to the others.

A. kind
B. nice
C. sharp
D. weak

SECTION II. QUANTITATIVE SKILLS

1. Look at the series: 3, 6, 9, 12, ... What number should come next?

   A. 13
   B. 14
   C. 15
   D. 16

2. Calculate and compare the values for I, II, and III in order to select the best answer.

   I. $4 + 6 + 6 - 8$
   II. $9 + 8 - 3 - 6$
   III. 8

   A. I ≤ II ≤ III
   B. I ≥ II ≥ III
   C. I + II = III
   D. I = II = III

3. Which sequence is in the correct order from least to greatest?

   A. −10, 0, 1, 8
   B. 0, 1, 8 −10
   C. −10, 8, 1, 0
   D. 8, 1, 0, −10

4. Look at the series: 10, 20, 30, ___, 50... What number is missing?

   A. 31
   B. 35
   C. 40
   D. 45

5. Calculate and compare the values for I, II, and III in order to select the best answer.

   I. $5 + 4 - 7 + 6$
   II. $3 - 12 + 8 + 4$
   III. 2

   A. I ≤ II ≤ III
   B. I ≥ II ≥ III
   C. I + II = III
   D. I = II = III

6. What is the difference between two equal numbers?

   A. Negative
   B. Positive
   C. Zero
   D. Not enough information

7. Look at the series: Z, Y, X, ___, V... Which letter is missing?

   A. L
   B. S
   C. W
   D. Z

8. Calculate and compare the values for I, II, and III in order to select the best answer.

   I. 3×5
   II. $15 \div 3$
   III. 1

   A. I ≤ II ≤ III
   B. I ≥ II ≥ III
   C. I + II = III
   D. I = II = III

9. What is the quotient of a number divided by itself?

   A. −1
   B. 0
   C. 1
   D. Not enough information

10. Look at the series: A, B, C, D... Which letter would come next?

    A. E
    B. Z
    C. F
    D. G

11. Calculate and compare the values for I, II, and III in order to select the best answer.

    I. 14×2
    II. 4×7
    III. 28

    A. I ≤ II ≤ III
    B. I ≥ II ≥ III
    C. I + II = III
    D. I = II = III

12. **What points in the diagram are collinear?**

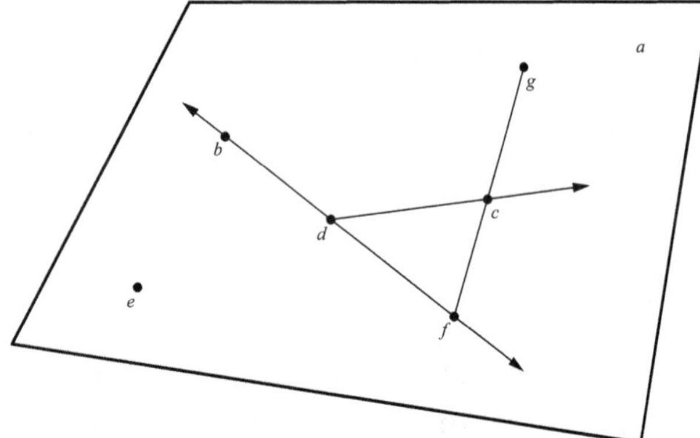

A. Points *D*, *C*, and *F*
B. Points *B*, *D*, and *F*
C. Points *B*, *C*, and *E*
D. Points *B*, *C*, and *D*

13. **Look at the series: X, X2, X3,X4... What variable that would come next in the series?**

A. X^3
B. X^4
C. X^5
D. X^6

14. **Calculate and compare the values for I, II, and III in order to select the best answer.**

I. 0.01
II. 0.90 – 0.81
III. 10 ÷ 100

A. I ≤ II ≤ III
B. I ≥ II ≥ III
C. I + II = III
D. I = II = III

15. **Which fraction is the greatest?**

A. $\frac{5}{12}$
B. $\frac{1}{3}$
C. $\frac{1}{6}$
D. $\frac{1}{4}$

16. **Look at the series: $\sqrt{400}$, $\sqrt{200}$, _____, $\sqrt{50}$...Which number is missing?**

A. $\sqrt{300}$
B. $\sqrt{250}$
C. $\sqrt{100}$
D. $\sqrt{150}$

17. **Calculate and compare the values for I, II, and III in order to select the best answer.**

I. $\frac{1}{2}$
II. $\frac{1}{4}$
III. $\frac{3}{4}$

A. I ≤ II ≤ III
B. I ≥ II ≥ III
C. I + II = III
D. I = II = III

18. **In a backyard, $\frac{1}{6}$ of the yard is a garden, $\frac{2}{5}$ is landscaped, and $\frac{1}{3}$ is for play. How much of the yard is available for other use?**

A. $\frac{1}{10}$
B. $\frac{2}{15}$
C. $\frac{13}{15}$
D. $\frac{9}{10}$

19. **Look at the series: $x^4y^3z^2$, $x^5y^4z^3$, $x^6y^5z^4$, $x^7y^6z^5$... Which expression comes next?**

A. $x^8y^7z^6$
B. $x^8y^8z^8$
C. $x^8y^9z^{10}$
D. $x^8y^{10}z^{12}$

20. **Calculate and compare the values for I, II, and III in order to select the best answer.**

I. $\frac{1}{8}$
II. $\frac{3}{9}$
III. $\frac{9}{10}$

A. I ≤ II ≤ III
B. I ≥ II ≥ III
C. I + II = III
D. I = II = III

21. **A person has $250 in a checking account and writes checks for $70, $85, $60, and $100. There is also a fee of $20. What is the balance of the account?**

A. –$335
B. –$85
C. $335
D. $685

22. **Look at the series: √9, √16, √25, √36... Which number comes next?**

A. √38
B. √42
C. √49
D. √53

23. **Calculate and compare the values for I, II, and III in order to select the best answer.**

I. $\frac{4}{12}$

II. $\frac{5}{5}$

III. $\frac{9}{6}$

A. I ≤ II ≤ III
B. I ≥ II ≥ III
C. I + II = III
D. I = II = III

24. **What shape is used to measure the distance between two cities on a map?**

A. A ray
B. A line
C. A point
D. A line segement

25. **Look at the series: x + 4, x + 8, ______, x + 16, x + 20... Which expression is missing?**

A. x + 10
B. x + 12
C. x + 14
D. x + 16

26. **Calculate and compare the values for I, II, and III in order to select the best answer.**

I. $\frac{2}{3} \times \frac{1}{7}$

II. $\frac{3}{5} \times \frac{5}{6}$

III. $\frac{3}{4}$

A. I ≤ II ≤ III
B. I ≥ II ≥ III
C. I + II = III
D. I = II = III

27. **Which statement about multiplication is true?**

A. The order of two factors in multiplication has no effect on the product.
B. The signs of the two factors in multiplication have no effect on the product.
C. Memorizing a multiplication table is sufficient by itself to determine any product.
D. None of the above.

28. **Look at the series: 0.1, 0.19, ____, 0.35, 0.43... Which decimal is missing?**

A. 0.20
B. 0.23
C. 0.27
D. 0.32

29. **Calculate and compare the values for I, II, and III in order to select the best answer.**

I. $\frac{4}{7} \div \frac{4}{7}$

II. $\frac{1}{6} \div \frac{2}{4}$

III. $\frac{1}{8}$

A. I ≤ II ≤ III
B. I ≥ II ≥ III
C. I + II = III
D. I = II = III

30. **Multiply $\frac{2}{5} \times 3$.**

A. $\frac{2}{15}$
B. $1\frac{1}{5}$
C. $2\frac{3}{5}$
D. $3\frac{2}{5}$

31. **Look at the series: 1.6, 1.2, 0.8, 0.4... Which decimal comes next?**

A. 0.3
B. 0.2
C. 0.1
D. 0

32. Calculate and compare the values for I, II, and III in order to select the best answer.

I. $\frac{3}{5} \times \frac{2}{3}$

II. $\frac{1}{3} \div \frac{5}{9}$

III. $\frac{14}{15}$

A. I ≤ II ≤ III
B. I ≥ II ≥ III
C. I + II = III
D. I = II = III

33. Write $83.\overline{3}\%$ as a decimal.

A. $8.\overline{3}$
B. $0.8\overline{3}$
C. $0.08\overline{3}$
D. 0.0083

34. Look at the series: 7, 14, ____, 28, 35... Which number is missing?

A. 19
B. 21
C. 23
D. 25

35. Calculate and compare the values for I, II, and III in order to select the best answer.

I. The total number of miles walked in a week when Adam walks 1.5 miles, to and from school every day including weekends for sports practice.

II. The number of hours worked if Stacy works from 7AM-1PM on Friday, Saturday, and Sunday.

III. 15

A. I ≤ II ≤ III
B. I ≥ II ≥ III
C. I + II = III
D. I = II = III

36. Divide $1\frac{9}{14} \div \frac{3}{5}$.

A. $\frac{69}{70}$
B. $1\frac{1}{3}$
C. $1\frac{27}{70}$
D. $2\frac{31}{42}$

37. Look at the series: 6%, 18%, 54%... Which percentage comes next?

A. 60%
B. 75%
C. 162%
D. 180%

38. Calculate and compare the values for I, II, and III in order to select the best answer.

I. A paycheck for $60

II. Interest accumulated on an account of $3200 with a 15% rate

III. $540

A. I ≤ II ≤ III
B. I ≥ II ≥ III
C. I + II = III
D. I = II = III

39. Three vertices of a square are $(3,-8)$, $(8,-3)$, $(8,-8)$. What is the fourth coordinate?

A. (3, 3)
B. (–3, 3)
C. (3,–3)
D. (–3, –3)

40. Look at the series: 3:6, ____, 5:10, 6:12... Which ratio is missing?

A. 3:8
B. 4:8
C. 5:8
D. 6:8

41. Calculate and compare the values for I, II, and III in order to select the best answer.

I. The number of inches in a foot

II. The number of feet in a yard

III. 15

A. I ≤ II ≤ III
B. I ≥ II ≥ III
C. I + II = III
D. I = II = III

42. Which number is a prime factor of 108?

A. 3
B. 7
C. 11
D. 13

43. Look at the series: 1:2, 1:4, 1:6, 1:8... Which ratio comes next?

A. 1:10
B. 1:100
C. 2:10
D. 2:100

44. Calculate and compare the values for I, II, and III in order to select the best answer.

I. 9

II. $(-2)^2$

III. $(-3)^3$

A. I ≤ II ≤ III
B. I ≥ II ≥ III
C. I + II = III
D. I = II = III

45. Given the coordinates for a square $(-6,6), (6,6), (6,-6)(-6,-6)$, find the length of each side of the square.

A. 0 units
B. 6 units
C. 12 units
D. 18 units

46. Look at the series: 30°F, 26°F, 22°F, 18°F... Which temperature comes next?

A. 14°F
B. 16°F
C. 17°F
D. 40°F

47. Calculate and compare the values for I, II, and III in order to select the best answer.

I. 12^1

II. $(5)^2$

III. $(4)^3$

A. I ≤ II ≤ III
B. I ≥ II ≥ III
C. I + II = III
D. I = II = III

48. Look at the series: 40π, ___, 46π, 49π, 52π... Which quantity is missing?

A. 41π
B. 42π
C. 43π
D. 44π

49. Calculate and compare the values for I, II, and III in order to select the best answer.

I. $\sqrt{121}$

II. 7^2

III. 45

A. I ≤ II ≤ III
B. I ≥ II ≥ III
C. I + II = III
D. I = II = III

50. What is the prime factorization of 99?

A. 9, 9
B. 9, 11
C. 3, 3, 10
D. 3, 3, 11

51. Calculate and compare the values for I, II, and III in order to select the best answer.

I. 15^2

II. $\sqrt{225}$

III. 240

A. I ≤ II ≤ III

B. I ≥ II ≥ III

C. I + II = III

D. I = II = III

52. Identify an arc of the circle.

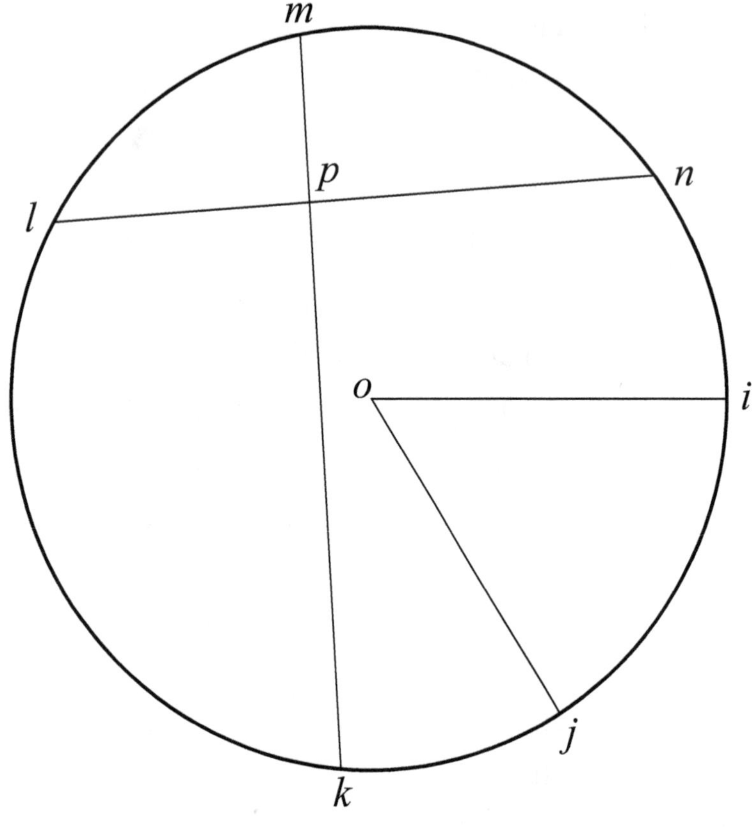

A. $\widehat{LM}$

B. $\widehat{PN}$

C. $\widehat{OJ}$

D. $\widehat{LP}$

SECTION III. READING AND VOCABULARY

Part 1: Reading

Directions: *Each passage (or pair of passages) below is followed by a number of questions. Read each passage (or pair), then choose the best answer to each question based on what is stated or implied in the passage (or passages), and in any graphics that may accompany the passage.*

Read the passages below and answer questions 1-9.

Electroconvulsive therapy was pioneered in the 1930s as a method for combatting severe psychiatric symptoms such as intractable depression and paranoid schizophrenia. This procedure, which involves delivering a deliberate electrical shock to the brain, was controversial from the beginning because it caused pain and short-term memory loss. It fell strongly out of public favor after the 1962 publication of Ken Kesey's novel *One Flew Over the Cuckoo's Nest,* which featured an unprincipled nurse using electroconvulsive therapy as a means of control over her patients. Paradoxically, medical advances at the time of the novel's publication made electroconvulsive therapy significantly safer and more humane.

Although the public is still generally opposed to electroconvulsive therapy, it remains a genuine option for psychiatric patients whose symptoms do not improve with medication. Medical professionals who offer this option should be especially careful to make clear distinctions between myth and reality. On this topic, unfortunately, many patients tend to rely on fiction rather than fact.

*

We were led into a stark exam room, where three doctors positioned themselves so Mama and I had no direct path to the door. The one in charge cleared his throat and told me my mother needed electroshock. My brain buzzed—almost as if it was hooked up to some crackpot brainwashing machine—as Big Doctor droned on about his sadistic intentions. I didn't hear any of it. All I could think was that these people wanted to tie my mother down and stick wires in her ears.

When Big Doctor was finished, he flipped through the papers on his clipboard and asked if I had questions. I mumbled something noncommittal. Then, when he and his silent escort left, I grabbed Mama and beat it out of that wacko ward as fast as I could make her go.

1. **What is the purpose of the first paragraph of Passage 1?**

   A. To inform
   B. To distract
   C. To persuade
   D. To entertain

2. **What is the purpose of the second paragraph of Passage 1?**
   A. To inform
   B. To distract
   C. To persuade
   D. To entertain

3. **What is the primary purpose of Passage 2?**
   A. To inform
   B. To distract
   C. To persuade
   D. To entertain

4. **With which statement would the author of Passage 1 likely agree?**
   A. Patients who suffer from mental illness should sue Ken Kesey for libel.
   B. Electroconvulsive therapy is a ready solution for every psychiatric complaint.
   C. No twenty-first century patient should ever receive electroconvulsive therapy.
   D. Medical patients should try options such as medication before electroconvulsive therapy.

5. **Which detail from Passage 1 supports the conclusion that patients should try other options before electing to undergo electroconvulsive therapy?**
   A. This procedure...was controversial from the beginning because it caused pain and short-term memory loss.
   B. Ken Kesey's novel *One Flew Over the Cuckoo's Nest*...featured an unprincipled nurse using electroconvulsive therapy as a means of control over her patients.
   C. Electroconvulsive therapy...remains a genuine option for patients whose symptoms do not improve with medication.
   D. Paradoxically, medical advances at the time of the novel's publication made electroconvulsive therapy significantly safer and more humane.

6. **The author of Passage 1 would most likely criticize the author of Passage 2 for:**
   A. failing to listen to the doctor's explanations.
   B. making no attempt to protect her ailing mother.
   C. feeling threatened by her physical circumstances.
   D. asking too many questions and wasting the doctor's time.

7. **The author of Passage 1 would most likely criticize the doctor in Passage 2 for:**

   A. revealing medical information to the patient's family members.

   B. denying the patient and her family the chance to ask questions.

   C. taking control of the meeting instead of letting underlings speak.

   D. neglecting to anticipate the feelings of his patient and her family.

8. **Which details from Passage 2 suggest that the author has a negative outlook about medical professionals?**

   A. She describes feeling trapped in a room by doctors, one of whom she calls "sadistic."

   B. She describes feeling outnumbered when she makes reasoned arguments to a doctor she calls "wacko."

   C. She describes feeling bored by the idea that the doctor wants to "tie [her] mother down and stick wires in her ears."

   D. She describes feeling excited by the prospect of seeing her mother hooked up to a pseudo-medical "brainwashing machine."

9. **The author of Passage 1 supports her points primarily by:**

   A. telling humanizing stories.

   B. relying on facts and logic.

   C. pointing to expert sources.

   D. using fear tactics and manipulation.

Read the paragraph below and answer questions 10-17.

Until about 1850, few people living in temperate climates had ever had the opportunity to taste a banana. Only after the invention of the steamship could importers and exporters reliably transport this fruit to North America and Europe. Railways and refrigeration were two other vital components in the development of the banana trade. Today, bananas are a major export in several Central and South American countries as well as the Philippines. Around the world, people in climates that cannot support banana production now have access to plentiful inexpensive bananas.

10. **Which sentence provides an effective summary of the text above?**

    A. The author of this paragraph really likes bananas and researched them thoroughly.

    B. Shipping and refrigeration technology helped bananas become a major export crop.

    C. This paragraph should include more detail about the development of the banana trade.

    D. Before 1850, most Americans and Europeans had never had the opportunity to taste a banana.

11. Read the following summary of the paragraph above.

According to John K. Miller, the invention of shipping and refrigeration technology helped bananas become a major export crop. The banana trade is an important source of income for many countries around the world, and consumers can buy bananas easily even in places where bananas do not grow.

What makes this summary effective?

A. It makes a judgment on the original text without being unfair.

B. It restates the ideas of the original text in completely new words.

C. It rearranges the ideas of the original text into a different sequence.

D. It highlights ideas from the original text that were not stated explicitly.

12. Which summary sentence retains language too close to the original text?

A. The author of this paragraph really likes bananas and researched them thoroughly.

B. This paragraph should include more detail about the development of the banana trade.

C. Before 1850, most Americans and Europeans had never had the opportunity to taste a banana.

D. The technological developments of the Industrial Revolution helped create a global banana trade.

13. Which summary sentence fails to be objective?

A. The author of this paragraph really likes bananas and researched them thoroughly.

B. This paragraph should include more detail about the development of the banana trade.

C. Before 1850, most Americans and Europeans had never had the opportunity to taste a banana.

D. The technological developments of the Industrial Revolution helped create a global banana trade.

14. Read the following sentence.

Nobody would eat bananas today if modern shipping and refrigeration technology had never been invented.

Why does this sentence NOT belong in a summary of the paragraph above?

A. It concerns supporting details and not main ideas.

B. It adheres too closely to the original author's language.

C. It fails to make a clear judgment about the original text.

D. It does not accurately state an idea from the original text.

15. Reread the opening sentence from lines 1-3 ("Until about 1850, ... banana"). What type of sentence is this, and why?

A. Fact; the research of the passage explains why countries around the world did not have access to bananas.

B. Fact; the writing suggests that the author is likely a primary source to discuss the topic of the passage.

C. Opinion; the people from this time period cannot verify if banana trade could reach countries with temperate climates.

D. Opinion; the research and data the author used makes the sentence an educated assumption.

16. Where would a reader likely have found this passage?

A. A fantasy novel

B. A history textbook

C. A science magazine discussing fruit trade

D. A geography study about plantations

17. What type of data would best help support the main idea of the passage?

A. A survey of whether or not consumers like bananas in cold climate countries

B. A pie chart of where banana exports go from the Philippines

C. A line graph displaying the value of banana exports from Central America since 1800

D. A bar graph of banana export values from Central America, South America and the Philippines in 2018

Read the following passage and answer questions 18-25.

You know what I hate? Businesses that rely on contract workers and freelancers instead of regular employees.

Don't hit me with arguments about grater freedom for workers. Freedom isn't free if your bleeding out in the street.

Sound the alarm, people! Workers are suffering! No benefits means you're out of luck if you get sick and can't do your job. Plus, studies show freelancers don't make as much money as regular employees.

--From Rod's Job Blog at rodtalksaboutjobs.com

18. Which of the following is NOT a sign that the reader should be skeptical of this source?

A. The passage contains typos and spelling errors.

B. The author presents opinion information as if it is fact.

C. There is no clear information about the author's credentials.

D. The passage comes from a personal blog with a .com address.

19. Why should a reader be skeptical of the point about freelancers not making as much money as regular employees?

A. The argument is not based in logic.

B. Some freelancers make plenty of money.

C. The source of the information is not clear.

D. The sentence contains grammatical errors.

20. A reader should be skeptical of lines 5-6 ("Freedom isn't free ... street") because it:

A. appears to use objective language but is actually hiding gender bias.

B. uses emotional language without responding to the opposing argument.

C. seems to present an expert point of view but does not name the source.

D. makes no attempt to defend regular workers in a discussion of the economy.

21. A student is writing a paper on employment trends and wants to quote an expert's opinion. What type of site would provide the most credible alternative to Rod's Job Blog?

A. A different post on Rod's Jobs Blog

B. A different blog with a .net address

C. An opinion article by a recognized expert in the field

D. A government website tracking employment statistics

22. In line 7, what does the author mean by "Sound the alarm, people!"?

A. The author is asking for help about changing the working conditions for contract workers.

B. The author is dramatizing how the "Workers are suffering!"

C. The author is trying to increase the urgency of the problem by yelling at the audience.

D. The author is calling attention to the idea that businesses are reaping benefits while contract workers are being taken advantage of.

23. What could the author of this blog do to make his argument stronger?

A. Edit the passage to get rid of the spelling errors and exclamatory sentences.

B. Elaborate on their own experience as a contract worker.

C. Select a business that relies on freelancers and expose the salary difference with their contracted work and a regular employee.

D. Explain more clearly that businesses save tons of money by not having to pay large salaries for contracted workers.

24. Reread the following sentence from lines 4-5 ("Don't hit ... workers") Which of the following would be a more formal way to rewrite the sentence?

A. I disagree with the argument about contract workers having greater freedom.

B. Stop telling me that freelancers have more freedom!

C. Is there actually greater freedom for workers?

D. I've already heard arguments about greater freedom for workers.

25. What is the author's intended purpose of the blog post?

A. To expose how the author was personally taken advantage of as a contract worker.

B. To argue that freelancers are not enjoying the perks of contract work most businesses would argue they have.

C. To increase awareness that non-benefitted workers are suffering.

D. To make the argument that minimum wages for freelancers need to be increased.

Please read the text below and answer questions 26-34.

A global temperature change of a few degrees is more significant than it may seem at first glance. This is not merely a change in weather in any one location. Rather, it is an average change in temperatures around the entire surface of the planet. It takes a vast amount of heat energy to warm every part of our world—including oceans, air, and land—by even a tiny measurable amount. Moreover, relatively small changes in the earth's surface temperatures have historically caused enormous changes in climate. In the last ice age 20,000 years ago, when much of the northern hemisphere was buried under huge sheets of ice, mean global temperatures were only about five degrees Celsius lower than they are now. Scientists predict a temperature rise of two to six degrees Celsius by 2100. What if this causes similarly drastic changes to the world we call home?

26. Which sentence is the topic sentence?

A. What if this causes similarly drastic changes to the world we call home?

B. A global temperature change of a few degrees is more significant than it may seem at first glance.

C. It takes a vast amount of heat energy to warm every part of our world—including oceans, air, and land—by even a tiny measurable amount.

D. In the last ice age 20,000 years ago, when much of the northern hemisphere was buried under huge sheets of ice, mean global temperatures were only about five degrees Celsius lower than they are now.

27. In the paragraph above, global temperature change is:

A. the topic.

B. the main idea.

C. a supporting detail.

D. the topic sentence.

28. Which sentence summarizes the main idea of the paragraph?

A. A small change in weather at any one location is a serious problem.

B. The author is manipulating facts to make global warming sound scary.

C. People should be concerned by even minor global temperature change.

D. It takes an enormous amount of energy to warm the earth even a little.

29. What function does the information about temperature differences in the last ice age play in the paragraph?

A. Topic
B. Opinion
C. Main idea
D. Supporting detail

30. Which sentence would best function as a supporting detail in this paragraph?

A. Electricity and heat production create one quarter of all carbon emissions globally.
B. The world was only about one degree cooler during the Little Ice Age from 1700 to 1850.
C. China has surpassed the United States as the single largest producer of carbon emissions.
D. Methane emissions are, in some ways, more concerning than carbon dioxide emissions.

31. The author wants to include a line graph demonstrating the mean global temperature changes between the last ice age to the present. Why should the author not do this?

A. The mean global temperature changes are small and would not visually add emphasis to the argument.
B. The mean global temperature changes are small, but the majority of the difference, and basis of the argument, comes from changes in cold weather locations.
C. The temperature rise predicted for 2100 is between two and six degrees Celsius, but cannot go into the graph because it has not happened yet.
D. The temperature rise predicted for 2100 is between two and six degrees Celsius, but the line graph would not show the temperature change between each element of ocean, air, and land.

32. What graphic(s) would best assist the passage to support the author's argument?

A. Images related to the ice age and cold weather locations now.
B. A pie chart to show where the polar bear populations live.
C. A graph to demonstrate the global volume of ice sheets and glaciers over the past fifty years.
D. A line graph of the volume of sun rays on the Earth through the protective ozone layer throughout the past fifty years.

33. **Select a more formal rewrite for the sentence from lines 7-10 ("It takes ... measureable amount").**

A. It takes a lot of heat energy from the sun to move the temperature up for the entire globe.

B. Every part of the world- including oceans, air, and land- requires a crazy amount of sunlight.

C. A lot of heat energy is required to push the temperature scale upwards for our globe, which is defined by the oceans, air, and land.

D. Between the oceans, air, and land, it takes a vast amount of heat energy to shift every part of our world to a warmer measurable temperature.

34. **The author of the passage has written the argument in a formal manner. Why does it end with a question?**

A. The question cannot be answered by the author because the impact is unknown.

B. The question is meant to leave a reader with an open-ended question to think critically about global temperature change affects for the future.

C. The scientific prediction for a global temperature rise is meant to guide a reader to the answer that global temperature changes may be fatal to the earth's surface.

D. It is a rhetorical question and is meant to show the author's frustration with scientists who do not support the argument.

Read the passage below and answer questions 35-42.

When my 13-year-old daughter entered the house, the door slammed open with a celebratory "bang!" I was instantly dismayed to see that my first-born stomped right by me as I held my arms open for a warm hug.

"How was your day, honey?" I asked as she gave me her quintessential eye roll.

I sat across from her ready to hear how marvelous her day was. However, I only got an earful of all the drama that had ensued at school: "So-and-so said this," "gym was a drag," "Mr. Fletcher doesn't like me because I am not a math genius."

My head ached from nodding so much, so I got up quickly to bring her something.

"Mom! How could you get up when I'm in the middle of telling you about my life?" she barked.

Despite her protest, her eyes could not help but light up when I brought her a freshly baked chocolate chip cookie on a plate.

I guess life isn't all that bad, is it?

35. **Which adjectives best describe the tone of the passage?**

A. Ironic, furious

B. Honest, furious

C. Ironic, amusing

D. Honest, amusing

36. Which sentence from the passage is clearly ironic?

A. "How was your day, honey?"

B. I sat across from her ready to hear how marvelous her day was.

C. My head ached from nodding so much, so I got up quickly to bring her something.

D. "Mom! How could you get up when I'm in the middle of telling you about my life?"

37. The author of the passage first establishes the ironic tone by:

A. describing the slamming of the door as "celebratory."

B. quoting the daughter's words.

C. explaining how the mother got up to get the daughter cookie.

D. having the mother state that life "isn't all that bad."

38. Which adjective could describe an effective reader's mood when reading line 25 ("I guess life ..., is it?") **in the passage?**

A. Entertained

B. Frustrated

C. Empathetic

D. Dismissive

39. Which word or phrase does *not* function as a transition in the passage?

A. Instantly

B. However

C. So

D. Despite

40. The transitions "however" and "despite" link ideas in the passage by showing:

A. when events happen in time.

B. how certain ideas contrast.

C. examples that illustrate ideas.

D. cause-and-effect relationships.

41. Reread lines 7-8 ("How was ... roll").

Which transition would you use if the next sentence describes the daughter *also* making a "tsk" sound to show her frustration?

A. Finally

B. Furthermore

C. To illustrate

D. Nevertheless

42. The author details how her daughter states, "Mr. Fletcher doesn't like me because I am not a math genius." Why does the author not take this statement seriously?

A. The daughter is being rude to the author.

B. The author knows what her daughter's math skills truly are.

C. The author cannot verify how Mr. Fletcher feels about her daughter at the moment.

D. It is her daughter's opinion stated as if it is a fact because her daughter is being dramatic.

Part 2: Vocabulary

Directions: *Vocabulary knowledge is a key component for reading comprehension. This section focuses on vocabulary usage in a variety of ways. Read each question carefully and choose the best option.*

1. **Select the meaning of the underlined word in the sentence.**

   When an egg gets fertilized, a number of traits are predetermined by the natural genetic processes, including gender.

   A. verified during a process
   B. concluded at a later date
   C. decided before something happens
   D. determined right after something occurs

2. **Irascible most nearly means:**

   A. easily angered
   B. easily swayed
   C. easily amused
   D. easily embarrassed

3. **Select the meaning of the underlined word in the sentence.**

   Spending the day getting pampered at a spa will rejuvenate anyone.

   A. Make someone feel sleepy
   B. Make someone feel relaxed
   C. Make someone feel young again
   D. Make someone feel appreciative

4. **A neophyte is someone who:**

   A. works hard
   B. knows a lot
   C. is very curious
   D. is new to something

5. **Something that is dysfunctional is:**

   A. not working right
   B. working too hard
   C. working smoothly
   D. not working enough

6. **Circumvent means to:**

   A. find a way over
   B. find a way under
   C. find a way around
   D. find a way through

7. **Select the meaning of the underlined word in the sentence.**

   There was much discord between the two political parties.

   A. Support
   B. Conflict
   C. Disrespect
   D. Collaboration

8. **What is the best definition of the word genuflect?**

   A. Sit
   B. Bow
   C. Stroll
   D. Stand

9. **What is the best definition of the word transcontinental?**

   A. Near the continent
   B. Inside the continent
   C. Across the continent
   D. Outside the continent

10. Select the meaning of the underlined word in the sentence.

Susan is known as a business magnate and is at the top of her industry.

A. A mischievous and evil person

B. A wealthy and powerful person

C. A giving and supportive person

D. A knowledgeable and informed person

11. What is the best definition of the word loquacious?

A. Selfish

B. Friendly

C. Talkative

D. Resentful

Directions: *The synonyms below consist of a word in capital letters followed by four answer choices. Select the one word that is most nearly the same in meaning as the word in capital letters.*

12. FLACCID

A. firm

B. limp

C. stiff

D. taut

13. HAPLESS

A. blessed

B. favored

C. well-off

D. woeful

14. RETRACT

A. admit

B. reaffirm

C. sanction

D. withdraw

15. TORRID

A. arctic

B. arid

C. damp

D. frigid

16. PRESUMPTUOUS

A. arrogant

B. cautious

C. modest

D. rash

17. COMPEL

A. block

B. deter

C. force

D. impede

18. DUTIFUL

A. betraying

B. faithless

C. irresponsible

D. obedient

19. SORDID

A. clean

B. dirty

C. incorrupt

D. unacquisitive

20. INNATE

A. acquired

B. extrinsic

C. inherent

D. learned

Section IV. Mathematical Skills

1. Identify the diameter of the circle.

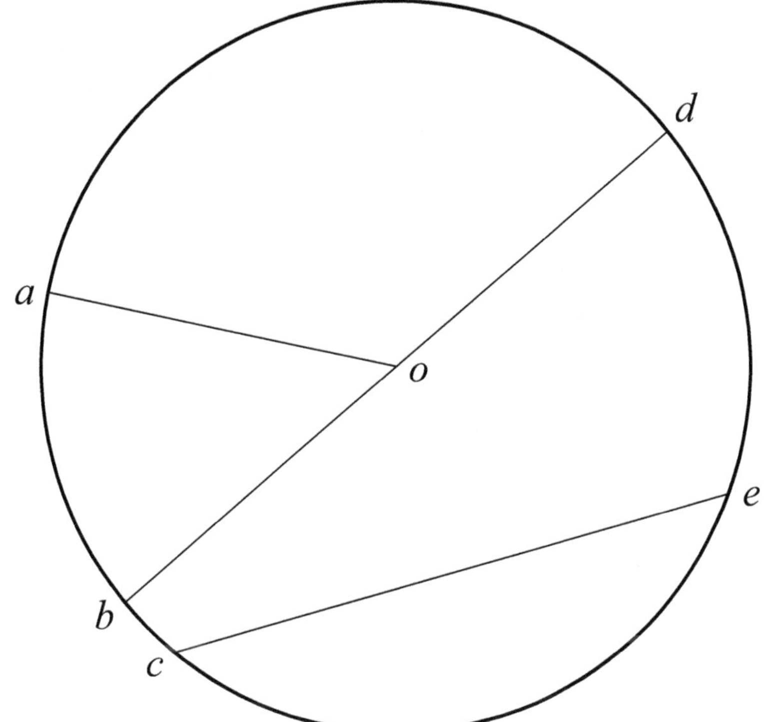

A. $\bar{AO}$

B. $\bar{BD}$

C. $\bar{CE}$

D. $\bar{AC}$

2. If Professor Markham has 127 students in her calculus course but 37 drop out because it is too difficult, how many students remain?

   A. 37 C. 127

   B. 90 D. 164

3. 1,004 + 110

   A. 2,104 C. 1,204

   B. 1,411 D. 1,114

4. (−224) ÷ 14

   A. −210 C. 16

   B. −16 D. 210

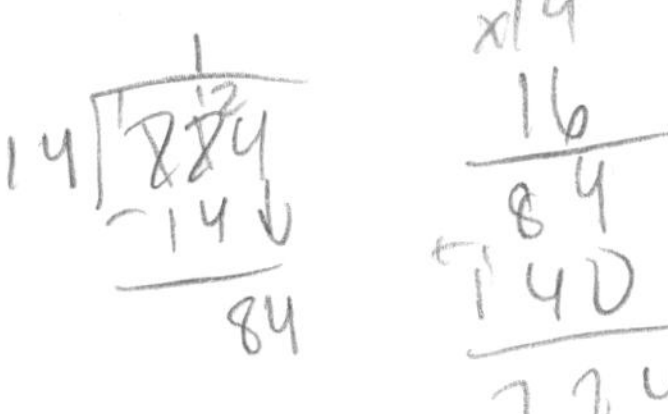

5. Which statement about multiplication is true?

   A. Multiplication is impossible.

   B. Multiplication is repeated division.

   C. Multiplication is repeated addition.

   D. Multiplication is repeated subtraction.

6. A rug is shaped in a half circle. The curved edge of the rug has a circumference of 74 inches. Find the area of the rug to the nearest tenth of a square inch. Use 3.14 for π.

   A. 296.0 C. 1,113.9

   B. 874.4 D. 1,748.9

7. **Find the circumference in centimeters of a circle with a radius of 11 centimeters. Use 3.14 for π.**

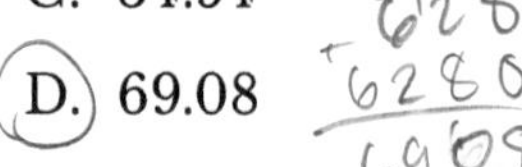

A. 3.14
B. 6.28
C. 34.54
D. 69.08

8. **Select the figure that is rotated 90° counterclockwise about the origin.**

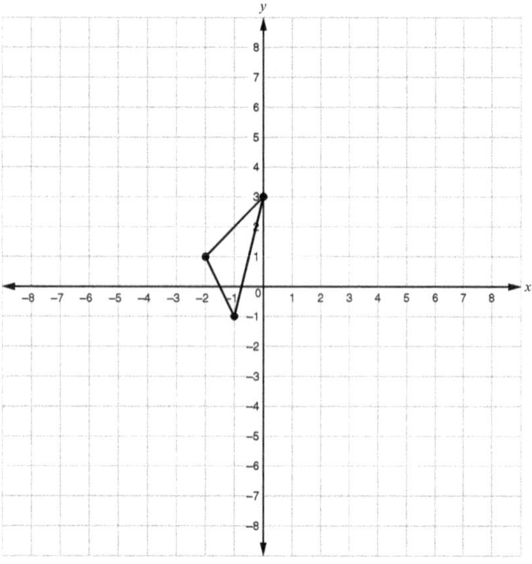

A.

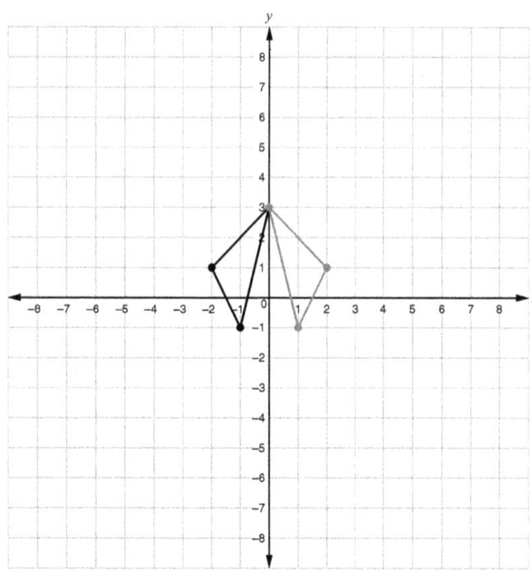

B.

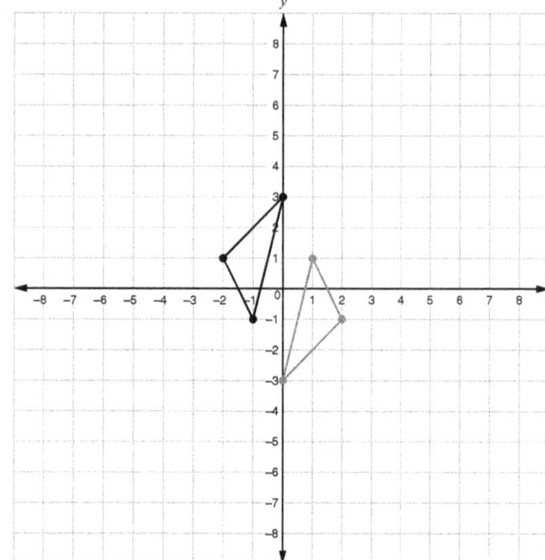

C.

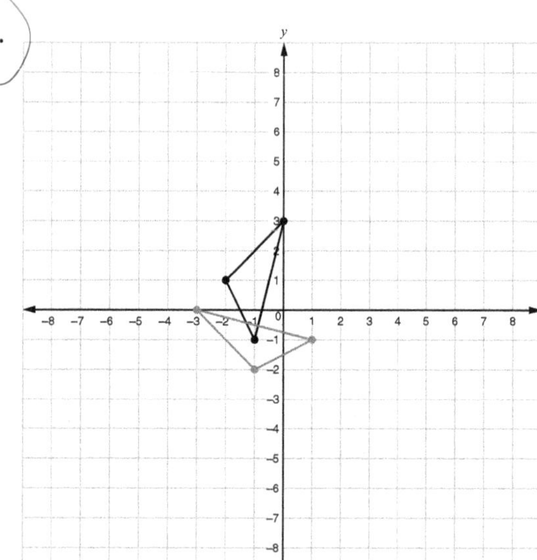

D.

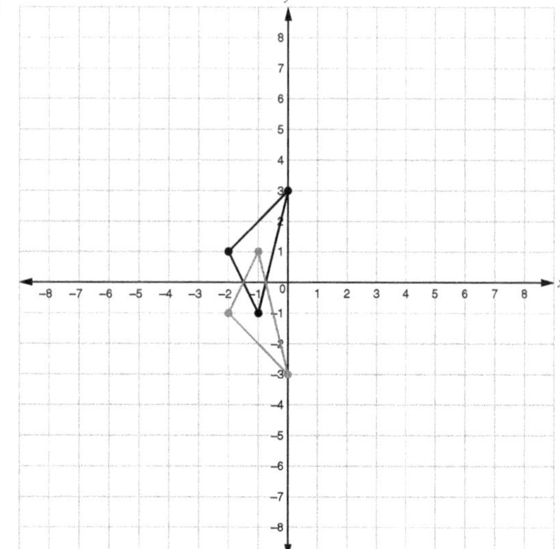

9. ΔDEF has points $D(-3, 6)$, $E(-2, -4)$, and $F(5, 0)$. After a transformation, the points are $D'(6, 3)$, $E'(-4, 2)$, and $F'(0, -5)$. What is the transformation between the points?

A. Reflection across the x-axis

B. Reflection across the y-axis

C. Rotation of 90° counterclockwise

D. Rotation of 270° counterclockwise

10. Select the figure that is translated $(x + 2, y + 1)$.

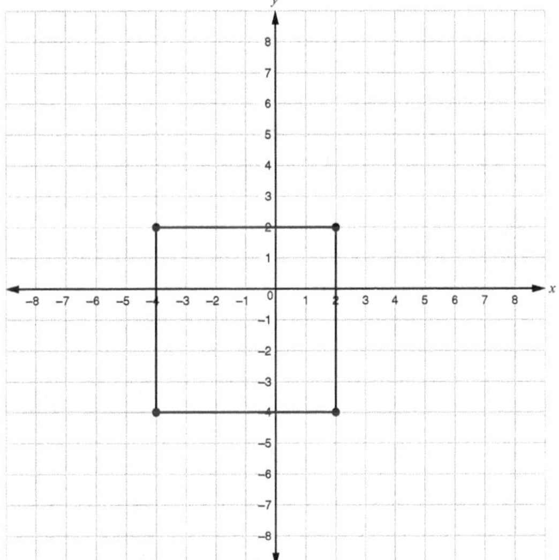

A.

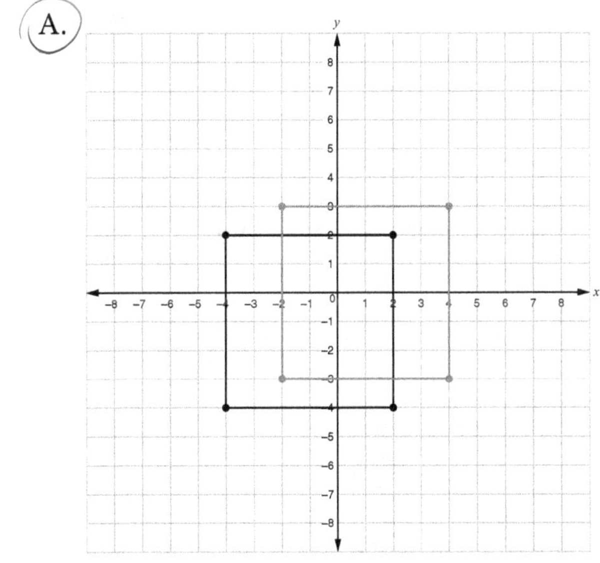

B.

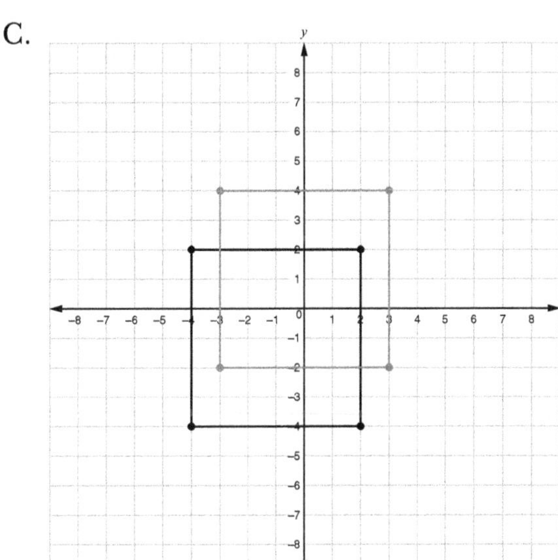

C.

D.

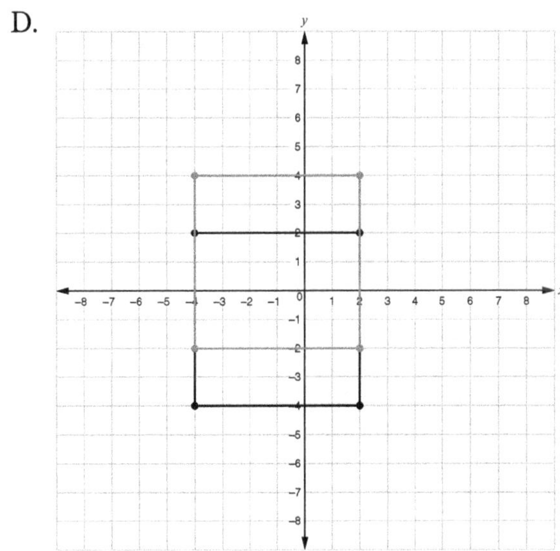

11. Write 1.5 as a percent.

A. 0.15%

B. 1.5%

C. 15%

D. 150%

12. Write 290% as a fraction.

A. $2\frac{9}{200}$

B. $2\frac{9}{100}$

C. $2\frac{9}{20}$

D. $2\frac{9}{10}$

13. Change $7\frac{13}{20}$ to a decimal. Simplify completely.

A. 7.55

B. 7.6

C. 7.65

D. 7.7

14. Solve the equation for the unknown, $\frac{x}{2} + 5 = 8$.

A. $\frac{3}{2}$

B. $\frac{5}{2}$

C. 6

D. 26

15. Solve the inequality for the unknown.

$2(3x-1) + 5 \geq 3x-4-4x$

A. $x > -7$

B. $x > -4$

C. $x > -1$

D. $x > 0$

16. Solve the equation for *c*.

$2a(b + c) = c$

A. $\frac{2ab}{1-2a} = c$

B. $\frac{2ab}{1+2a} = c$

C. $\frac{2ab}{2a} = c$

D. $\frac{2ab}{a} = c$

17. Solve the system of equations.

$-4x + 3y = 30$
$3x + 4y = 15$

A. (3, -6)

B. (-3, 6)

C. (-3, -6)

D. (3, 6)

18. Which number is *not* a factor of 1,155?

A. 22

B. 33

C. 55

D. 77

19. Solve the system of equations.

$y = -2x$
$x^2 + y^2 = 5$

A. (1, -2) and (-1, 2)

B. (1, 2) and (-1, -2)

C. (2, -1) and (-2, 1)

D. (2, 1) and (-2, -1)

20. The dot plot shows the results of rolling a dice for a game. Which statement is true for the dot plot?

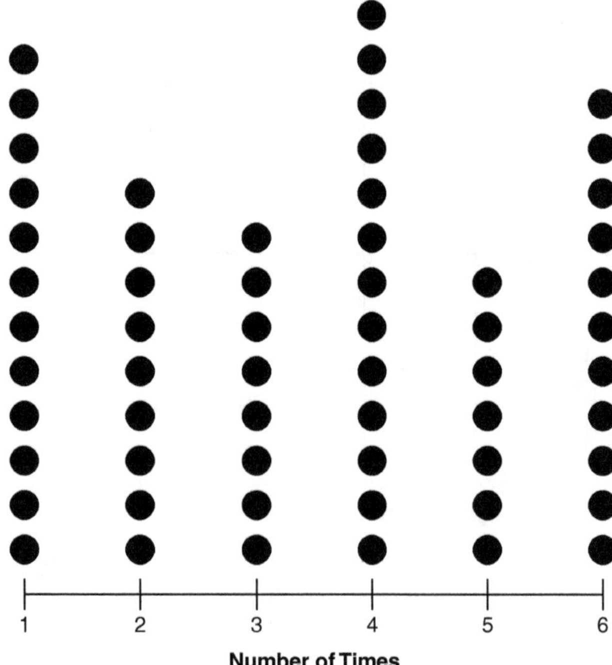

A. There were 60 turns in the game.

B. More than half of the turns were 3 or less.

C. 1 and 6 occurred the same number of times.

D. The difference between the lowest and highest frequency is 3.

21. If a number has 3 and 5 as factors, which statement best describes that number?

A. The number is 15.

B. The number is prime.

C. The number has 15 as a factor.

D. The number has only two prime factors.

22. Solve the system of equations by graphing.

$y = -x + 7$
$y = 2x - 8$

A.

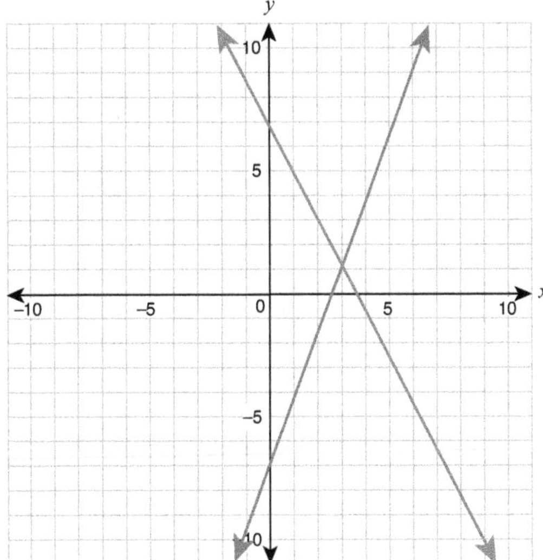

B.

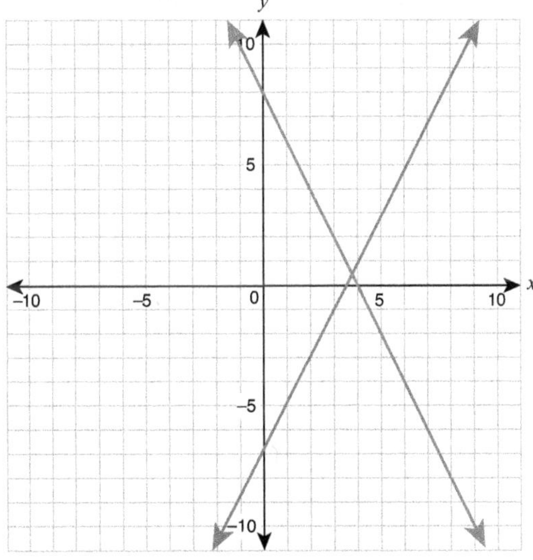

C.

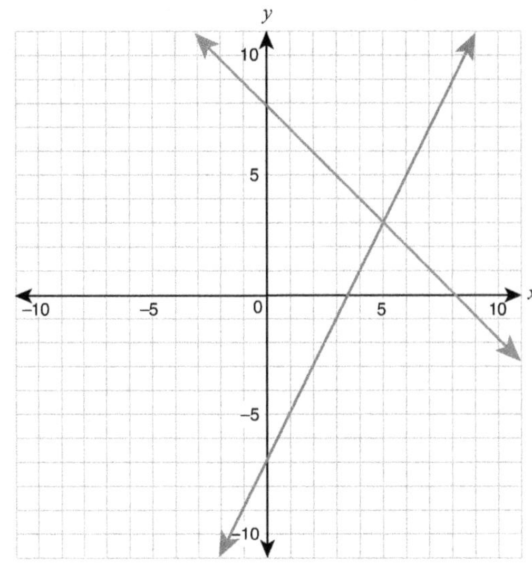

D.

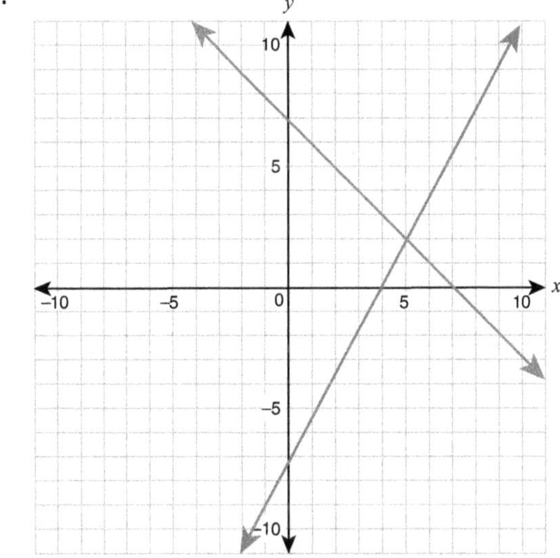

23. The last 8 transactions at a shoe store in dollars are 5, 39, 49, 50, 52, 35, 44, 100. What is the effect of removing the outliers on the mean and median?

A. The mean and median increase.

B. There is no effect on the mean or median.

C. The mean decreases, but the median does not change.

D. The median decreases, but the mean does not change.

24. The double line chart shows the number of points scored and points given up by a basketball team over the first 10 games. Which statement is true?

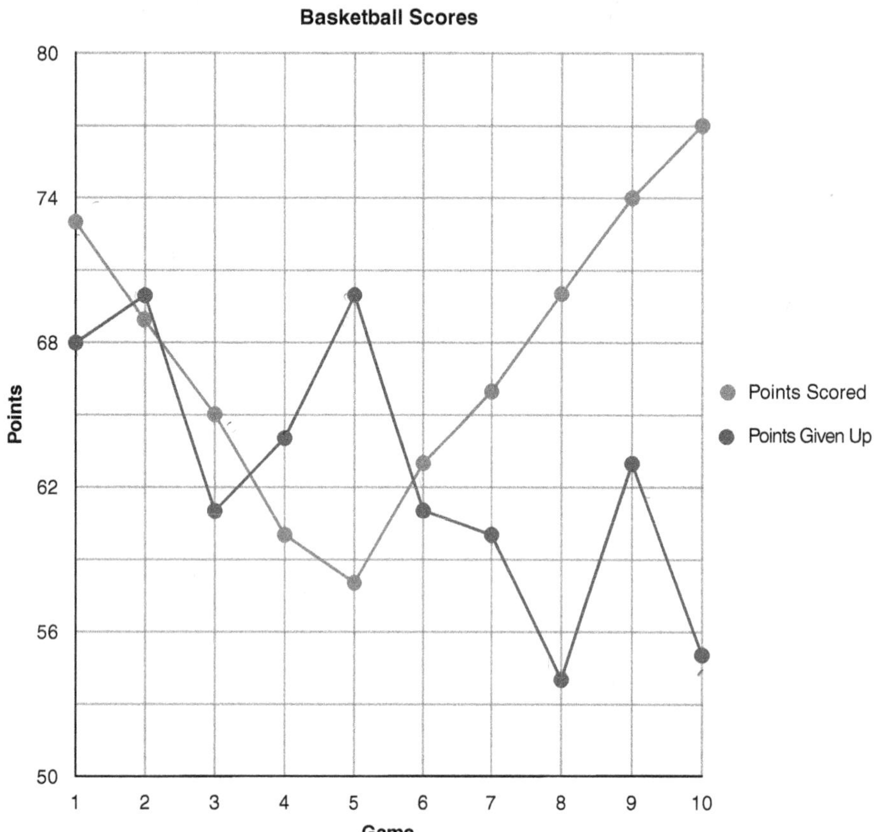

A. The team scored more than 62 points in a majority of games and gave up fewer than 62 points in a majority of games.

B. The team scored more than 65 points in a majority of games and gave up fewer than 65 points in a majority of games.

C. The team scored more than 68 points in a majority of games and gave up fewer than 68 points in a majority of games.

D. The team scored more than 70 points in a majority of games and gave up fewer than 65 points in a majority of games.

25. A mixture for a cake has various parts. Select the correct circle graph for the data.

Part	Eggs	Water	Oil	Mixture	Vanilla
Parts	2	3	2	7	1

A.

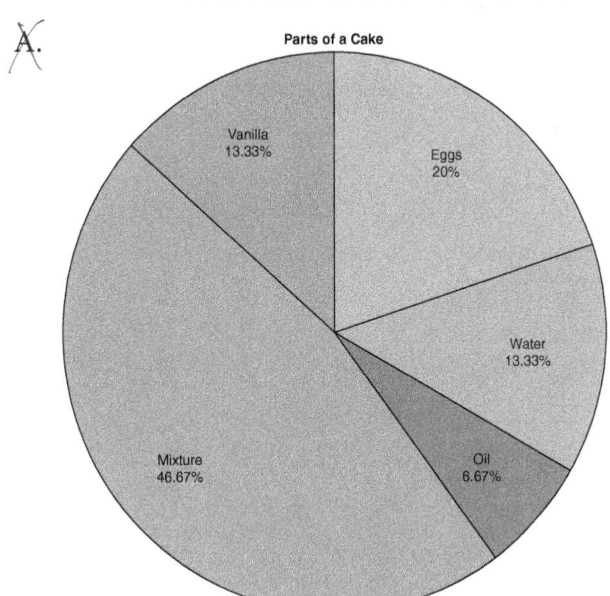

C.

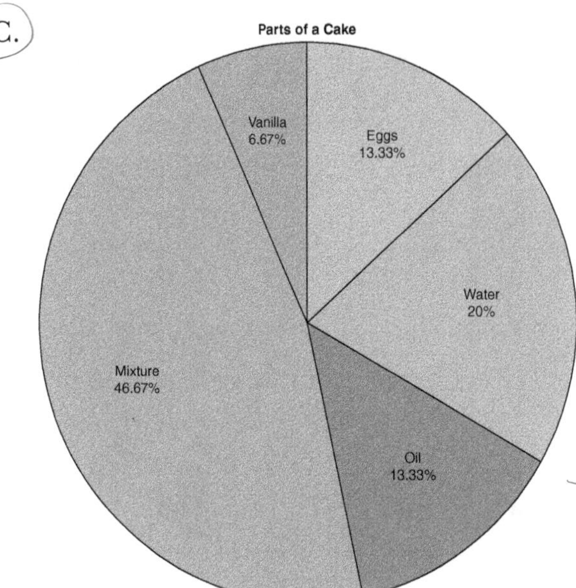

B.

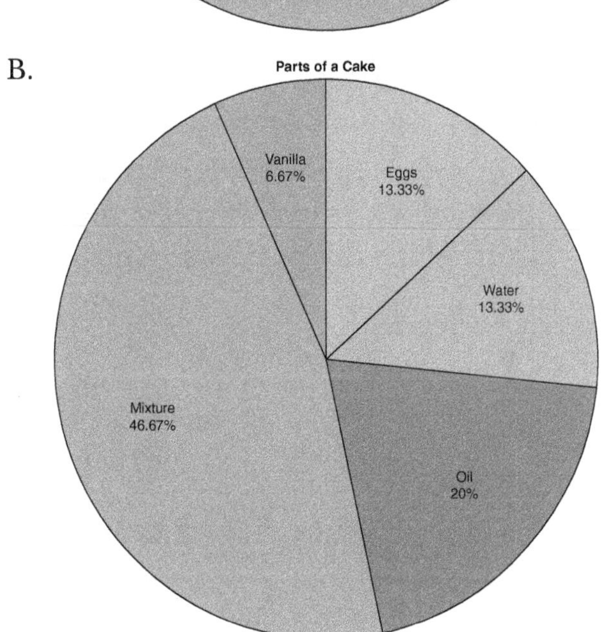

D.

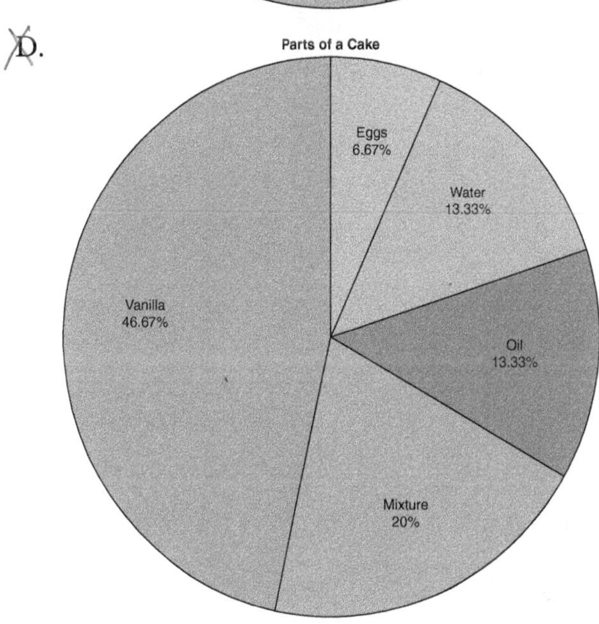

26. **Identify the variable from a study on cereal that is quantitative.**

A. Fat calories
B. Cereal name
C. Manufacturer
D. Target audience

27. **A gymnastics team has the following scores for an event:**

12.3, 12.7, 14.1, 14.5, 13.8, 13.6, 14.2, 15.2, 14.8, 13.9, 15.4, 14.3

Find the mean score for the team to the nearest hundredth.

A. 14.07
B. 14.15
C. 14.57
D. 14.71

28. A basketball has a diameter of 10 inches. What is the volume in cubic inches inside the ball? Use 3.14 for π.

A. 261.67
B. 523.33
C. 1,046.67
D. 2,093.33

29. The volume of a hemi-sphere is $\frac{16}{3}\pi$ cubic feet. What is the diameter in feet?

A. 1
B. 2
C. 3
D. 4

30. A jar of salsa has a diameter of 12 centimeters and a height of 10 centimeters. There are 4 centimeters of salsa left in the jar. How much salsa was used if the jar was originally filled to the top? State the answer in cubic centimeters in terms of π.

A. 216π
B. 360π
C. 864π
D. 1,440π

31. $2 \times \frac{3}{4}$

A. $\frac{1}{4}$
B. $\frac{3}{8}$
C. $1\frac{1}{2}$
D. $2\frac{3}{4}$

32. $1\frac{6}{7} \div \frac{3}{14}$

A. $\frac{39}{91}$
B. $1\frac{1}{2}$
C. $7\frac{1}{14}$
D. $8\frac{2}{3}$

33. $\frac{3}{14} \div 3$

A. $\frac{1}{42}$
B. $\frac{1}{14}$
C. $\frac{1}{3}$
D. $\frac{9}{14}$

34. Multiply.

$(2y^2 - 1)(y^2 - 3y + 5)$

A. $2y^4 - 6y^3 + 10y^2 + 3y - 5$
B. $2y^4 - 6y^3 + 9y^2 + 3y - 5$
C. $2y^4 - 6y^3 + 11y^2 + 3y - 5$
D. $2y^4 - 6y^3 + 8y^2 + 3y - 5$

35. Perform the operation.

$(-2x^2 + 8x) + (3x^3 - 4x^2 + 1)$

A. $3x^3 - 6x^2 + 8x + 1$
B. $3x^3 - 2x^2 + 8x + 1$
C. $3x^3 + 6x^2 + 8x + 1$
D. $3x^3 + 2x^2 + 8x + 1$

36. Apply the polynomial identity to rewrite the expression.

$x^2 - 100$

A. $(x-10)^2$
B. $(x-10)(x+10)$
C. $(x+10)^2$
D. $x^2 - 10^2$

37. Simplify.

$\left(\frac{x^0}{y^{-2}}\right)^2$

A. $\frac{1}{y^4}$
B. $\frac{x}{y^4}$
C. y^4
D. x^4y^4

38. The land area of Colorado about 1×10^5 square miles, and the land area of Ohio is about 4×10^4 square miles. How many times larger is the land area of Colorado?

A. 2
B. 3
C. 4
D. 5

39. Solve.

$x^3 = -8$

A. −4
B. −2
C. 2
D. 4

40. Which percent is closest to the ratio 7:3?

A. 23%
B. 43%
C. 73%
D. 233%

41. If a company's revenue changes from \$123 million to \$118 million in a month, how quickly is it increasing in a year?

A. −\$60 million
B. −\$5 million
C. \$5 million
D. \$60 million

42. The number 36 is what percent of 16?

A. 31%
B. 44%
C. 69%
D. 225%

43. Given the coordinates for a rectangle $(-4,-1), (-9,-1), (-9,-8)(-4,-8)$, find the length of each side of the rectangle.

A. 2 units and 3 units
B. 2 units and 7 units
C. 5 units and 3 units
D. 5 units and 7 units

44. A box in the shape of a right rectangular prism has dimensions of 6 centimeters by 7 centimeters by 8 centimeters. What is the volume in cubic centimeters?

A. 280
B. 336
C. 560
D. 672

45. A sign stating "Do Not Enter" is in the shape of a square with side lengths of 75 centimeters. What is the area in square centimeters?

A. 150
B. 300
C. 5,325
D. 5,625

46. Solve the equation by any method.

$x^2 + 4x - 15 = 0$

A. $2 \pm \sqrt{19}$
B. $-2 \pm \sqrt{19}$
C. $2 \pm \sqrt{15}$
D. $-2 \pm \sqrt{15}$

47. Solve the equation by the quadratic formula.

$12x^2 + x - 3 = 0$

A. −0.46 and −0.54
B. 0.46 and −0.54
C. −0.46 and 0.54
D. 0.46 and 0.54

48. Solve the equation by the square root method.

$x^2 + 10 = 110$

A. ±8
B. ±9
C. ±10
D. ±11

49. The level of a river during a flood was 39.45 feet. After a week, the water level declined to 18.97 feet. What was the amount of decrease in feet?

A. 20.38
B. 20.48
C. 21.38
D. 21.48

50. An even roll of a number cube results in +2 points, and an odd roll of a number cube is −3 points. If there are 14 even numbers and 11 odd numbers, then how many points are scored?

A. −61
B. −5
C. 5
D. 61

51. In a state, the highest elevation is 1,450 feet and the lowest elevation is −80 feet. What is the difference in the elevations in feet?

A. 1,370
B. 1,430
C. 1,530
D. 1,570

52. Convert 1,000 fluid ounces to gallons.

A. 7.8125 gallons
B. 15.625 gallons
C. 31.25 gallons
D. 62.5 gallons

53. Convert 6 meters to feet.

A. 1.52 feet
B. 1.72 feet
C. 18.68 feet
D. 19.68 feet

54. Convert 0.5 kiloliter to milliliters.

A. 50,000 milliliters

B. 500,000 milliliters

C. 5,000,000 milliliters

D. 50,000,000 milliliters

55. A group of researchers is studying dog behavior. They study the number of hours dogs sleep when music is playing and when it is not playing. What type of study is this?

A. Census

B. Survey

C. Experiment

D. Observational study

56. A coin is flipped 10 times, and the results are 5 heads and 5 tails. Choose the statement that correctly explains why or why not this result questions this model of probability.

A. Yes, because there are not enough simulations.

B. Yes, because there are only two options, heads or tails.

C. No, because the probability is the same as the simulation.

D. No, because each flip of the coin is independent of all others.

57. A survey group wants to ask the daily commute time for workers at a large company who use a car to get to work. What is the sample for the survey?

A. Employees who work from home

B. Employees who drive to work daily

C. Employees who work for the company

D. Employees who drive on a highway to work daily

58. There are 12 boys' and 14 girls' names in a hat. What is the probability of selecting a boy's name twice in a row without replacement?

A. $\frac{33}{169}$

B. $\frac{66}{325}$

C. $\frac{11}{25}$

D. $\frac{6}{13}$

59. Which option results in the greatest gain on an investment?

A. 60% of gaining \$5,000 and 40% of gaining \$0

B. 70% of gaining \$4,500 and 30% of gaining \$0

C. 80% of gaining \$4,000 and 20% of gaining \$0

D. 90% of gaining \$3,500 and 10% of gaining \$0

60. Students were surveyed on if they liked math, social studies, or science as a subject. Describe an intersection of the events.

A. Students who like math or social studies

B. Students who like math and social studies

C. Students who do not like math, social studies, or science

D. Students who like math

Section V. Language

1. **Select the correct word to complete the following sentence.**

   It was a treacherous route, and they traveled more _____ when they had a guide.

   A. safe
   B. safer
   C. safest
   D. safely

2. **Which of the following spellings is correct?**

   A. Argument
   B. Arguemint
   C. Arguement
   D. Arguemant

3. **Which word is not a conjunction?**

   A. Or
   B. The
   C. So
   D. But

4. **Select the word from the following sentence that has more than one meaning.**

   They need to prune the bushes every year or else they will lose their shape.

   A. Need
   B. Prune
   C. Lose
   D. Shape

5. **Select the verb that acts on the underlined direct object.**

   We decided that we should walk the dog before going to the restaurant.

   A. decided
   B. should
   C. walk
   D. going

6. **Which word does the underlined modifier describe?**

   I looked up to Marvin, who was a year older.

   A. I
   B. looked
   C. up
   D. Marvin

7. **Which of the following spellings is correct?**

   A. Posibility
   B. Possibility
   C. Possibilitie
   D. Possibillity

8. **Which word in the following sentence is a pronoun?**

   Alexi's grandfather was a well-known lawyer who won many cases.

   A. was
   B. won
   C. who
   D. Alexi's

9. **Which sentence is incorrect?**

   A. I hate you!
   B. When does the movie start?
   C. I go to bed early so I do not feel tired.
   D. You should drink eight glasses of water a day.

10. **Which of the following prefixes means too much?**

    A. sub-
    B. non-
    C. mis-
    D. over-

11. **Which of the following spellings is correct?**

    A. Criticim
    B. Criticism
    C. Kriticism
    D. Critisism

12. **Select the verb to complete the following sentence.**

    Do you think the automobile or the personal computer ____ changed our lives more?

    A. have
    B. haves
    C. has
    D. his

13. Fill in the blank with the correct subordinating conjunction.

I had a bad stomach flu but started to regain my appetite, _____ is good news.

A. So
B. That
C. Which
D. Whereas

14. Which of the following options would complete the sentence below to make it a simple sentence?

The house at the top of the hill ____________________________.

A. is very old.
B. it is very old
C. is very old despite having a modern feel.
D. is very old, and it has a very modern feel.

15. Which of the following is correct?

A. *Gone With The Wind*
B. *Gone With the Wind*
C. *Gone with the Wind*
D. *Gone with the wind*

16. What part of speech is the underlined word in the following sentence?

Douglas served on the <u>Supreme Court</u> for 36 years.

A. Noun
B. Pronoun
C. Adjective
D. Preposition

17. Which of the following spellings is correct?

A. Acomodation
B. Accomodation
C. Accomudation
D. Accommodation

18. Fill in the blank with the correctly capitalized form.

______ is part of the United Kingdom.

A. northern ireland
B. Northern Ireland
C. Northern ireland
D. northern Ireland

19. Identify the nouns in the following sentence.

Marie Curie won the Nobel Prize in 1911.

A. won, in, 1911
B. won, Nobel Prize, 1911
C. Marie Curie, won, Nobel Prize
D. Marie Curie, Nobel Prize, 1911

20. Identify the direct object of the underlined verb in the following sentence.

Tommy <u>watched</u> a movie with Mary.

A. Tommy
B. watched
C. a movie
D. with Mary

21. Identify the likely misplaced modifier in the following sentence.

The man in blue wore a large, gaudy hat on his head, which was ugly.

A. in blue
B. large
C. gaudy
D. which was ugly

22. Select the pronoun that *cannot* be used in the following sentence.

____ coat is so warm!

A. My
B. Her
C. This
D. Hers

23. **Which word in the following sentence is an adjective?**

Mrs. Washington loves red roses.

A. Mrs. Washington

B. loves

C. red

D. roses

24. **What part of speech are the underlined words in the following sentence?**

Twelve students passed the exam, but seven did not, so the teacher is letting them retake it.

A. Adjective

B. Preposition

C. Conjunction

D. Adverb

25. **Which of the following is correct?**

A. american civil liberties union

B. American civil liberties union

C. American civil liberties Union

D. American Civil Liberties Union

26. **Which of the following sentences is correct?**

A. Ashley cant ride a bike.

B. Ashleys parents never taught her.

C. Its an impossible task for her.

D. Ashley's determined to learn.

27. **Select the parts of speech of the underlined words in the following sentence.**

That man is quite tall.

A. Adverb, adverb

B. Adjective, adverb

C. Adverb, adjective

D. Adjective, adjective

28. **What is the correct plural of half?**

A. Half

B. Halfs

C. Halfes

D. Halves

29. **Select the response that correctly describes both of the underlined verbs.**

When a buyer offered 5% below our asking price, our realtor advised us to accept the offer.

A. Helping verbs

B. Past tense verbs

C. Present tense verbs

D. Progressive tense verbs

30. **Which of the following suffixes means having characteristics of?**

A. -ic

B. -ed

C. -er

D. -ist

31. **Which word does the underlined modifier describe?**

Hoping to improve his grade, he took the test again.

A. he

B. took

C. test

D. again

32. **What is missing from the following sentence?**

Classical music helps with studying, I always listen to it before a test.

A. There needs to be a colon after studying.

B. There needs to be a semicolon after studying.

C. There should be an exclamation point at the end.

D. Nothing is missing.

33. Which of the following is correct?

A. senate
B. congress
C. White House
D. Supreme court

34. Which word in the following sentence is a possessive pronoun?

Are you sure that it's yours?

A. it's
B. you
C. that
D. yours

35. Which word is <u>not</u> a preposition?

A. It
B. At
C. For
D. In

36. Select the subject with which the underlined verb must agree.

Everyone I know <u>has</u> the day off, but my boss wants me to work.

A. Everyone
B. I
C. day
D. boss

37. What is the correct plural of shelf?

A. Shelf
B. Shelfs
C. Shelfes
D. Shelves

38. Choose the correct plural noun to complete the following sentence.

It was surprising to suddenly see some _____ as we drove along the deserted road.

A. mooses
B. churchs
C. cactuses
D. passersby

39. What is the sentence with the most correct use of punctuation?

A. Wait!
B. Wait,
C. Wait-
D. Wait;

40. Which of the following is correct?

A. Civil war
B. black death
C. World War I
D. Nineteenth Century

41. Identify the independent clause in the following sentence.

Although most people understand the benefits of exercise, people do not exercise as much as they should.

A. Although most people understand
B. The benefits of exercise
C. People do not exercise as much as they should
D. People do not exercise

42. Which of the following root words means <u>to throw</u>?

A. ject
B. dict
C. rupt
D. mort

43. What is the correct plural of waltz?

A. Waltzs
B. Waltzes
C. Waltzies
D. Waltzzes

44. Select the context clue from the following sentence that helps you define the multiple meaning word <u>operation</u>.

The family has always worked together to run their small farming <u>operation</u>.

A. "family"
B. "always"
C. "worked"
D. "farming"

45. Select the form of the verb that agrees with the following subject.

The people in the restaurant

A. Eats
B. Eat
C. Eating
D. Eaten

46. **Why is the following <u>not</u> a correct sentence?**

The clown sad.

A. It does not have a verb.

B. It does not have a noun.

C. The verb tense is incorrect.

D. The words are in the wrong order.

47. **How many adjectives are in the following sentence?**

The children love to play with the cute, furry kitten.

A. 0

B. 1

C. 2

D. 3

48. **What is the mistake in the following sentence?**

Hospital's can be scary, because they are filled with sick people and needles.

A. The comma is misplaced.

B. There should be a colon after *with*.

C. There should be a comma after *people*.

D. *Hospital's* does not need an apostrophe.

49. **Which of the following spellings is correct?**

A. Lonliness

B. Lonelines

C. Loneliness

D. Loneleness

50 **Which of the following verbs <u>cannot</u> take a direct object?**

A. Snore

B. Watch

C. Choose

D. Bake

51. **Which word(s) in the following sentence should be capitalized?**

My friend's birthday is december 25. she does not like that her birthday is on christmas.

A. christmas

B. december

C. december and christmas

D. december, she, and christmas

52. **Which of the following uses a conjunction to combine the sentences below so the focus is on Tony preparing for his job interview?**

Tony prepared well for his job interview. Tony ended up getting an offer.

A. Tony ended up getting an offer; he prepared for his job interview.

B. Tony prepared well for his job interview, he ended up getting an offer.

C. Tony prepared well for his job interview and he ended up getting an offer.

D. Tony ended up getting an offer because he prepared for his job interview.

53. **What tense are the underlined verbs in the following sentence?**

We <u>read</u> a book and <u>wrote</u> a paper about it.

A. Simple past

B. Past perfect

C. Simple present

D. Present perfect

54. How would you connect the following clauses?

The trial must begin.

She shows up or not.

A. The trial must begin and she shows up or not.

B. The trial must begin which she shows up or not.

C. The trial must begin because she shows up or not.

D. The trial must begin whether she shows up or not.

55. What is the correct plural of chair?

A. Chair

B. Chairs

C. Chaires

D. Chairies

56. Which of the following options correctly fixes the run-on sentence below?

Taking a foreign language class is important speaking another language allows us to connect with others in our world.

A. Taking a foreign language class is important, speaking another language allows us to connect with others in our world.

B. Taking a foreign language class is important. Speaking another language allows us to connect with others in our world.

C. Taking a foreign language class is important and speaking another language allows us to connect with others in our world.

D. Taking a foreign language class is important speaking. Another language allows us to connect with others in our world.

57. Select the verb that best completes the following sentence.

Katharina didn't ____ her job as an accountant, so she decided to change careers.

A. like

B. likes

C. liken

D. liked

58. What is the mistake in the following sentence?

He asked me, "What are you doing this weekend."

A. The comma is misplaced.

B. There should be a semicolon after *me*.

C. There shouldn't be any quotation marks.

D. There should be a question mark after *weekend*.

59. Since it is raining outside, I should _____ a raincoat.

A. wear

B. ware

C. where

D. whear

60. Select the correct definition of the underlined word having multiple meanings in the sentence.

Natalie's fingers were calloused after practicing her <u>bass</u>.

A. Kind of fish

B. Low and deep sound

C. Lowest male singing voice

D. A guitar with four strings that makes low sounds

HSPT Practice Exam 1
Answer Key with Explanatory Answers

Section I. Verbal Skills

1. **A.** The statements describe that both Mary and Sally attend Northern Heights. **See Lesson: Understanding Primary Sources, Making Inferences and Drawing Conclusions.**

2. **C.** A building is the result of constructing. Dinner is the result of cooking. **See Lesson: Synonyms, Antonyms, and Analogies.**

3. **A.** Abase means to lower, demean, or degrade. **See Lesson: Synonyms, Antonyms, and Analogies.**

4. **B.** Aggregate means to gather or collect. Distribute is an antonym to aggregate. **See Lesson: Synonyms, Antonyms, and Analogies.**

5. **B.** Ted could not have received an award if Kayla received one and the science fair only awards one per class. **See Lesson: Understanding Primary Sources, Making Inferences and Drawing Conclusions.**

6. **A.** Brazen means excessively bold or brash. **See Lesson: Synonyms, Antonyms, and Analogies.**

7. **A.** Buffet means to hit or strike. It does not mean to assist. **See Lesson: Synonyms, Antonyms, and Analogies.**

8. **B.** A couch belongs *in* a room like a stove is expected to be in a kitchen. **See Lesson: Synonyms, Antonyms, and Analogies.**

9. **A.** Captivate means to hold the interest or gain attention. **See Lesson: Synonyms, Antonyms, and Analogies.**

10. **D.** Dictate means to command or put into law. A request would be the opposite of dictate. **See Lesson: Synonyms, Antonyms, and Analogies.**

11. **C.** Although Taylor and Jacob arrive at each of their destinations at the same time, the statements do not indicate which direction they went or where their end location is. **See Lesson: Understanding Primary Sources, Making Inferences and Drawing Conclusions.**

12. **A.** Extravagant means indulgent, excessive, or over-the-top. **See Lesson: Synonyms, Antonyms, and Analogies.**

13. **A.** Indictment means to accuse of wrongdoing. To absolve would be to free or release someone of wrongdoing. **See Lesson: Synonyms, Antonyms, and Analogies.**

14. A. A shark is expected to be in the ocean, necessary for survival. Only a lion is expected to be in the jungle for survival. **See Lesson: Synonyms, Antonyms, and Analogies.**

15. A. Gregarious means affable, sociable, or outgoing. **See Lesson: Synonyms, Antonyms, and Analogies.**

16. B. Laud means to applaud or praise. Denounce means to blame or accuse. **See Lesson: Synonyms, Antonyms, and Analogies.**

17. A. The statements describe that Halloween will be in one week and that the day indicated is Saturday. **See Lesson: Understanding Primary Sources, Making Inferences and Drawing Conclusions.**

18. D. Inclination is a tendency or propensity. **See Lesson: Synonyms, Antonyms, and Analogies.**

19. B. Malleable means to be changeable. Firm does not relate to malleable. **See Lesson: Synonyms, Antonyms, and Analogies.**

20. D. Students are expected to learn in a school like customers are expected to shop in a store. **See Lesson: Synonyms, Antonyms, and Analogies.**

21. A. Malicious means detrimental or vicious. **See Lesson: Synonyms, Antonyms, and Analogies.**

22. A. Pariah means to be outcast. Friend is the only option not related to being an outsider or unaccepted. **See Lesson: Synonyms, Antonyms, and Analogies.**

23. A. If Tracy takes every envelope, the conclusion is that the box will have no more envelopes inside of it. **See Lesson: Understanding Primary Sources, Making Inferences and Drawing Conclusions.**

24. B. Pugnacious means belligerent or violent. **See Lesson: Synonyms, Antonyms, and Analogies.**

25. C. Only lean is not related to portly which means chubby or round. **See Lesson: Synonyms, Antonyms, and Analogies.**

26. B. Uniform means to conforming or unvarying. **See Lesson: Synonyms, Antonyms, and Analogies.**

27. A. Stripes can be found on a tiger like leaves can be found on a tree. **See Lesson: Synonyms, Antonyms, and Analogies.**

28. D. Retaliate means to get even with someone. Sympathize is an antonym of retaliate. **See Lesson: Synonyms, Antonyms, and Analogies.**

29. B. The first statement describes that Henry only went to one portion of the tournament since it began before he arrived, and ended after he must have left. **See Lesson: Understanding Primary Sources, Making Inferences and Drawing Conclusions.**

30. D. Weaken is not related to the other words which describe mobility and liveliness. **See Lesson: Synonyms, Antonyms, and Analogies.**

31. B. Critical is unrelated to the words which describe being soft or unaggressive. **See Lesson: Synonyms, Antonyms, and Analogies.**

32. D. Comatose means sleepy or lethargic. **See Lesson: Synonyms, Antonyms, and Analogies.**

33. B. Distressing is not related. The other words describe tolerability or being sanguine. **See Lesson: Synonyms, Antonyms, and Analogies.**

34. A. A fern is a type of plant. While a crop is a descriptor for plants, crops are plants that are harvested for use. **See Lesson: Synonyms, Antonyms, and Analogies.**

35. D. Terse means abrupt, brief, or short. **See Lesson: Synonyms, Antonyms, and Analogies.**

36. B. The third statement is contradictory since the first statement provides an absolute indication that Garfield *always* finishes his dinner. **See Lesson: Understanding Primary Sources, Making Inferences and Drawing Conclusions.**

37. A. Adept means capable of. **See Lesson: Synonyms, Antonyms, and Analogies.**

38. C. Pacify means to assuage or ease. **See Lesson: Synonyms, Antonyms, and Analogies.**

39. D. Sagacious means shrewd or wise. **See Lesson: Synonyms, Antonyms, and Analogies.**

40. C. Steep means excessive which is the opposite of cheap. **See Lesson: Synonyms, Antonyms, and Analogies.**

41. C. These words are associated by how a person may act. To be amiable is to be friendly; to be sadistic is to be cruel. **See Lesson: Synonyms, Antonyms, and Analogies.**

42. C. While it is possible the tree described is an oak tree, there are other trees that grow to be over one hundred feet tall. The statements do not indicate that it is the only possibility. **See Lesson: Understanding Primary Sources, Making Inferences and Drawing Conclusions.**

43. A. Cheerful is an antonym to the other words that describe being sad. **See Lesson: Synonyms, Antonyms, and Analogies.**

44. A. Inclement means stormy, severe, or bitter. **See Lesson: Synonyms, Antonyms, and Analogies.**

45. D. Transparent means to be seen clearly. The other descriptors do not indicate clarity. **See Lesson: Synonyms, Antonyms, and Analogies.**

46. D. Shameful means deserving criticism. **See Lesson: Synonyms, Antonyms, and Analogies.**

47. B. The first statement describes that lady bugs have spots, but does not indicate if there is an absolute number. **See Lesson: Understanding Primary Sources, Making Inferences and Drawing Conclusions.**

48. C. To pacify means to ease or soothe. A person would properly kindle, or ignite, a fire. **See Lesson: Synonyms, Antonyms, and Analogies.**

49. B. Effortless is the only word that does not indicate a level of difficulty. **See Lesson: Synonyms, Antonyms, and Analogies.**

50. A. Consolidate means to combine. **See Lesson: Synonyms, Antonyms, and Analogies.**

51. B. Rancid means spoiled, disgusting to the smell or taste, or rotten. **See Lesson: Synonyms, Antonyms, and Analogies.**

52. D. Lucky means to occur by chance. **See Lesson: Synonyms.**

53. A. The word *half* indicates that Sally must be awake, since she was already asleep for half of it. **See Lesson: Understanding Primary Sources, Making Inferences and Drawing Conclusions.**

54. A. Perspicuous means clear. **See Lesson: Synonyms, Antonyms, and Analogies.**

55. D. A psychic will predict the future; a judge will analyze information to make a conclusion. **See Lesson: Synonyms, Antonyms, and Analogies.**

56. C. Infiltrate means to pervade. **See Lesson: Synonyms, Antonyms, and Analogies.**

57. C. Foreboding is not related as it means to foreshadow evil. While stealthy is not a positively connotated word choice, it does not have the same indication of evil. **See Lesson: Synonyms, Antonyms, and Analogies.**

58. D. To (give) respect is to (give) honor. Complimenting or flattering is going beyond a relationship of respect. **See Lesson: Synonyms, Antonyms, and Analogies.**

59. A. Demolish is not related as it is the only negatively connotated word. **See Lesson: Synonyms, Antonyms, and Analogies.**

60. C. Sharp is not related as it indicates a level of aggression that the other options do not. **See Lesson: Synonyms, Antonyms, and Analogies.**

Section II. Quantitative Skills

1. C. The series is increasing by adding positive three to the previous number in the series. **See Lesson: Basic Addition and Subtraction.**

2. D. Following the order of operations, all values are equivalent to the value 8. **See Lesson: Basic Addition and Subtraction.**

3. A. The correct solution is –10, 0, 1, 8. One approach is to place the numbers on the number line and make sure they appear from left to right in the same order they appear in the answers above. Alternatively, note that negative numbers are less than positive numbers (and 0), then order the remaining numbers. **See Lesson: Basic Addition and Subtraction.**

4. C. The series is increasing by 10. **See Lesson: Basic Addition and Subtraction.**

5. B. Value I is equal to 8 and Value II is equal to 3. **See Lesson: Basic Addition and Subtraction.**

6. C. The correct solution is zero. Try a few examples: 6 – 6, 100 – 100, (–5) – (–5). All are equal to zero. **See Lesson: Basic Addition and Subtraction.**

7. C. The missing letter is W. The series is the alphabet in reverse order. **See Lesson: Interpreting Categorical and Qualitative Data.**

8. B. Value I is equal to 15 while Value II is equal to 5. **See Lesson: Basic Multiplication and Division.**

9. C. Since division yields a positive quotient when the signs of the dividend and divisor are the same, the answer must be positive. Pick any nonzero number: 231 ÷ 231, for example. The quotient is always 1. **See Lesson: Basic Multiplication and Division.**

10. A. The next letter in the series would be E. **See Lesson: Interpreting Categorical and Qualitative Data.**

11. D. All values are equal to 28. **See Lesson: Basic Multiplication and Division.**

12. B. The correct solution is points B, D, and F because these points are line $\overleftrightarrow{BF}$. **See Lesson: Congruence.**

13. C. The exponent is increasing by 1 within the series. **See Lesson: Powers, Exponents, Roots, and Radicals.**

14. C. Value II is equivalent to 0.09. Value III is equivalent to 0.10 which is the value of I and II added together. **See Lesson: Decimals and Fractions.**

15. A. The correct solution is $\frac{5}{12}$ because $\frac{5}{12}$ has the largest numerator when comparing to the other fractions with the same denominator. The fractions with a common denominator of 12 are $\frac{5}{12} = \frac{5}{12}, \frac{1}{3} = \frac{4}{12}, \frac{1}{6} = \frac{2}{12}, \frac{1}{4} = \frac{3}{12}$. **See Lesson: Decimals and Fractions.**

16. C. The series is the square root of a number divided by 2. **See Lesson: Powers, Exponents, Roots, and Radicals.**

17. C. Value I is equivalent to the fraction $\frac{2}{4}$. Adding Value I and II together equals $\frac{3}{4}$. **See Lesson: Decimals and Fractions.**

18. A. The correct solution is $\frac{1}{10}$ because $1-(\frac{1}{6} + \frac{2}{5} + \frac{1}{3}) = 1-(\frac{5}{30} + \frac{12}{30} + \frac{10}{30}) = 1-\frac{27}{30} = 1-\frac{9}{10} = \frac{1}{10}$ of the yard remaining. **See Lesson: Solving Real World Mathematical Problems.**

19. A. Each exponent within the series is increasing by 1. **See Lesson: Polynomials.**

20. A. Value II converted into lowest common terms is equivalent to $\frac{1}{3}$. **See Lesson: Decimals and Fractions.**

21. B. The correct solution is –\$85 because 250–(70 + 85 + 60 + 100+ 20) = 250 – 335 = –\$85. **See Lesson: Solving Real World Mathematical Problems.**

22. C. The series numbers are increasing perfect squares. **See Lesson: Powers, Exponents, Roots, and Radicals.**

23. C. Value I is equivalent to $\frac{1}{3}$ and Value II is equivalent to 1. Value III is an improper fraction but is equal to $1\frac{1}{3}$ when converted to a mixed number. **See Lesson: Decimals and Fractions.**

24. D. The correct solution is line segment because the cities represent the endpoints and the segment is the distance between the two points. **See Lesson: Congruence.**

25. B. The variable stays consistent throughout the series, but the constant number increases by 12. **See Lesson: Polynomials.**

26. A. Value I equals $\frac{2}{21}$ and Value II equals $\frac{15}{30}$ or $\frac{1}{2}$. **See Lesson: Multiplication and Division of Fractions.**

27. A. Regardless of the order of the factors, the product is the same. For instance, 12 × 13 = 13 × 12 = 156. **See Lesson: Basic Multiplication and Division.**

28. C. The series is increasing by 0.08. **See Lesson: Decimals and Fractions.**

29. B. Value I is equal to 1 and Value II is equal to $\frac{4}{12}$ or $\frac{1}{3}$. **See Lesson: Multiplication and Division of Fractions.**

30. B. The correct solution is $1\frac{1}{5}$ because $\frac{2}{5} \times \frac{3}{1} = \frac{6}{5} = 1\frac{1}{5}$. **See Lesson: Multiplication and Division of Fractions.**

31. D. The series is decreasing by four tenths, which would make the next number in the series 0. **See Lesson: Decimals and Fractions.**

32. B. The correct solution for Value I is $\frac{3}{5} \times \frac{2}{3} = \frac{6}{15}$. The correct solution for Value II is $\frac{1}{3} \times \frac{9}{5} = \frac{9}{15}$. **See Lesson: Multiplication and Division of Fractions.**

33. B. The correct answer is $0.8\overline{3}$ because $83.\overline{3}\%$ as a decimal is $0.8\overline{3}$. **See Lesson: Decimals and Fractions.**

34. B. The series increases by seven with each succession. **See Lesson: Basic Addition and Subtraction.**

35. B. Value I is equal to 21 because Adam walks a total of 3 miles each day. 3 × 7 = 21. Stacy works 6 hours each day for 3 days for a total of 18 hours. **See Lesson: Solving Real World Mathematical Problems.**

36. D. The correct answer is $2\frac{31}{42}$ because $\frac{23}{14} \div \frac{3}{5} = \frac{23}{14} \times \frac{5}{3} = \frac{115}{42} = 2\frac{31}{42}$. **See Lesson: Multiplication and Division of Fractions.**

37. C. The percentages are increasing by a factor 3. **See Lesson: Ratios, Proportions, and Percentages.**

38. C. Value II is equal to \$480 because $3200 \times 0.15 = 480$. **See Lesson: Solving Real World Mathematical Problems.**

39. C. The correct solution is (3, –3) because this point shows a square has a side length of 5. **See Lesson: Similarity, Right Triangles, and Trigonometry.**

40. B. The series has each number increase by 1 so that the ratio is always equivalent to $\frac{1}{2}$. **See Lesson: Ratios, Proportions, and Percentages.**

41. C. There are 12 inches in a foot and 3 feet in a yard. $12 + 3 = 15$. **See Lesson: Standards of Measure.**

42. A. To determine whether a number is a factor of another number, divide the second number by the first number. If the quotient is whole, the first number is a factor. In this case, all the numbers are prime, but 108 is only divisible by 3. **See Lesson: Factors and Multiples.**

43. A. The series is a fraction with 1 as the numerator and the denominator increases by 2. **See Lesson: Ratios, Proportions, and Percentages.**

44. B. Following the rules of exponents, Value II is equal to 4 and Value III is equal to -27. **See Lesson: Powers, Exponents, Roots, and Radicals.**

45. C. The correct solution 12 units. The difference between the x-coordinates is $6-(-6) = 12$ units and the difference between the y-coordinates is $6-(-6) = 12$ units. **See Lesson: Similarity, Right Triangles, and Trigonometry.**

46. A. The series is decreasing by 4°F. **See Lesson: Standards of Measure.**

47. A. Following the rules of exponents, Value I is equivalent to 12. Value II is 25 and Value III is 64. **See Lesson: Powers, Exponents, Roots, and Radicals.**

48. C. The series is increasing by increments of 3π. **See Lesson: Standards of Measure.**

49. A. Value I is 11 and Value II is 49. **See Lesson: Powers, Exponents, Roots, and Radicals.**

50. D. Use a factor tree to find the prime factors of 99. The factors are 3, 3, and 11. **See Lesson: Factors and Multiples.**

51. C. Value I is equal to 225 whereas the square root of 225 is 15. Add the two values together and the total is 240, or Value III. **See Lesson: Powers, Exponents, Roots, and Radicals.**

52. A. The correct solution is $\widehat{LM}$ because L and M are on the circle. **See Lesson: Circles.**

Section III. Reading and Vocabulary

Part 1: Reading

1. A. Passage 1 is intended to inform readers about electroconvulsive therapy. **See Lesson: Understanding the Author's Purpose, Point of View, and Rhetorical Strategies.**

2. C. The second paragraph of passage 1 makes opinion statements about what doctors should do. This is a sign of persuasive writing. **See Lesson: Understanding the Author's Purpose, Point of View, and Rhetorical Strategies.**

3. D. Passage 2 tells a story, which is meant to entertain. **See Lesson: Understanding the Author's Purpose, Point of View, and Rhetorical Strategies.**

4. D. Passage 1 says that electroconvulsive therapy is "a genuine option for patients whose symptoms do not improve with medication." This suggests that medication should be tried first. **See Lesson: Understanding the Author's Purpose, Point of View, and Rhetorical Strategies.**

5. C. The detail about electroconvulsive therapy as "a genuine option for patients whose symptoms do not improve with medication" suggests that patients should try an option like medication first, before contemplating electroconvulsive therapy. **See Lesson: Understanding the Author's Purpose, Point of View, and Rhetorical Strategies.**

6. A. The author of Passage 1 is aware that many people have negative preconceived ideas about electroconvulsive therapy. This is true of the author of Passage 2, who does not inform herself about the facts of the situation. **See Lesson: Understanding the Author's Purpose, Point of View, and Rhetorical Strategies.**

7. D. The author of Passage 1 specifically recommends extra care in communication about electroconvulsive therapy. The doctor in Passage 2 does not seem to make any extra effort to differentiate between myth and reality. **See Lesson: Understanding the Author's Purpose, Point of View, and Rhetorical Strategies.**

8. A. The author of Passage 2 describes doctors blocking her "direct path to the door," which suggests that she feels trapped in the room. This suggests a negative, fearful outlook which is further reinforced by the comment about Big Doctor being "sadistic." **See Lesson: Understanding the Author's Purpose, Point of View, and Rhetorical Strategies.**

9. B. The author of Passage 1 uses primarily facts and logic, although she could strengthen her points by clearly identifying sources or establishing her credentials. **See Lesson: Understanding the Author's Purpose, Point of View, and Rhetorical Strategies.**

10. B. A summary must restate the ideas of the original text, not comment on them with judgments or speculation, and without adhering too closely to the wording of the original.

This paragraph explains how shipping and refrigeration technology helped bananas become a major export crop. **See Lesson: Summarizing Text and Using Text Features.**

11. B. These sentences, like all effective summaries, restate the ideas of the original text in different words. Although a summary can sometimes state an implicit idea from the original text, this one does not need to do so. **See Lesson: Summarizing Text and Using Text Features.**

12. C. The structure and word choice of this sentence are so close to the original that it qualifies as plagiarism. **See Lesson: Summarizing Text and Using Text Features.**

13. B. This sentence comments on the original text rather than summarizing it. Some types of writing allow this, but it is not a summary. **See Lesson: Summarizing Text and Using Text Features.**

14. D. It would be inaccurate to say that nobody would eat bananas if modern shipping and refrigeration technology had never been invented. This is not in the original text, and logically speaking, bananas would still be eaten in the tropics regardless of changes in technology. **See Lesson: Summarizing Text and Using Text Features.**

15. A. The opening sentence of the passage makes a general claim to be read as fact since it is supported by the details of the passage. **See Lesson: Facts, Opinions, and Evaluating an Argument.**

16. C. Although this passage relates to history, a general history textbook is not highly specific to assert that the passage came from it. It likely came from a science magazine discussing fruit trade. **See Lesson: Types of Passages, Text Structure, Genre and Theme.**

17. C. The line graph would display how banana exports from Central America have risen since a time period before steamships, railways, and refrigeration to support the passage. **See Lesson: Evaluating and Integrating Data.**

18. B. This author is not very trustworthy, but he does not make any attempt to conceal the fact that he is sharing his personal opinions rather than facts. The fact that he begins with the sentence "You know what I hate?" is a clear cue that this is argumentative writing. **See Lesson: Understanding Primary Sources, Making Inferences and Drawing Conclusions.**

19. C. The sentence about freelancers not making as much money is one of the few logical points this blog post makes, but the writer does not share his sources. This makes it difficult for the reader to verify the information. **See Lesson: Understanding Primary Sources, Making Inferences and Drawing Conclusions.**

20. B. The passage raises the opposing argument that freelancing provides greater freedom for workers, but the writer does not respond to this argument. Instead, he makes a manipulatively emotional argument. **See Lesson: Understanding Primary Sources, Making Inferences and Drawing Conclusions.**

21. C. A government website tracking statistics might be a good source, but it would provide facts rather than opinions. An opinion article by an expert in the field would more likely offer what the student is looking for. **See Lesson: Understanding Primary Sources, Making Inferences and Drawing Conclusions.**

22. D. The author demonstrates a frustration with business relying on contract workers because they supposedly do not have to support employees with health benefits and still pay a smaller wage. **See Lesson: Facts, Opinions, and Evaluating an Argument.**

23. C. Using a specific example to support the author's claim would help make the argument stronger, despite making a manipulatively emotional argument. **See Lesson: Facts, Opinions, and Evaluating an Argument.**

24. A. Throughout the passage, the author is sharing personal opinions without many facts to show their reasoning. Stating "I disagree" is a more formal way to share that concluded opinion. **See Lesson: Formal and Informal Language.**

25. B. While the author of the passage is misguided in creating a compelling argument, the purpose of the writing is meant to discuss how freelancers cannot enjoy workplace freedom due to their unbenefited health and lower wages. **See Lesson: Types of Passages, Text Structure, Genre and Theme.**

26. B. The first sentence of this paragraph expresses the main idea that people should be concerned by even a small amount of climate change. This makes it the topic sentence. **See Lesson: Main Ideas, Topic Sentences, and Supporting Details.**

27. A. The topic of a sentence is a word or phrase that describes what the text is about. **See Lesson: Main Ideas, Topic Sentences, and Supporting Details.**

28. C. This paragraph argues that a small change in global temperatures could have a major result. This idea is expressed in a topic sentence at the beginning of the paragraph. **See Lesson: Main Ideas, Topic Sentences, and Supporting Details.**

29. D. The information about temperature differences in the last ice age supports the main idea that people should be concerned by global climate change. This makes it a supporting detail. **See Lesson: Main Ideas, Topic Sentences, and Supporting Details.**

30. B. All of the above sentences relate to the topic of global climate change, but only the sentence about the Little Ice Age relates directly to the main idea that a small amount of climate fluctuation is cause for concern. **See Lesson: Main Ideas, Topic Sentences, and Supporting Details.**

31. A. The author's argument discusses how small temperature changes have a large impact on the planet. A line graph to show the small change in mean global temperatures. **See Lesson: Evaluating and Integrating Data.**

32. C. A graph with the change in volume of ice on Earth's surface would show the most change to add visual emphasis to the passage. While all options have an element related to global temperature change, the graphic(s) would not provide dramatic evidence for a reader. **See Lesson: Evaluating and Integrating Data.**

33. D. To make the sentence more formal, the rewrite should avoid choppy sentence structure and unnecessary definitions or jargon. **See Lesson: Formal and Informal Language.**

34. B. The author describes how the ice age occurred with a global temperature that is five degrees less than today. With the scientific prediction that the same level of temperature change is possible, the ending question harmonizes the details and adds emphasis to the argument. **See Lesson: Formal and Informal Language.**

35. C. This passage ironically is an amusing description of an adolescent written by an adult who has enough experience to know that her daughter's huge emotions will pass and the little girl inside her will poke out. **See Lesson: Tone, Mood, and Transition Words.**

36. B. Authors use irony when their words do not literally mean what they say. The daughter is clearly having an awful day based on her words and actions, and the use of the word "marvelous" adds an ironic tone to the passage. **See Lesson: Tone, Mood, and Transition Words.**

37. A. This passage establishes irony in the opening sentence by applying a positive adjective, "celebratory" to an ordinary occurrence that is usually negative, such as the banging of a door. **See Lesson: Tone, Mood, and Transition Words.**

38. A. Effective readers would likely know this is just the life of an adolescent since we have all been through this time in our lives. Entertained would be a more likely reaction. **See Lesson: Tone, Mood, and Transition Words.**

39. A. The word "instantly" explains how quickly the mother felt "dismayed" but does not transition between ideas. **See Lesson: Tone, Mood, and Transition Words.**

40. B. "However" and "despite" both indicate a difference between ideas. **See Lesson: Tone, Mood, and Transition Words.**

41. B. "Furthermore" would be the transition to use as in: *Furthermore, she made a "tsk" sound.* This would show how the author is building on an established line of thought. **See Lesson: Tone, Mood, and Transition Words.**

42. D. The author wrote this passage to show how her daughter is being dramatic with descriptions of being "stomped right by" and being given a "quintessential eye roll". The author is not concerned about the statement because her daughter is making an assumption about her teacher because she had a bad day. **See Lesson: Facts, Opinions, and Evaluating an Argument**

Part 2: Vocabulary

1. C. The prefix *pre-* means "before," so, predetermined means decided before something happens. **See Lesson: Root Words, Prefixes, and Suffixes.**

2. A. The root *irasc* means "to be angry" and the suffix *-ible* means "able to be," so irascible means easily angered. **See Lesson: Root Words, Prefixes, and Suffixes.**

3. C. The prefix *re-* means "again," and the root word *juven* means "young," so rejuvenate means to make someone feel young again. **See Lesson: Root Words, Prefixes, and Suffixes.**

4. D. The root *neo* means "new and recent," so a neophyte is someone who it new to something. **See Lesson: Root Words, Prefixes, and Suffixes.**

5. A. The root *funct* means "perform, work," and the prefix *dys-* means "faulty or bad," so something that is dysfunctional is not working right. **See Lesson: Root Words, Prefixes, and Suffixes.**

6. C. The root word *circum* means "around," so circumvent means to find a way around. **See Lesson: Root Words, Prefixes, and Suffixes.**

7. B. The prefix *dis-* means "not" and the root word *cord* means "heart," so discord means conflict. **See Lesson: Root Words, Prefixes, and Suffixes.**

8. B. The root word *flect* means "to bend," so genuflect means to bow. **See Lesson: Root Words, Prefixes, and Suffixes.**

9. C. The root word *trans* mean "across," so transcontinental means across the continent. **See Lesson: Root Words, Prefixes, and Suffixes.**

10. B. The root word *magn* mPeans "great or large," so, a magnate would be a wealthy and powerful person. **See Lesson: Root Words, Prefixes, and Suffixes.**

11. C. The root *locu* means "speak," so a loquacious person would be talkative. **See Lesson: Root Words, Prefixes, and Suffixes.**

12. B. Flaccid means limp. **See Lesson: Synonyms, Antonyms, and Analogies.**

13. D. Hapless means unlucky or woeful. **See Lesson: Synonyms, Antonyms, and Analogies.**

14. D. Retract means to withdraw. **See Lesson: Synonyms, Antonyms, and Analogies.**

15. B. Torrid means very hot, or arid. **See Lesson: Synonyms, Antonyms, and Analogies.**

16. A. Presumptuous means disrespectfully bold or arrogant. **See Lesson: Synonyms, Antonyms, and Analogies.**

17. C. Compel means to force. **See Lesson: Synonyms, Antonyms, and Analogies.**

18. D. Dutiful means careful to fulfill obligations, or obedient. **See Lesson: Synonyms, Antonyms, and Analogies.**

19. B. Sordid means dirty. **See Lesson: Synonyms, Antonyms, and Analogies.**

20. C. Innate means inborn, native, or inherent. **See Lesson: Synonyms, Antonyms, and Analogies.**

Section IV. Mathematical Skills

1. B. The correct solution is $\bar{BD}$ because B and D are on the circle and the segment goes through the center of the circle. **See Lesson: Circles.**

2. B. The correct solution is 90. This situation requires finding the difference between 127 and 37. Use the subtraction algorithm if necessary: 127 – 37 = 90. **See Lesson: Basic Addition and Subtraction.**

3. D. The correct solution is 1,114. Use the addition algorithm or note the two numbers never have nonzero digits in the same place. This fact allows addition by inspection. **See Lesson: Basic Addition and Subtraction.**

4. B. When dividing signed numbers, remember that if the dividend and divisor have different signs, the quotient is negative. Other than the sign, the process is the same as dividing whole numbers. Use the division algorithm to divide 224 by 14. **See Lesson: Basic Multiplication and Division.**

5. C. Instead of adding the same number over and over (for example, 5 + 5 + 5 + 5 + 5 + 5), multiplication enables a more concise expression. In this example, because the expression adds 6 terms of 5, it becomes 6 × 5, or 30. **See Lesson: Basic Multiplication and Division.**

6. B. The correct solution is 874.4. $C = \frac{1}{2}(2\pi r); 74 = 3.14r; r \approx 23.6$ inches. $A = \frac{1}{2}\pi r^2 \approx \frac{1}{2}(3.14)(23.6)^2 \approx \frac{1}{2}3.14(556.96) \approx 874.4$ square inches. **See Lesson: Circles.**

7. D. The correct solution is 69.08 because $C = 2\pi r \approx (2)3.14(11) \approx 69.08$ centimeters. **See Lesson: Circles.**

8. C. The correct solution is C. This is a rotation of 90° counterclockwise because the point (x, y) becomes $(-y, x)$. **See Lesson: Congruence.**

9. D. The correct solution is a rotation of 270° counterclockwise because the points (x, y) become $(y, -x)$. **See Lesson: Congruence.**

10. A. The correct solution is A. The translation for the points is $(x + 2, y + 1)$. The points of the original square, (–4, –4), (–4, 2), (2, 2), and (2, –4), become (–2, –3), (–2, 3), (4, 3), and (4, –3). **See Lesson: Congruence.**

11. D. The correct answer is 150% because 1.5 as a percent is $1.5 \times 100 = 150\%$. **See Lesson: Decimals and Fractions.**

12. D. The correct answer is $2\frac{9}{10}$ because 290% as a fraction is $2\frac{90}{100} = 2\frac{9}{10}$. **See Lesson: Decimal and Fractions**

13. C. The correct answer is 7.65 because $\frac{13}{20} = 13.00 \div 20 = 0.65$. **See Lesson: Decimals and Fractions.**

14. C. The correct solution is 6.

$\frac{x}{2} = 3$	Subtract 5 from both sides of the equation.
$x = 6$	Multiply both sides of the equation by 2.

See Lesson: Equations with One Variable.

15. C. The correct solution is $x > -1$.

$6x + 2 + 5 \geq 3x - 4 - 4x$	Apply the distributive property.
$6x + 3 \geq -x - 4$	Combine like terms on both sides of the inequality.
$7x + 3 \geq -4$	Add x to both sides of the inequality.
$7x \geq -7$	Subtract 3 from both sides of the inequality.
$x \geq -1$	Divide both sides of the inequality by 7.

See Lesson: Equations with One Variable.

16. A. The correct solution is $\frac{2ab}{1-2a} = c$.

$2ab + 2ac = c$	Apply the distributive property.
$2ab = c - 2ac$	Subtract $2ac$ from both sides of the equation.
$2ab = c(1 - 2a)$	Factor c from the right side of the equation.
$\frac{2ab}{1-2a} = c$	Divide both sides of the equation by $1-2a$.

See Lesson: Equations with One Variable.

17. B. The correct solution is (-3, 6).

$-12x + 9y = 90$	Multiply all terms in the first equation by 3.
$12x + 16y = 60$	Multiply all terms in the second equation by 4.
$25y = 150$	Add the equations.
$y = 6$	Divide both sides of the equation by 25.
$3x + 4(6) = 15$	Substitute 6 in the second equation for y.
$3x + 24 = 15$	Simplify using order of operations.
$3x = -9$	Subtract 24 from both sides of the equation.
$x = -3$	Divide both sides of the equation by 3.

See Lesson: Equations with Two Variables.

18. A. To determine whether a number is a factor of another number, divide the second number by the first number. If the quotient is whole, the first number is a factor. In this case, 1,155 is not divisible by 22. **See Lesson: Factors and Multiples.**

19. A. The correct solutions are (1, -2) and (-1, 2).

$x^2 + (-2x)^2 = 5$	Substitute $-2x$ in for y in the second equation.
$x^2 + 4x^2 = 5$	Apply the exponent.
$5x^2 = 5$	Combine like terms on the left side of the equation.
$x^2 = 1$	Divide both sides of the equation by 5.
$x = \pm 1$	Apply the square root to both sides of the equation.
$y = -2(1) = -2$	Substitute 1 in the first equation and multiply.
$y = -2(-1) = 2$	Substitute -1 in the first equation and multiply.

See Lesson: Equations with Two Variables.

20. A. The correct solution is there were 60 turns in the game. The sum of the results is 12 + 9 + 8 + 13 + 7 + 11, which is 60 turns. **See Lesson: Interpreting Categorical and Quantitative Data.**

21. C. Because 3 and 5 are prime factors of the number, its prime factorization includes them. Furthermore, because a number is the product of all its prime factors, the number in this question must either be 15 or have 15 as a factor. It may or may not be 15, so it may have more than two prime factors. **See Lesson: Factors and Multiples.**

22. D. The correct graph has the two lines intersect at (5, 2). **See Lesson: Equations with Two Variables.**

23. C. The correct solution is the mean decreases, but the median does not change. The mean decreases from 46.75 to 44.83, but the median does not change from 46.5. **See Lesson: Interpreting Categorical and Quantitative Data.**

24. B. The correct solution is the team scored more than 65 points in a majority of games and gave up fewer than 65 points in a majority of games. From the graph, there are 6 games during which the team scored more than 65 points and 6 games during which it gave up fewer than 65 points. **See Lesson: Interpreting Graphics.**

25. C. The correct solution is C because each of the percent values is calculated correctly. There are 15 parts for the mix. The percentages for eggs and oil are each $\frac{2}{15} = 0.1333 = 13.33\%$. The percent for water is $\frac{3}{15} = \frac{1}{5} = 0.20 = 20\%$. The percent for mixture is $\frac{7}{15} = 0.4667 = 46.67\%$. The percent for vanilla is $\frac{1}{15} = 0.0667 = 6.67\%$. **See Lesson: Interpreting Graphics.**

26. A. The correct solution is fat calories because this is a numerical value. **See Lesson: Interpreting Categorical and Quantitative Data.**

27. A. The correct solution is 14.07. The sum of the scores is 168.8, and the average is 14.07 for the 12 scores. **See Lesson: Interpreting Graphics.**

28. B. The correct solution is 523.33 cubic inches. The radius is 5 inches. Substitute the values into the formula and simplify using the order of operations, $V = \frac{4}{3}\pi r^3 = \frac{4}{3}(3.14)\,5^3 = \frac{4}{3}(3.14)(125) =$ 523.33 cubic inches. **See Lesson: Measurement and Dimension.**

29. D. The correct solution is 4 feet. Substitute the values into the formula $\frac{16}{3}\pi = \frac{2}{3}\pi r^3$, multiply both sides by the reciprocal, $8 = r^3$. Apply the cube root, $r = 2$ feet, and double the radius to find the diameter of 4 feet. **See Lesson: Measurement and Dimension.**

30. A. The correct solution is 216π. The radius is one-half of the diameter, 6 centimeters. The height of the used salsa is $10 - 4$, or 6 centimeters. Substitute the values into the formula and simplify using the order of operations, $V = \pi r^2 h = \pi 6^2(6) = \pi(36)(6) = 216\pi$ cubic centimeters. **See Lesson: Measurement and Dimension.**

31. C. The correct solution is $1\frac{1}{2}$ because $\frac{2}{1} \times \frac{3}{4} = \frac{6}{4} = 1\frac{2}{4} = 1\frac{1}{2}$. **See Lesson: Multiplication and Division of Fractions.**

32. D. The correct answer is $8\frac{2}{3}$ because $\frac{13}{7} \div \frac{3}{14} = \frac{13}{7} \times \frac{14}{3} = \frac{182}{21} = 8\frac{14}{21} = 8\frac{2}{3}$. **See Lesson: Multiplication and Division of Fractions.**

33. B. The correct answer is $\frac{1}{14}$ because $\frac{3}{14} \times \frac{1}{3} = \frac{3}{42} = \frac{1}{14}$. **See Lesson: Multiplication and Division of Fractions.**

34. B. The correct solution is $2y^4–6y^3 + 9y^2 + 3y–5$.

$(2y^2–1)(y^2–3y + 5) = (2y^2–1)(y^2) + (2y^2–1)(–3y) + (2y^2–1)(5) = 2y^4–y^2–6y^3 + 3y + 10y^2–5 = 2y^4–6y^3 + 9y^2 + 3y–5$

See Lesson: Polynomials.

35. A. The correct solution is $3x^3–6x^2 + 8x + 1$.

$(–2x^2 + 8x) + (3x^3–4x^2 + 1) = 3x^3 + (–2x^2–4x^2) + 8x + 1 = 3x^3–6x^2 + 8x + 1$

See Lesson: Polynomials.

36. B. The correct solution is $(x–10)(x + 10)$. The expression $x^2–100$ is rewritten as $(x–10)(x + 10)$ because the value of a is x and the value of b is 10. **See Lesson: Polynomials.**

37. C. The correct solution is y^4 because $\left(\frac{x^0}{y^{-2}}\right)^2 = \frac{x^{0\times2}}{y^{-2\times2}} = \frac{x^0}{y^{-4}} = \frac{1}{y^{-4}} = y^4$. **See Lesson: Powers, Exponents, Roots, and Radicals.**

38. B. The correct solution is 3 because the land area of Colorado is about 100,000 square miles and the land area of Ohio is about 40,000 square miles. So, the land area is about 3 times larger. **See Lesson: Powers, Exponents, Roots, and Radicals.**

39. B. The correct solution is –2 because the cube root of –8 is –2. **See Lesson: Powers, Exponents, Roots, and Radicals.**

40. D. To convert a ratio to a percent, divide the numbers in the ratio (noting that its equivalent fraction is $\frac{7}{3}$) to get approximately 2.33. Then, multiply by 100%. **See Lesson: Ratios, Proportions, and Percentages.**

41. A. The company's revenue is decreasing –\$60 million in a year. Begin by calculating the revenue decrease, which is the difference between \$118 million and \$123 million, or –\$5 million. That decrease is for one month. Next, set up a proportion to find the equivalent rate of change for a year, noting that a year is 12 months:

$$\frac{-\$5\ million}{1\ month} = \frac{?}{12\ months}$$

Because the denominator on the right is 12 times the denominator on the left, find the unknown rate of change by multiplying –\$5 million by 12 to get –\$60 million. Because the question asked for a rate of increase but the revenue is decreasing, the negative sign is critical. **See Lesson: Ratios, Proportions, and Percentages.**

42. D. The fraction $\frac{36}{16}$ is 225%, meaning 36 is 225% of 16. **See Lesson: Ratios, Proportions, and Percentages.**

43. D. The correct solution is 5 units and 7 units. The difference between the x-coordinates is $-4-(-9) = 5$ units, and the difference between the y-coordinates is $-1-(-8) = 7$ units. **See Lesson: Similarity, Right Triangles, and Trigonometry.**

44. B. The correct solution is 336. Substitute the values into the formula and simplify using the order of operations, $V = lwh = 6(7)(8)$ cubic centimeters. **See Lesson: Similarity, Right Triangles, and Trigonometry.**

45. D. The correct solution is 5,625. Substitute the values into the formula and simplify using the order of operations, $A = s^2 = 75^2 = 5{,}625$ square centimeters. **See Lesson: Similarity, Right Triangles, and Trigonometry.**

46. B. The correct solutions are $-2 \pm \sqrt{19}$. The equation can be solved by completing the square.

$x^2 + 4x = 15$	Add 15 to both sides of the equation.
$x^2 + 4x + 4 = 15 + 4$	Complete the square, $(\frac{4}{2})^2 = 2^2 = 4$.
	Add 4 to both sides of the equation.
$x^2 + 4x + 4 = 19$	Simplify the right side of the equation.
$(x + 2)^2 = 19$	Factor the left side of the equation.
$x + 2 = \pm\sqrt{19}$	Apply the square root to both sides of the equation.
$x = -2 \pm \sqrt{19}$	Subtract 2 from both sides of the equation.

See Lesson: Solving Quadratic Equations.

47. B. The correct solutions are 0.46 and –0.54.

$x = \frac{-1 \pm \sqrt{1^2-4(12)(-3)}}{2(12)}$	Substitute 12 for *a*, 1 for *b*, and –3 for *c*.
$x = \frac{-1 \pm \sqrt{1-(-144)}}{24}$	Apply the exponent and perform the multiplication.
$x = \frac{-1 \pm \sqrt{145}}{24}$	Perform the subtraction.
$x = \frac{-1 \pm 12.04}{24}$	Apply the square root.
$x = \frac{-1 + 12.04}{24}, x = \frac{-1-12.04}{24}$	Separate the problem into two expressions.
$x = \frac{11.04}{24} = 0.46, x = \frac{-13.04}{24} = -0.54$	Simplify the numerator and divide.

See Lesson: Solving Quadratic Equations.

48. C. The correct solution is ± 10.

$x^2 = 100$	Subtract 10 from both sides of the equation.
$x \pm 10$	Apply the square root to both sides of the equation.

See Lesson: Solving Quadratic Equations.

49. B. The correct solution is 20.48 because 39.45–18.97 = 20.48 feet. **See Lesson: Solving Real World Mathematical Problems.**

50. B. The correct solution is –5 because 14(2) + 11(–3) = 28 + (–33) = –5 points. **See Lesson: Solving Real World Mathematical Problems.**

51. C. The correct solution is 1,530 because 1,450–(–80) = 1,450 + 80 = 1,530 feet. **See Lesson: Solving Real World Mathematical Problems.**

52. A. The correct solution is 7.8125 gallons. $1{,}000\, fl\ oz \times \frac{1\ pt}{16\ fl\ oz} \times \frac{1\ qt}{2\ pt} \times \frac{1\ gal}{4\ qt} = \frac{1{,}000}{128} = 7.8125\ gal$. **See Lesson: Standards of Measure.**

53. D. The correct solution is 19.68 feet. $6\ m \times \frac{3.28\ ft}{1\ m} = 19.68\ ft$. **See Lesson: Standards of Measure.**

54. B. The correct solution is 500,000 milliliters. $0.5\ kL \times \frac{1{,}000\ L}{1\ kL} \times \frac{1{,}000\ mL}{1\ L} = 500{,}000\ mL$. **See Lesson: Standards of Measure.**

55. C. The correct solution is experiment because the number of hours of sleep are observed with and without music. **See Lesson: Statistical Measures.**

56. A. The correct solution is yes, because there are not enough simulations. Only 10 simulations can lead to questioning the probability because there are a small number of simulations. **See Lesson: Statistical Measures.**

57. B. The correct solution is employees who drive to work daily because this sample represents an accurate sample from the population of all employees. **See Lesson: Statistical Measures.**

58. B. The correct solution is $\frac{66}{325}$. There are 12 out of 26 boys' name on the first draw and 11 out of 25 boys' name on the second draw. The probability of the event is $\frac{12}{26} \times \frac{11}{25} = \frac{132}{650} = \frac{66}{325}$. **See Lesson: Statistics & Probability: The Rules of Probability.**

59. C. The correct solution is 80% of gaining $4,000 and 20% of gaining $0. The expected value is 0.80(40) = $3,200. **See Lesson: Statistics & Probability: The Rules of Probability.**

60. B. The correct solution is students who like math and social studies because it is the intersection of two events. **See Lesson: Statistics & Probability: The Rules of Probability.**

Section V. Language

1. D. *Safely* is an adverb that describes the verb *traveled.* **See Lesson: Adjectives and Adverbs.**

2. A. *Argument* is the only correct spelling. **See Lesson: Spelling.**

3. B. *The* is an article, not a conjunction. **See Lesson: Conjunctions and Prepositions.**

4. B. The word "prune" has more than one meaning. **See Lesson: Context Clues and Multiple Meaning Words.**

5. C. *The dog* is the direct object of the verb *walk.* **See Lesson: Direct Objects and Indirect Objects.**

6. D. *Who was a year older* describes *Marvin.* **See Lesson: Modifiers, Misplaced Modifiers, and Dangling Modifiers.**

7. B. *Possibility* is the only correct spelling. **See Lesson: Spelling.**

8. C. *Who* is a relative pronoun. **See Lesson: Pronouns.**

9. C. *I go to bed early so I do not feel tired.* There should be a comma before so as it is a coordinating conjunction. **See Lesson: Punctuation.**

10. D. The prefix that means "too much" is *over.* **See Lesson: Root Words, Prefixes, and Suffixes.**

11. B. *Criticism* is the only correct spelling. **See Lesson: Spelling.**

12. C. *The automobile* and *the personal computer* are both singular subjects connected by *or,* so they take a singular verb form. **See Lesson: Subject and Verb Agreement.**

13. C. *Which.* The word "which" signifies the beginning of a dependent clause and is the only conjunction that makes sense in the sentence. **See Lesson: Types of Clauses.**

14. A. This option would make the sentence a complete thought with a subject and a predicate. **See Lesson: Types of Sentences.**

15. C. Gone with the Wind. Publication titles are capitalized. Shorter prepositions, articles, and conjunctions within titles are not capitalized. **See Lesson: Capitalization.**

16. A. *Supreme Court* is a noun. **See Lesson: Nouns.**

17. D. *Accommodation* is the only correct spelling. **See Lesson: Spelling.**

18. B. *Northern Ireland.* Directional words like northern are capitalized when it is a part of the official name. **See Lesson: Capitalization.**

19. D. *Marie Curie, Nobel Prize,* and *1911* are nouns. **See Lesson: Nouns.**

20. C. *A movie* is the direct object of the verb *watched.* **See Lesson: Direct Objects and Indirect Objects.**

21. D. *Which was ugly* most likely refers to *hat,* so it should be placed after that word, not after *head.* **See Lesson: Modifiers, Misplaced Modifiers, and Dangling Modifiers.**

22. D. *Hers* cannot be used to modify a noun. **See Lesson: Pronouns.**

23. C. *Red* is an adjective that describes the noun *roses.* **See Lesson: Adjectives and Adverbs.**

24. C. *But* and *so* are coordinating conjunctions. These two conjunctions connect three independent clauses in this sentence. **See Lesson: Conjunctions and Prepositions.**

25. D. American Civil Liberties Union. National organizations need to be capitalized. **See Lesson: Capitalization.**

26. D. *Ashley's determined to learn.* Ashley's stands for Ashley is and is the only correct use of an apostrophe in the examples. **See Lesson: Punctuation.**

27. C. *Quite* is an adverb that describes the adjective *tall. Tall* is an adjective that describes the noun *man.* **See Lesson: Adjectives and Adverbs.**

28. D. With a word ending in -f, you drop the -f and add -ves. **See Lesson: Spelling.**

29. B. *Offered* and *advised* are simple past tense verb forms. **See Lesson: Verbs and Verb Tenses.**

30. A. The suffix that means "having characteristics of" is *ic.* **See Lesson: Root Words, Prefixes, and Suffixes.**

31. A. *Hoping to improve his grade* refers to *he.* **See Lesson: Modifiers, Misplaced Modifiers, and Dangling Modifiers.**

32. B. *There needs to be a semicolon after studying.* A semicolon is used to connect two related sentences. **See Lesson: Punctuation.**

33. C. White House. The White House is capitalized because it is an important governmental building. **See Lesson: Capitalization.**

34. D. *Yours* is a possessive pronoun. **See Lesson: Pronouns.**

35. A. *It* is a pronoun, not a preposition. **See Lesson: Conjunctions and Prepositions.**

36. A. The verb *has* must agree with the subject *everyone.* **See Lesson: Subject and Verb Agreement.**

37. D. With words ending in -f, drop the -f and add -ves. **See Lesson: Spelling.**

38. D. *Passersby* is the only correct plural form offered. It is the plural of the noun *passerby.* **See Lesson: Nouns.**

39. A. *Wait!* Exclamation points are placed at the end of a sentence and indicate strong feelings, shouting, or emphasis. **See Lesson: Punctuation.**

40. C. World War I. Specific wars and historical eras are capitalized. General historical eras like nineteenth century are not capitalized. **See Lesson: Capitalization.**

41. C. People do not exercise as much as they should. It is independent because it has a subject, verb, and expresses a complete thought. **See Lesson: Types of Clauses.**

42. A. The root that means "to throw" is *ject.* **See Lesson: Root Words, Prefixes, and Suffixes.**

43. B. With words ending in -z, add -es. **See Lesson: Spelling.**

44. C. The meaning of operation in this context is "a small business." The phrase "worked" helps you figure out which meaning of operation is being used. **See Lesson: Context Clues and Multiple Meaning Words.**

45. B. The verb eat agrees with the subject people. In the restaurant is a prepositional phrase; it is not the main subject. **See Lesson: Subject and Verb Agreement.**

46. A. A complete sentence must have a verb. **See Lesson: Verbs and Verb Tenses.**

47. C. *Cute* and *furry* are adjectives that describe the noun *kitten.* **See Lesson: Adjectives and Adverbs.**

48. *D. Hospital's does not need an apostrophe.* Hospitals is plural and is not possessive in this sentence. **See Lesson: Punctuation.**

49. C. *Loneliness* is the only correct spelling. **See Lesson: Spelling.**

50. A. *Snore* is intransitive and cannot take a direct object. **See Lesson: Direct Objects and Indirect Objects.**

51. D. *december, she, and christmas.* All months and holidays are capitalized. She is the beginning of a sentence and needs to be capitalized. **See Lesson: Capitalization.**

52. D. The subordinate conjunction "because" combines the sentences and puts the focus on Tony preparing for his job interview. **See Lesson: Types of Sentences.**

53. A. Read and wrote are in simple past tense. **See Lesson: Verbs and Verb Tenses.**

54. D. The trial must begin whether she shows up or not. With an independent and dependent clause, a subordinating conjunction is used to connect them. "Whether" is the only choice that makes sense. **See Lesson: Types of Clauses.**

55. B. For words ending in most consonants, add -s. **See Lesson: Spelling.**

56. B. This sentence correctly fixes the run-on sentence. **See Lesson: Types of Sentences.**

57. A. This is a past tense negative, so it takes the helping verb *did* with the base form *like*. **See Lesson: Verbs and Verb Tenses.**

58. D. *There should be a question mark after weekend.* What is a common question word. **See Lesson: Punctuation.**

59. A. *Wear* is the only correctly spelled form of the word that fits with the sentence. **See Lesson: Spelling.**

60. D. The meaning of bass in the context of this sentence is "a guitar with four strings that makes low sounds." **See Lesson: Context Clues and Multiple Meaning Words.**

HSPT Practice Exam 2

Section I. Verbal Skills

1. **Every child in Miss Smith's class has read a book written by Dr. Seuss. Dr. Seuss wrote The Cat in the Hat. Every child in Miss Smith's class has read The Cat in the Hat. If the first to statements are true, the third is**

   A. true.
   C. uncertain.
   B. false.

2. **Car : Traffic**

   A. Girl : Crowd
   C. Water : Bottle
   B. Pencil : Box
   D. Lunch : Bag

3. **Select the one word that is most nearly the same in meaning as the word in capital letters.**

   ACCOMODATING

   A. Hinder
   C. Prevent
   B. Impede
   D. Welcome

4. **Select the one word that does not have the same meaning as the word in capital letters.**

   ALLEVIATE

   A. Ease
   C. Pacify
   B. Irritate
   D. Relieve

5. **Vince and Amanda verse each other in the final round of a chess tournament. The tournament awards the top two players. Vince was the champion of the tournament. If the first to statements are true, the third is**

   A. true.
   C. uncertain.
   B. false.

6. **Select the one word that is most nearly the same in meaning as the word in capital letters.**

   BENIGN

   A. Disadvantageous
   B. Hostile
   C. Mild
   D. Severe

7. **Select the one word that does not have the same meaning as the word in capital letters.**

   CHASTISE

   A. Berate
   C. Praise
   B. Criticize
   D. Scold

8. **Cup : Coffee**

   A. Canvas : Paint
   C. Bag : Book
   B. Sign : Door
   D. Blanket : Bed

9. **Select the one word that is most nearly the same in meaning as the word in capital letters.**

   CALLOUS

   A. Concerned
   C. Tender
   B. Merciful
   D. Tough

10. **Select the one word that does not have the same meaning as the word in capital letters.**

    FICKLE

    A. Changeable
    C. Steady
    B. Fitful
    D. Whimsical

11. Stan only buys vanilla ice cream. Stan's favorite ice cream flavor is vanilla. Stan has never had chocolate ice cream. If the first to statements are true, the third is

A. true. C. uncertain.

B. false.

12. Select the one word that is most nearly the same in meaning as the word in capital letters.

CLAIRVOYANT

A. Careless C. Insensitive

B. Dense D. Perceptive

13. Select the one word that does not have the same meaning as the word in capital letters.

INDIGNATION

A. Calm C. Scorn

B. Exasperate D. Wrath

14. Row : Boat

A. Ticket : Airplane

B. Gas : Car

C. Subway : Train

D. Pedal : Bike

15. Select the one word that is most nearly the same in meaning as the word in capital letters.

FEIGN

A. Differ C. Oppose

B. Imitate D. Reverse

16. Select the one word that does not have the same meaning as the word in capital letters.

LETHARGIC

A. Comatose C. Languid

B. Idle D. Vivacious

17. The spider crawling on the wall next to Ben scared him. Children are scared of spiders. Ben is a child. If the first to statements are true, the third is

A. true. C. uncertain.

B. false.

18. Select the one word that is most nearly the same in meaning as the word in capital letters.

HIATUS

A. Consistent C. Invariable

B. Gap D. Uniform

19. Select the one word that does not have the same meaning as the word in capital letters.

MEAGER

A. Barren C. Substantial

B. Insufficient D. Spare

20. Money : Bank

A. Bus : School C. Desk : Office

B. Sick : Hospital D. Books : Library

21. Select the one word that is most nearly the same in meaning as the word in capital letters.

INUNDATE

A. Disappoint C. Hollow

B. Empty D. Overwhelm

22. Select the one word that does not have the same meaning as the word in capital letters.

PERVASIVE

A. Common C. Scarce

B. Prevalent D. Widespread

23. **Carly and Sam have identical collections. Carly collects rocks. Sam collects spoons. If the first to statements are true, the third is**

A. true. C. uncertain.

B. false.

24. **Select the one word that is most nearly the same in meaning as the word in capital letters.**

MOLLIFY

A. Anger C. Mellow

B. Exasperate D. Prolong

25. **Select the one word that does not have the same meaning as the word in capital letters.**

RADIANT

A. Beaming C. Glowing

B. Dull D. Lucent

26. **Select the one word that is most nearly the same in meaning as the word in capital letters.**

STAGNANT

A. Dormant C. Moving

B. Hustle D. Productive

27. **Broom : Clean**

A. Fold : Laundry C. Pencil : Write

B. Stack : Books D. File : Papers

28. **Select the one word that does not have the same meaning as the word in capital letters.**

REVEL

A. Celebrate C. Relish

B. Ignore D. Savor

29. **Penguins must live in in areas with cold weather. Penguins live in Antarctica. Antarctica has a cold weather environment. If the first to statements are true, the third is**

A. true. C. uncertain.

B. false.

30. **Select the one word that is not related to the others.**

A. amend C. damage

B. corrupt D. upset

31. **Select the one word that is most nearly the same in meaning as the word in capital letters.**

PLACATE

A. incite C. stroke

B. soothe D. trouble

32. **Select the one word that is not related to the others.**

A. mope C. romp

B. pout D. stew

33. **Select the one word that is most nearly the same in meaning as the word in capital letters.**

WANE

A. develop C. lessen

B. enhance D. reach

34. **Oliver finished taking his science test before Sarah. Sarah finished taking the test before Ally. Oliver finished his test before Ally. If the first to statements are true, the third is**

A. true. C. uncertain.

B. false.

35. Select the one word that is most nearly the same in meaning as the word in capital letters.

REFRAIN

A. abstain
B. allow
C. help
D. release

36. Select the one word that is not related to the others.

A. corporeal
B. deceptive
C. palpable
D. tangible

37. Hazard : Road :: Inclement : ________

A. Danger
B. Weather
C. Car
D. Location

38. Select the one word that is not related to the others.

A. approve
B. flatter
C. honor
D. scorn

39. Child : Curious :: Employee : ________

A. Late
B. Docile
C. Paid
D. Frantic

40. Select the one word that is not related to the others.

A. dissuade
B. hinder
C. promote
D. starve

41. Connor has three best friends who are boys. Connor has two best friends who are girls. Connor has five best friends. If the first to statements are true, the third is

A. true.
B. false.
C. uncertain.

42. Select the one word that is not related to the others.

A. forgive
B. laud
C. praise
D. scold

43. Select the one word that is not related to the others.

A. do
B. rest
C. stand
D. tilt

44. Select the one word that is most nearly the same in meaning as the word in capital letters.

FRENETIC

A. calm
B. hectic
C. placid
D. sound

45. Select the one word that is not related to the others.

A. block
B. check
C. provoke
D. suppress

46. Select the one word that is not related to the others.

A. definite
B. formed
C. shapely
D. vague

47. Ross is Rachel's brother. Rachel has a daughter named Sophie. Ross and Sophie are not related. If the first to statements are true, the third is

A. true.
B. false.
C. uncertain.

48. Summary : Book :: Results : ________

A. Report
B. Experiment
C. Conclusion
D. Situation

49. Select the one word that is not related to the others.

A. inspiring
B. ominous
C. remarkable
D. suggestive

50. Select the one word that is most nearly the same in meaning as the word in capital letters.

DISCRETE

A. connected
B. distinct
C. joined
D. similar

51. Select the one word that is not related to the others.

A. accurate
B. incorrect
C. sound
D. valid

52. Select the one word that is most nearly the same in meaning as the word in capital letters.

TIMOROUS

A. bold
B. brazen
C. fearful
D. forthcoming

53. A cat gives birth to a litter of five boy kittens. Two kittens are orange. Three kittens are white. If the first to statements are true, the third is

A. true.
B. false.
C. uncertain.

54. Select the one word that is not related to the others.

A. aloof
B. chatty
C. garrulous
D. fluent

55. Pollinate : Garden :: Reproduce : __________

A. Family
B. Multiply
C. Copy
D. Factory

56. Select the one word that is not related to the others.

A. heedless
B. foolish
C. sensible
D. unwise

57. Select the one word that is not related to the others.

A. assisting
B. destructive
C. devoted
D. empathetic

58. Isolate : Island :: Collective : __________

A. Bunch
B. Crowd
C. Country
D. Coast

59. Select the one word that is not related to the others.

A. active
B. engaged
C. lethargic
D. vivacious

60. Select the one word that is not related to the others.

A. pithy
B. succinct
C. terse
D. wordy

Section II. Quantitative Skills

1. **Look at the series: 72, 70, 68, 66 ... What number should come next?**

   A. 64
   C. 68
   B. 66
   D. 70

2. **Calculate and compare the values for I, II, and III in order to select the best answer.**

   I. $5 + 3 - 7 + 2$
   II. $3 - 4 + 9 - 2$
   III. 16

   A. I ≤ II ≤ III
   C. I + II = III
   B. I ≥ II ≥ III
   D. I = II = III

3. **What is the difference between natural numbers and whole numbers?**

   A. They are the same.
   B. The whole numbers include zero, but the natural numbers exclude zero.
   C. The natural numbers only go to 10, but the whole numbers have no limit.
   D. The whole numbers include negative numbers, but the natural numbers do not.

4. **Look at the series: 1000, ____, 10, 1, 0.1... What number is missing?**

   A. 1000
   C. 10
   B. 100
   D. 0.1

5. **Calculate and compare the values for I, II, and III in order to select the best answer.**

   I. $18 - 9 + 4 - 3$
   II. $23 - 6 + 1 - 14$
   III. 14

   A. I ≤ II ≤ III
   C. I + II = III
   B. I ≥ II ≥ III
   D. I = II = III

6. **Which statement is true?**

   A. A numeral is a symbol that represents a number.
   B. A number is a symbol that represents a numeral.
   C. Numerals and numbers are the same.
   D. None of the above.

7. **Look at the series: P, ___, R, S... Which letter is missing?**

   A. T
   C. Q
   B. X
   D. F

8. **Calculate and compare the values for I, II, and III in order to select the best answer.**

   I. 3×4
   II. $100 \div 10$
   III. 9

   A. I ≤ II ≤ III
   C. I + II = III
   B. I ≥ II ≥ III
   D. I = II = III

9. **How many numbers are on the complete number line?**

   A. 7
   C. 1,000,000
   B. 100
   D. None of the above

10. Look at the series: C, E, G, I, ... Which letter would come next?

A. H
B. K
C. L
D. N

11. Calculate and compare the values for I, II, and III in order to select the best answer.

I. $72 \div 9$

II. $56 \div 7$

III. 8

A. I ≤ II ≤ III
B. I ≥ II ≥ III
C. I + II = III
D. I = II = III

12. What are the prime factors of 30?

A. 5, 6
B. 2, 3, 5
C. 1, 3, 10
D. 2, 3, 5, 6, 10, 15

13. Look at the series: $y = x^3$, $y = x^6$, $y = x^9$, $y = x^{12}$... What will y be equal to next?

A. x^{13}
B. x^{15}
C. x^{24}
D. x^{36}

14. Calculate and compare the values for I, II, and III in order to select the best answer.

I. $9 \div 90$

II. $0.05 + 0.05$

III. 0.20

A. I ≤ II ≤ III
B. I ≥ II ≥ III
C. I + II = III
D. I = II = III

15. Which expression yields a quotient with no remainder?

A. $5 \div 5$
B. $26 \div 5$
C. $81 \div 40$
D. $365 \div 87$

16. Look at the series: 3x + 5, 6x + 10, 12x + 20, 24x + 40... Which equation would come next?

A. 36x + 50
B. 36x + 60
C. 48x + 40
D. 48x + 80

17. Calculate and compare the values for I, II, and III in order to select the best answer.

I. 1

II. $\frac{6}{7}$

III. $\frac{2}{5}$

A. I ≤ II ≤ III
B. I ≥ II ≥ III
C. I + II = III
D. I = II = III

18. A cube has a surface area of 54 square feet. What is the side length in feet?

A. 2
B. 3
C. 4
D. 5

19. Look at the series: 0.125, 0.25, ____, 0.50, 0.625... Which decimal is missing?

A. 0.305
B. 0.315
C. 0.350
D. 0.375

20. Calculate and compare the values for I, II, and III in order to select the best answer.

I. $\frac{2}{5}$

II. $\frac{8}{20}$

III. $\frac{20}{25}$

A. I ≤ II ≤ III
B. I ≥ II ≥ III
C. I + II = III
D. I = II = III

21. Which decimal is the least?

A. 5.2304
B. 5.3204
C. 5.2403
D. 5.3024

22. **Look at the series: 0.45, 0.60, 0.75, 0.90... Which decimal comes next?**

A. 0.92
B. 0.96
C. 1.05
D. 1.20

23. **Calculate and compare the values for I, II, and III in order to select the best answer.**

I. $1\frac{4}{5}$

II. $\frac{8}{7}$

III. $\frac{1}{15}$

A. I ≤ II ≤ III
B. I ≥ II ≥ III
C. I + II = III
D. I = II = III

24. **Ron is training for a marathon. If he trains by running 57.5 miles every 5 days, then about how many miles will he run in 43 days?**

A. 120
B. 300
C. 480
D. 60

25. **Look at the series: $\frac{4}{2}, \frac{4}{3}$, ___, $\frac{4}{5}, \frac{4}{6}$...Which fraction is missing?**

A. $\frac{5}{2}$
B. $\frac{5}{3}$
C. $\frac{4}{4}$
D. $\frac{4}{8}$

26. **Calculate and compare the values for I, II, and III in order to select the best answer.**

I. $\frac{4}{9} \times \frac{3}{4}$

II. $\frac{6}{7} \times \frac{8}{9}$

III. $1\frac{1}{9}$

A. I ≤ II ≤ III
B. I ≥ II ≥ III
C. I + II = III
D. I = II = III

27. **A teacher buys 4 bottles of water for class. Each bottle of water contains 3 liters. Each cup holds $\frac{2}{5}$ of a liter. How many cups can be filled?**

A. 12
B. 30
C. 42
D. 60

28. **Look at the series: $\frac{1}{3}, \frac{2}{6}, \frac{3}{9}, \frac{4}{12}$...Which fraction comes next?**

A. $\frac{1}{12}$
B. $\frac{4}{15}$
C. $\frac{5}{12}$
D. $\frac{5}{15}$

29. **Calculate and compare the values for I, II, and III in order to select the best answer.**

I. $2 \times \frac{3}{4}$

II. $\frac{5}{7} \div \frac{4}{7}$

III. 1

A. I ≤ II ≤ III
B. I ≥ II ≥ III
C. I + II = III
D. I = II = III

30. **Multiply $\frac{3}{16} \times \frac{4}{7}$.**

A. $\frac{3}{28}$
B. $\frac{1}{9}$
C. $\frac{1}{6}$
D. $\frac{7}{9}$

31. **Look at the series: 48, 24, 12, 6... Which number comes next?**

A. 5
B. 4
C. 3
D. 2

32. Calculate and compare the values for I, II, and III in order to select the best answer.

I. $\frac{2}{3} \times \frac{4}{15}$

II. $\frac{1}{3} \div \frac{5}{8}$

III. $\frac{2}{3}$

A. I ≤ II ≤ III
B. I ≥ II ≥ III
C. I + II = III
D. I = II = III

33. Divide $2\frac{9}{10} \div 3\frac{1}{2}$.

A. $\frac{2}{7}$
B. $\frac{9}{20}$
C. $\frac{2}{3}$
D. $\frac{29}{35}$

34. Look at the series: 5, 20, ___, 320...Which number is missing?

A. 40
B. 60
C. 80
D. 100

35. Calculate and compare the values for I, II, and III in order to select the best answer.

I. $25 shirt

II. $18 pants with a 8% sales tax

III. $5 sandwich, $3 chips, $2 water and a $4 food service fee

A. I ≤ II ≤ III
B. I ≥ II ≥ III
C. I + II = III
D. I = II = III

36. Look at the series: 2, 14, ___, 686... Which number is missing?

A. 21
B. 49
C. 98
D. 320

37. Calculate and compare the values for I, II, and III in order to select the best answer.

I. 10% sales tax on a $300 item

II. 20% tip on a $150 bill

III. $30

A. I ≤ II ≤ III
B. I ≥ II ≥ III
C. I + II = III
D. I = II = III

38. If the captain of a search party evenly assigns 242 people into 11 groups, how many people are in each group?

A. 11
B. 22
C. 24
D. 37

39. Look at the series: 50%, ____, 2%, 0.4% ... Which percentage is missing?

A. 40%
B. 25%
C. 10%
D. 8%

40. Calculate and compare the values for I, II, and III in order to select the best answer.

I. The number of pounds in a ton

II. The number of ounces in a pound

III. 1

A. I ≤ II ≤ III
B. I ≥ II ≥ III
C. I + II = III
D. I = II = III

41. Select the figure that is reflected across the *y*-axis.

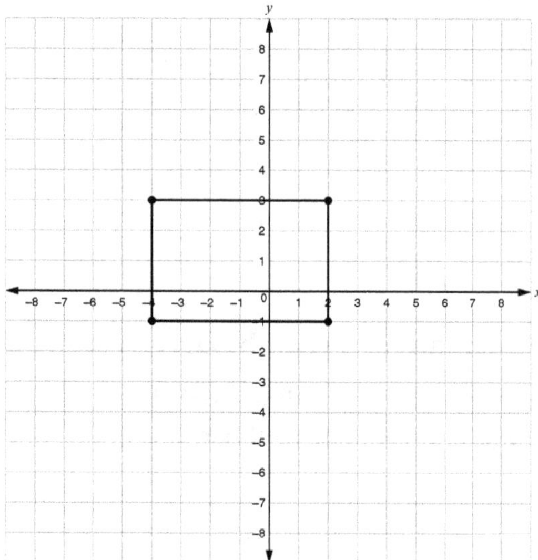

A.

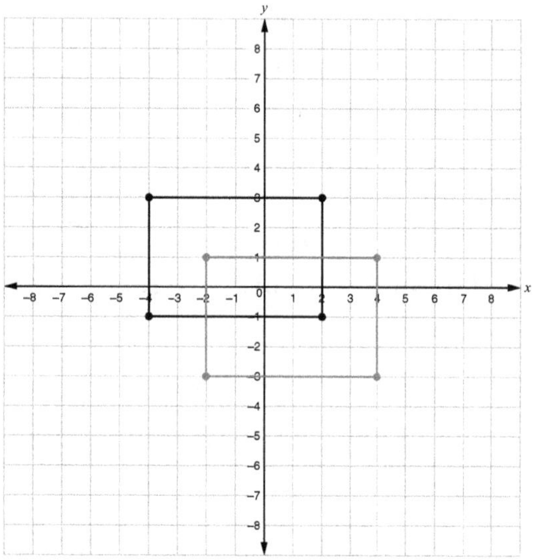

B.

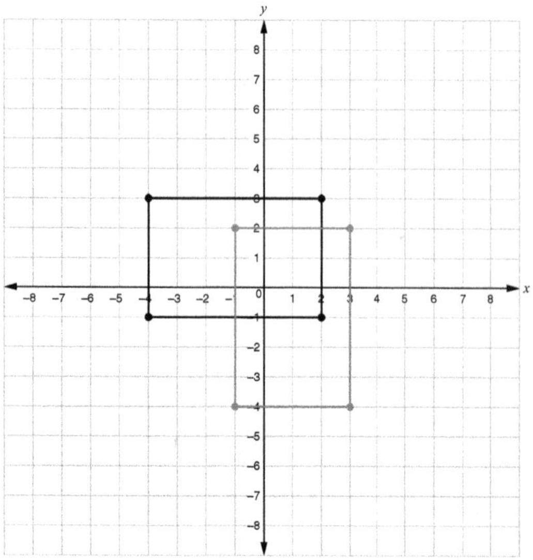

C.

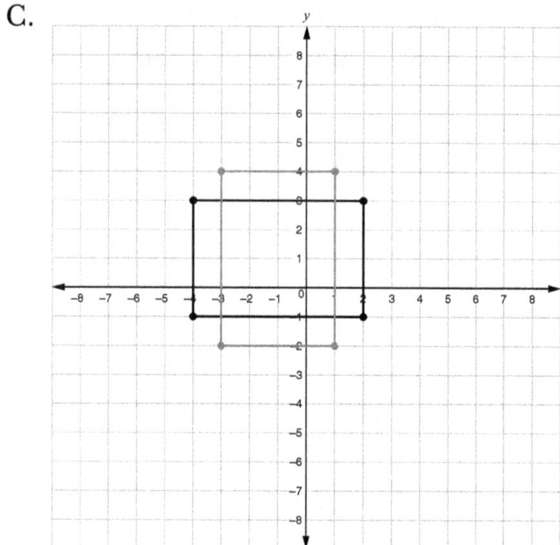

D.

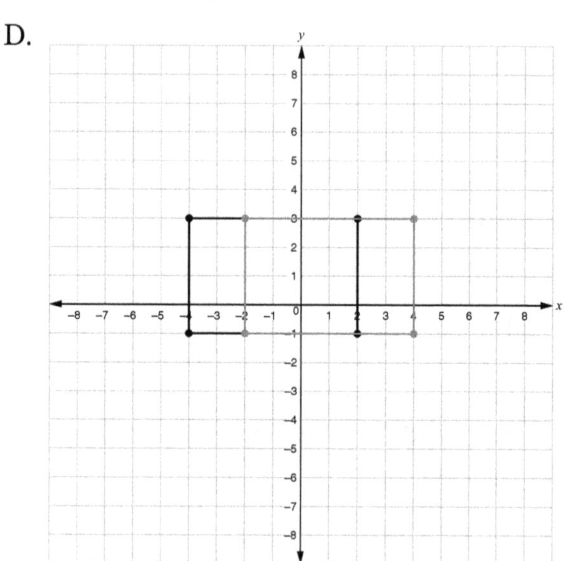

42. Look at the series: 2%, 5%, 12.5%, 31.25%... Which percentage comes next?

A. 38.5%

B. 53.75%

C. 65.125%

D. 78.125%

43. Select the right isosceles triangle with the correct lines of symmetry.

A.

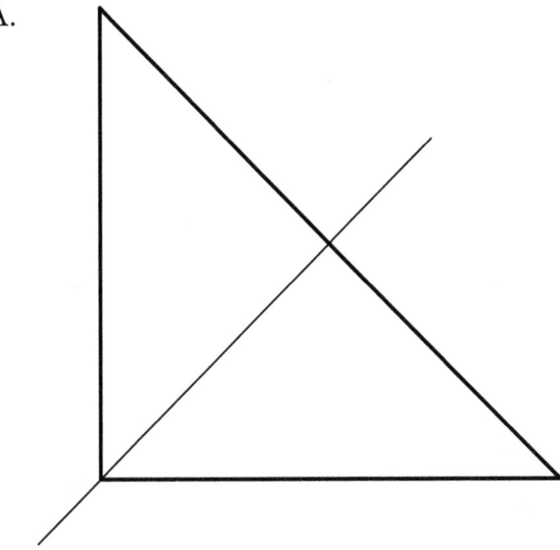

B.

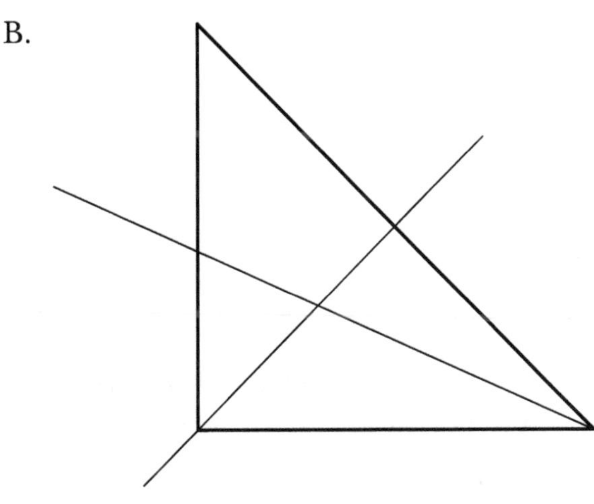

C.

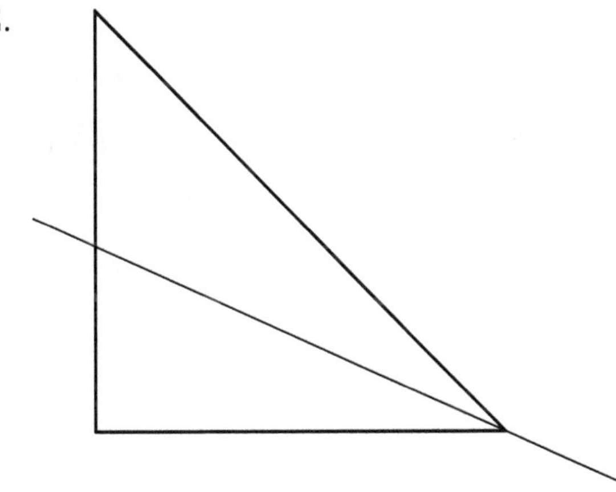

D.

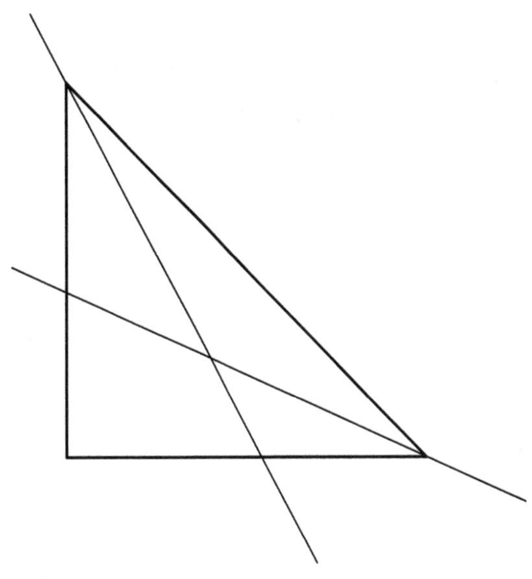

44. Calculate and compare the values for I, II, and III in order to select the best answer.

I. $(6)^3$

II. 40

III. $(-4)^4$

A. I ≤ II ≤ III

B. I ≥ II ≥ III

C. I + II = III

D. I = II = III

45. Write 145.5% as a decimal.

A. 1.455

B. 14.55

C. 145.5

D. 1455

46. Look at the series: 36π, 18π, 9π, 4.5π... Which quantity comes next?

A. 27π

B. 4π

C. 3.5π

D. 2.25π

47. Calculate and compare the values for I, II, and III in order to select the best answer.

I. 9^2

II. 3^4

III. 486 ÷ 6

A. I ≤ II ≤ III

B. I ≥ II ≥ III

C. I + II = III

D. I = II = III

48. Identify a chord of the circle.

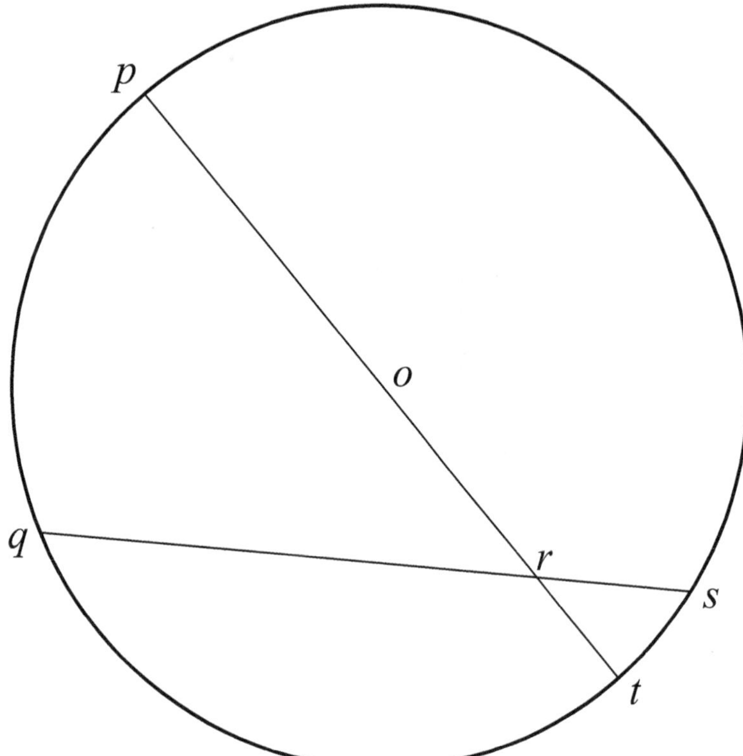

A. $\bar{QS}$

B. $\bar{RS}$

C. $\bar{PO}$

D. $\bar{PT}$

49. Look at the series: 0°C, ___, 100°C, 150°C...What temperature is missing?

A. 25°C

B. 50°C

C. 75°C

D. 100°C

50. Calculate and compare the values for I, II, and III in order to select the best answer.

I. $\sqrt{49}$

II. $\sqrt{64}$

III. $\sqrt{225}$

A. I ≤ II ≤ III

B. I ≥ II ≥ III

C. I + II = III

D. I = II = III

51. A cube has a side length of 10 inches. What is the surface area in square inches?

A. 400

B. 600

C. 800

D. 1,000

52. Which number is *not* a multiple of 11?

A. −121

B. 0

C. 11

D. 131

SECTION III. READING AND VOCABULARY

Part 1: Reading

Directions: *Each passage (or pair of passages) below is followed by a number of questions. Read each passage (or pair), then choose the best answer to each question based on what is stated or implied in the passage (or passages), and in any graphics that may accompany the passage.*

Read the following text and answer questions 1-9.

WiseWear gear provides you with cutting-edge technology to enhance your performance and optimize your training. WiseWear products include sensors to track your heart rate, activity level, and calorie burn during workouts. Information is automatically uploaded to your phone and organized so you can track your improvement over time with just a tap of the screen.

Concerned about comfort? We've got you covered. WiseWear clothing is made with high-tech synthetic compression fabrics to promote circulation and wick away sweat while you work out.

Top-level pro athletes, like ultra-marathoner Uri Schmidt, rely on WiseWear for training and competition. Shouldn't you do the same?

1. **The purpose of this passage is to:**

   A. decide.
   B. inform.
   C. persuade.
   D. entertain.

2. **With which statement would the author of this passage most likely agree?**

   A. Americans who work out put too much emphasis on performance and not enough on enjoyment.
   B. People who do not buy high-end exercise gear do not deserve to get a good workout and stay healthy.
   C. The best way to achieve a healthy body is to follow a simple exercise plan and avoid hyped-up gadgets.
   D. Consumers want help pushing their bodies to the limit and gathering information about their exercise performance.

3. **Which detail from the passage, if true, is factual?**

   A. WiseWear transforms the user into a better and more informed athlete.
   B. WiseWear gear is the most comfortable exercise clothing on the market.
   C. WiseWear products contain sensors that track the user's body signals.
   D. WiseWear users are bound to improve at the sport of their choice over time.

4. **The author of the passage includes details about WiseWear's comfort and ease of use in order to appeal to the reader's:**

   A. reason.
   B. trust.
   C. feelings.
   D. knowledge.

5. **The author most likely includes the detail about a famous ultra-marathoner in order to make readers:**

   A. understand that WiseWear gear is factually the best on the market.
   B. take a weak position when they attempt to argue against the point.
   C. trust that scientists have really studied WiseWear gear and proven it worthy.
   D. feel an association between WiseWear products and a person they admire.

6. **Where would the author best place this passage to serve its purpose?**

   A. In a fashion blog
   B. In a scientific journal
   C. In the sports section of a magazine
   D. As part of a research study on runners

7. **What graphic(s) should the author use to best assist the passage's argument?**

   A. A picture of the products offered
   B. A picture of Uri Schmidt wearing WiseWear gear in an ultra-marathon
   C. A phone screenshot for some of the tracked performance provided by the sensors of the products
   D. A graphic showing performance without WiseWear gear and with WiseWear gear

8. **Reread lines 11-12 ("Concerned about ... covered"). Who is the "We" referring to?**

   A. The author and any co-authors
   B. Ultra-marathoner Uri Schmidt and other top-level pro athletes
   C. The makers of WiseWear clothing
   D. The synthetic compression fabrics that help make the clothing comfortable

9. **The author poses an informal question at the end of the passage. Why?**

   A. It is meant to be a simply ironic question that entices a reader to buy the product.
   B. The entire passage is informal and it would be out of the text structure to make the question formalized.
   C. The author is switching the passage voice to be one of a pro athlete.
   D. The author proposed a question earlier within the passage and wants to keep the passage consistent with more informal questions.

Read the following text and summary. Then answer questions 10-17.

Original Text:

Nobody groaned when Candace arrived at the door. Several people's smiles did look a bit plastic for a moment, but they could hardly be blamed for that.

Poor Gladys, who had to sit right next to Candace on the couch, accepted her fate with good grace. Afterward she developed a hilarious and highly popular impression of Candace's donkey bray laugh, but in the moment Gladys was the picture of welcome and friendliness.

All of the *invited* guests took their cue from Gladys and showed Candace a good time. By the time Candace went home, she looked pink with pleasure at how well she'd been treated. It was quite inspiring. After all, well-bred kids should never be unkind.

Summary:

When a widely disliked girl named Candace arrives uninvited to a party, all the invited guests pretend to welcome her. Because they resist the urge to be cruel to her face, they congratulate themselves on their so-called kindness.

10. Which detail in the summary is implicitly but not explicitly included in the original text?

A. A girl named Candace arrives at a party.

B. The invited guests feel the urge to be cruel.

C. The invited guests pretend to welcome Candace.

D. Candace is pink with pleasure when she goes home.

11. Which detail from the original text most clearly implies that the invited guests dislike Candace?

A. It describes Candace looking "pink with pleasure."

B. It states that "well-bred kids should never be unkind."

C. It says the invited guests "showed Candace a good time."

D. It mentions "poor Gladys" who "had to" be near Candace.

12. Why wouldn't an effective summary comment on Candace's personality?

A. Only the invited guests really know who Candace is.

B. Her personality is irrelevant to the events of the story.

C. That would express a judgment about the original text.

D. The original text does not describe Candace's personality.

13. Which sequence shows in what order the events occurred?

A. Candace looks pink with pleasure, people's smiles look plastic, Candace leaves.

B. Candace arrives, Candace leaves, Gladys mocks Candace's "donkey bray laugh."

C. Candace arrives, Gladys accepts her fate with good grace, people's smiles look plastic.

D. Gladys pretends to welcome Candace, Gladys mocks Candace's "donkey bray laugh," Candace leaves.

14. **What does the expression "Poor Gladys" from line 6 mean in the passage?**
    A. Gladys does not have any wealth
    B. The author is ironically making fun of Gladys
    C. Gladys is pitied for sitting next to Candace
    D. Gladys is disliked by Candace because Candace purposefully sat next to her on the couch

15. **What is the author implying in the summary by describing the actions of the invited guests as "so-called kindness" in line 26?**
    A. *So* is acting as adjective. The guests were excessively kind which is highlighted by Candace being "pink with pleasure" in the original text.
    B. The guests are only considered kind because they resisted the urge to be cruel to Candace's face.
    C. The summary can explicitly describe the guests being kind, while the original text must only imply their kindness with the guests' actions.
    D. The expression shows that the guests believed that they were kind to Candace when they actually weren't because they made fun of her behind her back.

16. **Based on the original text, which of the following is a fact?**
    A. The party-goers dislike Candace
    B. Candace knew she was not invited to the party
    C. Everyone at the party is a well-bred kid
    D. Candace was treated cruelly at the party

17. **The author uses several expressions that demonstrate that the invited guests hid their displeasure for Candace's presence at the party well. Which of the following phrases does not support this?**
    A. she looked pink with pleasure
    B. she developed a hilarious and highly popular impression of Candace's donkey bray laugh
    C. smiles did look a bit plastic for a moment
    D. well-bred kids should never be unkind

Read the following passage and answer questions 18-25.

Adelia stood on the porch in her bathrobe.

"Mr. Snuggles?" she called. "Mr. Snuggles! Come on in, you little vermin."

She peered up and down the street. Sighing, she went back inside and, a moment later, emerged with a metal bowl and a spoon. She rapped on the bowl several times.

"Mr. Snuggles? Breakfast!"

When Mr. Snuggles did not appear, Adelia reached inside and grabbed some keys off a low table. Cinching her bathrobe tightly around her waist, she climbed into the car.

"It's not like I have anything better to do than look for you again," she said.

18. From the text above, you can infer that Adelia is:

A. looking for a pet.

B. calling her son home.

C. a kindhearted person.

D. unconcerned for Mr. Snuggles.

19. Which detail does not provide evidence to back up the conclusion that Adelia is feeling frustrated?

A. She calls Mr. Snuggles "you little vermin."

B. She has not yet gotten dressed for the day.

C. She complains about having to search for Mr. Snuggles.

D. She sighs when Mr. Snuggles does not immediately appear.

20. Which detail from the text supports the inference that Adelia cares what happens to Mr. Snuggles, even if she is angry at him?

A. She goes out to look for him.

B. She keeps her car keys near the door.

C. She is joking when she calls him "vermin."

D. She says she wants to be doing something else.

21. Which sentence of dialogue, if added to the passage, would support the conclusion that Mr. Snuggles actually belongs to someone else?

A. "What ever possessed me to adopt a cat?"

B. "You shed on my sheets, you pee on my couch, and now *this*."

C. "Next time Raul goes out of town, I'm going to babysit his plants instead."

D. "If you make me late again, I'm going to lose my job. Then how will we eat?"

22. Which detail provides evidence that Adelia is an adult?

A. Adelia uses advanced vocabulary such as the word "vermin".

B. She called out to Mr. Snuggles and rapped on the metal bowl.

C. She grabbed keys and climbed into the car.

D. She went to look for Mr. Snuggles in her bathrobe.

23. Which clue from the text serves as evidence that Mr. Snuggles has done this before?

A. She calls out, "Mr. Snuggles! Come on in, you little vermin."

B. Adelia rapped on the bowl several times.

C. She knew where the keys were without looking.

D. She says, "It's not like I have anything better to do than look for you again."

24. In line 10, Adelia yells out "Breakfast!" Why is this acceptable?

A. Adelia must yell out louder than she raps on the metal bowl with a spoon.

B. She is calling out to Mr. Snuggles and trying to grab his attention wherever he is.

C. Since Adelia is wearing a bathrobe, it is acceptable to speak informally.

D. It is not acceptable. A reader can infer this because the name she calls out includes the title "Mr."

25. How would this passage best be described and why?

A. Serious, the passage shows that Mr. Snuggles is gone and is in danger

B. Comedic, the passage displays relatable details about how Adelia handles not knowing where Mr. Snuggles is

C. Formal, the passage includes direct quotes from what Adelia is yelling and her actions in between

D. Emotional, Adelia's yelling shows how uncontrollably angry she is

Please read the text below and answer questions 26-35.

It is perhaps unsurprising that fad diets are so common given the level of obesity in American society. But over the long term, most fad diets are harmful both to the health and to the waistline. Many such diets advocate cutting out one major nutrient, such as fats or carbohydrates. Others suggest fasting over long periods or eating from fixed menu options that may not meet the body's needs. Most of these diets are highly impractical, and many lead directly or indirectly to binge eating and other unhealthy behaviors.

26. The topic of this paragraph is:

A. fasting.

B. obesity.

C. fad diets.

D. binge eating.

27. The topic sentence of this paragraph is:

A. But over the long term, most fad diets are harmful both to the health and to the waistline.

B. Many such diets advocate cutting out one major nutrient, such as fats or carbohydrates.

C. It is perhaps unsurprising that fad diets are so common given the level of obesity in American society.

D. Most of these diets are highly impractical, and many lead directly or indirectly to binge eating and other unhealthy behaviors.

28. **If the author added a description of a man who attempted several fad diets and ended up heavier than ever, what type of information would this be?**

A. A main idea

B. A topic sentence

C. A supporting detail

D. An off-topic sentence

29. **Read the following description of the paragraph:**

The author argues unfairly against fad diets without taking their good qualities into account.

Why is this *not* a valid description of the main idea?

A. It is not accurate; the author of the paragraph is stating facts, not opinions.

B. It is not objective; the person summarizing the main idea is adding a judgment.

C. It is not accurate; the author of the paragraph does not argue against fad diets.

D. It is not objective; the person summarizing the main idea ignores a sentence about the benefits of dieting.

30. **Why doesn't a statistic about early childhood obesity rates belong in this paragraph?**

A. It does not directly support the main idea that fad diets are harmful.

B. Readers might feel hopeless to solve the problem the author identifies.

C. Statistics should never be used as supporting details in persuasive writing.

D. It would act as a second topic sentence and confuse readers about the main idea.

31. **The author finds a scientific survey that reveals over 75% of adults quit a fad diet before they've reached four weeks of following one. Why would this be useful?**

A. It is not useful because it is a survey.

B. Any statistic above 50% that supports a claim is beneficial information for the argument.

C. The author has yet to incorporate any data from scientific studies.

D. The survey shows a popular opinion that fad diets are impractical.

32. Reread lines 10-13 ("Most of these diets ... behaviors.") Why does the author need to elaborate further on this?

A. The sentence is only an opinion until the author provides factual evidence to support the claim.

B. The author has only explained why fad diets are impractical, but not given evidence that they lead to unhealthy behaviors.

C. The sentence is unrelated and the author needs to relate the idea back to the passage for it to make sense.

D. The author has not given any specific examples of a fad diet.

33. The author states that eating from a narrow selection of menu options may not meet the body's needs. Based on the passage, should this statement be considered an opinion or a fact?

A. Opinion because the author does not give a direct example of a fad diet that does not meet the body's needs.

B. Opinion because the author does not mention that a fad diet could meet the body's needs but still have a negative affect by oversupplying certain nutrition values.

C. Fact because the passage is meant to be informative about negative health effects of fad dieting.

D. Fact because the passage clearly only makes verifiable claims in support of their argument.

34. The author finds the following information in a related article:

"Many fat adults fail their diets because cutting out nutrients during the day leads them to eat a crazy amount of gross food before bed."

How could the author rewrite the quote to formalize it for the passage and properly support their argument?

A. Related articles suggest that binge eating before bed is directly related to impractical fad diets.

B. Fad diets lead adults who are fat to eat uncontrollably since they don't eat nutrients like fats or carbohydrates.

C. Further information concludes that overweight adults will likely to binge eat late at night when they cut out nutrients from their diet.

D. One study shows that eating gross foods late at night will continue a cycle of failed fad diets for adults.

35. **The author decides to incorporate information about three different adults: two who tried a fad diet and one who followed a diet plan from a dietician. How might the author use this to shift the text structure to best support the argument?**

A. The author can compare and contrast all of the results to reveal, if the evidence concludes, that all fad diets lead to unhealthy behaviors.

B. The information could be used, if the evidence concludes, as proof that fad diets are not the solution for overweight adults trying to lose weight.

C. The adults who tried a fad diet, if evidence concludes, did not succeed in their dieting goals could be depicted by each adult's physical description before and after their diet regime.

D. The author can create a cause and effect piece to prove, if evidence concludes, that fad diets are harmful to a person's health.

Read the passage and answer questions 36-42.

Dear Mr. O'Hara,

I am writing to let you know how much of a positive impact you have made on our daughter. Before being in your algebra class, Violet was math phobic. She would shut down when new concepts would not come to her easily. As a result, she did not pass many tests. Despite this past struggle, she has blossomed in your class! Your patience and dedication have made all the difference in the world. Above all, your one-on-one sessions with her have truly helped her in ways you cannot imagine. She is a more confident and capable math student, thanks to you. We cannot thank you enough.

Fondly,

Bridgette Foster

36. **Which adjective best describes the tone of this passage?**

A. Arrogant
B. Hopeless
C. Friendly
D. Appreciative

37. **Which phrase from the passage has an openly appreciative and warm tone?**

A. I am writing to let you now
B. you have made on our daughter
C. made all the difference
D. We cannot thank you enough

38. **What mood would this passage most likely evoke in the math teacher, Mr. O'Hara?**

A. Calm
B. Grateful
C. Sympathetic
D. Embarrassment

39. Which transition word or phrase from the passage adds emphasis to the writer's point?

A. Being

B. As a result

C. Despite

D. Above all

40. This passage is best described as:

A. a formal letter because it is properly addressed and signed.

B. a formal letter because it is about a parent's daughter to the math teacher.

C. an informal letter because it expresses an appreciative tone.

D. an informal letter because it is signed with "Fondly".

41. Based on the passage, a reader could assume that:

A. Mr. O'Hara enjoyed teaching Violet.

B. Bridgette Foster could not help her daughter in math.

C. Violet passed her math class with Mr. O'Hara.

D. Mr. O'Hara taught Violet to love math.

42. If Bridgette Foster wanted to submit another copy of her letter to the school, which of the following would help show the principal how good a teacher Mr. O'Hara is?

A. A description of Violet's test scores before and after Mr. O'Hara taught her

B. A letter from Violet saying thank-you to Mr. O'Hara

C. Additional signatures from Violet's family members on the letter

D. A record of the lessons Mr. O'Hara tutored Violet in

Part 2: Vocabulary

Directions: *Vocabulary knowledge is a key component for reading comprehension. This section focuses on vocab usage in a variety of ways. Read each question carefully and choose the best option.*

1. **What is the best definition of the word egocentric?**

   A. Selfish
   B. Friendly
   C. Focused
   D. Resentful

2. **A kleptomaniac is someone who:**

   A. steals
   B. overeats
   C. lights fires
   D. pretends to be sick

3. **Something that is amorphous is:**

   A. toxic
   B. shapeless
   C. beneficial
   D. enormous

4. **Select the meaning of the underlined word in the sentence.**

   A horse or a cow is an example of a quadruped.

   A. An animal that has fur
   B. An animal that is a mammal
   C. An animal that helps man
   D. An animal that has four feet

5. **What is the best definition of the word spherical?**

   A. Hard
   B. Round
   C. Rough
   D. Absorbent

6. **What is the best definition of the word endotherm?**

   A. A plant-eating animal
   B. A meat-eating animal
   C. A cold-blooded animal
   D. A warm-blooded animal

7. **Fallible most nearly means capable of:**

   A. falling down
   B. making errors
   C. being dishonest
   D. talking loudly

8. **Select the meaning of the underlined word in the sentence.**

   The man studies extraterrestrial beings. What kind of beings does the man study?

   A. Ones that are not of this earth
   B. Ones that are similar to humans
   C. Ones that live in tropical habitats
   D. Ones that live high in the mountains

9. **What is the best definition of the word synchronize?**

   A. To cause to occur at a later time
   B. To cause to occur at different times
   C. To cause to occur at an earlier time
   D. To cause to occur at the same time

10. **Select the meaning of the underlined word in the sentence.**

    He loves to use hyperbole in his writing to make his pieces more interesting.

    A. Details
    B. Dialogue
    C. Mystery
    D. Exaggeration

11. **A person who is a miscreant is a:**

    A. has-been
    B. do-gooder
    C. loudmouth
    D. troublemaker

Directions: *The synonyms below consist of a word in capital letters followed by four answer choices. Select the one word that is most nearly the same in meaning as the word in capital letters.*

12. FORESTALL

A. delay
B. forward
C. leave
D. permit

13. QUOTIENT

A. exciting
B. extraordinary
C. mundane
D. unusual

14. RUSTIC

A. city
B. cultured
C. pastoral
D. refined

15. JUBILANT

A. crestfallen
B. defeated
C. disconsolate
D. joyful

16. TRITE

A. impressive
B. ordinary
C. original
D. relevant

17. CORPULENT

A. haggard
B. obese
C. slender
D. willowy

18. IMPUDENT

A. bold
B. meek
C. retiring
D. shy

19. STEADFAST

A. afraid
B. irresolute
C. loyal
D. pliant

20. ENVIOUS

A. content
B. generous
C. jealous
D. pleased

SECTION IV. MATHEMATICAL SKILLS

1. How many millimeters are in a measurement that is 4 centimeters, 3 meters, and 7 millimeters long? (Note that a centimeter is 10 millimeters and a meter is 1,000 millimeters.)

A. 347 C. 3,047

B. 437 D. 3,407

2. Which statement is true?

A. The sum of a positive number and a negative number is always negative.

B. The sum of a positive number and a negative number is always positive.

C. The sum of a positive number and a negative number is always zero.

D. None of the above.

3. $462 \div 53$

A. 1R3 C. 8R38

B. 8R0 D. 8R53

4. $96 \div 12$

A. 8 C. 960

B. 84 D. 1,152

5. A half circle has an area of 45 square centimeters. Find the diameter to the nearest tenth of a centimeter. Use 3.14 for π.

A. 2.7 C. 10.8

B. 5.4 D. 16.2

6. Half of a circular garden with a radius of 11.5 feet needs weeding. Find the area in square feet that needs weeding. Round to the nearest hundredth. Use 3.14 for π.

A. 207.64 C. 519.08

B. 415.27 D. 726.73

7. The circumference of a circle is 92 centimeters. Find the area of the circle to the nearest tenth of a square centimeter. Use 3.14 for π.

A. 669.3 C. 1,338.6

B. 858.5 D. 2,695.7

8. Select the statement that is true for the angles.

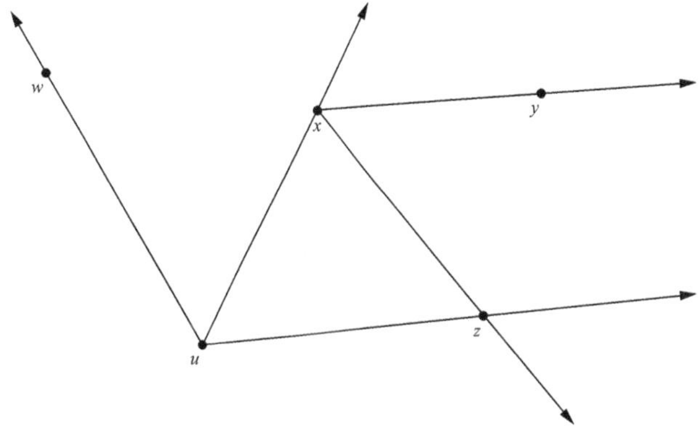

A. Points X and Y are vertices of angles.

B. Points X and U are vertices of angles.

C. Points W and Y are vertices of angles.

D. Points W and U are vertices of angles.

9. ΔMNO has points $M(2, 6)$, $N(3, -1)$, and $O(0, -2)$. After a transformation, the points are $M'(-1, 2)$, $N'(0, -5)$, and $O'(-3, -6)$. What is the transformation between the points?

A. Translation right 3 units and up 4 units

B. Translation left 3 units and up 4 units

C. Translation right 3 units and down 4 units

D. Translation left 3 units and down 4 units

10. Select the figure that is translated $(x - 4, y + 4)$.

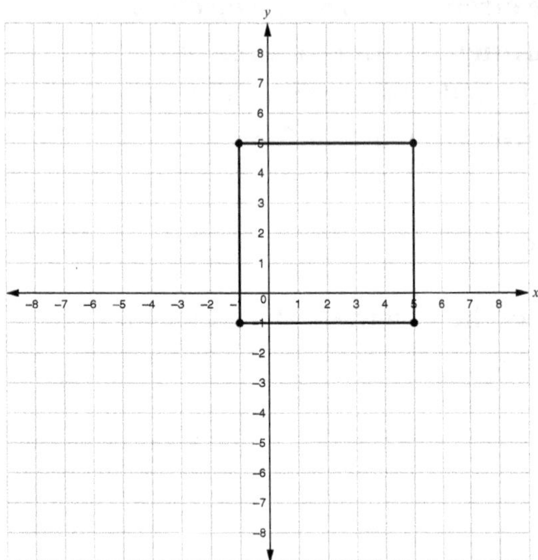

A.

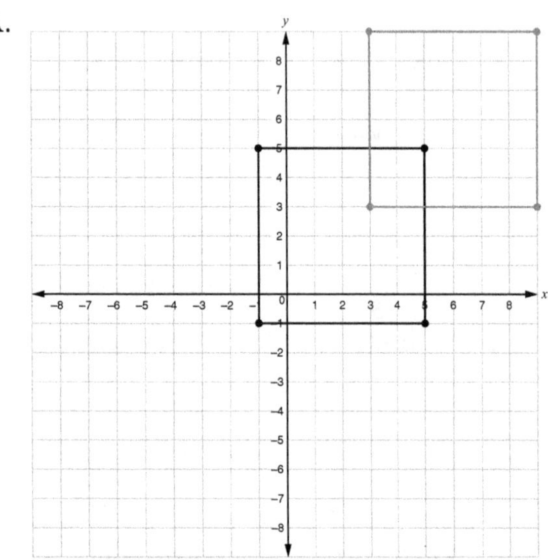

B.

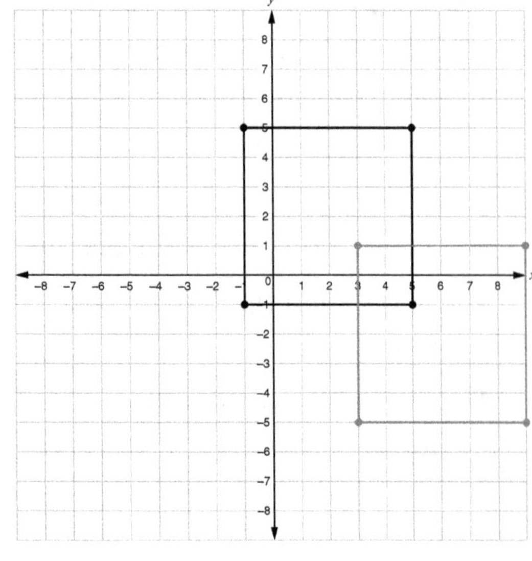

C.

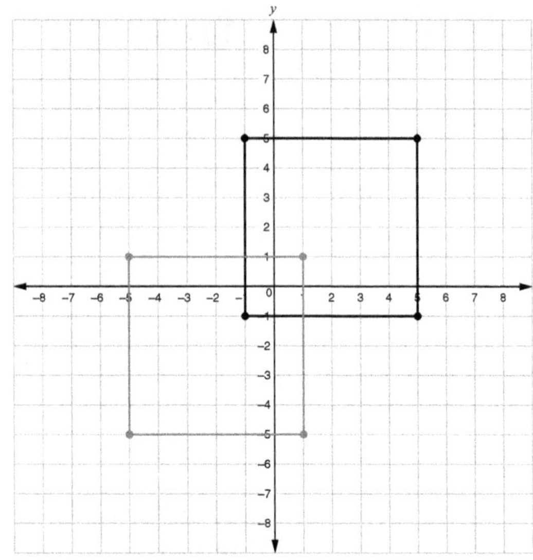

D.

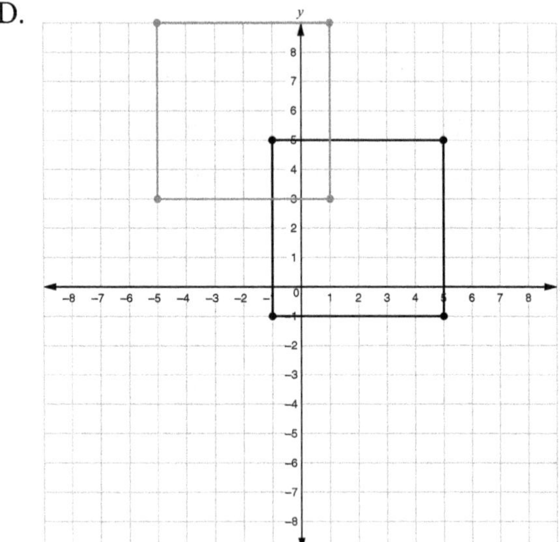

11. Change $5\frac{3}{8}$ to a decimal. Simplify completely.

A. 5.275
B. 5.325
C. 5.375
D. 5.425

12. Write 12.5% as a fraction.

A. $\frac{1}{12}$
B. $\frac{1}{9}$
C. $\frac{1}{8}$
D. $\frac{1}{7}$

13. Write 0.21 as a percent.

A. 2.1%
B. 20%
C. 20.1%
D. 21%

14. **Solve the inequality for the unknown.**

$3(4x-1) > 5(2x+3)$

A. x > 2 C. $x > 10$

B. $x > 9$ D. $x > 18$

15. **Solve the equation for the unknown.**

$\frac{1}{2}x + 3 = \frac{1}{4}x - 2$

A. −20 C. 10

B. −10 D. 20

16. **Solve the equation for the unknown.**

$6x - 12 = -24$

A. −4 C. 2

B. −2 D. 4

17. **Solve the system of equations.**

$x = -3y + 10$
$x = 3y - 8$

A. (-1, 3) C. (1, -3)

B. (-3, 1) D. (3, 1)

18. **Solve the system of equations by graphing.**

$y = \frac{1}{3}x + 2$

$y = \frac{2}{3}x + 5$

A.

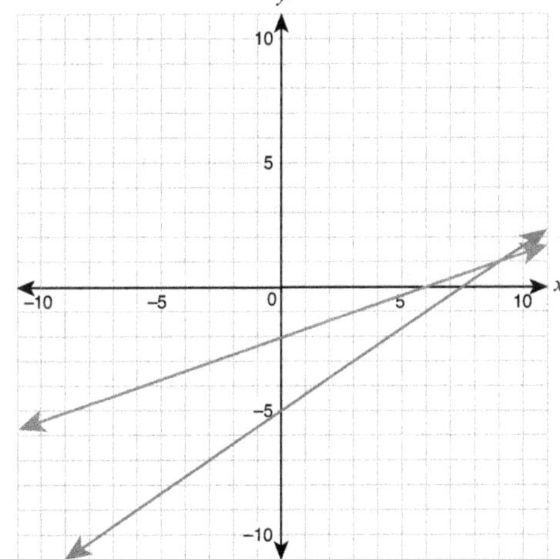

B.

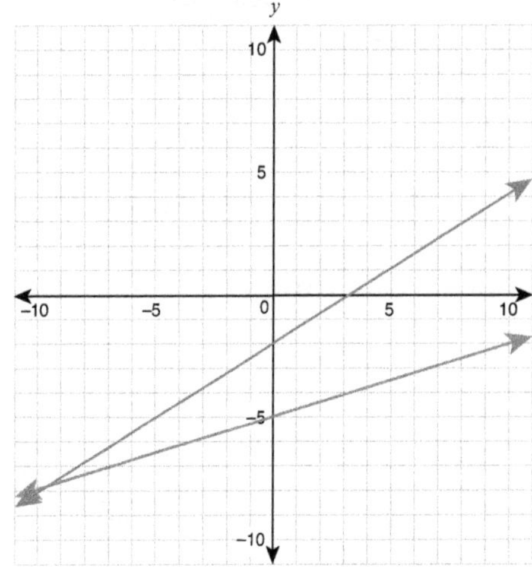

C.

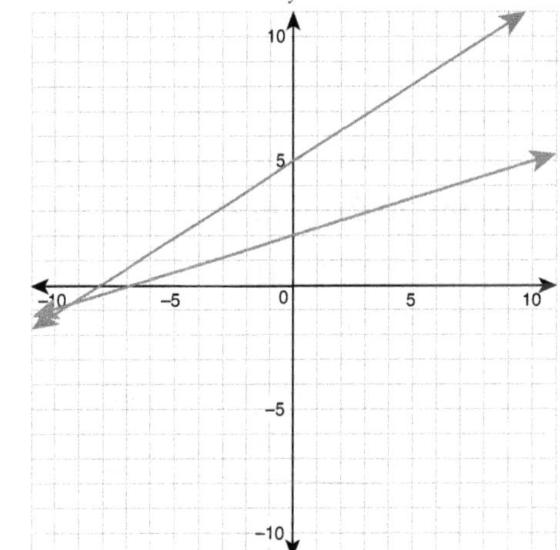

D.

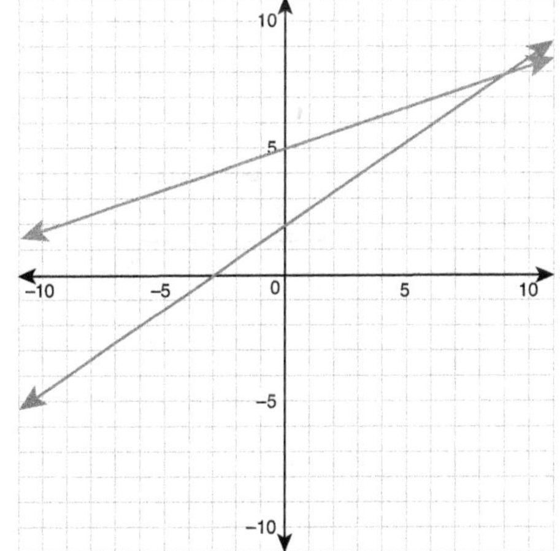

19. Solve the system of equations.

$$x + 3y = 34$$
$$-3x + y = -12$$

A. (-7, -9)

B. (-9, -7)

C. (7, 9)

D. (9, 7)

20. What are the unique prime factors of 56?

A. 2, 7

B. 1, 2, 7

C. 2, 5, 7

D. 2, 4, 7, 8, 14, 16, 28

21. Which number is composite?

A. 2

B. 11

C. 73

D. 91

22. The data below shows a class's quiz scores out of 20 points.

5, 5, 6, 7, 8, 8, 9, 10, 11, 12, 13, 14, 15, 15, 16, 18, 18, 19, 20, 20

Select a box plot for the data.

A.

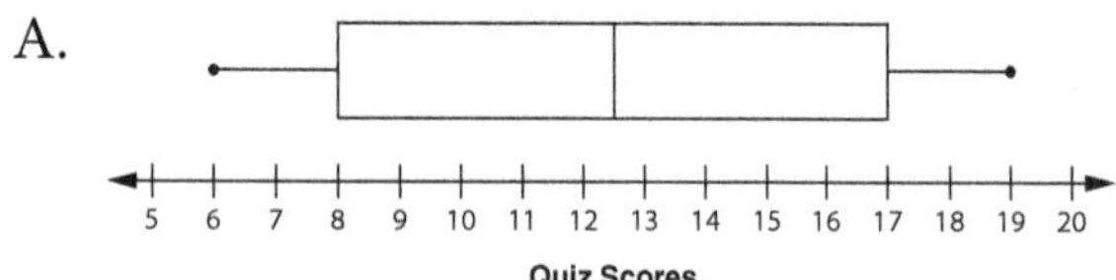

B.

5 6 7 8 9 10 11 12 13 14 15 16 17 18 19 20
Quiz Scores

C.

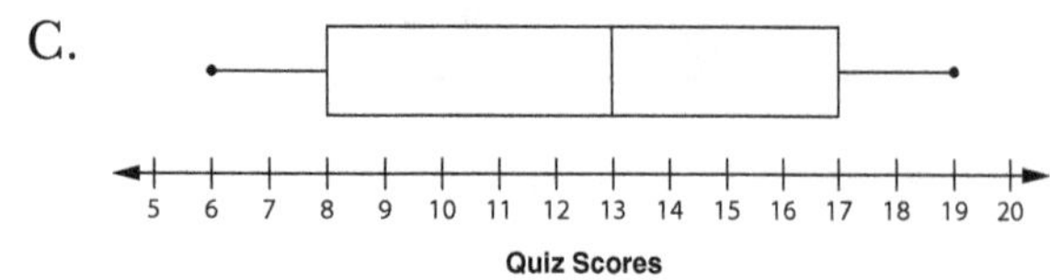

D.

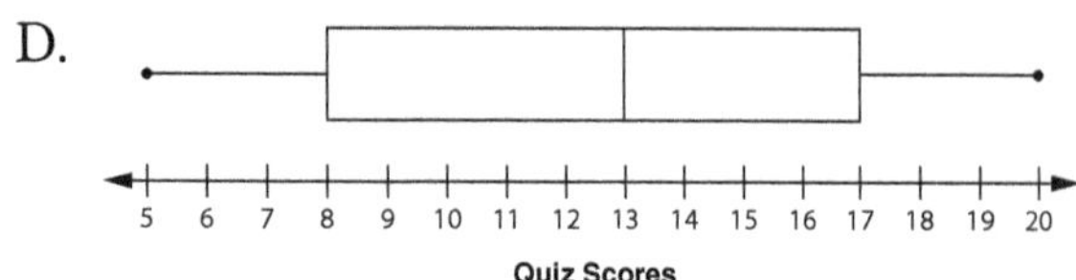

23. The histogram below shows the number of text messages between a group of friends in a week. Which statement is true for the histogram?

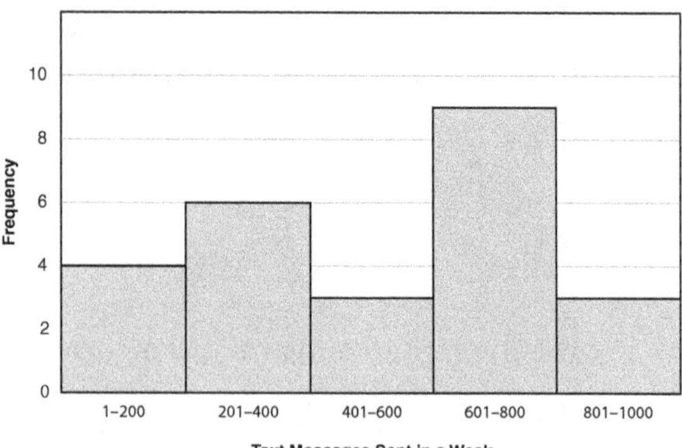

A. There are 30 friends in the group.

B. The highest frequency is 8 friends.

C. The bin size is 1,000 text messages.

D. Two bins have the same frequency.

24. The test scores in a class are 82, 83, 84, 84, 85, 86, 88, 89, 90. The last test is a score of 105. Compare the mean and median before and after the last test score is included.

A. The mean and median increase.

B. The mean and median decrease.

C. The mean increases, and the median does not change.

D. The mean decreases, and the median does not change.

25. The bar chart shows the number of boys and girls who participate in sports. What year had the most participants?

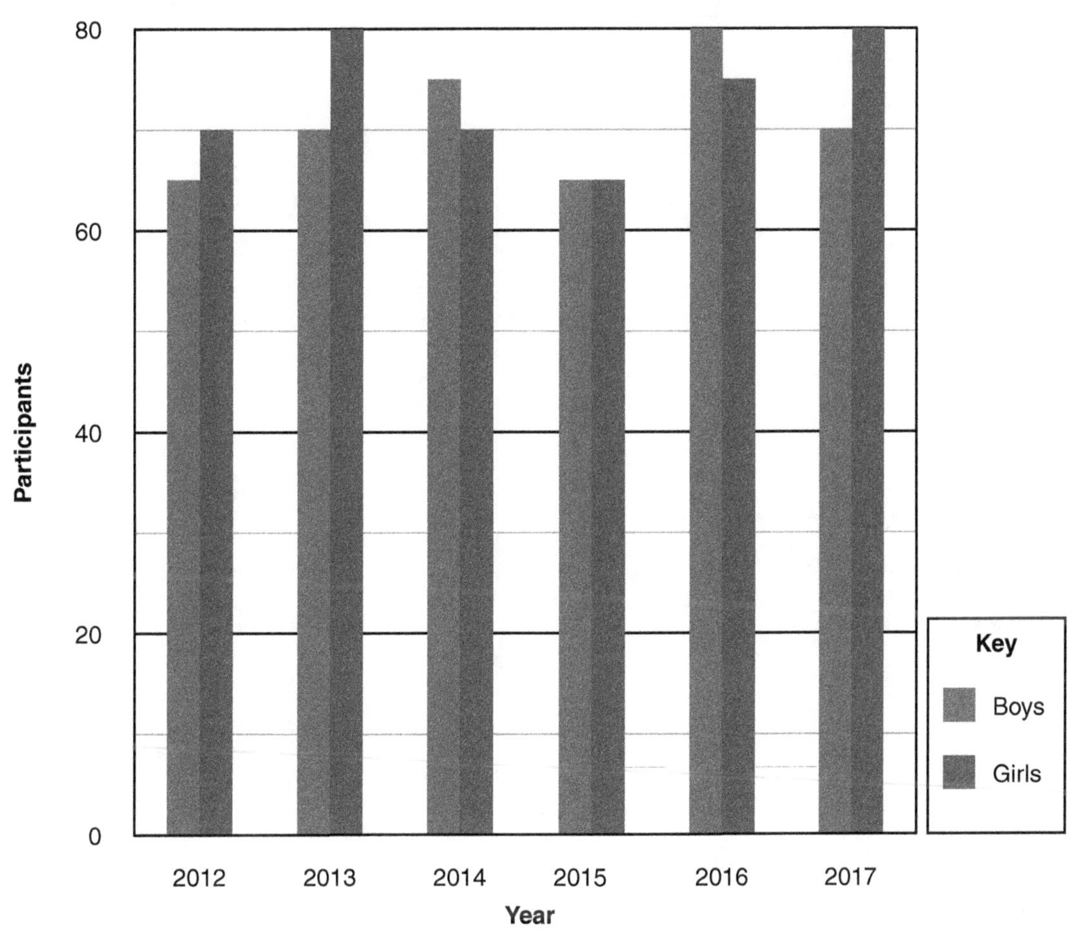

A. 2013

B. 2014

C. 2016

D. 2017

26. The table shows the speed in miles per hour of different roller coasters at an amusement park. Select the correct line graph for this data.

Amusement Park Roller Coasters	1	2	3	4	5	6	7	8
Speed (miles per hour)	120	105	75	100	60	85	110	90

A.

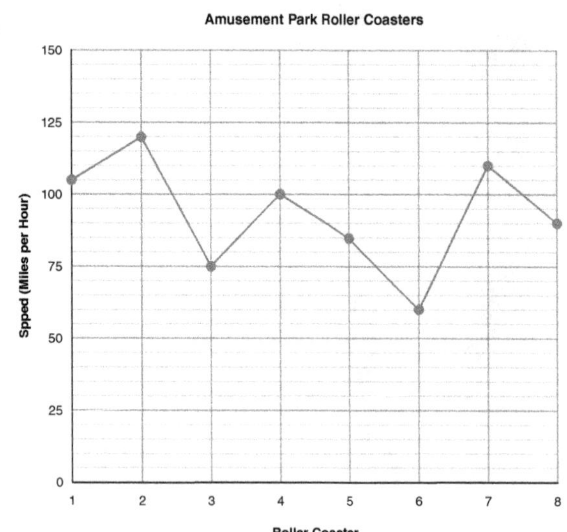

C.

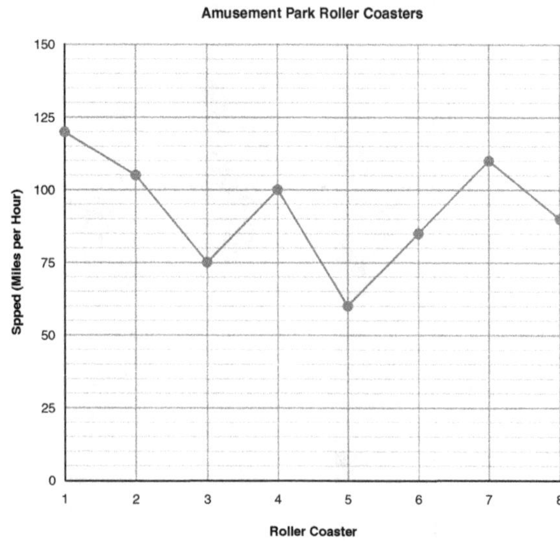

B.

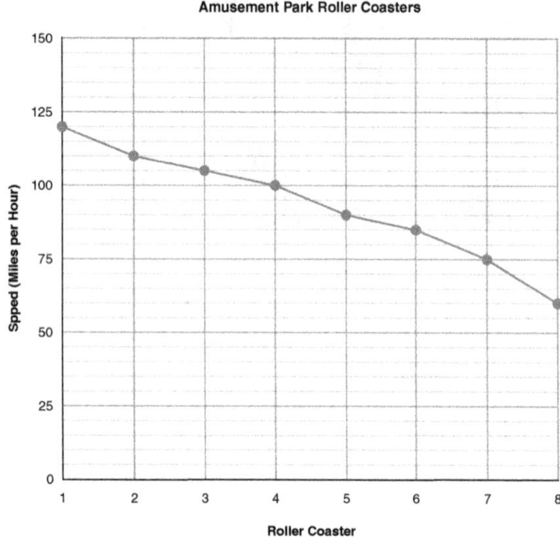

D.

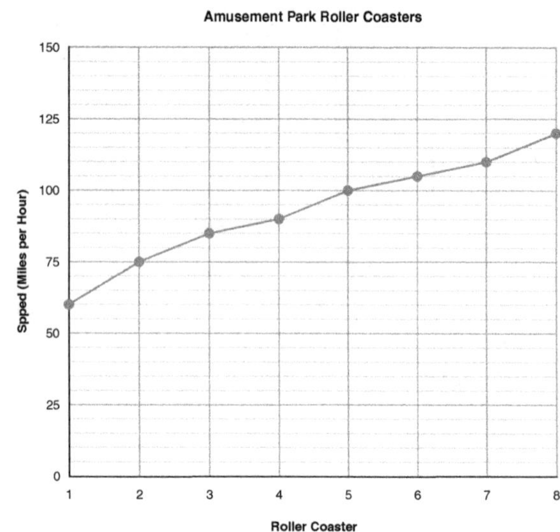

27. Find the median for the data set 20, 22, 23, 24, 25, 21, 20, 22, 24, 25, 23, 22, 25, 26, 22, and 20.

A. 22

B. 22.25

C. 22.5

D. 22.75

28. The base of an equilateral triangular pyramid has side lengths of 9 centimeters. The height of the triangular base is $3\sqrt{3}$ centimeters, and the pyramid has a height of 10 centimeters. Find the volume of the pyramid in cubic centimeters.

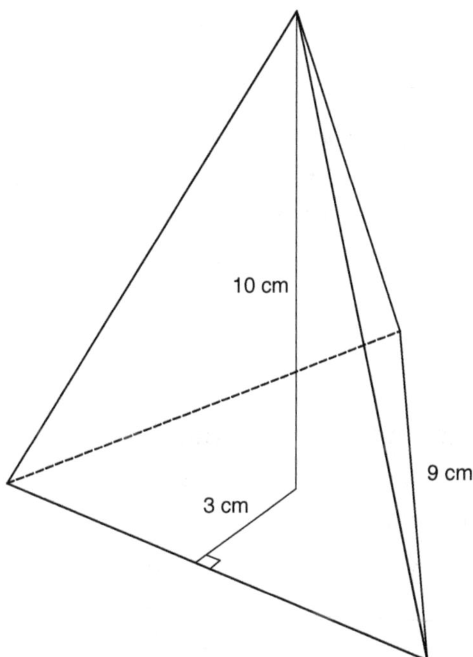

A. $45\sqrt{3}$

B. $90\sqrt{3}$

C. $135\sqrt{3}$

D. $180\sqrt{3}$

30. A paper cup in the shape of a cone has a diameter of 8 centimeters and a height of 11 centimeters. How much liquid does the cup hold if filled to the top? Use 3.14 for π.

A. 92.11 cubic centimeters

B. 184.21 cubic centimeters

C. 368.42 cubic centimeters

D. 736.84 cubic centimeters

29. A cylinder has an outer radius of 6 inches. There is a hole cut out of the center with a radius of 4 inches. The volume of the solid part is 260π cubic inches. Find the height of the cylinder.

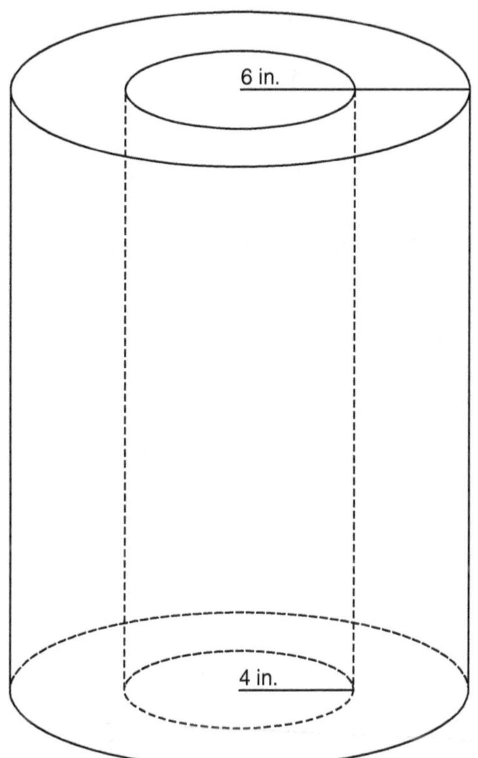

A. 2 inches

B. 9 inches

C. 13 inches

D. 26 inches

31. $2\frac{1}{2} \times 3\frac{3}{4}$

A. $5\frac{3}{8}$

B. $6\frac{3}{8}$

C. $7\frac{3}{8}$

D. $9\frac{3}{8}$

32. $\frac{2}{3} \times \frac{4}{15}$

A. $\frac{3}{20}$

B. $\frac{1}{6}$

C. $\frac{8}{45}$

D. $\frac{1}{3}$

33. $8 \div \frac{2}{9}$

A. 9

B. 18

C. 36

D. 72

34. Multiply.

$(4x + 5)(3x-2)$

A. $12x^2-7x+10$
C. $12x^2+7x-10$
B. $12x^2+7x+10$
D. $12x^2-7x-10$

35. Perform the operation.

$(-3x + 5xy-6y)-(4x + 2xy-5y)$

A. $-7x+7xy-y$
C. $-7x+3xy-y$
B. $-7x+7xy-11y$
D. $-7x+3xy-11y$

36. Apply the polynomial identity to rewrite the expression.

$x^2 + 20x + 100$

A. x^2+100
C. $(x^2+10)^2$
B. $(x+10)^2$
D. $(10x)^2$

37. Simplify.

$(4x^3)^2$

A. $8x^5$
C. $16x^5$
B. $8x^6$
D. $16x^6$

38. The error on one manufacturing machine is 2×10^{-4}, and the error on a second machine is 8×10^{-5}. How many times larger is the error on the first machine?

A. 1
C. 3
B. 2
D. 4

39. Solve.

$x^3 = 64$

A. 2
C. 4
B. 3
D. 5

40. If a company's automobile fleet includes 132 cars of brand A and 48 cars of brand B, what is the fleet's ratio of brand B to brand A?

A. 4:11
C. 15:11
B. 11:15
D. 11:4

41. What is 36% as a ratio?

A. 9:25
C. 18:40
B. 36:100
D. 25:9

42. If 1 out of every 250 people will contract a certain disease, what percent of people will contract it?

A. 0.004%
C. 2.5%
B. 0.4%
D. 25%

43. A stop sign is a regular octagon with an area of 27,000 square centimeters and an apothem of 90 centimeters. What is the length in centimeters of one side?

A. 38
C. 300
B. 75
D. 600

44. Three vertices of a parallelogram are (8,5), (–2,5), $(-1,1)$. What is the fourth coordinate?

A. (9, 1)
C. (9,–1)
B. (8, 1)
D. (8, –1)

45. A right triangular prism has a triangular base with legs of 5 centimeters and 12 centimeters and a hypotenuse of 13 centimeters. What is the surface area in square centimeters if the height is 2 centimeters?

A. 60
C. 180
B. 120
D. 240

46. Solve the equation by any method.

$x^2 + 16x + 33 = 0$

A. $-8 \pm \sqrt{31}$
C. $-8 \pm \sqrt{33}$
B. $8 \pm \sqrt{31}$
D. $8 \pm \sqrt{33}$

47. Solve the equation by the square root method.

$2x^2 = 162$

A. ± 8
C. ± 10
B. ± 9
D. ± 11

48. Solve the equation by factoring.

$x^2 + 15x + 54 = 0$

A. –6, –9
C. 6, –9
B. –6, 9
D. 6, 9

49. Karida has a part-time job. She works 4.25 hours on Thursday and Friday and 6.5 hours on Saturday and Sunday. What is her hourly rate if her check is $268.75?

A. $8.50
C. $14.50
B. $12.50
D. $21.50

50. Eric buys $2\frac{2}{5}$ pounds of apples each week for four weeks. How many total pounds does he buy?

A. $7\frac{3}{5}$
C. $9\frac{3}{5}$
B. $8\frac{2}{5}$
D. $10\frac{2}{5}$

51. Four walls in a room need to be painted. The dimensions of two walls are 12 $\frac{1}{2}$ feet by $11\frac{3}{4}$ feet, and the other two walls are $11\frac{3}{4}$ feet by $10\frac{1}{8}$ feet. What is the estimated area in square feet to be painted?

A. 242
C. 484
B. 276
D. 552

52. Convert 0.75 kilograms to grams.

A. 0.0075 grams
C. 75 grams
B. 0.075 grams
D. 750 grams

53. Convert 9 meters to yards.

A. 4.09 yards
B. 8.23 yards
C. 9.84 yards
D. 12.28 yards

54. Convert 16 gallons to liters.

A. 12.21 liters
C. 58.28 liters
B. 19.79 liters
D. 60.64 liters

55. A doctor wants to study the effects of a low-fat diet in patients. What would be needed to create an observational study?

A. Ask how many fat calories were eaten and track weight.

B. Ask about the amount of weight patients have gained or lost.

C. Have one-half of the patients eat a high-fat diet and the other eat a low-fat diet.

D. Select a group of patients with a low-fat diet and ask how they feel being on the diet.

56. Identify the study that is a census.

A. A restaurant asks all customers what they want to add to the menu.

B. A restaurant asks some of its customers what they want to add to the menu.

C. A restaurant asks all customers on a Friday what they want to add to the menu.

D. A restaurant asks random customers by email what they want to add to the menu.

57. A teacher wants to know if seat location affects test scores. What data needs to be collected for an experiment?

A. The teacher should collect data on one seat for every class.

B. The teacher should collect data on one student for every class.

C. The teacher should collect data on a random sample of students for the final exam.

D. The teacher should collect data on a random sample of students of test scores and seat location.

58. A bag contains 10 red marbles, 8 black marbles, and 7 white marbles. What is the probability of selecting a white marble twice in a row without replacement?

A. $\frac{49}{625}$

B. $\frac{49}{600}$

C. $\frac{14}{25}$

D. $\frac{343}{600}$

59. In a deck of 20 number cards, cards 1–5 are green, cards 6–10 are red, cards 11–15 are yellow, and cards 16–20 are blue. Describe the union of the first 10 cards.

A. Green cards

B. Cards 1, 2, 3, 4, 5, 6, 7, 8, 9, 10

C. Green cards and Red cards; 1, 2, 3, 4, 5, 6, 7, 8, 9, 10

D. Green cards 1, 2, 3, 4, 5; Red cards 6, 7, 8, 9, 10

60. A club wants to meet once a week. The available times are Tuesday, Wednesday, and Thursday at 2:00 p.m., 3:00 p.m., and 4:00 p.m. How many outcomes are there for the sample space?

A. 3

B. 6

C. 9

D. 12

SECTION V. LANGUAGE

1. **Which is the sentence with the correct use of punctuation?**

   A. I cooked so I could eat dinner.

   B. I cooked so, I could eat dinner.

   C. I cooked so I, could eat dinner.

   D. I cooked, so I could eat dinner.

2. **Select the part of speech of the underlined words in the following sentence.**

   Like the Wind is a <u>fast</u> racehorse, but *On the Mark* is <u>faster</u>.

   A. Noun C. Adjective

   B. Verb D. Adverb

3. **Which of the following suffixes means <u>act, process</u>?**

   A. -able C. -less

   B. -tion D. -ible

4. **What is the correct plural of century?**

   A. Centurys C. Centuries

   B. Centures D. Centuryies

5. **Which exclamation contains a verb?**

   A. Oh no! C. So true!

   B. Not me! D. That's great!

6. **Which of the following options would complete the sentence below to make it a simple sentence?**

   You can see the wonders of our country

   ____

   A. on a road trip.

   B. take a road trip.

   C. and, on a road trip.

   D. rather than taking a road trip.

7. **Fill in the blank with the correct coordinating conjunction.**

   Desert climates are hot and dry, ______ many plants grow there.

   A. So C. For

   B. Yet D. And

8. **Which verbs in the following sentence have indirect objects?**

   I told them my opinion when I said that giving their daughter a gerbil for her birthday was a bad idea.

   A. told, said C. said, was

   B. told, giving D. giving, was

9. **Which of the following is correct?**

   A. europe C. Sweden

   B. oregon D. barcelona

10. **Select the word from the following sentence that has more than one meaning.**

    The teacher was content with the quality of her students' work on their math exam.

    A. Teacher C. Quality

    B. Content D. Math

11. **How would you connect the following clauses?**

    They went to dinner.

    The movie.

    A. They went to dinner after the movie.

    B. They went to dinner until the movie.

    C. They went to dinner since the movie.

    D. They went to dinner because the movie.

12. They ____ lunch together yesterday.

A. eit
B. ate
C. aet
D. eight

13. Which sentence is correct?

A. What is wrong.
B. Honesty is the best policy.
C. You dont need an umbrella.
D. A band needs a guitarist singer and drummer.

14. Which word does the underlined modifier describe?

The young children shouted <u>loudly</u>.

A. The
B. young
C. children
D. shouted

15. Which sentence combines all of the information below using a parallel structure?

Dental care requires brushing. You should also floss. Rinse with a fluoride wash.

A. Dental care requires to brush, floss, and rinsing.
B. Dental care requires brushing, to floss, and rinse.
C. Dental care requires brushing, flossing, and rinse.
D. Dental care requires brushing, flossing, and rinsing.

16. Select the context clue from the following sentence that helps you define the multiple meaning word <u>formula</u>.

The mother gave her baby his <u>formula</u> after he woke up from his nap in the car.

A. “mother”
B. “baby”
C. “nap”
D. “car”

17. Identify the direct object in the following sentence.

William's sister painted a portrait for him.

A. William's
B. sister
C. portrait
D. him

18. What is the plural form for the noun *crisis*?

A. Crisii
B. Crisis
C. Crises
D. Crisises

19. Every runner needs a good _____ of shoes.

A. pair
B. piar
C. pear
D. pare

20. How many indirect objects are in the following sentence?

Nigel drove his father's car to their country house.

A. 0
B. 1
C. 2
D. 3

21. Which of the following is correct?

A. fourth of July
B. Fourth of July
C. Fourth of july
D. Fourth Of July

22. Which modifier could <u>not</u> be added before the underlined word?

The <u>workers</u> ate lunch.

A. hungrily
B. hungry
C. laughing
D. uniformed

23. Which is <u>not</u> a prepositional phrase?

A. On the bus
B. Against the wall
C. Oh no
D. To him

24. **Which of the following sentences is correct?**

A. No; I did not do that.

B. Yes: I ate the leftovers.

C. No, I am not leaving yet.

D. Yes I finished my homework.

25. **Which of the following spellings is correct?**

A. Prununciation

B. Pronuncietion

C. Pronunciation

D. Pronounciation

26. **Which of the following is correct?**

A. *Wall Street Journal*

B. *Catcher In The Rye*

C. *To kill A mockingbird*

D. "look what you made me do"

27. **What verb tense are the underlined words in the following sentence?**

I am going out.

A. Past perfect

B. Present perfect

C. Past progressive

D. Present progressive

28. **Select the correct verb to complete the following sentence.**

Dolphins and fish ____ in that large tank.

A. swim   C. swims

B. swum   D. swimming

29. **What is the role of the pronoun *him* in a sentence?**

A. Object   C. Possessive

B. Subject   D. Any of these

30. **Which of the following spellings is correct?**

A. Comitment   C. Comitmment

B. Comitmant   D. Commitment

31. **What part of speech is the underlined word in the following sentence?**

Professor Allen estimated that his research could be completed in two weeks, but he soon realized that his estimate was incorrect.

A. Verb   C. Adverb

B. Noun   D. Adjective

32. **Select the helping verb that completes the following sentence.**

Millions of people watched the news story on TV as it ____ unfolding.

A. is   C. was

B. did   D. would

33. **Which word does the underlined modifier modify?**

She gave me a gift, which I opened before my birthday.

A. She   C. me

B. gave   D. gift

34. **Which of the following prefixes means not?**

A. im-   C. con-

B. re-   D. pre-

35. **Which word in the following sentence is an adjective?**

Washington, Jefferson, and Adams were founding fathers of the United States.

A. and   C. fathers

B. founding   D. of

36. What is the correct plural of theory?

A. Theores
B. Theorys
C. Theories
D. Theoryes

37. Which word in the following sentence is an interjection?

"Yikes!" he shouted, as he slipped on the ice.

A. Yikes
B. shouted
C. as
D. on

38. Which subject is third person singular?

A. I
B. He
C. We
D. You

39. Which word in the following sentence does the underlined adverb describe?

The news is <u>so</u> upsetting.

A. The
B. news
C. is
D. upsetting

40. A _____ is sixty seconds.

A. minit
B. minute
C. muinet
D. mionute

41. Which words in the following sentence are common nouns?

The crowd cheered as Dr. King gave an inspiring speech.

A. cheered, gave
B. crowd, speech
C. inspiring, speech
D. crowd, Dr. King, speech

42. Fill in the blank with the correctly capitalized form.

Everyone wants to live in _____ _______, because it has nice weather and beaches.

A. southern California
B. Southern California
C. Southern california
D. southern california

43. Which word in the following sentence is a possessive pronoun?

That's our new house.

A. our
B. new
C. That's
D. house

44. Which word in the following sentence is an adjective?

That gymnast is so talented.

A. gymnast
B. is
C. so
D. talented

45. Which word(s) in the following sentence should NOT be capitalized?

The President Is Elected By The People.

A. The, Is, By, and The
B. Is, Elected, By, The
C. Is, Elected, By, The, People
D. President, Is, Elected, By, The, People

46. Which of the following spellings is correct?

A. Judgmant
B. Judgment
C. Judgement
D. Judgemant

47. Select the context clue from the following sentence that helps you define the multiple meaning word bind.

The mayonnaise is the key ingredient that will bind the egg salad together.

A. "key"

B. "ingredient"

C. "salad"

D. "together"

48. How many pronouns are in the following sentence?

I wanted to call you last night, but I couldn't find my phone.

A. 2

B. 3

C. 4

D. 5

49. Select the sentence that best describes something that is happening at this moment.

A. The chef roasts a chicken.

B. The chef roasted a chicken.

C. The chef is roasting a chicken.

D. The chef was roasting a chicken.

50. Identify the dependent clause in the following sentence.

When I lived in New York City, I took the subway to work every day.

A. When I lived in New York City

B. I took the subway

C. To work every day

D. In New York City

51. Choose a proper noun to complete the following sentence.

_____ walked to work.

A. We

B. Sharon

C. The girls

D. My mom and dad

52. What is the sentence with the correct use of punctuation?

A. The bookstore has three types of books: fiction, nonfiction, and biography.

B. The bookstore has three types of books, fiction, nonfiction, and biography.

C. The bookstore: has three types of books fiction, nonfiction, and biography.

D. The bookstore has three: types of books fiction, nonfiction, and biography.

53. What is the sentence with the correct use of punctuation?

A. The bookstore has three types of books: fiction, nonfiction, and biography.

B. The bookstore has three types of books, fiction, nonfiction, and biography.

C. The bookstore: has three types of books fiction, nonfiction, and biography.

D. The bookstore has three: types of books fiction, nonfiction, and biography.

54. Which word(s) in the following sentence should be capitalized?

she asked, "do you like indian food?"

A. she and do

B. do and indian

C. she and indian

D. she, do, and indian

54. People have ____ arms and legs.

A. to
B. tu
C. too
D. two

55. Select the correct verb to complete the following sentence.

Each of these children ____ special in his or her own way.

A. is
B. be
C. am
D. are

56. What is the mistake in the following sentence?

Today the new movie premiered, and it was a hit.

A. The comma is misplaced.
B. There should be a comma after *today.*
C. There should be a colon after *premiered.*
D. There should be a semicolon after *today.*

57. Which of the following root words means <u>to build</u>?

A. sect
B. script
C. sol
D. struct

58. Which of the following options correctly fixes the fragment below?

Rather than go skiing.

A. Rather than go skiing Sasha opted to go snowboarding.
B. Rather than go skiing, Sasha opted to go snowboarding.
C. Rather than go skiing. Sasha opted to go snowboarding.
D. Rather than go skiing, so Sasha opted to go snowboarding.

59. What is the mistake in the following sentence?

It's unfortunately raining outside today.

A. *It's* does not need an apostrophe.
B. There should be a comma after *outside.*
C. There should be a period after *unfortunately.*
D. There should be commas before and after *unfortunately.*

60. I went to the butcher for some _____.

A. met
B. mete
C. meat
D. meet

HSPT Practice Exam 2
Answer Key with Explanatory Answers

Section I. Verbal Skills

1. B. The statements explain that the children have read *a* book written by Dr. Seuss, but does not indicate which one. **See Lesson: Understanding Primary Sources, Making Inferences and Drawing Conclusions.**

2. A. One car can be a part of traffic like a girl can be a part of crowd. **See Lesson: Synonyms, Antonyms, and Analogies.**

3. D. To accommodate is to be helpful, welcome, or oblige. **See Lesson: Synonyms, Antonyms, and Analogies.**

4. B. Alleviate means to soothe or ease. Irritate is the opposite of alleviate. **See Lesson: Synonyms, Antonyms, and Analogies.**

5. C. Although both Vince and Amanda are considered the top two players, the statements do not indicate who won the final match. **See Lesson: Understanding Primary Sources, Making Inferences and Drawing Conclusions.**

6. C. Benign means non-threatening or innocuous. **See Lesson: Synonyms, Antonyms, and Analogies.**

7. C. Chastise means to critique. Praise is to offer compliment or reward. **See Lesson: Synonyms, Antonyms, and Analogies.**

8. C. A book can go *into* a bag like coffee can go into a cup. **See Lesson: Synonyms, Antonyms, and Analogies.**

9. D. Callous means harsh, tough, or unfeeling. **See Lesson: Synonyms, Antonyms, and Analogies.**

10. C. Fickle means to be changeable or whimsical. Steady is an antonym to whimsical. **See Lesson: Synonyms, Antonyms, and Analogies.**

11. C. Even though Stan only buys his favorite flavor ice cream, the statements do not indicate what flavors he has tried. The third statement would be true only if the first statement stated that Stan has only ever bought vanilla ice cream. **See Lesson: Understanding Primary Sources, Making Inferences and Drawing Conclusions.**

12. D. Clairvoyant means to be able to see things that others cannot. **See Lesson: Synonyms, Antonyms, and Analogies.**

13. A. Indignation means anger and unfairness. Calm is an antonym. **See Lesson: Synonyms, Antonyms, and Analogies.**

14. D. Rowing in an action completed to make a boat move like pedaling makes a bike move. **See Lesson: Synonyms, Antonyms, and Analogies.**

15. B. To be feign is to fake or pretend. **See Lesson: Synonyms, Antonyms, and Analogies.**

16. D. Lethargic means slow or in a sleepy manner. Vivacious means lively. **See Lesson: Synonyms, Antonyms, and Analogies.**

17. C. It is possible for Ben to be a child, but the statements do not indicate that only children can be scared of spiders. **See Lesson: Understanding Primary Sources, Making Inferences and Drawing Conclusions.**

18. B. Hiatus means a break or an interruption. **See Lesson: Synonyms, Antonyms, and Analogies.**

19. C. Meager means poor or lacking in quality. Substantial means over abundant. **See Lesson: Synonyms, Antonyms, and Analogies.**

20. D. A bank's main purpose is to deal with money. While desks can be found in an office, a library's main purpose is to provide books to the public. **See Lesson: Synonyms, Antonyms, and Analogies.**

21. D. Inundate is to flood or overwhelm. **See Lesson: Synonyms, Antonyms, and Analogies.**

22. C. Pervasive means to spread or be common. Scarce is not related to pervasive. **See Lesson: Synonyms, Antonyms, and Analogies.**

23. B. Since Carly and Sam have identical collections, Sam must collect the same items as Carly. Sam cannot be collecting spoons. **See Lesson: Understanding Primary Sources, Making Inferences and Drawing Conclusions.**

24. C. Mollify is to soften in temper or calm down. **See Lesson: Synonyms, Antonyms, and Analogies.**

25. B. Radiant means shining or glowing. Dull is an antonym. **See Lesson: Synonyms, Antonyms, and Analogies.**

26. A. Stagnant means not flowing, or still. **See Lesson: Synonyms, Antonyms, and Analogies.**

27. C. A broom is used to clean like a pencil is used to write. **See Lesson: Synonyms, Antonyms, and Analogies.**

28. B. Revel means to enjoy. Ignore is not related to revel. **See Lesson: Synonyms, Antonyms, and Analogies.**

29. A. The statements indicate that the Penguins have to live in an area with cold weather, so Antarctica must have cold weather. **See Lesson: Understanding Primary Sources, Making Inferences and Drawing Conclusions.**

30. A. Amend means to set right, rather than disturb or corrupt. **See Lesson: Synonyms, Antonyms, and Analogies.**

31. A. Placate means to appease or soothe. **See Lesson: Synonyms, Antonyms, and Analogies.**

32. C. Romp means to frolic or prance. The other words relate to being mild or unmoving. **See Lesson: Synonyms, Antonyms, and Analogies.**

33. C. Wane means to decrease gradually, or lessen. **See Lesson: Synonyms, Antonyms, and Analogies.**

34. A. By order of the statements, Oliver finished his test before Sarah and Ally. **See Lesson: Understanding Primary Sources, Making Inferences and Drawing Conclusions.**

35. A. Refrain means to hold oneself back, or abstain. **See Lesson: Synonyms, Antonyms, and Analogies.**

36. B. Deceptive means to deceive or produce an illusion of sorts. **See Lesson: Synonyms, Antonyms, and Analogies.**

37. B. Inclement means stormy or severe and is generally associated with describe the weather. **See Lesson: Synonyms, Antonyms, and Analogies.**

38. D. Scorn means to disapprove rather than give compliment. **See Lesson: Synonyms, Antonyms, and Analogies.**

39. B. A child is expected to be curious and an employee, although expected to be paid for their work, would be expected to act docile, or obedient. **See Lesson: Synonyms, Antonyms, and Analogies.**

40. C. All of the word options have a negative connotation, except promote which means to encourage in a positive manner. **See Lesson: Synonyms, Antonyms, and Analogies.**

41. A. The statements describe that Connor has five best friends because three are boys and two are girls. **See Lesson: Understanding Primary Sources, Making Inferences and Drawing Conclusions.**

42. D. Scold is not related to the other words as it has a negative connotation. The other options have positive connotations of acceptance and praise. **See Lesson: Synonyms, Antonyms, and Analogies.**

43. B. Rest is unrelated to the other words which indicate movement or further action. **See Lesson: Synonyms, Antonyms, and Analogies.**

44. B. Frenetic means frenzied or hectic. **See Lesson: Synonyms, Antonyms, and Analogies.**

45. C. Provoke means to encourage in an irritating manner. The other words relate to hindrance. **See Lesson: Synonyms, Antonyms, and Analogies.**

46. D. Vague demonstrates a lack of definition or shape. **See Lesson: Synonyms, Antonyms, and Analogies.**

47. B. Any relationship Rachel has will be related to her brother Ross. Sophie and Ross are related. **See Lesson: Understanding Primary Sources, Making Inferences and Drawing Conclusions.**

48. B. A summary is a shortened version of information from, or about, a book. Results would display all the necessary information from an experiment. **See Lesson: Synonyms, Antonyms, and Analogies.**

49. B. Ominous means foreboding rather than inspiring or promotion. **See Lesson: Synonyms, Antonyms, and Analogies.**

50. B. Discrete means separate, distinct, or individual. **See Lesson: Synonyms, Antonyms, and Analogies.**

51. B. Incorrect or mistaken is not related to being sound or having logic. **See Lesson: Synonyms, Antonyms, and Analogies.**

52. C. Timorous means timid or fearful. **See Lesson: Synonyms, Antonyms, and Analogies.**

53. C. The statements do not indicate what the expected color of the cats should be. **See Lesson: Understanding Primary Sources, Making Inferences and Drawing Conclusions.**

54. A. Taciturn means not inclined to talk, aloof. **See Lesson: Synonyms, Antonyms, and Analogies.**

55. A. The result of reproducing would be a family. **See Lesson: Synonyms, Antonyms, and Analogies.**

56. C. Sensible is having a sense of practicality. **See Lesson: Synonyms, Antonyms, and Analogies.**

57. B. Destructive implies harmful rather than being helpful or empathetic. **See Lesson: Synonyms, Antonyms, and Analogies.**

58. B. It is common to describe being isolated, or alone, on an island. Similarly, it is possible to be collective in a crowd. **See Lesson: Synonyms, Antonyms, and Analogies.**

59. C. Lethargic means lazy or sleepy. **See Lesson: Synonyms, Antonyms, and Analogies.**

60. D. Wordy is not related to the other options which imply being short or precise. **See Lesson: Synonyms, Antonyms, and Analogies.**

Section II. Quantitative Skills

1. A. The series is decreasing by increments of 2. **See Lesson: Basic Addition and Subtraction.**

2. A. Value I is equal to 3 and Value II is equal to 10. **See Lesson: Basic Addition and Subtraction.**

3. B. The correct solution is the whole numbers include zero, but the natural numbers exclude zero. The natural or "counting" numbers are 1, 2, 3, 4,.... To get the whole numbers, just include 0 with the natural numbers. **See Lesson: Basic Addition and Subtraction.**

4. B. Each number in the series is being divided by 10. **See Lesson: Factors and Multiples.**

5. C. Value I is equal to 10 and Value II is equal to 4. Adding the values together is equivalent to Value III. **See Lesson: Basic Addition and Subtraction.**

6. A. The correct solution is a numeral is a symbol that represents a number. Recall that numbers are abstract quantities, but a numeral is a symbol that represents a number. **See Lesson: Basic Addition and Subtraction.**

7. C. The letter Q is missing from the series. **See Lesson: Interpreting Categorical and Qualitative Data.**

8. B. Value I is equivalent to 12. Value II is equivalent to 10. **See Lesson: Basic Multiplication and Division.**

9. D. The correct solution is none of the above. The complete number line comprises all possible numbers, including fraction/decimal numbers. This is an infinite number of numbers. **See Lesson: Basic Addition and Subtraction.**

10. B. The series is alternating letters. The next letter would be K. **See Lesson: Interpreting Categorical and Qualitative Data.**

11. D. All values are equal to 8. **See Lesson: Basic Multiplication and Division.**

12. B. Answers A, C, and D all contain composite numbers (6, 10, and 15). Therefore, answer B is correct. See **Lesson: Factors and Multiples.**

13. B. The exponent in the series is increasing by 3. **See Lesson: Powers, Exponents, Roots, and Radicals.**

14. C. Value I and Value II are equal to 0.01. Adding the values together equals Value III. **See Lesson: Decimals and Fractions.**

15. A. By inspection, $5 \div 5 = 1$, so it has no remainder. Using the division algorithm on the other expressions produces a remainder. **See Lesson: Basic Multiplication and Division.**

16. D. The series is being multiplied by a factor of 2. **See Lesson: Polynomials.**

17. B. Doing a quick comparison, it is easy to determine that Value II is almost equivalent to 1 and Value III is a little less than $\frac{1}{2}$. **See Lesson: Decimals and Fractions.**

18. B. The correct solution is 3. Substitute the values into the formula $54 = 6s^2$. Solve the equation by dividing both sides of the equation by 6 and applying the square root, $9 = s^2; s = 3$ feet. **See Lesson: Similarity, Right Triangles, and Trigonometry.**

19. D. The series is increasing by 0.125. **See Lesson: Decimals and Fractions.**

20. D. Value I and II are equal, but adding them together equals Value III which is equivalent to $\frac{4}{5}$. **See Lesson: Decimals and Fractions.**

21. A. The correct solution is 5.2304 because 5.2304 contains the smallest values in the tenths and the hundredths places. **See Lesson: Decimals and Fractions.**

22. C. The series increases by increments of 0.15. **See Lesson: Decimals and Fractions.**

23. B. Value I is a mixed number that converts to $\frac{9}{5}$ or $\frac{63}{35}$. Value II is an improper fraction that is equivalent to $\frac{56}{35}$. **See Lesson: Decimals and Fractions.**

24. C. The correct solution is 480 because by estimation Ron runs about $60(8) = 480$ miles. **See Lesson: Solving Real World Mathematical Problems.**

25. C. The numerator stays constant through the series while the denominator increases by 1. **See Lesson: Decimals and Fractions.**

26. A. Value I is equal to $\frac{12}{36}$ or $\frac{1}{3}$. Value II is equal to $\frac{48}{63}$ or $\frac{16}{21}$. By doing a quick comparison, Value III is more than 1 making the answer option A. **See Lesson: Multiplication and Division of Fractions.**

27. B. The correct solution is 30 because $4(3) \div \frac{2}{5} = 12 \div \frac{2}{5} = \frac{12}{1} \times \frac{5}{2} = \frac{60}{2} = 30$ cups of water. **See Lesson: Solving Real World Mathematical Problems.**

28. D. The series numerator increases by 1, but the series consistently stays as $\frac{1}{3}$. **See Lesson: Decimals and Fractions.**

29. B. The correct solution for Value I is $\frac{2}{1} \times \frac{3}{4} = \frac{6}{4} = 1\frac{2}{4} = 1\frac{1}{2}$. The correct solution for Value II is $\frac{5}{7} \times \frac{7}{4} = \frac{35}{28} = 1\frac{7}{28} = 1\frac{1}{4}$. **See Lesson: Multiplication and Division of Fractions.**

30. A. The correct solution is $\frac{3}{28}$ because $\frac{3}{16} \times \frac{4}{7} = \frac{12}{112} = \frac{3}{28}$. **See Lesson: Multiplication and Division of Fractions.**

31. C. The series is being divided by 2. **See Lesson: Basic Multiplication and Division.**

32. A. The correct solution for Value I is $\frac{2}{3} \times \frac{4}{15} = \frac{8}{45}$. The correct solution for Value II is $\frac{1}{3} \times \frac{8}{5} = \frac{8}{15}$ Use a common denominator of 45 to compare the fractions and convert, $\frac{8}{15} \times \frac{3}{3} = \frac{24}{45}$. Value III is equal to $\frac{30}{45}$. **See Lesson: Multiplication and Division of Fractions.**

33. D. The correct answer is $\frac{29}{35}$ because $\frac{29}{10} \div \frac{7}{2} = \frac{29}{10} \times \frac{2}{7} = \frac{58}{70} = \frac{29}{35}$. **See Lesson: Multiplication and Division of Fractions.**

34. C. The series is increasing by a factor of 4. **See Lesson: Basic Multiplication and Division.**

35. B. Value II is equal to \$19.44 because \$18 + (\$18 × 0.08) = \$18 + \$1.44 = \$19.44. Value II totals to \$14. **See Lesson: Solving Real World Mathematical Problems.**

36. C. The series is increasing by a factor of 7. **See Lesson: Basic Multiplication and Division.**

37. D. Value I and II are both equal to \$30. \$300 x 0.10 = \$30 and \$150 x 0.20 = \$30. **See Lesson: Solving Real World Mathematical Problems.**

38. B. Because the question indicates that the 11 groups have the same number of people, division is appropriate. The 242 people are divided evenly among 11 groups. This can be expressed as 242 ÷ 11 = 22 people in each group. The division algorithm is helpful here. **See Lesson: Basic Multiplication and Division.**

39. C. The series is decreasing by a divisor of 5. **See Lesson: Ratios, Proportions, and Percentages.**

40. B. There are 1000 pounds in a ton and 16 ounces in a pound. **See Lesson: Standards of Measure.**

41. D. The correct solution is D. A reflection of any point (x, y) becomes $(-x, y)$. The points of the original rectangle, (−4, 3), (2, 3), (2, −1), and (−4, −1), become (4, 3), (−2, 3), (−2, −1), and (4, −1). **See Lesson: Congruence.**

42. C. The series is increasing by a multiple of 2.5. **See Lesson: Ratios, Proportions, and Percentages.**

43. A. The correct solution is the triangle with one line of symmetry. There is a line of symmetry from the right angle through the midpoint of the hypotenuse that maps the triangle onto itself. **See Lesson: Congruence.**

44. C. Following the rules of exponents, Value I is 216 and Value III is 256. **See Lesson: Powers, Exponents, Roots, and Radicals.**

45. A. The correct answer is 1.455 because 145.5% as a decimal is 145.5 ÷ 100 = 1.455. **See Lesson: Decimals and Fractions.**

46. D. Each number within the series is being divided by 2. **See Lesson: Standards of Measure.**

47. D. Following the rules of exponents, Value I and II are both 81. Using the division algorithm, Value III is also 81. **See Lesson: Powers, Exponents, Roots, and Radicals.**

48. A. The correct solution is $\bar{QS}$ because Q and S are on the circle and the segment does not go through the center of the circle. **See Lesson: Circles.**

49. B. The temperature is increasing by increments of 50. **See Lesson: Standards of Measure.**

50. C. The square root of 49 is 7 and the square root of 64 is 8. The added values are 15, which is the square root of 225. **See Lesson: Powers, Exponents, Roots, and Radicals.**

51. B. The correct solution is 600. Substitute the values into the formula and simplify using the order of operations, $SA = 6s^2 = 6(10^2) = 6(100) = 600$ square inches. **See Lesson: Similarity, Right Triangles, and Trigonometry.**

52. D. Any product of a number and an integer is a multiple of that number. In the case of 11, only 131 is not a multiple. Note that the product of 11 and 11 is 121. Therefore, the next multiple is 132, not 131. **See Lesson: Factors and Multiples.**

Section III. Reading and Vocabulary

Part 1: Reading

1. C. This is an advertisement. Although it includes some information its primary purpose is to convince you to buy something. This makes it a persuasive text. **See Lesson: Understanding the Author's Purpose, Point of View, and Rhetorical Strategies.**

2. D. It is difficult to know much about the true feelings of advertising writers because it's their job to sell products, not say what they believe. However, it is a fair bet that advertising writers believe people will pay money for products presented the way they describe. **See Lesson: Understanding the Author's Purpose, Point of View, and Rhetorical Strategies.**

3. C. Much of the information in this advertisement is not verifiable, but the fact that the clothing tracks the body's signals with sensors is a fact. **See Lesson: Understanding the Author's Purpose, Point of View, and Rhetorical Strategies.**

4. C. The advertisement highlights several aspects of WiseWear gear, such as the comfort and ease of use, that suggest the potential customer will feel good using the products. These details appeal to the emotions. **See Lesson: Understanding the Author's Purpose, Point of View, and Rhetorical Strategies.**

5. D. Celebrity endorsements in advertisements appeal to the emotions by associating a product for sale with a person who is widely admired. **See Lesson: Understanding the Author's Purpose, Point of View, and Rhetorical Strategies.**

6. C. The passage is an advertisement for sports clothing. The audience it would appeal to would be interested in sports. **See Lesson: Types of Passages, Text Structure, Genre and Theme.**

7. D. Although a screenshot of what the gear can provide, it would only be a portion for the data the gear is said to provide and would not be the most compelling graphic for the advertisement. A sensor tracked performance graphic would be better utilized because the author is arguing that WiseWear gear enhances training and sport performance. Of the options given, the author should use a graphic showing the difference of athletic performance with and without the product. **See Lesson: Evaluating and Integrating Data.**

8. C. The passage is an advertisement meant to appeal to an audience on behalf of the brand name. **See Lesson: Understanding the Author's Purpose, Point of View, and Rhetorical Strategies.**

9. A. The passage is structured around appealing to a reader that would buy the WiseWear products. **See Lesson: Formal and Informal Language.**

10. B. The original text says explicitly that the invited guests welcome Candace, but it only implies that they want to be cruel to her. The original text shows this partly by saying that Gladys and the other guests mock Candace when she is gone. **See Lesson: Summarizing Text and Using Text Features.**

11. D. The original text shows the guests' dislike for Candace partly by expressing sympathy for the girl who has to sit next to her. **See Lesson: Summarizing Text and Using Text Features.**

12. D. The original text clearly implies that the invited guests at the party are being cruel, but it does not clearly show how Candace thinks or feels. **See Lesson: Summarizing Text and Using Text Features.**

13. B. The word "afterward" and the phrase "in the moment" indicate Gladys mocks Candace's laugh only after Candace is out of earshot. **See Lesson: Summarizing Text and Using Text Features.**

14. C. Gladys is pitied because she had to sit next to the uninvited guest. **See Lesson: Summarizing Text and Using Text Features.**

15. D. The author is emphasizing that the guests believed they were kind because the led Candace to believe she was welcomed at the party while everyone else knew that she wasn't. **See Lesson: Summarizing Text and Using Text Features.**

16. A. The original text describes how the party-goers hid how they felt about Candace to her face. However, it details that they took cues from Gladys to treat her well contrary to their feelings and made fun of her after she left. **See Lesson: Facts, Opinions, and Evaluating an Argument.**

17. C. Although Gladys made fun of Candace's laugh, Candace never saw that behavior because it happened *after* the party. Even if Candace did not see, the detail about several people's smiles looking plastic shows the instance that the guests did not hide their feelings. **See Lesson: Facts, Opinions, and Evaluating an Argument.**

18. A. Adelia is attempting to call a pet, not a child. You can infer this because she calls Mr. Snuggles "vermin" and bangs on a bowl with a spoon to get his attention. **See Lesson: Understanding Primary Sources, Making Inferences and Drawing Conclusions.**

19. B. Adelia's bathrobe is not evidence that she is frustrated at Mr. Snuggles. **See Lesson: Understanding Primary Sources, Making Inferences and Drawing Conclusions.**

20. A. Adelia tries repeatedly to call Mr. Snuggles, and when he does not come, she goes out to look for him. This implies that she does care about him, even if she is angry at him. **See Lesson: Understanding Primary Sources, Making Inferences and Drawing Conclusions.**

21. C. The line about Raul and his plants does not explicitly say Adelia is babysitting Mr. Snuggles, but it suggests that she is caring for the pet for someone else. **See Lesson: Understanding Primary Sources, Making Inferences and Drawing Conclusions.**

22. C. A reader can infer the Adelia is looking for a pet. A reader can also conclude that she is an adult looking for a pet because she goes to look for him in a car. **See Lesson: Understanding Primary Sources, Making Inferences and Drawing Conclusions.**

23. D. Adelia's statement using the word "again" provides evidence that she has had to go out and look for him in the past. **See Lesson: Understanding Primary Sources, Making Inferences and Drawing Conclusions.**

24. B. The reader can infer that Adelia is trying to get Mr. Snuggles to come home by offering breakfast and making sounds associated with being fed. **See Lesson: Formal and Informal Language.**

25. B. While a reader can infer that Mr. Snuggles is missing, Adelia's reaction shows that she is not overly concerned because he has gone missing before. Her actions display an annoyance, but the idea that she prioritizes finding him despite not being dressed provides clues that the passage is meant to entertain the reader. **See Lesson: Types of Passages, Text Structure, Genre and Theme.**

26. C. The topic of this paragraph is related to obesity, but it is more narrowly focused on the fad diets people use as they try to control their weight. **See Lesson: Main Ideas, Topic Sentences, and Supporting Details.**

27. A. The first sentence of this paragraph leads the reader toward the main idea, which is expressed next in a topic sentence about the harmfulness of fad diets. **See Lesson: Main Ideas, Topic Sentences, and Supporting Details.**

28. C. A description of a failed experience with fad diets would function as a supporting detail in this paragraph about the negative consequences of fad diets. **See Lesson: Main Ideas, Topic Sentences, and Supporting Details.**

29. B. Although this description of the paragraph would be valid in an opinion response, it is not merely a statement of the main idea because it adds the reader's judgment about the paragraph. **See Lesson: Main Ideas, Topic Sentences, and Supporting Details.**

30. A. Although a statistic about early childhood obesity might belong in a passage focusing on obesity rates, it would be off-topic information in this paragraph on the harm of fad dieting. **See Lesson: Main Ideas, Topic Sentences, and Supporting Details.**

31. D. Even though the author has not yet provided specific examples, it is not a requirement to use scientific data studies to strengthen an argument. If adults dislike following fad diets, the survey proves that fad diets are impractical in support of the author's claims. **See Lesson: Evaluating and Integrating Data.**

32. B. The author has not provided evidence to support the claim that fad diets may go beyond a failed diet, but actually lead to unhealthy behaviors. **See Lesson: Facts, Opinions, and Evaluating an Argument.**

33. C. The author describes that a fixed menu option *may* not meet a body's needs, to make it a more general statement, rather than an opinion. The passage has not provided any details to make a reader skeptic of their argument, but still lacks supporting evidence and details. **See Lesson: Facts, Opinions, and Evaluating an Argument.**

34. C. The author should be careful in utilizing the quote because of its highly informal language in respect to a more formal passage. However, if the author wanted to rewrite it, C is the only option that gets rid of all informal descriptions such as "fat adults" and "gross food" while not falsifying the quote. **See Lesson: Formal and Informal Language.**

35. D. The new found information could be utilized in many ways to shift the text structure, but only the last option describes how the author can use it to support their argument that fad diets are harmful. **See Lesson: Types of Passages, Text Structure, Genre and Theme.**

36. D. The tone of this letter is appreciative as the author openly thanks the teacher for all he has done for her daughter. **See Lesson: Tone, Mood, and Transition Words**

37. D. The author of the letter uses a lot of respectful and admiring language, but the line "We cannot thank you enough" has an especially appreciative and warm tone. **See Lesson: Tone, Mood, and Transition Words**

38. B. A teacher receiving a note like this would likely feel grateful. **See Lesson: Tone, Mood, and Transition Words**

39. D. The phrase "above all" adds emphasis to the writer's point that the teacher has made a significant impact on the daughter. **See Lesson: Tone, Mood, and Transition Words**

40. B. The relationship between the letter writer and who it is addressed to reveals that the letter would be considered formal, even if it did or did not follow formal writing patterns. **See Lesson: Formal and Informal Language.**

41. C. The letter describes how Mr. O'Hara was very patient and helped Violet into being a capable math student, but does not give direct insight to how either of them feel. It can be assumed that Violet passed her class because she "blossomed" and Bridgette Foster feels extreme gratitude. **See Lesson: Facts, Opinions, and Evaluating an Argument.**

42. A. Showing the principal how Mr. O'Hara's instruction improved Violet's test scores would be the best argument for demonstrating his teaching skills. **See Lesson: Facts, Opinions, and Evaluating an Argument.**

Part 2: Vocabulary

1. A. The root *ego* means "self," so egocentric means selfish. **See Lesson: Root Words, Prefixes, and Suffixes.**

2. A. The root *klept* means "steal," so a kleptomaniac is someone who steals. **See Lesson: Root Words, Prefixes, and Suffixes.**

3. B. The root *morph* means "form," and the prefix *a-* means "without or not," so something that is amorphous is shapeless. **See Lesson: Root Words, Prefixes, and Suffixes.**

4. D. The prefix *quad-* means "four," and the root word "ped" means "foot," so a quadruped is an animal that has four feet. **See Lesson: Root Words, Prefixes, and Suffixes.**

5. B. The root word *spher* means "ball-like," so spherical means round. **See Lesson: Root Words, Prefixes, and Suffixes.**

6. D. The root word *therm* means "heat, or warm," so endotherm is a warm-blooded animal. **See Lesson: Root Words, Prefixes, and Suffixes.**

7. B. The root word *fal* means "false," and the suffix *-ible* means able to, so fallible means capable of making errors. **See Lesson: Root Words, Prefixes, and Suffixes.**

8. A. The root word *terr* means "earth," and the prefix *extra-* means "beyond," so, extraterrestrial beings are ones that are not of this earth. **See Lesson: Root Words, Prefixes, and Suffixes.**

9. D. The root *syn* means "same," and *chron* means "time," so to synchronize means to cause to occur at the same time. **See Lesson: Root Words, Prefixes, and Suffixes.**

10. D. The prefix *hyper-* means "above or excessively," so hyperbole would be exaggeration. **See Lesson: Root Words, Prefixes, and Suffixes.**

11. D. The prefix *mis-* means "wrong," so a miscreant is a troublemaker. **See Lesson: Root Words, Prefixes, and Suffixes.**

12. A. Forestall means to impede or delay. **See Lesson: Synonyms, Antonyms, and Analogies.**

13. C. Quotient means happening every day, or mundane. **See Lesson: Synonyms, Antonyms, and Analogies.**

14. C. Rustic means relating to country life, or pastoral. **See Lesson: Synonyms, Antonyms, and Analogies.**

15. D. Jubilant means happy or joyful. **See Lesson: Synonyms, Antonyms, and Analogies.**

16. B. Trite means overused, hackneyed, or ordinary. **See Lesson: Synonyms, Antonyms, and Analogies.**

17. B. Corpulent means very fat or obese. **See Lesson: Synonyms, Antonyms, and Analogies.**

18. A. Impudent means rude, improper, or bold. **See Lesson: Synonyms, Antonyms, and Analogies.**

19. C. Steadfast means fixed, unchanging, or loyal. **See Lesson: Synonyms, Antonyms, and Analogies.**

20. C. Envious means jealous. **See Lesson: Synonyms, Antonyms, and Analogies.**

Section IV. Mathematical Skills

1. C. The correct solution is 3,047. Place the digits in base-10 format, using the number of meters in the thousands place, the number of centimeters in the tens place, and the number of millimeters in the ones place. The measurement is 3,047 millimeters long. **See Lesson: Basic Addition and Subtraction.**

2. D. The correct solution is none of the above. Try some test cases. For example, $-1 + 5 = 4$, but $-5 + 1 = -4$. Also, $-5 + 5 = 0$. Counterexamples therefore show that statements A, B, and C are false. **See Lesson: Basic Addition and Subtraction.**

3. C. Because 462 is not evenly divisible by 53, remainder division is necessary. Use the division algorithm to obtain 8R38. **See Lesson: Basic Multiplication and Division.**

4. A. Use the division algorithm. Knowing the multiplication table well helps you recognize these numbers. **See Lesson: Basic Multiplication and Division.**

5. C. The correct solution is 10.8 because $A = \frac{1}{2}\pi r^2; 45 = (\frac{1}{2})3.14\,r^2; 45 = 1.57\,r^2 = 28.66 = r^2\ ; r \approx 5.4$. The diameter is twice the radius, or about 10.8 centimeters. **See Lesson: Circles.**

6. A. The correct solution is 207.64 because $A = \frac{1}{2}\pi r^2 \approx \frac{1}{2}(3.14)(11.5)^2 \approx \frac{1}{2}(3.14)(132.25) \approx 207.64$ square feet. **See Lesson: Circles.**

7. A. The correct solution is 669.3. $C = 2\pi r; 92 = 2(3.14)r; 92 = 6.28r; r \approx 14.6$ centimeters. $A = \pi r^2 \approx 3.14(14.6)^2 \approx 3.14(213.16) \approx 669.3$ square centimeters. **See Lesson: Circles.**

8. B. The correct solution is points X and U are vertices of angles because these points are the intersection of two rays. **See Lesson: Congruence.**

9. D. The correct solution is a translation left 3 units and down 4 units because the points (x, y) become $(x - 3, y - 4)$. **See Lesson: Congruence.**

10. D. The correct solution is D. The translation for the points is $(x - 4, y + 4)$. The points of the original square, (–1, 5), (–1, –1), (5, –1) and (5, 5), become (–5, 9), (–5, 3), (1, 3) and (1, 9). **See Lesson: Congruence.**

11. C. The correct answer is 5.375 because $\frac{3}{8} = 3.000 \div 8 = 0.375$. **See Lesson: Decimals and Fractions.**

12. C. The correct answer is $\frac{1}{8}$ because 12.5% as a fraction is $\frac{12.5}{100} = \frac{125}{1000} = \frac{1}{8}$. **See Lesson: Decimals and Fractions.**

13. D. The correct answer is 21% because 0.21 as a percent is $0.21 \times 100 = 21\%$. **See Lesson: Ratios, Proportions, and Percentages.**

14. B. The correct solution is $x > 9$.

$12x-3 > 10x + 15$	Apply the distributive property.
$2x-3 > 15$	Subtract $10x$ from both sides of the inequality.
$2x > 18$	Add 3 to both sides of the inequality.
$x > 9$	Divide both sides of the inequality by 2.

See Lesson: Equations with One Variable.

15. A. The correct solution is −20.

$2x + 12 = x-8$	Multiply all terms by the least common denominator of 4 to eliminate the fractions.
$x + 12 = -8$	Subtract x from both sides of the equation.
$x = -20$	Subtract 12 from both sides of the equation.

See Lesson: Equations with One Variable.

16. B. The correct solution is −2.

$6x = -12$	Add 12 to both sides of the equation.
$x = -2$	Divide both sides of the equation by 6.

See Lesson: Equations with One Variable.

17. C. The correct solution is (1, -3).

	The first equation is already solved for x.
$-3y + 10 = 3y - 8$	Substitute $-3y + 10$ in for x in the second equation.
$6y + 10 = -8$	Subtract $3y$ from both sides of the equation.
$6y = -18$	Subtract 10 from both sides of the equation.
$y = -3$	Divide both sides of the equation by 6.
$x = -3(-3) + 10$	Substitute -3 in the first equation for y.
$x = -9 + 10 = 1$	Simplify using order of operations.

See Lesson: Equations with Two Variables.

18. C. The correct graph has the two lines intersect at (-9, -1). **See Lesson: Equations with Two Variables.**

19. C. The correct solution is (7, 9).

$x = -3y + 34$	Solve the first equation for x by subtracting $3y$ from both sides of the equation.
$-3(-3y + 34) + y = -12$	Substitute $-3y + 34$ in for x in the second equation.
$9y - 102 + y = -12$	Apply the distributive property.
$10y - 102 = -12$	Combine like terms on the left side of the equation.
$10y = 90$	Add 102 both sides of the equation.
$y = 9$	Divide both sides of the equation by 10.
$x + 3(9) = 34$	Substitute 9 in the first equation for y.
$x + 27 = 34$	Simplify using order of operations.
$x = 7$	Subtract 27 from both sides of the equation.

See Lesson: Equations with Two Variables.

20. A. The prime factorization of 56—for example, using a factor tree—yields the numbers 2, 2, 2, and 7. Ignoring repeats of 2, the unique prime factors are 2 and 7. **See Lesson: Factors and Multiples.**

21. D. A composite number has factors other than 1 and itself. Note that 2 is prime by definition: it only has itself and 1 as factors. Answer B is easy to confirm as prime. That leaves answers C and D. One approach is to start at 2 and test each successive whole number to determine whether it is a factor by dividing. If the quotient is a whole number, it is a factor. In this case, 91 has 7 as a factor. Therefore, it is composite. **See Lesson: Factors and Multiples.**

22. B. The correct response is B. The median value is 12.5, the first quartile value is 8, and the third quartile value is 17. The minimum is 5, and the maximum is 20. **See Lesson: Interpreting Categorical and Quantitative Data.**

23. D. The correct solution is two bins have the same frequency. The bins 400–600 and 800–1,000 have three friends. **See Lesson: Interpreting Categorical and Quantitative Data.**

24. A. The correct solution is the mean and median increase. The test score of 105 increases the mean from 85.67 to 87.6 and increases the median from 85 to 85.5. **See Lesson: Interpreting Categorical and Quantitative Data.**

25. C. The correct solution is 2016 because there were 155 total participants. **See Lesson: Interpreting Graphics.**

26. C. The correct solution is C. The line graph has the correct values for each roller coaster. **See Lesson: Interpreting Graphics.**

27. C. The correct solution is 22.5. The data set written in order is 20, 20, 20, 21, 22, 22, 22, 22, 23, 23, 24, 24, 25, 25, 25 and 26. The middle two numbers are 22 and 23, and the mean of these numbers is 22.5. **See Lesson: Interpreting Graphics.**

28. A. The correct solution is $45\sqrt{3}$. Substitute the values into the formula and simplify using the order of operations, $V=\frac{1}{3}Bh=\frac{1}{3}(\frac{1}{2}bh)h=\frac{1}{3}\left(\frac{1}{2}(9)(3\sqrt{3})\right)10=45\sqrt{3}$ cubic centimeters. **See Lesson: Measurement and Dimension.**

29. C. The correct solution is 13 inches. Substitute the values into the formula, $260\pi=\pi 6^2h-\pi 4^2h$ Apply the exponent and combine like terms, $260\pi=\pi 36h-\pi 16h; 260\pi=20\pi h$. Divide both sides of the equation by 20π, $h=13$ inches. **See Lesson: Measurement and Dimension.**

30. B. The correct solution is 184.21 cubic centimeters. The radius is 4 centimeters. Substitute the values into the formula and simplify using the order of operations, $V=\frac{1}{3}\pi r^2h=\frac{1}{3}(3.14)4^2(11)$ $=\frac{1}{3}(3.14)(16)(11)=184.21$ cubic centimeters. **See Lesson: Measurement and Dimension.**

31. D. The correct solution is $9\frac{3}{8}$ because $\frac{5}{2}\times\frac{15}{4}=\frac{75}{8}=9\frac{3}{8}$. **See Lesson: Multiplication and Division of Fractions.**

32. C. The correct solution is $\frac{8}{45}$ because $\frac{2}{3}\times\frac{4}{15}=\frac{8}{45}$. **See Lesson: Multiplication and Division of Fractions.**

33. C. 36 is the correct answer because $\frac{8}{1}\times\frac{9}{2}=\frac{72}{2}=36$. **See Lesson: Multiplication and Division of Fractions.**

34. C. The correct solution is $12x^2+7x-10$.

$$(4x+5)(3x-2)=4x(3x-2)+5(3x-2)$$
$$=12x^2-8x+15x-10=12x^2+7x-10$$

See Lesson: Polynomials.

35. C. The correct solution is $-7x + 3xy-y$.

$$(-3x + 5xy-6y)-(4x + 2xy-5y)$$
$$= (-3x + 5xy-6y) + (-4x-2xy + 5y)$$
$$= (-3x-4x) + (5xy-2xy) + (-6y + 5y)$$
$$= -7x + 3xy-y$$

See Lesson: Polynomials.

36. B. The correct solution is $(x + 10)^2$. The expression $x^2 + 20x + 100$ is rewritten as $(x + 10)^2$ because the value of a is x and the value of b is 10. **See Lesson: Polynomials.**

37. D. The correct solution is $16x^6$ because $(4x^3)^2 = 4^2x^{3\times2} = 4^2x^6 = 16x^6$.**See Lesson: Powers, Exponents, Roots, and Radicals.**

38. C. The correct solution is 3 because 2×10^{-4} is 0.0002 and 8×10^{-5} is 0.00008. So, the error on the first machine is about 3 times larger. **See Lesson: Powers, Exponents, Roots, and Radicals.**

39. C. The correct solution is 4 because the cube root of 64 is 4. **See Lesson: Powers, Exponents, Roots, and Radicals.**

40. A. The ratio is 4:11. A ratio is like a fraction of two numbers, although in this case the answer uses colon notation. The ratio of brand B to brand A is the number of brand-B cars divided by the number of brand-A cars. Reduce to lowest terms:

$$\frac{48}{132} = \frac{4}{11}$$

See Lesson: Ratios, Proportions, and Percentages.

41. A. As a ratio, 36% is 9:25. The most direct route is to convert 36% to a fraction, $\frac{36}{100}$, then reduce to lowest terms: $\frac{9}{25}$. The equivalent ratio in colon notation is 9:25. **See Lesson: Ratios, Proportions, and Percentages.**

42. B. If 1 out of every 250 contract a disease, the fraction of people is $\frac{1}{250}$, which is equal to 0.004. Multiply by 100% to get 0.4%. **See Lesson: Ratios, Proportions, and Percentages.**

43. B. The correct solution is 75. Substitute the values into the formula, $27{,}000 = \frac{1}{2}(90)p$ and simplify using the order of operations, $27{,}000 = 45p$. Divide both sides of the equation by 45 to find the perimeter, $p = 600$ centimeters. Divide the perimeter by 8 to find the length of 75 centimeters for each side. **See Lesson: Similarity, Right Triangles, and Trigonometry.**

44. A. The correct solution is (9, 1) because this point shows a parallelogram with a base length of 10 units. **See Lesson: Similarity, Right Triangles, and Trigonometry.**

45. B. The correct solution is 120. Substitute the values into the formula and simplify using the order of operations, $SA = (2)\left(\frac{1}{2}\right)(5)(12) + (2)(5) + 2(12) + 2(13) = 60 + 10 + 26 + 24 = 120$ square centimeters. **See Lesson: Similarity, Right Triangles, and Trigonometry.**

46. A. The correct solutions are $-8 \pm \sqrt{31}$. The equation can be solved by completing the square.

$x^2 + 16x = -33$	Subtract 33 from both sides of the equation.
$x^2 + 16x + 64 = -33 + 64$	Complete the square, $(\frac{16}{2})^2 = 8^2 = 64$.
	Add 64 to both sides of the equation.
$x^2 + 16x + 64 = 31$	Simplify the right side of the equation.
$(x + 8)^2 = 31$	Factor the left side of the equation.
$x + 8 = \pm\sqrt{31}$	Apply the square root to both sides of the equation.
$x = -8 \pm \sqrt{31}$	Subtract 8 from both sides of the equation.

See Lesson: Solving Quadratic Equations.

47. B. The correct solution is ± 9.

$x^2 = 81$	Divide both sides of the equation by 2.
$x = \pm 9$	Apply the square root to both sides of the equation.

See Lesson: Solving Quadratic Equations.

48. A. The correct solutions are -6 and -9.

$(x + 6)(x + 9) = 0$	Factor the equation.
$(x + 6) = 0$ *or* $(x + 9) = 0$	Set each factor equal to 0.
$x + 6 = 0$	Subtract 6 from both sides of the equation to solve for the first factor.
$x = -6$	
$x + 9 = 0$	Subtract 9 from both sides of the equation to solve for the second factor.
$x = -9$	

See Lesson: Solving Quadratic Equations.

49. B. The correct solution is \$12.50 because she worked a total of $4.25(2) + 6.5(2) = 8.5 + 13 = 21.5$ hours. The hourly rate is $268.75 \div 21.50 = \$12.50$. **See Lesson: Solving Real World Mathematical Problems.**

50. C. The correct solution is $9\frac{3}{5}$ because $2\frac{2}{5} \times 4 = \frac{12}{5} \times \frac{4}{1} = \frac{48}{5} = 9\frac{3}{5}$ pounds of apples. **See Lesson: Solving Real World Mathematical Problems.**

51. D. The correct solution is 552 because the dimensions of the walls are approximately 13 feet by 12 feet and 12 feet by 10 feet. The area is $2(13)(12) + 2(12)(10) = 312 + 240 = 552$ square feet. **See Lesson: Solving Real World Mathematical Problems.**

52. D. The correct solution is 750 grams. $0.75\ kg \times \frac{1{,}000\ g}{1\ kg} = 750\ g$. **See Lesson: Standards of Measure.**

53. C. The correct solution is 9.84 yards. $9\ m \times \frac{3.28\ ft}{1\ m} \times \frac{1\ yd}{3\ ft} = \frac{29.52}{3} = 9.84\ yd$. **See Lesson: Standards of Measure.**

54. D. The correct solution is 60.64 liters. $16\ gal \times \frac{3.79\ L}{1\ gal} = 60.64\ L$. **See Lesson: Standards of Measure.**

55. A. The correct solution is to ask how many fat calories patients eat and track patients' weight because the researcher is observing the number of fat calories eaten and the weight. **See Lesson: Statistical Measures.**

56. A. The correct solution is a restaurant asking all customers what they want to add to the menu because all customers are being asked their opinion. **See Lesson: Statistical Measures.**

57. D. The correct solution is that the teacher should collect data on a random sample of students of test scores and seat location because there are specific groups based on seat location. **See Lesson: Statistical Measures.**

58. A. The correct solution is $\frac{49}{625}$. There are 7 white marbles out of 25 in the bag. The probability of the event is $\frac{7}{25} \times \frac{7}{25} = \frac{49}{625}$. **See Lesson: Statistics & Probability: The Rules of Probability.**

59. D. The correct solution is Green cards 1, 2, 3, 4, 5; Red cards 6, 7, 8, 9, 10. The union is listing out all options of the sample space. **See Lesson: Statistics & Probability: The Rules of Probability.**

60. C. The correct solution is 9 possible outcomes. There are three days and three times available, or 3 times 3, which is 9 times. **See Lesson: Statistics & Probability: The Rules of Probability.**

Section V. Language

1. D. *I cooked, so I could eat dinner.* Commas are placed before coordinating conjunctions. **See Lesson: Punctuation.**

2. C. These words are adjectives that describe the noun *racehorse.* **See Lesson: Adjectives and Adverbs.**

3. B. The suffix that means "capable of" is *tion.* **See Lesson: Root Words, Prefixes, and Suffixes.**

4. C. With a word ending in -y, you drop the -y and add -ies. **See Lesson: Spelling.**

5. D. *That's great* contains the contraction *That is. Is* is a verb. **See Lesson: Verbs and Verb Tenses.**

6. A. This option would make the sentence a simple sentence. **See Lesson: Types of Sentences.**

7. B. Yet. It is the only conjunction that fits within the context of the sentence. **See Lesson: Types of Clauses.**

8. B. *Them* is the indirect object for told, and *their daughter* is the indirect object for *giving.* **See Lesson: Direct Objects and Indirect Objects.**

9. C. Sweden. Cities, states, countries, and continents need to be capitalized. **See Lesson: Capitalization.**

10. B. The word "content" has more than one meaning. **See Lesson: Context Clues and Multiple Meaning Words.**

11. A. They went to dinner after the movie. With an independent and dependent clause, a subordinating conjunction is used to connect them. "After" is the only choice that makes sense. **See Lesson: Types of Clauses.**

12. A. *Ate* is the correctly spelled form of the past tense of eat. **See Lesson: Spelling.**

13. B. *Honesty is the best policy.* All the other sentences are missing some punctuation. **See Lesson: Punctuation.**

14. D. *Loudly* is an adverb that describes *shouted.* **See Lesson: Modifiers, Misplaced Modifiers, Dangling Modifiers.**

15. D. This sentence combines the information using parallel structure. **See Lesson: Types of Sentences.**

16. B. The meaning of <u>formula</u> in this context is "a liquid that is given to babies." The phrase "baby" helps you figure out which meaning of <u>formula</u> is being used. **See Lesson: Context Clues and Multiple Meaning Words.**

17. C. *Portrait* is the direct object of the verb *painted.* **See Lesson: Direct Objects and Indirect Objects.**

18. C. *crises.* **See Lesson: Nouns.**

19. A. *Pair* is spelled correctly and has the appropriate meaning for the sentence. **See Lesson: Spelling.**

20. A. *His father's car* is a direct object of the verb *drove,* but there is no indirect object. **See Lesson: Direct Objects and Indirect Objects.**

21. B. Fourth of July. Holidays need to be capitalized. **See Lesson: Capitalization.**

22. A. *Hungrily* is an adverb that could modify *ate.* It could not be placed before *workers.* **See Lesson: Modifiers, Misplaced Modifiers, Dangling Modifiers.**

23. C. *Oh no* is an interjection. It does not contain a preposition. **See Lesson: Conjunctions and Prepositions.**

24. C. *No, I am not leaving yet.* Commas are used after yes or no. **See Lesson: Punctuation.**

25. C. *Pronunciation* is the only correct spelling. **See Lesson: Spelling.**

26. A. Wall Street Journal. Publication titles have to be capitalized, except for shorter prepositions, conjunctions, and articles. **See Lesson: Capitalization.**

27. D. *Am going* is present progressive tense. **See Lesson: Verbs and Verb Tenses.**

28. A. *Dolphins and fish* is a third person plural subject, so it takes the verb form *swim.* **See Lesson: Subject and Verb Agreement.**

29. A. *Him* is an object pronoun. **See Lesson: Pronouns.**

30. D. *Commitment* is the only one spelled correctly. **See Lesson: Spelling.**

31. B. The word *estimated* in this sentence functions as a verb, but here *estimate* is a noun. **See Lesson: Nouns.**

32. C. *Was unfolding* (past progressive) is the correct verb tense to use in this sentence. **See Lesson: Verbs and Verb Tenses.**

33. D. *Which I opened before my birthday* modifies *gift.* **See Lesson: Modifiers, Misplaced Modifiers, Dangling Modifiers.**

34. A. The prefix that means "not" is *im.* **See Lesson: Root Words, Prefixes, and Suffixes.**

35. B. *Founding* is an adjective that describes the noun *fathers.* **See Lesson: Adjectives and Adverbs.**

36. C. With words ending in -y, drop the -y and add -ies. **See Lesson: Spelling.**

37. A. *Yikes* is an interjection. **See Lesson: Conjunctions and Prepositions.**

38. B. *He* is third person singular. **See Lesson: Subject and Verb Agreement.**

39. D. *So* is an adverb that describes the adjective *upsetting.* **See Lesson: Adjectives and Adverbs.**

40. B. *Minute* is the only correctly spelled option. **See Lesson: Spelling.**

41. B. *crowd* and *speech* are common nouns. There is one more noun in the sentence, *Dr. King,* but it is a proper noun. **See Lesson: Nouns.**

42. A. *southern California.* Words such as southern are not capitalized unless they are a part of the official name. States are always capitalized. **See Lesson: Capitalization.**

43. A. *Our* is a possessive pronoun, showing ownership of the noun *house.* **See Lesson: Pronouns.**

44. D. *Talented* is an adjective that describes the noun *gymnast.* See Lesson: Adjectives and Adverbs.

45. D. President, Is, Elected, By, The, People. Only the first word in this sentence is capitalized. The term president is used generally here and does not need to be capitalized. **See Lesson: Capitalization.**

46. B. *Judgment* is the correct answer. Alternative standards allow for a spelling option of *judgement,* but American standards state that when adding a suffix such as "-ment" to a word ending with a silent sounding "-e" as in the word *judge,* the mute "-e" is dropped, making *judgment* the only correct option. **See Lesson: Spelling.**

47. D. The meaning of <u>bind</u> in this context is "to form a mass that stays connected." The word "together" helps you figure out which meaning of <u>bind</u> is being used. **See Lesson: Context Clues and Multiple Meaning Words.**

48. C. *I, you, I, and my* are pronouns. **See Lesson: Pronouns.**

49. C. This sentence is in present progressive tense, and it describes something that is happening at this moment. **See Lesson: Verbs and Verb Tenses.**

50. A. When I lived in New York City. It is dependent because it does not express a complete thought and relies on the independent clause. The word "when" also signifies the beginning of a dependent clause. **See Lesson: Types of Clauses.**

51. B. *Sharon* is the only proper noun offered. **See Lesson: Nouns.**

52. A. *The bookstore has three types of books: fiction, nonfiction, and biography.* Colons are used after the last word before introducing a list. **See Lesson: Punctuation.**

53. A. *The bookstore has three types of books: fiction, nonfiction, and biography.* Colons are used after the last word before introducing a list. **See Lesson: Punctuation.**

54. D. *she, do, and indian.* She is at the beginning of the sentence and needs to be capitalized. Do is at the beginning of a quoted sentence and also needs to be capitalized. Nationalities such as Indian should always be capitalized. **See Lesson: Capitalization.**

54. D. *Two* is the correctly spelled form of the number. **See Lesson: Spelling.**

55. A. *Each* is a third person singular subject, so it takes the verb form *is.* **See Lesson: Subject and Verb Agreement.**

56. B. *There should be a comma after today.* Commas are used after introductory phrases. **See Lesson: Punctuation.**

57. D. The root that means "to build" is *struct.* **See Lesson: Root Words, Prefixes, and Suffixes.**

58. B. This sentence correctly fixes the fragment. **See Lesson: Types of Sentences.**

59. D. *There should be commas before and after unfortunately.* Commas are used to set off thoughts and emotions. **See Lesson: Punctuation.**

60. C. *Meat* is the correctly spelled form for the sentence. **See Lesson: Spelling.**

CPSIA information can be obtained
at www.ICGtesting.com
Printed in the USA
BVHW080208110919
557987BV00002B/2/P

9 781949 147304